Spirit in the Dark

Spirit in the Dark
A Religious History of Racial Aesthetics

Josef Sorett

OXFORD
UNIVERSITY PRESS

OXFORD
UNIVERSITY PRESS

Oxford University Press is a department of the University of Oxford. It furthers
the University's objective of excellence in research, scholarship, and education
by publishing worldwide. Oxford is a registered trade mark of Oxford University
Press in the UK and certain other countries.

Published in the United States of America by Oxford University Press
198 Madison Avenue, New York, NY 10016, United States of America.

Library of Congress Cataloging-in-Publication Data
Names: Sorett, Josef, author.
Title: Spirit in the dark : a religious history of racial aesthetics / Josef Sorett.
Description: New York : Oxford University Press, 2016. |
Includes bibliographical references and index.
Identifiers: LCCN 2015039265 | ISBN 9780199844937 (hardback : alk. paper)
Subjects: LCSH: American literature—African American authors—History and criticism. |
Religion and literature—United States—History—20th century. | Religion in literature. |
African Americans in literature. | Blacks—Race identity—United States.
Classification: LCC PS153.N5 S646 2016 | DDC 810.9/896073—dc23
LC record available at http://lccn.loc.gov/2015039265

1 3 5 7 9 8 6 4 2
Printed by Sheridan Books, Inc., United States of America

Special thanks to Indiana University Press for permission to reprint portions of chapter
1, which appeared in different form as "'We Build Our Temples for Tomorrow': Racial
Ecumenism and Religious Liberalism in the Harlem Renaissance," in Leigh Schmidt and Sally
Promey, Eds. American Religious Liberalisms (Bloomington: Indiana University Press, 2012).

Excerpts from The Leroi Jones/Amiri Baraka Reader by Amiri Baraka, copyright © 1993.

Reprinted by permission of Basic Books, a member of The Perseus Books Group.

Excerpts from "If We Must Die" © 1919, "Cycle Poem 11" © 2004, and "Cycle Poem 23"
also known as "Look Within" © 2004 by Claude McKay are used with the permission of the
Literary Estate for the Works of Claude McKay.

"Neo-Hoodoo Manifesto" by Ishmael Reed excerpted from Los Angeles Free Press. Copyright
© 1970 by Ishmael Reed. Permission granted by Lowenstein Associates, Inc.

"Sermonette" by Ishmael Reed excerpted from Catechism of d neomamerican hoodoo church.

Copyright © 1970 by Ishmael Reed. Permission granted by Lowenstein Associates, Inc.

In memory of my mother, Patricia Ann Wallace

CONTENTS

PROLOGUE

Are You Getting the Spirit?

Over the course of the 1960s, the Queen of Soul earned her crown by powerfully blurring the lines between sensuality and spirituality to great effect. She continued in this vein when she recorded "Spirit in the Dark" in 1970. Even still, so much more was at stake by the end of the 1960s, when Aretha Franklin wondered out loud before audiences around the world:

"Are you getting the spirit?"

The chart-topping singer surely found herself in the midst of personal transition. Her first marriage had recently come to an end. With regard to personal sorrow, Franklin secured her honorific on the most familiar of terms. Soul music's "Queen" was intimately acquainted with sorrow.

Yet the daughter of celebrated Detroit preacher C. L. Franklin was, like so many others, deeply impacted by the political upheaval and cultural transformations that had taken place during the preceding decade. As cries of "black is beautiful," echoed across the nation, Aretha had gone "natural" around the same time that she recorded "(You Make Me Feel Like) A Natural Woman." By 1970 she had taken to sporting a short Afro and often adorned herself in African-inspired attire. Her own image on the album's jacket drew a strong resemblance to the beautiful brown-skinned woman who graced the book cover of Toni Cade Bambara's anthology, *The Black Woman*, which was published the same year as "Spirit in the Dark" reached record stores. Increasingly, Franklin's music took on the political intonations of the period as well.

In one view, "Spirit in the Dark" was emblematic of the shifting generational winds that blew from Civil Rights to Black Power as the 1960s came to an end. Franklin's next album, *Young, Gifted and Black* (1972), seemed to make a more explicit political statement. But the reverberations of a new racial consciousness were already apparent in her music before 1970. The narrative arc toward Black Power has typically been taken to be secularizing—that is, a move away from the church and its civil rights-preaching clergy. Yet the same year that she recorded *Young, Gifted and Black*, Franklin also returned to her church roots with the live album *Amazing Grace*. Gospel music, in the form of this album, would give the Queen of Soul her best-selling album ever. And while these two albums suggested separate trajectories for Soul and Gospel, Aretha Franklin knew better. Indeed, albeit in the subtle codes of a sultry songstress, she had brilliantly blurred the two genres just two years earlier when she invited her listeners to move with the spirit (in the dark).

"Spirit in the Dark," in this way, represented a rapprochement between the competing visions of Black Power and Civil Rights, Soul and Gospel, politics and religion, secular and sacred. The common adage is that all black musicians come out of the church. Such singers as Sam Cooke, Marvin Gaye, and Stevie Wonder, each with their unique performances of black masculinity, were all influenced by the spiritual and cultural traditions of Afro-Protestantism. Still, no one has so brilliantly and boldly navigated the waters of black music to achieve mass popularity and critical acclaim as the daughter of "the preacher-man." And, at least in this instance, Aretha Franklin brought the church to the nightclub; and she called it spirit. Yet when Aretha sang the words to the album's title track, her now-classic single "Spirit in the Dark," what exactly was she asking of her audience? What might Aretha have meant by her invocation of "the spirit"?

Beyond the sheer musical power of her performance, there are multiple readings that might be rendered of this song. Perhaps she was raising a theological question concerning the nature of what precisely took place when a standard black church performance moved from the bright light of a Sunday church service to the dimly lit rooms of the nightclub where this song was so often performed. What exactly happened when a dance associated with the light of Sunday morning moved to the darkened halls of Saturday night? Or when a cultural repertoire cultivated within the segregated sacred space of the first independent black institution ended up in front of a primarily white audience and at the center of the American cultural marketplace? Aretha Franklin sang about the spirit with simplicity even as she simultaneously crossed multiple lines, ignoring orthodoxies of all sorts along the way.

Or perhaps "Spirit in the Dark" would better be received as an ode to a newly inaugurated black identity. After all, it was released during the same year that Toni Cade's *The Black Woman* was published and just two years before Addison Gayle's *The Black Aesthetic*. Both of these landmark anthologies of black writing came in the wake of a decade in which Africa was rediscovered outside of a colonial discourse on the so-called "Dark Continent." Both texts issued clarion calls for a new kind of black culture and identity. Perhaps Franklin was announcing her take on Black Power or, better yet, declaring a distinctive vision of black feminism. Such speculations, in truth, invite countless prospects.

Although Aretha Franklin's meditation on the spirit neither requires nor provides any single meaning, most of the answers proposed above are more than arbitrary, random, or unrelated possibilities. On the contrary, juxtapositions of churches and nightclubs, of Saturday sinners and Sunday saints and of blurred lines between black and white or between religious inspiration and economic incentive were all by 1970 familiar themes in African American literature. Indeed, the literary visions cast by Toni Cade and Addison Gayle shared much more in common with Aretha Franklin's album than one might first suppose. A closer reading reveals that all three shared a spiritual impulse that animated much of black literature and culture at the time.

To be clear, as much as this book draws inspiration from her music, *Spirit in the Dark* has much more to say about writers like Toni Cade and Addison Gayle than it does about Aretha Franklin. It is less concerned with black music, per se, than it is with the African American literary tradition. Although music always seems to be lurking nearby, *Spirit in the Dark* explores how a set of ideas about religion animated the literary imaginings of black artists and intellectuals. The actual investment here is not in discerning or imputing any particular meaning to a single song. Instead, here "Spirit in the Dark," even in its title, serves as an invitation to wrestle with a set of questions about the relationships (real and imagined) between the aesthetics of black churches—which were so powerfully put on display when Aretha Franklin performed this song—and appeals to "the spirit." Indeed, the anxiety and anticipation attendant on the prospect that one might catch, feel, or be moved by the spirit—whether in broad daylight or the dark of night—accounts, at least in part, for what has made black culture so popular. And though "the spirit" has certainly animated the singing, shouting, and dancing of black churchgoers on Sunday mornings, it has also extended far beyond the confines of any one institutional formation or theological formulation.

One thing that the song does, to be sure, is suggest a notion of spirit that knows no boundaries. It implies an excess of spiritual powers that traverse popular oppositions (i.e., sacred and secular) and which confound the more specific Christian distinction between "the church" and "the world." Aretha Franklin's soulful rumination on the spirit suggests a more complicated rendering of the cultural and political powers of black churches—of the spirit spilling out into the world in unpredictable ways. "Spirit in the Dark" was not performed *in* the church. Yet as a performance, it was still very much *of* the church. And this is what makes the song both emblematic of the afterlives of Afro-Protestantism and an apt metaphor for Afro-modernity, in general. Ultimately, the song provided a brilliant, beautiful, and definitive enactment of Afro-modernity in all its complexities, contradictions, and creative possibilities. Lyrical substance and musical composition, content and form, serendipitously came together in Aretha Franklin's performance of "Spirit in the Dark." In this way, the song bears witness to the manner in which modern black life—even under the sign of the secular—has continued to adhere to the logics of a familiar Protestantism and, in this way, is quintessentially American.

ACKNOWLEDGMENTS

Across the span of the past few years during which this book was finished, I repeatedly drew energy and inspiration by watching video footage on YouTube of Aretha Franklin's many performances of "Spirit in the Dark." As much as Franklin is known to be the preacher's daughter who came out of the black church tradition, part of the appeal of this particular song—as a scholar of religion—is that it also strikes me as being especially emblematic of the subtle ways in which (Afro) Protestantism—the repertoires and registers of black churches—continues to animate the shape and form of (Afro) modernity, in general.

I can admit that, maybe, some of what I have found in the song may also be a product of long hours spent staring at the computer screen (yes, often in the dark). Perhaps such speculations are the result of scholarly projections as much as anything self-evident in the song itself, or certainly anything intentionally envisioned by Aretha Franklin. To be sure, personal biography is always lurking somewhere close by, haunting the objectives of academic inquiry. True to form, long before I began this book or heard a rendition of "Spirit in the Dark," the first germinating seeds for the ideas and arguments that unfold on the following pages were inspired by my own travels between churches and nightclubs. However, the context of my journeys back and forth between church and club was more obviously literary than what is readily apparent in Aretha Franklin's original performance.

The earliest inspiration for this project came almost two decades ago when I was studying at Boston University's School of Theology and a student intern at Charles Street African Methodist Episcopal Church in Boston's Roxbury neighborhood. On many a Wednesday evening I found myself in conversation with a dynamic group of teenagers (and sometimes their elementary-school-aged younger siblings) who challenged me to make interesting, let alone make sense of, any number of biblical passages. Often, shortly after our discussions I would drive across town to attend Afrocentrics, then the biggest weekly event in a vibrant local Spoken Word scene. Each week the crowd for Afrocentrics packed out Estelle's, one of the largest black nightclub venues in the city, which was situated on Tremont Street at the border between Boston's South End and Roxbury neighborhoods.

On one particular Wednesday that still stands out in my memory, a member of Boston's Black Hebrew Israelite community rose to the microphone to recite a poem entitled "For All You Church-Going Black Folks." Dressed in white from head to toe, the poet rehearsed in verse the familiar critique of Christianity as "the white man's religion," as if to settle the matter once and for all. In a crowd of young, mostly black and brown poets and fans, the poem received a generally positive response, but it wasn't an especially impressive performance. However, later that night, after going home and quickly falling asleep, I found myself awake, unsettled, and typing away on my keyboard at 3:30 a.m. After I finished what amounted to a few pages of words on the computer screen, I named my impassioned rejoinder, "Unapologetically Church!"—a rant of a defense against the Black Hebrew poet's polemic. The substance of my late-night poem merits no mention in detail here. Rereading it now, it is quite clear why I never presented it in public. Nevertheless, those rather unartful verses eventually evolved into a set of questions regarding the intersections of religion, race, and the arts. Those questions, in turn, slowly took the form of the arguments that unfold on the following pages.

It goes without saying that during the ensuing years of researching and writing this book, I have been the beneficiary of intellectual, emotional, social, and financial support from more people than I could name if I tried. Protocol and genuine gratitude requires that I give it my best effort. First, I want to thank my editor at Oxford University Press, Theo Calderara—for his faith in this project over the long haul and his patience in waiting for a manuscript to be delivered—and the team at OUP: Gina Chung, Marcela Maxfield and Alyssa Bender Russell. I also want to thank Theo for passing along the name of Jana Riess, an editor extraordinaire and scholar of American religion in her own right. Without Jana's keen editorial eye this book would be both much longer and significantly less clear. Thank you also to Kate Babbitt, who created the index and provided a fresh set of eyes at just the right moment.

The research that went into this book began, in earnest, as a dissertation in the Department of African and African American Studies at Harvard University. Very little about *Spirit in the Dark*, in terms of its structure and arguments, resembles that dissertation. Still, what follows is very much a result of my time at Harvard, where I was fortunate to be supervised by a group of faculty who took the responsibility of mentoring graduate students as seriously as their own research. As a dissertation advisor, Evelyn Brooks Higginbotham's generosity has yet to be matched. The "tough love" with which she treated all of my writing will not soon be forgotten. Robert Orsi affirmed my research questions from the moment I sat down in his Religion 2001 seminar in the fall of 2001. He was the first to suggest that my own religious biography, via Pentecostal-Charismatic preachers, Prosperity Gospel, and Oral Roberts University, was an analytical resource. I am also indebted to Werner Sollors's encyclopedic knowledge of the sources that organize this study. *Spirit in the Dark* would be a decidedly different book without sharp critiques of the dissertation. Then and since, David Carrasco has consistently gone out of his way to support my research and professional development.

In addition to an exemplary committee, a number of other faculty and graduate students made Harvard a warm institutional home. Lawrence Bobo, Marla Frederick, Henry Louis Gates Jr., Tommie Shelby, the late Ron Thiemann, and Preston Williams all offered crucial support along the way. I am also grateful for the encouragement (and employment!) that Marcyliena Morgan provided and the intellectual community she built through the Hiphop Archive. Members of the North American Religions Colloquium at Harvard Divinity School commented on portions of this work in its earliest stages. Thanks as well to my Ph.D. cohort, the first in what was then the Department of Afro-American Studies: David Brighouse, Surhid Gajendrakar, Akin Hubbard, Angel Ismail-Beigi, and Thembi Scott. And to those with whom I walked across the commencement stage: Michael Jeffries and Laura Murphy. This project would have taken much longer to complete without the help of many others at Harvard, including Mary Anne Adams, Barbara Boles, Kathleen Cloutier, Josiah Epps, Gisele Jackson, Terri Oliver, Bob Lapointe, Stephanie Parsons (and the Du Bois Graduate Society), Suzanne Smith, and Sally Wilson.

Upon moving to New York in 2004, I had the privilege of serving on the faculty of Medgar Evers College in the City University of New York for two years. During this time I grew tremendously as a teacher and thinker, and for that opportunity I am thankful to Edison O. Jackson. While there, I found community among faculty, administrators, and students, including Fontaine Davis, Samantha Gregoire-James, Tracy Grenville, Linda Susan Jackson, Hakim Lucas, Darryl Trimiew, and Vivaldi Jean-Marie, who remains a colleague and close friend.

Since joining the faculty of Columbia University, I have been surrounded by yet another group of amazing scholars who have supported this book in countless ways. I am especially indebted to my colleagues in the Religion Department and the Institute for Research in African-American Studies, who have provided me with two congenial intellectual homes. In particular, Mark Taylor has both read and championed my work from day one. Courtney Bender has helped me learn Columbia's peculiar institutional landscape. She also closely read and offered feedback on the entire manuscript (and much more). Gil Anidjar did as well, more than once, and provided generous comments. Farah Jasmine Griffin has consistently made herself available as an advisor, including to read and comment on this entire manuscript.

An early version of the book's introduction benefited from suggestions offered during an IRAAS Salon attended by June Cross, Fredrick Harris, Carl Hart, Kimberley Johnson, Valerie Purdie-Vaughns, Sam Roberts, Carla Shedd, and Venise Wagner. A number of other colleagues at Columbia, and across Morningside Heights, have commented on various parts of this book at different stages or listened to me think out loud about some of the ideas outlined herein. Thank you Marcellus Blount, Robert Gooding-Williams, Obery Hendricks, Kellie Jones, and Alondra Nelson. In her capacity as director of the Institute for Religion, Culture and Public Life (IRCPL), Karen Barkey generously made space for my intellectual vision. Julie Crawford, the Reverend Jewelnel Davis, Geraldine Downey, Flores Forbes, Samuel Freedman, David Haidju, and Marcia Sells each encouraged the work in less formal ways.

This book would never have been completed without assistance, in ways large and small, from other colleagues at Columbia, including Lennida Almanzar, Jaime Bradstreet, Emily Brennan, Julia Clark-Spohn, Walid Hamman, Sharon Harris, Jessica Lilien, Meryl Marcus, and Shawn Mendoza. Elizabeth Ross and Grace Tan provided invaluable research assistance. As part of a graduate seminar, Andrew Jungclaus and Laura McTighe read two chapters. Andrew also proved to be an archival sleuth of the first order, helping me track down key sources at just the right time.

Beyond Columbia's campus I have been fortunate to find a community of colleagues (and readers). Conversations with colleagues at Union Theological Seminary, especially Fred Davie, Gary Dorrien, and Serene Jones, were invaluable. Email exchanges with Richard Rosengarten about the evolution of religion and literature were incredibly helpful. Anthony Pinn encouraged this project early on. Josh Guild and Judith Weisenfeld each read portions of the manuscript in an earlier stage and offered clarifying questions. Jonathan Walton read a much earlier iteration of the entire manuscript and made several recommendations that led to what is now, I hope, a much stronger book. Eddie Glaude deserves special thanks for reading the entire manuscript more than once and for offering constructive criticism that helped me clarify the book's core claims and ambitions. Barbara Dianne Savage read a draft at a crucial moment and provided feedback that was as helpful as it was timely. Barbara has also extended herself in ways that do not necessarily show up in a book but for which I am no less appreciative. Over several years and multiple drafts, Lerone Martin has been a generous reader, a consistent conversation partner, and, most importantly, a good friend.

The 2013–15 cohort in the Young Scholars in American Religion program provided new friends and an opportunity to reconnect with old ones. Shelby Balik, Rosemary Corbett, Omri Elisha, Alison Greene, Katie Holscher, Hillary Kaell, David King, Anthony Petro, John Seitz—and our mentors, Courtney Bender and Bob Orsi—offered conversation, a structured space for our professional angst and practical advice, a cutting room for a bloated draft of an introduction, and so much more. Thank you, as well, to Philip Goff, Art Farnsley, Rebecca Vasko, and the Center for the Study of Religion and American Culture at IUPUI for creating the conditions for this community to come to be.

This book has also benefited from feedback received in response to presentations I have made over the past several years. At Columbia I shared portions of the book at Religion Unwound, the Religion in New York City University Seminar (thanks again, Courtney), and the Religion in America University Seminar (thank you, Randy Balmer). I also presented excerpts at the Cultures of American Religious Liberalism conference at Yale, Princeton's Religion in the Americas colloquium, the Black American Popular Religion conference sponsored by the CUNY Graduate Center's Committee for the Study of Religion, the Keep Your Eyes on the Prize conference at the University of Wisconsin–Madison, the Danforth Center at Washington University in St. Louis's Beyond the Culture Wars conference, and the North American Religions section of the American Academy of Religion. For these invitations I am grateful to Wallace Best, Darren Dochuck, Marie Griffith, Adrienne Lotson, Sally Promey, Leigh Schmidt, Bryan Turner, and Craig Werner. Sylvester Johnson also offered helpful comments on a version of chapter 1 that was presented at the 2011 national meeting of the American Studies Association.

I was challenged to reconsider many of my claims while giving talks at several churches in the Greater New York City area, including Abyssinian Baptist Church (Harlem, NY), Grace Baptist Church (New Rochelle, NY), and Union Baptist Church (Hackensack, NJ). Thank you to Rev. Calvin Butts, Rev. Gregory Jackson, Rev. William Mizell, Rev. Franklin Richardson, and Rev. Dr. Eboni Marshall Turman for these invitations.

Anonymous readers provided by Yale University Press and Oxford University Press submitted in-depth comments with their reviews, which helped me clarify what I was (and was not) trying to say.

The research and writing that led to this book, of course, was also made possible by generous financial support from several organizations. Thank you to the Fund for Theological Education (FTE, now the Forum for Theological Exploration), the Louisville Institute for the Study of American Religion (for both a dissertation and first book grant), what was then the Program in African American Studies at Princeton, Harvard's Charles Warren Center for American History, the Woodrow Wilson National Fellowship Foundation, and the Columbia University Summer Grant Program in the Humanities. Additionally, the Center for Religion and Media at New York University provided me with a quiet office to write in and the reprieve of friendly conversation while I was on research leave from Columbia during the 2013–2014 academic year. Special thanks are due here to Sharon Watson Fluker, Jim Lewis, Stephen Lewis, Caryl McFarlane, Terry Muck, Don Richter, Noliwe Rooks, Matthew Williams, Angela Zito as well as to Suzanne Case, Pamala Collins, Kali Handelman, Keri Liechty, Ina Noble, and Janine Paolucci.

FTE, the Louisville Institute and the Woodrow Wilson Career Enhancement program also provided spaces for substantive feedback on the work in progress. I am thankful to Patrick Alexander, Tobin Miller Shearer, and Sheila McCarthy, who each provided formal comments on my work in these contexts. Additionally, the scholars who attended each of these retreats were a tremendous encouragement, as were Alford Young and members of the Ford Network for Scholarship on Black Masculinity and Manhood. Librarians at several archives offered key assistance. Thank you to Emily Holmes in the Rare Books and Manuscripts Library at Columbia University, Karen Nagle at Yale University's Beinecke Rare Book and Manuscript Library, JoEllen ElBashir and Ida Jones in the Moorland-Spingarn Research Center at Howard University, Stephen Fullwood at the New York Public Library's Schomburg Center for Research in Black Culture, and Curtis Small at the University of Delaware's Library and Archives.

A very special word of appreciation is due to the community of scholars, activists, and clergy who participated in the work that led to the founding of the Center on African-American Religion, Sexual Politics and Social Justice (CARSS) at Columbia. Without our work together this book would certainly have been finished much sooner, but because of this work, I am a more sane human being. There are too many names to list here, and this work has been a collective labor, but I will mention a few: participants in the Roundtable on the Sexual Politics of Black Churches, the Columbia Advisory Group, the Community Advisory Group, strategists extraordinaire (Melinda Weekes-Laidlow and Curtis Ogden), the original planning team (Brad Braxton, Michael Brown, Mandy Carter, Barbara Savage, and Christine and Dennis Wiley), and especially Jennifer Leath and Derrick McQueen. THANK YOU!

There are, of course, a host of relationships that are not easily associated with the roles of reader or colleague but who were no less key to the completion of this book. For all the intangible ways—from encouragement to harassment—that they supported me in finishing this book, I am thankful for Jamil Drake, Warren Dillon, Gregory Ellison, Chapin Garner, Barry Goggans, Melanie Harris, Derek Hicks, Jennifer Hunt, David Kim, Darnell Moore, Luke Powery, Jerome Sealey and Nicole Thomas and the Harlem Renaissance radio show team (Jim and Genevieve Luce, Sally Placksin, Duke Marcos, and Norris Chumley).

Several churches offered existential support along the way, and for that I will always be grateful: Charles Street AME Church (Roxbury, MA); Allen AME Church (Providence, RI); Grant AME Church in Boston, MA; and Memorial West United Presbyterian Church (Newark, NJ). And I would be remiss if I did not thank the church in which I spent most of my youth, Faith Fellowship Ministries (Winchester, MA)—now International Family Church. I remain indebted to the early lessons and love I received there, which subtly show up in my writing in ways that I am even now just beginning to recognize.

Finally, I want to thank members of my immediate family, who were a consistent source of encouragement and understanding long before this book was even a question. My father, Howard Sorett (now joined by his wife, Mabel), has been my loudest one-man cheering section as long as I can remember. My brother, Tarek Mroue, has been there through thick and thin. My grandmother, Belva Wallace, never stopped asking me how the book was coming along; although she probably did not think she would live long enough to see it reach print. Evan, Wendy, and Max Sorett, as well as Brenda Wallace, round out this circle. Through marriage I was welcomed into a family as large as my own is few in numbers. Bert and Marlyn Rogers, Lebone and Anthony Wiggins, Shawina Mclean, Sekou Mclean, and scores of aunts and uncles, cousins, nieces and nephews have treated me as one of their own.

This book would not have been possible without the encouragement, prayers, and unwavering confidence of my mother Patricia Ann Wallace. Though it was written almost entirely after her death in 2006, my mother's spirit continued to spur me on every single step of the way. *Spirit in the Dark* is dedicated to her memory.

Ayanna, Jacob, and Elliot are my everything, plain and simple. Ayanna has been my most loyal supporter, my fiercest critic, and my most patient partner, shouldering more than her fair share of the load during the seemingly unending process of finishing this book. Jacob and Elliot have introduced me to a depth of joy (and anxiety) previously unimaginable. My love for you both, and for you, Ayanna—infinity, and then some!

Spirit in the Dark

Introduction

Church, Spirit, and the History of Racial Aesthetics

In the absence of a viable ideology, we settle with spirit; with spirit at our sides, we seek its signs . . .

Joe Wood

When Benjamin Elijah Mays published *The Negro's God as Reflected in His Literature* in 1938, there was nothing like it in circulation. To this day the fields of religion and literature largely proceed along separate trajectories, and this was all the more the case when *The Negro's God* first went to press. Religion was an object of theological reflection (and practice) presided over by divinity schools and denominational seminaries. Literature, in turn, belonged to the arena of humanistic inquiry. Such divisions had shaped the disciplinary conventions of modern American universities like the University of Chicago where Mays first wrote the dissertation that became *The Negro's God*. Mays's approach both complicated and confirmed the powers of this sacred/secular distinction.

As a student of literature, Mays cast a wide net of sources that included everything from sermons, Sunday School curricula, hymns, and prayers to poems, novels, and literary criticism. In this regard, he blurred the perceived lines between sacred and secular to make a "comprehensive" claim concerning the theological impulses in Negro literature. Yet as a theologian and Protestant preacher, Mays also reinforced a facile, if familiar, opposition between sacred and secular literatures, especially in his treatment of the modern literary scene. *The Negro's God* reached bookstands not long after the period of black cultural flourishing of the 1920s and early 1930s that came to be known as the Negro Renaissance. With regard to this recent phenomenon, Mays drew much clearer lines. He argued that now "there is a tendency or threat to abandon the idea of God 'as a useful instrument.'"[1] Whereas classical literatures had once adhered to a faith in God, some black writers now doubted and denied the existence of a divinity. Others suggested that God had "outlived his usefulness," Mays opined. This development left forward-thinking Christians such as himself with a clear charge.

Benjamin Mays acknowledged in the text itself that his Christian commitments might be at odds with his stated aim of evenly analyzing literary depictions of God. His belief that "the Negro's firm faith in God had saved him" and that this faith also served as a basis for social activism was "beside the point," he conceded.[2] Even so, Mays went on to call for a more radicalized form of religious activism for racial equality. "Unless liberal prophetic religion moves more progressively to the left," he warned, African Americans would increasingly continue on a path toward atheism. Mays staged a brewing confrontation between religion and secularism on the pages of Negro literature. The storied past of Afro-Protestantism was giving way, in the present, to such modern forces as communism, reason, and science. An emerging generation of writers, "New Negroes" was making this clear.

Despite arguments to the contrary, African American literature has since its advent and across its history been cut from a religious cloth—even during the moment in which Benjamin Mays diagnosed a growing secularization. To be sure, there is a robust tradition of religious dissent and critique within African American letters. Black writers have certainly documented the ways that Christianity helped authorize the social order embedded in white supremacy. Yet the relationship between Christianity and literature in African American culture has been anything but exclusively one of oppositions. In fact, the very organizing logics, aesthetic practices, and political aspirations of the African American literary tradition have been decidedly religious. In short, black literature is religious. Better yet, it is an extension of the practice of Afro-Protestant Christianity.

To date, roughly eighty years later, there is still nothing quite like *The Negro's God* in its ambition to make a grand claim about the religious dimensions of African American literature. While I harbor no desire to delineate how ideas of God have continued to develop across the African American literary tradition in the years since Mays's book, *Spirit in the*

Dark does attempt to account for the ways in which religion has remained formative to the very idea and aspirations of African American literature across much of the twentieth century. The following pages represent an effort to track and interpret the contours of a literary history that continued to unfold in the image of Afro-Protestantism even as most of its authors and critics hailed the tradition as secular and secularizing and, at times, profane.

Where Benjamin Mays was concerned with ideas about God that appeared in Negro literature, *Spirit in the Dark* explores how the very idea of African American literature and culture has adhered to Christianity and has been animated by a concern with religion, more broadly construed. Although I initially set out to write something other than a church history, it became clear that the African American literary tradition was not simply an alternative to Christian hegemony. Despite Mays's worries, Afro-Protestantism would not be undone anytime soon, even without the urgency, renewed energy, or fresh insights of "liberal prophetic religion."[3] Black writers were not the ideal counters to "the Black Church" I had once hoped they would be. Nor were they dramatically opposed to Christianity, at least in the ways that I first imagined. Working with literary sources did not mean that religion would be left behind. Afro-Protestantism persisted, I discovered, even in presumably secular black literary imaginations.

To my surprise, I began to see that the history of religion in America shared much in common with African American literary history. Over time I landed upon a set of questions that emerged from these unexpected connections and encountered a litany of literary sources that were the product of such entanglements. To help make sense of this messy cultural terrain, *Spirit in the Dark* offers a narrative in which religious and literary histories are understood as necessarily entangled. I also came to realize that I was less interested in the individual biographies of particular black artists and intellectuals than I was curious about a particular set of ideas—better yet, a single idea—that brought such figures into conversation, even when some of them were not directly in dialogue with one another in time and space. Why or what they believed (or didn't) was less interesting to me than the languages employed, sources engaged, and the structure and boundaries of the debate as it took shape. Indeed, this project rests upon (and wrestles with) a single idea, albeit a vigorously disputed one, which I refer to here and throughout as "racial aesthetics."

In lay terms, the phrase racial aesthetics is used to name the ongoing discussion that has attempted to answer such questions as: What precisely is blackness? What are its sources? What does it signify? What it is comprised by? What does it represent? And, ultimately, what might it become?

Most simply, as the late Stuart Hall once phrased the question, "What is this 'Black'?"[4] Tracing the ebb and flow of a debate about the aims, innovations in, and imagined ends of African American literature and culture from the age of the New Negro (circa 1920) through the era of the Black Arts (circa 1970), I show religion to be a consistent and vital—yet always contested—ingredient in efforts to define (as well as debunk) the idea of a distinctive black literature and culture. *Spirit in the Dark* is in short, a religious history of racial aesthetics.

Any aesthetic, most simply, is a philosophy of art and culture. So, then, the history of racial aesthetics is the story of an evolving effort to offer a compelling or persuasive philosophy (or theory) of black culture. As much as the idea of racial aesthetics was intended to theorize "the beautiful," as all aesthetics are taken to do, it has also always entertained a more specific concern with offering a normative definition of black art and culture. To be sure, this is a topic that is most firmly tethered to the field of African American literary studies. What I have named racial aesthetics was initially articulated as "race literature." Yet even in its earliest formulations, race literature sought to communicate something about the relationships between the literary imagination (and the arts in general) and the lived realities of black life. Notably, in its earliest iterations, "race literature," as it was first called, was also envisaged as a religious project.[5] To name the politics of the history in which black literature was produced and received is not to impose a political or racial norm onto a cultural form. However, it does mean acknowledging that no art and culture is conceived, produced, or received in a vacuum from social forces. To do so is to call attention to the contingencies of the historical and social contexts in which such creative work takes place. Politics and culture are necessarily entangled, and not just for black writers.

Given the politics of race in the modern world, the norms embedded in appeals to a racial aesthetic have often served both as a litmus test for measuring "real" black culture and as a means for harnessing that culture to address "legitimate" political ends. Otherwise put, the idea of a black literature or culture has often served as a proxy for assessing "racial progress, integrity and ability," to borrow Kenneth Warren's equation.[6] Racial aesthetics have carried the weight of race politics. Similar measures have been used to assess the value of African American religion. In this regard, racial aesthetics illumines a cultural and critical terrain in which religion and literature are indeed part of a shared history. By the end of this book, my hope is that readers will find it difficult to think of African American religious and literary histories as mutually exclusive, as disciplinary conventions would have us do. The respective fields of American religious history and African American literary history are much more intertwined than most academic accounts have acknowledged.

Although they often appear to not be in direct dialogue, scholars of religion and literature in America have, in fact, been preoccupied by many of the same concerns. Recent developments, in both fields, have highlighted the political context that underwrote the emergence of African American literature and the "Negro Church," respectively, during the early years of the twentieth century.[7] Barbara Dianne Savage's recent book *Your Spirits Walk Beside Us* perhaps most directly suggests the timeliness of the story narrated in *Spirit in the Dark*. Savage borrowed her book's title from the poetry of Robert Hayden—himself raised a Baptist and, as an adult, a member of the American Baha'i community—who would be appointed the Consultant in Poetry to the Library of Congress in 1976. In today's parlance, Hayden was the nation's first black Poet Laureate. His 1940 poem "We Have Not Forgotten" recalled the religious rituals (i.e., the "prayers you prayed" and "pageantries of faith") and the "spirits" that sustained black life under slavery and segregation.[8] To read Hayden fully is to encounter race, religion and literature as necessarily entangled. Here, black poetry narrated American religious history. And African American literature was imagined to carry spiritual significance. Conversely, the Negro Church came to be understood as a valuable social instrument.

While attentive to this always already impinging political metanarrative—of religion and literature equally in service to race politics—*Spirit in the Dark* attempts to analytically disentangle (or at least tease out) the multiple ways in which race and religion have been interwoven in the drama of American history. Here is a story wherein religion was invoked as a racial category and race was invested with religious meaning. Racial aesthetics, as such, offers a new avenue through which to reimagine the study of religion in America. In doing so, I also aim to remind readers of (or at least make it more difficult to forget) the aestheticized (Afro) Protestantism that many twentieth-century black writers both critiqued and advanced.

Spirit in the Dark illumines how a range of ideas about religion animated the history of racial aesthetics. As a rule, African American literature produced during the years from the New Negro to the Black Arts movements—roughly 1920 to 1970—has been identified with the broad rubrics of modernism, albeit with multiple variations on this theme. And while modernism signals anything but a singular cultural or ideological formation, it is generally framed in opposition to the (real and imagined) premodern, a past time when the primitive vestige of religion was comfortably located and left behind. For many a modernist, in fact, (secular) literature was supposed to supplant the spiritual authority previously accorded to religious institutions.[9] Similarly, black modernisms often assumed or endorsed a narrative of secularization. This orthodoxy has enshrined secularism as the appropriate, shared ideology of modern racial subjects and as the assumed substance of black literature. In short, Afro-modernity is imagined as secular.

Black literary and cultural production during the historical period that this book spans has generally been portrayed as unconcerned with, if not opposed to, religion writ large. This, of course, is by no means true of studies of black literature exclusively.[10] Scholarship (and popular coverage) has generally identified the aspirations and ideology of American literature under the sign of modernity as secular and secularizing, and in certain places and spaces as altogether profane.[11] Where religion has figured into the story, it has almost always appeared as inconsequential, tangential, or at the margins. Moreover, it has also often been claimed that racial aesthetics, in particular, would (or should) replace the rule of religion—really, churches—in black life. In this view, one might be tempted to read what follows as a history of African American secularism.

Yet on the contrary, *Spirit in the Dark* demonstrates that religion remained a fertile, dynamic, and formidable force in the history of black literature, including debates regarding racial aesthetics, across the twentieth century. Rather than a relic of a primitive past, religion persisted as a powerful presence in literary visions of modern black subjectivity and social life. As a history of ideas, *Spirit in the Dark* demonstrates that efforts to theorize a racial aesthetic bore witness to religious tensions in American culture. Black artists and intellectuals discussed religion in great detail as they theorized a racial aesthetic. They celebrated specific religious ideas and practices and critiqued others, and they did so in ways that reflected the constraints and possibilities of the historical contexts in which they wrote, lived, and died. Moreover, their words both reflected and revealed the impact of circulating, if shifting, ideas about religion in the modern world.

Religion and a range of more precise or related terms (e.g., Baptist, Botanica, Buddhism, church, Conjure, cult, Hoodoo, Islam, Protestant, sect, spirituality, storefront, Voodoo, and Yoruba, to name just a few) figured significantly in efforts to identify the constitutive ingredients and constructive hopes of what was put forward as a racial aesthetic. To this end, part of what follows involves a preliminary mapping of the wide array of religious images and ideas apparent in African American literary history. At the same time, I advance my own interpretive claims concerning the peculiar significance of religion, and (Afro) Protestantism in particular, to black literature and cultural expression. One key observation, in this regard, is that the diversity of black religious sources and practices that appeared across this history never entirely unsettled what scholars have identified as a Christian hegemony. Rather than simply celebrating religious diversity or a racialized spirituality, by engaging with artists and intellectuals who have typically been taken for granted as secular, *Spirit in the Dark* raises questions that trouble the boundaries of what counts as "religion."

This book is both a literary history of African American religion and a religious history of black literature. It is as much about racial aesthetics as it is about religion in America. Thus, as an interpretation of African American religious and literary histories, *Spirit in the Dark* suggests a theory of religion in black culture. This theory is, by all accounts, provisional, one advanced through illustration and narration. Admittedly, my end game is not a definitive or final statement. Rather, through the historical narrative provided herein I hope to provoke richer theoretical conversations about the relationships between religion—and perhaps especially, a privileged Afro-Protestantism—and the politics of black culture.

The primary contribution of *Spirit in the Dark*, then, is a novel historical account of religion as revealed in a critical debate—namely, racial aesthetics—populated by presumably secular sources. If nothing else, the individuals who appear on subsequent pages have not, for the most part, been received as the laity and clergy who lead and populate religious institutions. Most of these writers did not preside over what are recognized as sacred spaces. As such, they have not been understood as recognized subjects in the study of religion or as providing the acceptable source materials for religious history. Yet these allegedly secular artists and intellectuals, organized here under the rubric of racial aesthetics, have had much to say about religion. For scholars of literature, in turn, *Spirit in the Dark* sheds fresh light on an oft-ignored dimension in the work of the usual suspects. As much as it has been largely overlooked or obscured, religion has haunted the black literary imagination, often hiding in plain sight.

TOWARD A GENEALOGY OF SPIRIT IN THE DARK

As the title of this book suggests, the idea of spirituality, especially as it circulates throughout African American literature, is also a key point of interest. Much has been said in recent years about the now well-worn juxtaposition of religion and spirituality. "I'm not religious, but I am spiritual," is a common refrain. As the popular argument so often goes, a rise in personal spirituality replaced traditional religious ideas, identities, and affiliations. An ethic of individualist and eclectic spirituality trumped institutional allegiances and religious orthodoxy. *Spirit in the Dark* explores the relationship between these two terms—religion and spirituality—as it has been construed over the history of racial aesthetics. Just to clarify, my argument is not that racial aesthetics should be read as the literary equivalent of the "spiritual but not religious" phenomenon.[12] Rather than a relation of oppositions, spirituality (and a variety of related terms) is understood here as deeply dependent upon the idea and institution of church for its very articulation. As I've also often heard it said in church, "I'm not religious, but I love the Lord!" Church and spirit almost require each other; mutually exclusive they are not. As such, *Spirit in the Dark* narrates a spiritual history of race at the same time that it figures "secular" black artists and intellectuals in the story of American religion. By aligning oneself with spirituality, one does not necessarily escape from religion writ large or from the church in particular. This is my primary point in the prologue. Aretha Franklin's 1970 performance, "Spirit in the Dark," reminds us that one need not be IN an actual church to be OF the church. At least in Aretha's rendering, the spirit (in the dark) bore dramatic witness to the church even when it was performed or experienced outside the walls of the sanctuary.

So while not an entire departure from the church, the spiritual grammar cultivated within African American literature evinced an ambivalent attachment to Afro-Protestantism. More precisely, a celebratory ambivalence apparent across the history of racial aesthetics took the form of a frequent pairing of church and spirit. Thus, the structure in which this history of racial aesthetics unfolds is organized by engagements with religion across a spectrum that finds churches (never a singular entity) at one end and an often capacious, if vague, "spirit" at the other. In this way, "church" and "spirit" gave black artists and intellectuals access to a grammar through which they both celebrated and interrogated, critiqued and conjured, and revised and reimagined the idea of the "Negro Church" from the very first moment that such terminology was taking form.

Indeed, across the history of racial aesthetics one finds a prolific discourse on spirit that reflected different definitions of religion, drew upon a range of cultural sources, and emphasized diverse aspects and offered, competing interpretations of black life. Such appeals to spirit were at once influenced by the heterodox ethos of American spirituality and deeply indebted to the orthodoxies of Protestant Christianity. Indeed, the rhetorics of religious liberalism and racial ecumenism coalesced to help forge a tradition of racial aesthetics.[13] In this way, Afro-Protestantism, and African American religion more broadly, held together fundamental fissures attendant to the cultural and political strains of modern black intellectual life, social activism, and artistic production as expressed by New Negroes in the 1920s and Black Arts radicals of the late 1960s as well as during the intervening decades.

Historically, the business of black churches has been forced by the realities of white supremacy to straddle the spheres of culture and politics in American society.[14] A range of intellectual, literary, and political practices elevated a liberal—that is, literary and reasoning—Protestantism as representative of the spiritual life of "the race" and mobilized this institutional formation in service to the fight for social equality. Afro-Protestantism was made by a number of black leaders to discipline and downplay a number of other religious practices understood to be at odds with the desired end of equality and inclusion within the American body politic. At the same time, many artists and intellectuals valorized all of the attributes associated with black folk religion and culture in their efforts to theorize a distinctive racial aesthetic.

From the 1920s through the 1960s, the coupling of church and spirit provided a language for interpreting and negotiating the complicated cultural and social landscapes that resulted from the events transforming black life, whether those were the mass migrations of the first half of the twentieth century or the civil rights and Black Power movements that followed. The fact that this pairing was made to serve interests and arguments as different as the New Negro and the Black Arts reveals a significant tension between appeals to Christian faith and the claims other sources of cultural and spiritual authority made upon black lives. During these decades, religion provided crucial source material for constructing norms for a racial art and culture. At times, racial aesthetics assumed a decidedly religious tenor. Ultimately, appeals to church and spirit offered a rubric pliable and expansive enough for artists and intellectuals, and religious leaders and laypersons, to both affirm and disavow a wide range of religious ideas and practices. All the while, they were theorizing a racial aesthetic.

Ultimately, from the Negro Renaissance of the 1920s until the ascendance of the Black Arts in the 1960s, African American writers developed a grammar of spirit (i.e., spirit, spirits, spiritual, spirituality, etc.) in ways that reflected the constraints and possibilities of their particular contexts. As history marched forward, later generations exhibited an awareness of the terms of the debates defined by those who preceded them, even as they repurposed inherited vocabularies. If New Negroes identified a spirit in the arts that would aid racial advancement and help put an end to "the problem of the color line," then theorists of the Black Arts recognized a spiritual task of enunciating new myths to demolish the "double consciousness" within black minds and to conjure new, liberated black worlds. Along the way, others embraced their craft by refusing the restrictions of racial categories and insisting that the arts, by definition, were an experimental process in service to human equality and emancipation. In this view, all aesthetics should aspire to beauty on a universal scale, without the qualifiers of race politics or religious difference. Yet even in these instances, the business of aesthetics was still bound to the politics of race, if by nothing else than the social order in which such visions found a hearing and which they sought to transcend.

In this vein, spirit—simultaneously a signifier of race and religion, sacred and secular, and more—is the category that binds the history that follows. Often told as a sequence of movements, the spiritual grammars outlined during each of these moments were indeed distinct historical dramas. Yet together they comprise a genealogy of spirit that continues even to the present day. This genealogy links language, culture, and politics across history, time, and place through the shared and co-constituted modern discourses of race, religion, and literature. Moreover, this history of racial aesthetics—this genealogy of spirit (in the dark)—reveals the markings of a multitude of spirits.

As a discursive tradition, the history of racial aesthetics has been possessed by spiritual languages that trace their lineages back across multiple historical trajectories. It has inherited and carried on the stories, sacred and secular, of many peoples from many places. It was shaped by the breath (i.e., spirit) of God in the stories of the Hebrew Bible and the Holy Spirit of the New Testament and by the Zeitgeist prescribed by Georg Wilhelm Friedrich Hegel and the Volk spirit found in Johann Gottfried Herder's vision of romanticism. It has been animated by the mediating spirits of West Africa and those New World spirits that were creolized and created anew under the conditions of slavery and servitude in the Americas. It was also enfolded within the manifold spiritual traditions of antebellum North America: evangelical and liberal Protestantisms, native traditions, New Thought, Pentecostalism, Spiritualism, and more.

Spirit in the Dark takes up the task of putting flesh on the bones of this spiritual grammar—one wherein spirit itself was a heterodox formation that worked out its meanings in critical tension with, and in the shadows of, an especially prominent Protestant establishment. Not all spirits were imagined or received on equal terms. Asymmetries abounded. For now, in moving toward that genealogy of spirit (in the dark), just a few of the countless examples that litter the pages of African American literary history are worth considering.

Roughly two decades after W. E. B. Du Bois published his now classic text *The Souls of Black Folk* (1903), he offered a more extended discussion of what he took to be black people's special offerings to America in *The Gift of Black Folk* (1924). "The Gift of the Spirit" figured as the final, and most formidable, of nine distinct contributions that "the Negro" had made to the nation's culture. This "peculiar spiritual quality" was evidence of the "imprint of Africa" even as it was confirmation within the bodies of black folks "of that search for truth, of that strife toward God, of that body of belief which is the essence of true religion."[15] Du Bois noted that an ethical Christianity, an impulse toward freedom, and "the universal animism or fetishism of primitive peoples" were all evident in the gift of spirit that black folk offered modern society.

The following year, the sociologist George Edmund Haynes argued that "the church" was the institutional manifestation of the best of the "Negro spirit." In the context of a nascent Negro Renaissance, Haynes's Christian vision for the racial spirit was a minority report, which is not to say that religious ambitions were entirely absent from New Negro visions. Du Bois's move to privilege particular racial gifts anticipated the spiritual grammar of the literary movement that was taking shape just as *The Gift of Black Folk* was published. *The New Negro*, edited by Alain Locke and often referred to as "the bible" of the Harlem Renaissance, was also released in 1925. In the anthology's foreword Locke argued, "Negro life is not only establishing new contacts and founding new centers, it is finding a new soul. There is a fresh spiritual and cultural flourishing." Here, if soul signaled a fundamental transformation in the inner life of "the race," then spirit referenced the manifestation of that interior shift in the observable social world, especially in the artistic expressions of a new generation.[16]

For Locke and many others, the young artists who contributed to *The New Negro* were prophets of a novel "race-spirit." Indeed, this spiritual grammar not only inspired a novel reading of Afro-Protestantism (i.e., Haynes), but it was also repeatedly employed to advance arguments about the aesthetics of the New Negro. For instance, in his 1926 essay "The Negro Artist and the Racial Mountain," Langston Hughes asserted that an unnamed writer who desired not to be known as a "negro poet" was simply trying to "run away spiritually from his race."[17] In the same essay, Hughes also argued that some of the most distinctive cultural resources available to New Negro artists were to be found within the sanctuaries of black folk churches.

In his 1932 fictional elegy of the Harlem Renaissance, *Infants of the Spring*, Wallace Thurman troubled a number of assumptions about this movement, including the presumed sources of a racial spirit.[18] In satirizing a generational gap apparent at the time, Thurman staged an exchange between a young writer and an elder statesman who strongly resembled Alain Locke, who insisted that "the ancestral arts" of Africa should direct New Negro artists. In Thurman's fiction, the elder suggested to the youth that he should embrace an "inherited spirit" tied to "paganism based on African traditions." The response he received was curt: "I ain't got no African spirit."[19] For New Negro writers, no doubt, there was no singular formulation or source of spirit to be taken for granted as normative. Their spiritual grammar was capacious enough to contain the multiple meanings of religion, race, and culture that were up for grabs during the 1920s and 1930s. Spirit was the very site of contestation over their allegedly secular concerns.

That the 1940s and 1950s have often been treated as down moments in African American literary history does not square well with the sheer number of black writers who came to prominence in these decades.[20] Nor was there any ebb at this time in the steady flow of this genealogy of spirit in the making. On April 6, 1946, in his Chicago *Defender* column, Langston Hughes likened art to religion because they both appeared to "cross physical color lines with ease." Hughes was less than optimistic in his assessment of this commonality, as "neither seemed to have much effect on most white people's hearts."[21] Even though he recognized the social pressures that shaped both art and religion, neither was to be assessed primarily by political measures. Hughes argued that "truth alone glorifies the spirit," the implication being that religion (and art) ought to be able to transcend racial distinctions. This suggested a certain shift in his thinking since 1926.[22]

Langston Hughes's move to disentangle spirit from a particular politics of race in favor of the universal claims of art (and religion) was consistent with the times. A racial spirit, as seen in the culture and art that emerged out of the black experience, was not to be reduced to race politics. Renowned visual artist Romare Bearden captured the ethos of this era well in an essay that same year, "The Negro Artist's Dilemma." According to Bearden, "the true artist feels that there is only one art—and it belongs to all mankind."[23] To be sure, the subtleties of the African American experience and the aims of universal art were not mutually exclusive for Bearden and his contemporaries, many of whom crafted the latter, working with a variety of media, out of the former. The difference was that the particulars of black culture were increasingly lent in service to a claim for its catholicity, the universality of a racial aesthetic.

In this mid-century period, many artists offered a critique of the genre of "protest literature" and resisted the impositions of sociology onto art. For instance, James Baldwin proffered that a "spirit of medieval times which sought to exorcize evil by burning witches" animated literary genres and "the lynch mob" alike. Artistic appeals to racial caricatures and rigid binaries were "activated by what might be called a theological terror," Baldwin surmised. Short of producing great art, which could certainly draw inspiration from the history of racism in the United States, protest literature failed to unsettle, let alone transcend, the problem of race.[24] Baldwin knew all too well that "one writes out of one thing only—one's own experience."[25] Yet he found resources to resist the constraints of race politics within the religious cultures of the churches in which he had been immersed for much of his youth. Once again, the church proved to be a theater in which a racial spirit flourished. Throughout the 1950s, Baldwin enunciated this spiritual grammar in his fiction and nonfiction, including his 1962 tour de force, *The Fire Next Time*, which represented a high moment in his longer career as America's spiritual seer on race matters. It also signaled a major shift in racial aesthetics that was to culminate later that decade with the ascent of the Black Arts movement.

As described by one of the movement's key theorists, Larry Neal, the Black Arts was the "spiritual sister" of Black Power.[26] In its ancestry and origins, the Black Arts involved "an evocation of spirit," he explained. And in a moment of social upheaval, Neal argued that the arts should serve the purpose of "spiritual integration."[27] In this vision, the Black Arts advanced racial aesthetics—indeed, THE black aesthetic—as a spiritual practice. And because of the ability of drama to impact the collective, Neal elevated that medium. Plays, in particular, staged a "theater of the Spirit" that could replace the corporate function of black churches. The theater provided the possibility of transcendence, transformation, and "spiritual integration" to Black Arts congregants.

The Black Arts, more generally, were imagined as a social and cultural stage of possibility through which to enact a spirit-filled black subjectivity and social life. Regardless of form, genre, or medium, each performance possessed the potential to awaken, enliven, and transform—that is, to conjure—the spirits of a sleeping black nation. Black Arts writer Amiri Baraka acknowledged as much in his foreword to *Black Fire*, the movement's seminal anthology that he edited with Larry Neal. *Black Fire* aimed to provide a canon, in the full theological sense of the term. It would set "the standards . . . for the next thousand years." With the assembled collection of writings, Baraka and Neal presented—indeed, the Black Arts offered—"from God, a tone, your own."[28] James Stewart put it most simply in the anthology's lead essay when he observed, in short, "That spirit is black."

Most concisely, *Spirit in the Dark* is a historical project that engages with literary sources to wrestle with theoretical questions that are especially significant in the study of religion. First and foremost, it is written with scholars of African American religious history in mind. If the idea of a racial aesthetic is what holds this book together, my interests are guided by historical questions rather than constructive concerns. That is, how do various efforts at theorizing black art and culture open up insights into African American religion at particular moments in time and space? And what do the ways in which racial aesthetics were articulated and reimagined across the span of time between the New Negro (circa 1920s) and the Black Arts (circa 1960s) reveal about the workings of religion in North America during this chronological window?

To be sure, covering a five-decade span of time places clear constraints on how deeply I am able to dig down into the particulars of each decade. In a way, I have cast the kind of grand metanarrative that has long since gone out of fashion among historians. However, I trust that my sustained engagement with a single idea—namely, racial aesthetics—allows for a different kind of analytical depth even as it invites further historical inquiry into the overlapping periods that *Spirit in the Dark* surveys. I do not intend for the religious history of racial aesthetics that I provide here to be the final one. Rather, mine is but a preliminary gesture in this direction.

While close attention to literary texts and historical context are organizing principles for this project as a whole, recent theoretical debates concerning the very category of religion were pivotal to the development of my main arguments. By the end of this book, my aim is to have demonstrated that what I have called racial aesthetics is unthinkable without understanding the interlocking histories of terms like religion, secularism, and spirituality. I also hope that by foregrounding black artists and intellectuals, readers will think differently about the ways in which the history of the study of religion has held to its own (perhaps unstated) orthodoxies with regard to racial aesthetics. Substantial attention has already been given to what I have called racial aesthetics within the field of African American literary studies. Many of the key primary sources in this tradition appear in what are now considered classic anthologies such as *The New Negro* (1925), *The Negro Caravan* (1940), *Black Fire* (1968), *The Black Woman* (1970), and *The Black Aesthetic* (1972). Here, the substance of specific selections and the politics of editorial selection are both of interest. However, in addition to close readings of the ways that religion has figured in such representative texts, my arguments draw upon archival research (e.g., periodicals, journals, and correspondence) to offer a broader historical narrative.

Reframed through the theoretical insights of religious studies, these literary materials provide the "raw data" for narrating a religious history of racial aesthetics. They provide points of entry into particular moments in time and space. Moreover, the arguments and ideas found in these sources offer snapshots of individuals and groups attempting to make sense of their moment, including occasional efforts to imagine life outside the constraints of historical contingencies. Ultimately, I have tried to weave together history and literature, while also being attentive to theoretical concerns, in clear enough fashion to keep readers invested even if only one of these approaches suits a reader's interest.

Some of the people who are presented on the following pages only appear briefly. Others come and go, disappearing only to reappear at a later moment. A few remain present more or less throughout. As necessary, I provide biographical details to provide better understanding of a claim or question. However, more than the biographies of individual artists and intellectuals, my primary aim is to narrate the history of the idea of a racial aesthetic. I am less interested in imputing authorial intention or discerning obscured motivations or in proving what particular figures did (or did not) believe than I am in documenting and detailing the discursive terrain. In this regard, the texts stand on their own insofar as they encapsulate a specific claim about racial aesthetics in real time.

Even when particular writers were not in direct dialogue with one another (and many of them were), they were nonetheless participants in a larger set of exchanges that were actively cultivated and sustained over time. Such exchanges included formal and informal conversations, some that ended in agreement and others that were extended arguments. They took place at conferences and workshops. They were produced and staged in pamphlets, print publications, and publishing houses. They took shape within local organizations and institutions. Across space and time, a shared investment in the contested idea of a racial aesthetic helped bring about a community of black artists and intellectuals, which in the process also established a tradition of criticism. It is not insignificant that some of those who participated in this debate even explicitly imagined that their mode of collective engagement was spiritually significant. Indeed, the forging of a racial aesthetic took the form of a religious history.

CHAPTER OVERVIEW

Spirit in the Dark is structured to retell the history of African American literature from the 1920s to the end of the 1960s, with religion now at the center of the story. This chronology coheres around the question of how ideas about religion appeared in an extended critical debate about black art and culture and how these ideas evolved over the span of this particular period of time. Chapter 1 picks up with the New Negro movement of the 1920s. Commonly referred to as the Harlem Renaissance, this period of black literary and cultural flourishing was marked by a set of religious and cultural tensions that were amplified by the processes of mass migration and urbanization. Through a close analysis of the editorial process and composition of Alain Locke's 1925 anthology *The New Negro*, along with a selection of key essays written during this period, I call attention to how an investment in both Christian churches and growing race consciousness animated the cultural imagination of New Negro artists and intellectuals. Appeals to a racial spirit, on one hand, and the "Negro Church," on the other, provided an analytical frame through which many of the period's most celebrated writers made sense of a novel black religious pluralism and a nascent commercial culture.

In chapter 2, which attends to the decade of the 1930s, we see that black writers also managed to endorse and keep alive an ancestral spirit located both in the American South and the African past. Exploring especially the work of Zora Neale Hurston, along with Nancy Cunard's 1934 anthology *Negro*, I explain how an interest in African, Caribbean, and southern U.S. culture and history both challenged a dominant Christian tradition and called attention to how black Americans made something new, something perhaps not entirely Christian, with African-derived ideas, rituals, and expressive practices. The chapter ends by examining Richard Wright's elegy of the renaissance, which critiqued this racial logic, foregrounded the significance of the "Negro Church" as a primary institution organizing black social life and creative expression, and called on Negro writers to replace preachers in helping orient black life.

The 1940s and 1950s have often been framed as a valley between the high moments of the Negro Renaissance and the Black Arts movements. Recent scholarship has challenged this periodization, demonstrating that black literature "sustained vibrancy and power *throughout* the century."[29] Chapter 3 puts forward the idea of what I call racial catholicity by following Claude McKay's conversion to Catholicism to track the simultaneous numerical growth of black Catholics and the growing claim by black writers of the universality of black culture. I also provide a close reading and comparison of two transitional texts—Claude McKay's *Harlem: Negro Metropolis* (1940) and Roi Ottley's *New World A-Coming* (1943)—that tackled the complicated place of religion in black culture at the time. Ultimately, McKay's Catholic difference did not diminish the Judeo-Christian sensibility that was encoded in Ottley's first book, but a comparison of the two books offers a fascinating case study of the subtle ways in which Protestantism maintained a stronghold in the black literary imagination.

In chapter 4, I further extend this line of thinking but focus more specifically on the tension evident from the late 1940s through the mid-1950s between competing literary norms that were named as sociological, on one hand, and experimental, on the other. Black writers increasingly rode a wave of wartime liberal optimism that also drew inspiration from the early gains of a growing civil rights movement. In this view, sociology ceded victory to art. The dominant ethos in African American literature at this time espoused a rubric of universalism and experimentalism that was also entirely contingent on the particulars of the quotidian experience of black life. Examining a series of essays and articles by some of the most celebrated black writers of the period— including James Baldwin, Gwendolyn Brooks, Ralph Ellison, Lorraine Hansberry, Robert Hayden, Ann Petry, and Richard Wright—I highlight how they attempted to improvise on and play with the breaks in race politics. In doing so, they embraced a modernist aestheticism that still drew clear inspiration from (and often explicitly cited) the particular forms and context of Afro-Protestantism.

Chapter 5 explores the transition from racial catholicity during the mid-century years to the spiritual sensibilities of the Black Arts as emblematic of the broader international cultural and political ferment of the 1960s. Growing out of a historical moment in which the emergence of postcolonial Africa converged with the gains of the civil rights movement in the United States to foment an international racial (and religious) consciousness, I argue that theorists of the black aesthetic sought to conjure a spirit commensurate with the claims of Black Power and its critique of civil rights integrationism. More specifically, during the 1960s Black Arts writers aimed to reorder and re-direct the primary spiritual sensibilities in black culture by re-reading Christianity through the lens of radical blackness, embracing Islam as the true black religion and appealing to African-derived religions.

In chapter 6, I examine three anthologies associated with Black Power politics to illustrate how many figures associated with the Black Arts movement explicitly framed their creative and critical work as spiritual practice. Anthologies, in this view, were part of a broader set of efforts to erect a new black canon, and in this vein, I offer a close reading of Amiri Baraka and Larry Neal's *Black Fire: An Anthology of Afro-American Writing*, Addison Gayle's *The Black Aesthetic*, and Toni Cade-Bambara's *The Black Woman* not only to reveal how religion circulated throughout each of these anthologies but also to illumine how the masculinist politics associated with the Black Arts was often underwritten by the movement's spiritual aspirations.

Finally, in chapter 7, I address several "outliers" who challenged the nationalist orthodoxy of the Black Arts. In unique ways, Ishmael Reed, Alice Walker, Ralph Ellison, and Albert Murray each complicated narratives of blackness that were premised upon racial oppositions. They each also invited, in my reading, a sophisticated account of racial difference in American life—and the abiding significance of Afro-Protestantism for the politics of black culture—that anticipated more recent approaches to the study of black religion and culture.

Across the five decades spanned by this book, regardless of awareness or intentionality, Afro-modernity—its presumably secular subjectivities and social worlds and the cultural expressions they occasioned—continued to adhere to and inhabit the very structures and forms of the churches that gave black people in the New World their earliest breath of life. This is the perennial predicament: at once a theoretical problem, a historical possibility, and a literary polemic. Afro-modernity is haunted by the specter of the black church. And this is the social fact, of an Afro-Protestant modernity, that Aretha Franklin most powerfully performed in her now classic 1970 song, "Spirit in the Dark."

Spirit in the Dark, in turn, is the story of church, spirit, and the history of racial aesthetics.

CHAPTER 1

✕

The Church and the Negro Spirit

By shedding the old chrysalis of the Negro problem we are achieving something like a spiritual emancipation.

Alain Locke

By the beginning of the 1920s, the notion of a New Negro was anything but novel. In fact, the idea was more than two decades old. With roots in the final years of the nineteenth century, the idea of the New Negro encapsulated a set of cultural and political strategies that sought to counter the demise of Reconstruction. As lynchings reached an all-time high and the Supreme Court ruled in 1896 that segregation was the law of the land, African Americans responded by mobilizing politically on a national scale, which led to the formation of organizations like the Niagara movement and the National Association for the Advancement of Colored People (NAACP) in the first years of the twentieth century. At the same time, a group of black literary figures—including Charles Chesnutt, Paul Laurence Dunbar, and Victoria Earle Matthews—emerged forcefully, leading some to claim that the "nadir of race relations" was also the occasion of a Negro Renaissance.[1] Indeed, the failure of the nation to reconstitute itself as a racial democracy fomented the ascent of a New Negro.

Roughly twenty-five years later, in the wake of World War I, the epic population shift known as the Great Migration was well under way. As millions of African Americans moved north, ethnic and racial tensions arose in northern cities, evidenced in part by the resurgence of the Ku Klux Klan. Alongside this incendiary situation came the explosive growth of a commercial publishing market and cultural scene in New York City, including the neighborhood of Harlem. Although the New Negro movement dated back to the start of the century, something new was certainly in the making. Harlem was poised to become home to a novel and previously unimaginable black literary boom.

Most commonly referred to as the Harlem Renaissance, the period of black literary and cultural flourishing during the 1920s was marked by religious and cultural tensions that were amplified by the processes of mass migration and urbanization. Although the New Negro movement has been firmly established in both academic literature and the American cultural imagination, only scant attention has been paid to the ways in which religion influenced the black cultural performances that defined the moment. Although typically taken for granted as a secular (and secularizing) phenomenon, religion—more pointedly, Christianity—was a key dimension of the New Negro movement over the long haul. During the decade of the 1920s, black artists and intellectuals (as well as a number of Afro-Protestant preachers) cultivated a spiritual grammar that was delimited by an organizing trope of church and spirit. By all accounts a theological discourse, this frequent pairing of church and spirit provided an analytical frame through which to make sense, descriptively, of a novel black religious pluralism. Typically left undefined, this spiritual grammar also bore a family resemblance to the race consciousness and uplift ethic associated with the integrationist goals of the New Negro. Although its various invocations drew on everything from European Romanticism to a romanticized view of Africa, New Negroes assigned no less religious significance to racial aesthetics. This spiritual grammar functioned prescriptively by advancing a particular Protestant vision for black life during the interwar years, especially as the forces of migration, urbanization, and commercial culture coalesced to make the diversity of black life increasingly visible.

Such developments, no doubt, compounded the challenges attendant on forging a shared race politics, although the rule of segregation still prevailed. The spectrum of spiritual grammars—both church(es) and spirit(s)—was a ready and pliable resource in this regard. On one hand, the church was identified as a liberal, literate, and democratic institution and as an example and instrument of a modern racial spirit. Meanwhile, appeals to spirit suggested the presence and prospects of something more expansive than the institutional arrangements of Afro-Protestantism. The specific contents of this spiritual surplus, religious or otherwise, remained a vital question.

What follows in this chapter is an extended portrait of this pairing of church and spirit insofar as it appeared in several of the texts that were considered central to the making of a black literary movement in New York during the 1920s. Through a close engagement with Alain Locke's editorial process in compiling the period's pivotal text *The New Negro* (1925) and a selection of key essays written by several of the period's most prominent black artists and intellectuals (e.g., W. E. B. Du Bois, George Edmund Haynes, Langston Hughes, George Schuyler, and James Weldon Johnson), a spiritual grammar comes into view at the very center of the cultural imagining of the New Negro Renaissance.

Appeals to a racial spirit, on one hand, and the Negro Church, on the other, provided a discursive frame through which many of the period's most celebrated writers posited a distinctive black culture. Moreover, church and spirit were categories capacious enough to both endorse and underwrite (as well as undermine) the ideology of racial uplift associated with the political orthodoxies of the New Negro. If nothing else, the idea of the New Negro was shot through with spiritual significance. This fact was readily confirmed in the writings of the leading black literary lights and religious leaders of the day.

A NEW PREACHER FOR A NEW NEGRO

At the start of the same year that the Harlem Renaissance welcomed one of its most complicated texts, Jean Toomer's *Cane*, the movement also witnessed the publication of its most explicitly theological statement. In its first issue of 1923, the *New York Amsterdam News*, the city's leading black newspaper, published "The New Negro," a poem by the Reverend Reverdy Cassius Ransom.[2] Born in 1861 in Flushing, Ohio, Ransom received his education and ministerial training within his home state. While in college, he was licensed to preach in the African Methodist Episcopal (AME) Church. After graduating from Wilberforce University in 1886, Ransom began starting new congregations, referred to as "mission" churches; first, in Pennsylvania (where he was ordained) and then back in Ohio. During his time as a pastor in Ohio, he made a name for himself within the AME hierarchy and as a "race man" more generally. While there he developed relationships with other prominent Negroes, like the poet Paul Laurence Dunbar, who was from Dayton.[3] In the final years of the nineteenth century, Ransom was assigned to pastor Bethel AME Church in Chicago. Although he had already made a name for himself, Ransom's arrival in the city of Chicago afforded him access to a much larger stage.

Even before he moved to Chicago, Ransom had revealed himself to be a radical social thinker. As early as 1896 he publicly aligned himself with socialism in an essay printed in the *A.M.E. Church Review*.[4] Yet in Chicago he became enmeshed in the inner circles of the overlapping networks of Progressive Era activism organized around race, religion, and gender. There Ransom became an early advocate of the Social Gospel, which drew upon the newly developing social sciences to direct Christian churches toward social activism.[5] After four years at Bethel, Ransom once again decided to start a new church. When he founded the Institutional Church and Social Settlement House in Chicago in 1900, it was a first for African Methodism. Moreover, it established Ransom as a national player; and he would be among those involved in the founding of the Niagara movement and the NAACP.[6] Yet as an itinerant minister in the AME Church, Ransom was moved to a new church again four years later.

Later that decade, in New York City, Ransom immersed himself in local politics and founded the Church of Simon of Cyrene, which would be the last congregation he led. Although his one bid for Congress was unsuccessful, he achieved higher office within his denomination. First, he was elected as editor of the *A.M.E. Church Review*, which provided him a far-reaching platform to preach the Social Gospel with the resources of the Afro-Protestant press.[7] As an ordained minister, he was one of many American preachers of the era who worked deliberately to reconcile the dogma of the Christian tradition with the demands of the "modern" world. Ransom was in the vanguard of both American Protestantism and race politics.[8] He was not the only clergyperson to publish his thoughts about the New Negro. However, his 1923 poem "The New Negro" captured well several of the ways in which religious liberalism and racial ecumenism came together in the 1920s.[9]

Consonant with contemporary debates about racial aesthetics, which gained greater prominence via Alain Locke and others associated with the Negro Renaissance, "The New Negro" balanced an emphasis on Africa, on one hand, and slavery and segregation, on the other. By Ransom's account, both an African past and the harsh realities of American life had shaped the development of the culture of "the Negro" in the United States. He argued that the legacy of Africa had prepared black people for a unique role in the world. In his view, the New Negro descended from ancestors who "roamed the jungle and led the chase / Crystallized by the heat of Oriental suns." Now in the United States, Ransom explained, the Negro offered American society its last hope for peace. Much of the imagery in the poem perpetuated an image of a "primitive" Africa that was popular at the time.[10] Even so, Ransom posited a triumphalist vision of the New Negro as the "last reserve of God on earth."[11] In this regard, Ransom's New Negro bore the distinctive ambitions of an Afro-Protestant exceptionalism.

Ransom's assertion of a regal black ancestry that began long before the trauma of American slavery also resembled the pan-African theology of Marcus Garvey and his Universal Negro Improvement Association. Indeed, four years after publishing his poem Ransom would refer to Garvey as "the mightiest prophet who has appeared among us in fifty years."[12] At the same time, the Christian preacher acknowledged that racism in the New World played a formative role in the construction of racial identity. "The lyncher, mob, and stake" had both prepared "the Negro" to make a special contribution to the nation and had established black people as essential to America's national identity. The New Negro came "bearing rich gifts of science, religion, poetry and song," offerings upon which "America's unfinished arch of freedom waits." Yet it would be through Christian love, in particular, that they would arrive "ON EQUAL FOOTING everywhere with all mankind."[13]

A preacher and ardent champion of black equality, as a poet Reverdy Ransom added an overtly theological (and specifically Christian) dimension to the aspirations of the New Negro movement, even as both sacred and secular iterations of this idea were indebted to the common reserve of romantic racialism.[14] Still, Ransom's poem clarified at least one concrete way that religion informed the aesthetics and politics associated with the black cultural renaissance of the 1920s. The nomenclature "New Negro" is most commonly associated with Alain Locke's 1925 anthology *The New Negro*. By then, however, the term had a history that dated back almost three decades. The expression was commonly used by many of Ransom's contemporaries, including A. Philip Randolph and Marcus Garvey, as well as in prior years by a number of leading "race men" and women who witnessed the collapse of Reconstruction and the rise of legal segregation. Included in this group were Fannie Barrier Williams, Booker T. Washington, and N. B. Wood, who together edited a volume titled *A New Negro for a New Century* in 1900.[15]

Appeals to a New Negro circulated prominently in the intervening years across a range of cultural and political spaces. Moreover, the term would continue to carry salience for years to come until it was eventually eclipsed by the militancy associated with Black Power.[16] Across these decades, as well as in the high moment known as the Negro Renaissance, the New Negro was always as much a "coded system of signs complete with masks and mythology" as it was a reference to any concrete entity, group of people, or specific political program.[17] Race leaders hoped to create a new reality for "colored" people in America by constructing a fresh image of "the Negro" for America. However, the image of the New Negro was anything but singular. Decades later, recalling how the idea of a New Negro crystallized in Harlem during the 1920s, the poet Robert Hayden claimed that more than anything else it was "metaphysical."[18]

Reverdy Ransom's poem offered evidence that would seem to affirm Hayden's recollection. Religion was indeed a critical, if commonly overlooked, element in the aesthetic, institutional, and political manifestations of the New Negro Renaissance.[19] Ransom's broader ministry and social activism, rather than being exceptional, were in keeping with the activities of a cadre of black preachers at the time. Race leaders who were also churchmen, like Ransom, were by all accounts New Negro clergy. Such ministers crafted models of what amounted to New Negro ministries that negotiated the advances of modern society by creatively infusing racial aesthetics and race politics with aspects of traditional Afro-Protestantism.[20] In this light, Ransom was part of a movement to institutionalize the Social Gospel in northern black churches in order to address the demands of the Great Migration and the constraints imposed by Jim Crow.[21] As leaders and intellectuals hailed the coming of a novel racial spirit in the arts, these New Negro clergy claimed that their churches were the institutions best situated to help inaugurate a modern era for black people in the United States.

Elite churches led by men like Ransom, Adam Clayton Powell Sr. (Abyssinian Baptist Church in Harlem), and Lacey Kirk Williams (Olivet Baptist Church in Chicago) were by no means representative of most African American churches.[22] They were, in truth, a minority. W. E. B. Du Bois had argued that a "talented tenth" would represent the race to the world. Similarly, this relatively small group of clergy aspired to speak for black people from the institutional bases of Afro-Protestantism.[23] Like their secular counterparts, who defined the New Negro in opposition to the cultural stigmas associated with slavery, New Negro clergy sought to counter popular images of the "primitive" religiosity associated with the masses of black folk migrating from the South. Such caricatures had been used to justify racial segregation and its violent enforcement. In turn, it was argued, a new image of black religion would help remedy the political asymmetries and physical hostility that constrained black social life during the interwar years.[24]

As a pastor and a political activist, Reverdy Ransom embodied a broader effort to reform African American religion and culture—and black churches specifically—in line with a respectable New Negro politics. During the 1920s a number of black artists and intellectuals seconded the claims made by clergy like Ransom, in effect affirming the singularity of the Negro Church as it presided over black cultural and political life. At the same time, many of the same figures who valorized the Negro Church as an instrument of racial uplift maintained an abiding investment in the forms of black folk religion that New Negro politics often aimed to obscure.[25] Ransom's poem expressed the commitments of a cohort of New Negroes, religious and secular, who sought to interpret, present, and organize black cultural and political life during the interwar years. Ultimately, various kinds of black churches—folk and elite, institutional and storefront—figured as evidentiary sources and sites of contestation in efforts to define the spirit of the New Negro.

THE MAKING OF A RACIAL SPIRIT: ALAIN LOCKE AND THE MYTH OF THE NEW NEGRO

Reverdy Ransom's poem, written by a bishop in a black mainline denomination, encapsulated the specifically liberal Protestant aspirations of the New Negro. In contrast, Alain Locke's vision for the New Negro reflected the expansive rubrics of American religious liberalism. Yet as distinct as they were, the liberalisms of Ransom and Locke were by no means mutually exclusive. Rather, they were of a kind, indicative of a larger desire and a concerted effort during the early twentieth century to forge a decidedly modern religious sensibility.[26] The roster of individuals invested in forging a forward-thinking faith often worked in the same organizations and traveled in similar circles. It was not uncommon for a single person to identify with both traditions. This was certainly the case with Locke, the philosopher, editor, and cultural entrepreneur who helped launch the Harlem Renaissance.[27]

Although Reverdy Ransom was prominent in the overlapping circles of religious leadership and race politics, he was less influential on the New Negro literary scene. Alain Locke, the first black Rhodes Scholar and a Harvard-trained philosopher, played a more prominent role in shaping the presentation and reception of the New Negro during the 1920s. Playing both sides of the Protestant/religious liberal coin, Locke often minimized the significance of the former in favor of the ecumenism of the latter.

Within the primarily white circles of American religious liberalism, a key aim was to cultivate a spirituality that was more expansive and inclusive than what had been articulated by the Protestant establishment. For African Americans, it served this purpose as well. However, for "race men" such as Alain Locke, an all-embracing spirituality was also a resource for achieving the end of social recognition, if not full inclusion, within a nation where Christianity had all too often justified enslavement and racial segregation.[28] Christianity was both spiritual and social currency, but it was also a sign of oppression. In this regard, the egalitarianism preached by religious liberals squared well with the goal of social equality articulated by black artists, intellectuals, and the leadership of civil rights organizations. Locke stood squarely within this tradition when he framed his vision for the Harlem Renaissance as distinctly spiritual.

As one of the main architects organizing New Negro aesthetics and politics during the 1920s and 1930s, Alain Locke emphasized the role that secular organizations like the Urban League and the NAACP would play as the institutional launching pads for Negro literature. For instance, scholar and activist W. E. B. Du Bois and novelist and editor Jessie Fauset worked with the NAACP's magazine *Crisis* to cultivate and celebrate the talents of young artists. Similarly, sociologist and National Urban League research director Charles S. Johnson partnered with Alain Locke to provide comparable leadership in the realm of the arts. Through the organization's print outlet, *Opportunity*, they sponsored regular literary competitions. Indeed, the pages of *Opportunity* (as was also the case with *Crisis*) featured many of the race's rising literary stars. In 1924, under the auspices of the Urban League, Charles Johnson convened an affair at Manhattan's Civic Club that welcomed several of the most celebrated up-and-coming Negro writers, including Hughes, Gwendolyn Bennett, Countee Cullen, and Eric Walrond. Locke, then a professor of philosophy at Howard University in Washington, DC, was the master of ceremonies. The nascent Harlem Renaissance, a local flourishing of a longer New Negro movement that dated back to the final decade of the nineteenth century, appeared to be in full bloom.[29]

His work with *Opportunity* as well as his visible role presiding over the Civic Club dinner in 1924 helped establish Alain Locke as a dean of the Negro Renaissance. Locke edited *The New Negro* the following year. The anthology quickly became a definitive text, commonly considered the movement's "bible." The task of editing this most heralded document of the era required its own brand of artistic and political ingenuity.[30] Although the contributors were not exclusively Negroes, the collection was a virtual who's who of black artists and intellectuals during the 1920s. It included poetry, fiction, drama, music, the visual arts, and interpretive and historical essays.

Months prior to compiling hundreds of submissions into the more than four hundred pages of the anthology, Locke had first edited a special issue of the monthly periodical *Survey Graphic* titled "Harlem: Mecca of the New

Negro." Most of the March 1925 number of *Survey Graphic* became the core of the much larger book.[31] One of the most interesting stories of the New Negro movement concerns the process of expanding the *Survey Graphic* issue into *The New Negro* anthology. Perhaps unsurprisingly, like most scholarship on the New Negro, little energy has been devoted to exploring how religion figured as a site of contestation in the anthology's construction.[32] The one contribution in the *Survey Graphic* issue that focused directly on the subject of religion has been all but ignored. "The Church and the Negro Spirit," an essay by George Edmund Haynes, did not make the cut for the larger book. Haynes worked at the Urban League prior to Charles Johnson, Locke's collaborator at *Opportunity*. So perhaps his exclusion from the book was a matter of personal allegiances.[33] In any event, this excision suggests much about Locke's own commitments. It also provides an apt entrée into the politics of religion—of church and spirit(s)—at work during the decade.

In order to ascertain the significance of Haynes's omission from *The New Negro*, it is helpful to first consider those contributions to the *Survey Graphic* issue that mentioned religion in some form and were included in the anthology. Rudolph Fisher's series of short stories, "Vestiges," offers perhaps the most sustained attention to religion in *The New Negro*.[34] A particular form of Afro-Protestantism figured as central in the first and last of the four tales. The first, "Shepherd! Lead Us!," told the story of an old southern pastor, Ezekiel Taylor, who journeyed north in search of his migrating members. Having initially resisted the urge to move with the masses, Taylor now found himself combing Harlem's streets for members of his congregation. Lured into a storefront by the sounds of a familiar song, the migrant minister was there reunited with his former church, now worshipping under the direction of a new preacher, Shackleton Ealey. In contrast to the naïve southern sincerity he attributed to Taylor, Fisher portrayed Ealey as a prototypical northern con man who was "inspired to preach the Gospel by the draft laws of 1917" and sought "to make capital out of his conversion." Ealey's efforts were soon undone, however, as he learned that his congregants were leaving to reconstitute their old church under Taylor's leadership.

In "Shepherd! Lead Us!," the North figured as the place where a performance of faith became a financial hustle. Yet the religious scam at work in the city was ultimately trumped by an ancestral spirituality deeply shaped by southern kinship ties.[35] Fisher continued this line of thinking in the final story, "Revival," which featured Pete and Lucky, bored bootleggers who wound up at a revival because it presented the prospect of a "pretty good show." When the preacher's talk turned to hell, Lucky, who also happened to be the wayward son of a preacher, felt compelled to leave the service. In response to Pete's probing, Lucky explained, "Dam' 'f I know what it is—maybe because it makes me think of the old folks or somethin'—but—hell—it just sorter—gets me—."[36] In contrast to the first story, where the northern preacher was described as a con man, here a man who profited from vice proved unable to escape the ghosts of his religious past.

As quintessential migration narratives, Rudolph Fisher's stories provided an image of Afro-Protestantism as a relic of an authentic southern folk past that continued to exert significant cultural and theological power in northern cities.[37] Yet religion in the North was also simultaneously presented as a con, an absence of reason, a mindless amusement, and an object of ridicule. Additionally, the syntax that Fisher employed in the dialogue between the bootleggers raised the question of whether Lucky's reluctant religious experience was more a matter of familial ties than theological formation—a question of kinship rather than creed. Even Lucky appeared uncertain as to why the sermon preached at the revival moved him so deeply. Readers are left unclear about whether Lucky was concerned about his salvation (he was a bootlegger, after all) or because the hellfire message reminded him of "the old folks," presumably his mother and preacher father, and their shared southern past.

In Fisher's fiction, the spiritual and the social were entangled in an idyllic southern Afro-Protestantism that persisted in the North. Additionally, despite the changes facilitated by the migrations, the lines between fakery and "true" religion were not entirely clear in either region. For Locke, most simply, these fictional accounts of folk religion offered images of a cultural past from which New Negro politics departed. At best, these proverbial ghosts of Negroes past were raw material for a racial aesthetic. As a New Negro elder statesman, one might expect to find in Locke disdain for the "old-time religion" and an embrace of the liberal Afro-Protestantism of a man like Reverdy Ransom. But the New Negro never entailed a simple exchange of the old for the new or of a sacred past for a secular present and future. In this regard, Fisher's fictive portraits were at once playful caricatures and nostalgic tributes to a not-quite-bygone era.

In contrast to Fisher's "Vestiges," Alain Locke's own discussion of religion elsewhere in the volume helps explain the erasure of Haynes's essay. In addition to his duties as editor, Locke penned the foreword and title essay for *The New Negro*. He also published two of his own articles: "The Negro Spirituals" and "The Legacy of the Ancestral Arts." In the latter, Locke described Christianity as a particular challenge to his efforts to encourage black artists to draw inspiration from Africa. According to Locke:

> The American Negro, even when he confronts the various forms of African art expression with a sense of its ethnic claims upon him, meets them in as alienated and misunderstanding an attitude as the average European westerner. Christianity and all of the other European conventions operate to make this inevitable.[38]

In this view, churches socialized black people into cultural worlds that privileged Western norms and perpetuated a warped perspective on African culture. Convinced that the "ancestral arts" of Africa should direct New Negro artists, Locke was part of a wider conversation within modernism that found inspiration in "primitive" Africa, which also had certain reverberations within racial aesthetics.[39]

If not exceptional in this regard, as one especially formidable "European convention" among others, Christianity presented a particular impediment. Given the special prominence of Afro-Protestantism in black life, it was all the more difficult for New Negroes to embrace Africa as the source of a racial aesthetic. In his other essay, "The Negro Spirituals," Alain Locke displayed a similar ambivalence with regard to Christianity's undue influence on black musical expression. Locke created a hierarchical typology with four categories that, in his estimation, were unhelpfully lumped together under a single rubric. In Locke's schema, secular "work and labor songs" were mistakenly classified as spirituals and "Folk ballads," which had been fused with spirituals, were still something different. "Freer and more unrestrained evangelical shouts or Meeting songs" maintained a greater degree of authenticity. Yet the "pure spirituals" were "almost ritualistic prayer songs." At their artistic best, they expressed religious moods and motivations. When concerned with the mundane they became derivative, an altogether different genre of music. In short, beautiful art and true religion assumed each other. And the spirituals were, by definition, sacred music, akin to the Psalms of the Hebrew Bible.[40]

In his analysis of spirituals, Alain Locke awkwardly enfolded a peculiar sacred–secular binary into an argument for racial authenticity and American originality. Accordingly, he posited:

> The spirituals are really the most characteristic product of the race genius as yet in America. But the very elements which make them uniquely expressive of the Negro make them at the same time deeply representative of the soil

that produced them. Thus, as unique spiritual products of American life, they become nationally as well as racially characteristic.[41]

Echoing W. E. B. Du Bois's classic interpretation of "The Sorrow Songs" in *The Souls of Black Folk* (1903), Locke observed that the music was both Negro and American. However, his claim that Spirituals were singularly spiritual was, a bit ironically, a two-sided coin.

The music's mere persistence merited special praise and, in part, accounted for its dreadful beauty. Indeed, Negro Spirituals had outlasted both "the conventionalizations of formal religion, [and] the repressions of Puritanism," Locke observed. In this view, Christianity inflicted artistic violence upon the music (in addition to the actual violence of American slavery, out of which the music grew) at the same time that it provided the emotional and lyrical substance that defined the musical form. Ultimately though, according to Locke, the Spiritual was a kind of folk art. Thus, even in its "epic intensity and tragic profundity," the genre was more raw emotional material than refined cultural mastery. It would be required to "transcend[s] the level of its origin" if it were to truly represent the New Negro or receive unqualified recognition as universal art.[42] The artistic transcendence that Locke called for in Spirituals paired perfectly with what he claimed was already taking place with the race collectively (at least in Harlem). "Recall how suddenly the Negro spirituals revealed themselves; suppressed for generations under the stereotypes of Wesleyan hymn harmony," his lead essay to the anthology reminded readers.[43]

Together with Fisher's short stories, Locke's essays in *The New Negro* reveal an ambivalence toward the institutions and expressive forms associated with the Negro Church. The New Negro would be best served if Afro-Protestantism became a remnant of the past, Locke seemed to suggest, a historical determinant to be disentangled from Afro-Modernity. At a minimum, folk forms would have to be refined and elite arrangements less rigidly enforced for black people to fully and freely develop. Rather than an American-born Afro-Protestantism, Locke imagined that an emerging racial spirit would take its primary cultural cues from West Africa, which the ancestors of most Negroes, had once called home.

Alain Locke's appeal to Africa was consistent with the New Negro movement's desire to create distance from the stigmas attached to the period of legal enslavement. In circumventing the painfully intimate system of American chattel slavery, Locke also avoided mention of the emergence of the "invisible institution," the race's first independent and structural form of social life and the forerunner of what Benjamin

Elijah Mays and Joseph Nicholson would soon refer to as "the Negro's church."[44] In evading fuller discussion of Afro-Protestantism by exclud-ing Haynes's essay, Locke largely eluded any substantive treatment of the ethos of American evangelicalism, which defined most black congre-gations at the time and was a theological and cultural fault line during the 1920s.[45]

The secular myth-making function that informed the editing of *The New Negro* is made all the more evident upon examination of George Edmund Haynes's essay in the *Survey Graphic* number. Haynes had already earned degrees from Fisk and Yale when, in 1912, he became the first Negro to receive a PhD from Columbia University. While studying sociology at Columbia, he also played an instrumental role in the 1910 founding of the organization that became the National Urban League. Highly active in the Presbyterian Church, Haynes was serving as secretary of the Federal Council of Churches' Commission on Church and Race Relations when he penned his essay for *Survey Graphic*. George Haynes was as much a part of the Protestant establishment as any African American at the time.[46]

Alain Locke, in short, cast Christianity as one cause of racial alienation. By contrast, in "The Church and the Negro Spirit," Haynes argued that the church was an enduring and capable institution in northern cities as well as in the southern communities in which it had arisen. Extolling the edu-cational, social, and financial capital of black churches, Haynes affirmed that they were "visible evidence of the struggle of an aspiring people to express the best of life within them."[47] As these passages (and the essay's title) indicated, Haynes's analysis extended in two distinct yet interwoven directions. He lauded Afro-Protestant churches as the "most resource-ful and most characteristic organized force in the life of the Negro," and imagined them as the institutional embodiment of black inner life. To borrow the popular church refrain, the Negro Church, for Haynes, was the best evidence of "something on the inside, working on the outside" to effect change on behalf of the race.

As much as any other document of the decade, George Haynes's *Survey Graphic* essay most explicitly enunciated what has previously been identi-fied in this chapter as the trope of church and spirit. Indeed, his pairing of a religious institution (the church) and a collective race politics (the Negro spirit) provided Haynes with the organizing core of his main argument as well as the title of his article. Together, the inclusion of Rudolph Fisher's "Vestiges" and the exclusion of Haynes's essay offer a telling glimpse into Locke's sense of the limits of a black Christian modernism, in both its southern folk and liberal Protestant forms. Although "The Church and the Negro Spirit" was not republished in *The New Negro*, this trope of church and spirit was taken up and revised in the writings of a significant number of the Negro Renaissance's most celebrated artists and intellectuals, including Alain Locke himself. To be sure, most New Negro writers did not affirm the implicit normative order in Haynes's configuration of the trope; that is, church over spirit, racial spirit effectively channeled through the church. Yet even in dissent and disavowal, they confirmed the centrality of Afro-Protestantism in ordering the spirit(s) of the New Negro.

Like seminal research on "the Negro church" by W. E. B. Du Bois, Carter G. Woodson, and Benjamin Mays and Joseph Nicholson, George Edmund Haynes's essay was indicative of a nascent academic orthodoxy that posited a politically engaged Protestant church as the norm for black religious life. Alain Locke, however, was by no means an apologist for the rule of Afro-Protestantism. His own writing in *The New Negro* challenged the narrative of the triumphal ascent of a Christian hegemony. And his omission of the essay by George Haynes would seem to lend support to the idea that the New Negro was defined by a certain secularity. Alongside the more strident critiques of organized religion made by others during the 1920s, the image and aims of the New Negro have been understood as primarily secular and secularizing.

While less invested in institutional Afro-Protestantism as such, Locke's framing of the anthology accented the other side of Haynes's equation. That is, he availed himself of a spiritual grammar (e.g., spirit, race-spirit, spirituality) both to interpret the creative forces animating Harlem's artists and advance his own vision for the New Negro. If the New Negro was committed to a black secularism, in Locke's enunciation those commitments were no less spiritual. Although he was a lifelong Episcopalian, Locke also maintained active connections to the American Baha'i community from the 1910s until his death in 1954. He served on its National Interracial Amity committee, wrote for Baha'i publications, and eventually even made a pilgrimage to Baha'i holy places in the Middle East.[48] At least in part through his Baha'i activities, Locke cultivated a strong faith in the prospect that black people would make a unique contribution to the Western world.

In the cultural and political ambitions of the Harlem Renaissance, Alain Locke no doubt observed consonance between an emerging theory of cultural pluralism and the theological commitment to racial equality espoused by the Baha'i faith. While he did not explicitly invoke the Baha'i tradition in *The New Negro*, it may very well have provided a religious framework for the racial ecumenism and spiritual cosmopolitanism that he announced in the volume. In his introduction, Locke asserted: "Negro life is not only establishing new contacts and founding new centers, it is finding a new soul. There is a fresh spiritual and cultural flourishing."[49] He argued that black people in America were undergoing an analogous transformation. Once considered to be "more of a myth than a man ... more of a formula than a human being," Negroes were now gaining recognition as complex human subjects. This "sudden reorientation of view" amounted to no less than a "spiritual emancipation."[50]

As a philosopher of culture, Locke put forward an ambitious claim for racial ecumenism under the guise of social scientific observation in *The New Negro*. In 1920s Harlem, he detected the development of a collective intra-racial sensibility that was trumping any differences of ethnicity, class, and geography. Simultaneously interpreting and celebrating, Locke mobilized the familiar trope of church and spirit for his own purposes. "Each group has come with its own separate motives for its own special ends," he explained. "But their greatest experience has been the finding of one another. ... Harlem, I grant you, isn't typical—but it is significant." Locke continued, "It is prophetic." In light of the urban pluralism fostered by the migrations, Locke at once dispassionately observed and actively imagined the emergence of a shared "race-spirit." The "new spirit ... awake in the masses" was prophetic in anticipating that a "deep feeling of race" was becoming the "mainspring of Negro life."[51]

Significantly, Alain Locke's New Negro prophecy was construed as part of a larger national phenomenon of secularization. Allegiances to old "social nostrums and panaceas" such as religion were being diminished, if not discarded, in the face of a growing nascent "race-spirit."[52] This assessment of the declining role of Negro churches in the North was inadequate at best. Locke's philosophical training suggested a more active investment in myth-making than in the collection of empirical data. His claim that a "race-spirit" had begun to supplant religion confirmed his own constructive project, at once secular and spiritual, for *The New Negro*. Although Alain Locke insisted that the migrations were producing a "new spirit" among the masses, southern migrants more often than not interpreted their experience in the language of Afro-Protestantism.

Churches had played a significant role in shaping notions of selfhood and social life in the South. The structures and functions of the Negro Church certainly changed in Locke's Harlem. Yet the forms of Afro-Protestantism multiplied and diversified more than they declined in the North—the so-called Promised Land, as it was often named.[53] In this regard, Alain Locke and George Edmund Haynes had more in common than their essays might suggest. Both men argued that the movement of a modern spirit was increasingly evident in the lives of black people in the urban North. They diverged, however, in their assessment of which sites and sources of authority ought to have organizing power over this racial spirit. Haynes endorsed a literate and reasoning institutional Afro-Protestantism; Locke favored a form of racial reasoning that was unconstrained by Christian orthodoxy yet still devoutly spiritual. Ultimately, Haynes and Locke contributed to a larger debate about the role of the Christian church (and organized religion) in modern society even as they were theorizing a New Negro identity.[54]

THE EVIDENTIARY ENDS OF AFRO-PROTESTANTISM: DEBATING NEGRO ART IN *THE NATION*

By the mid-1920s, racial aesthetics had become a cause célèbre. Through *Opportunity* and other venues, Alain Locke continued to avidly support the next generation of Negro writers. One year after *The New Negro* went to press, W. E. B. Du Bois, Jessie Fauset, and the NAACP hosted an extended dialogue on the relationships between race, the arts, and popular culture. The civil rights organization had championed race literature since at least the 1910s. Its yearlong focus on the subject in 1926 helped put the arts at the forefront of the black reading public's imagination. Hosted on the pages of *The Crisis*, this discussion included such topics as representations of the Negro in American literature, the appropriate aims for black artists, and the prospects of a distinct tradition of racial art in the United States. By now the New Negro had also become a topic of national interest. In June 1926, one of the nation's leading weekly periodicals entered the debate. In back-to-back editions, *The Nation* published essays by George Schuyler and Langston Hughes, two of Harlem's most promising young writers.

Schuyler, who eventually became known as the "Sage of Sugar Hill," would create a name for himself as satirist par excellence on race matters with his 1931 debut novel *Black No More*. Part science fiction and part racial commentary, *Black No More* relayed the story of a scientist who created a machine capable of turning black skin white. The satire then proceeded to track the dramatic responses this invention evoked from black and white people alike. Even before *Black No More*, Schuyler had already begun to establish himself as an intellectual contrarian and journalistic provocateur. His sarcastic essay "The Negro-Art Hokum," which appeared in *The Nation* on June 16, 1926, fit squarely in this tradition.[55]

In short but theatrical fashion, Schuyler dismissed the very notion of a racial art. If one were to ever be developed, he opined, it would have to take place on the continent of Africa. Talk of a Negro art on North American soil was "self-evident foolishness."[56] He insisted that artistic expressions credited to "Aframericans"—such as spirituals, the blues, and jazz—were more accurately attributable to regional and class differences than to any particular racial characteristic. According to Schuyler, "this, of course, is easily understood if one stops to realize that the Aframerican is merely a lampblacked Anglo-Saxon." He continued, "Aside from his color, which ranges from very dark brown to pink, your American Negro is just plain American."[57]

Schuyler found religious life to be especially illustrative of this fact. Drawing comparisons across the color line, he explained that the Negro "reads the same Bible and belongs to the Baptist, Methodist and Episcopal and Catholic church. ... It is sheer nonsense to talk about 'racial differences' as between the American black man and the American white man."[58] Schuyler did not discount the reality of the racial history of the United States or the continued impact of slavery and segregation. Yet what mattered more in discussions of art was that black and white people alike were contributors to as well as heirs of a shared heritage. American culture was defined more by contact, encounter, and exchange than by any traditions discretely identifiable as black or white.[59] Moreover, that New Negro artists were well versed in European and American artistic traditions, for Schuyler, was more significant than any racial classification.

Acknowledging the significance of churches as tools of social and cultural formation, Schuyler emphasized that black people in the United States had more in common with their white Christian compatriots than they did with their distant ancestors from Africa. Although religious imagery appeared incidental to his critique of race, the pairing of race and religion here suggested the skeptical manner in which he treated both topics elsewhere. His essay "Ten Commandments," a clear reference to the Hebrew Bible, offered suggestions for dealing with "the Negro Problem." Yet he generally opposed the singularity of this sociological formulation. In contrast to Du Bois's notion of a "talented tenth," Schuyler was of the opinion that all "Aframericans" were obligated to wrestle with many human predicaments, some of which were shared by other black people.[60]

In his commandments, Schuyler advocated everything from reading the classics and practicing good hygiene to supporting black-owned businesses, joining a labor union, and purchasing real estate.[61] Provocation as much as practical advice, his seventh commandment specifically addressed the matter of religion. Here Schuyler implored his readers to "stop dealing in faith and face the facts. This is the age of materialism, not mysticism. Practice enlightened self-interest and develop intelligent skepticism. Examine all sides of every question. Be 'from Missouri.'"[62] Encouraging his newly urban audience to make the religious metaphysics of their rural roots a thing of the past, Schuyler's valorization of "doubt as a way of life" organized his broader discussions of religion. In other writings, he told fantastic tales of childhood deals with the devil and celebrated the gains of modern science.

However, Schuyler embraced a decidedly instrumentalist account of the social obligations of "the Negro Church."[63] Similar to George Haynes's argument in his 1925 *Survey Graphic* essay, Schuyler noted that churches were well situated to serve the social and economic interests of the race. In fact, the premise of his seventh commandment squared well with Haynes's notion of a Negro spirit. Both men valued literacy, reason, and economic self-sufficiency, attributes that Haynes hailed as animating institutional Afro-Protestantism. Yet as one quick to parody popular racial and religious assumptions, Schuyler mockingly described members of Negro churches as mimes of their white counterparts. In short, Afro-Protestants were "lampblacked Anglo-Saxons." If this were the case, then a distinctive racial aesthetic was implausible; never mind Haynes's idea (or Locke's, for that matter) of an independent "Negro spirit."[64]

Offering a rebuttal in the following week's issue of *The Nation*, Langston Hughes argued precisely the opposite.[65] In "The Negro Artist and the Racial Mountain," Hughes claimed that there was a distinct racial aesthetic and that it could be discerned in the folk cultures of American Negroes. More precisely, and perhaps taking a cue from Schuyler, he also pointed to black churches as evidence. Schuyler had argued that a shared American Christianity made the idea of a unique racial sensibility unfeasible. Hughes countered by clarifying that the "Negro Church" was not a monolith.

As much as any other New Negro writer, Langston Hughes touched on all points of the spectrum between church and spirit that framed discussions of religion during the decade. To date, relatively little attention has been paid to how extensively Hughes wrote about religion.[66] Over the course of a literary career that spanned more than half of the twentieth century, Hughes thoughtfully engaged the subject of religion in every genre in which he wrote, especially in his poems. Hughes also penned several gospel plays, including *Tambourines to Glory*, *Jericho-Jim Crow*, and *The Gospel Glory*. To this day his highly acclaimed *Black Nativity* is performed during the Christmas season in cities across the nation.[67] He spent significant energy discussing and portraying (and critiquing) both black churches and Christianity more broadly. He also assessed the sociological importance of churches and the practical value of specific religious practices in African American life.[68]

In addition to his critical and creative writing on the topic, Hughes candidly described his own personal experiences with churches in his autobiography, *The Big Sea* (1940), and elsewhere.[69] Yet ultimately, he was publicly noncommittal about whether he believed in God. If not a confession of faith, "The Negro Artist and the Racial Mountain" linked Hughes's appreciation for the aesthetics of Afro-Protestantism to his literary vocation. As his biographer Arnold Rampersad has explained, the essay functioned as a declaration of independence on behalf of a new breed of Negro artists.[70] *The Nation*'s readers were made privy to the author's understanding of the relationship between black churches and the racial spirit that others, like Locke and Haynes, had been hailing.

Hughes's essay refuted Schuyler's sharp dismissal of the idea of an "Aframerican" art. Moreover, he offered an apologia for creative freedom for Negro artists, as well as an argument in favor of a distinct tradition of racial aesthetics. Hughes articulated much of the sentiment that led his comrades, later that year, to publish the journal *Fire!!*, which endorsed the notion of a distinctive racial aesthetic evident in the ways of black "folk."[71]

Hughes framed his essay within a critique of an unnamed Countee Cullen, who was then perhaps the only comparably celebrated Negro poet. Hughes argued that Cullen's hope to be welcomed simply as a "poet" rather than a "negro poet" exposed a deeper desire: He wished to be white! Cullen's desire was important insofar as it revealed a wider sentiment shared by no small number of Negroes at the time. According to Hughes, Cullen's aspirations—and, by implication, Schuyler's denial— exposed "an urge within the race toward whiteness, the desire to pour racial individuality into the mode of American standardization, and to be as little Negro and as much American as possible." An interest in evading the adjectival "negro" was indicative of a latent "desire to run away spiritually" from the race, Hughes contended. Cullen equated the absence of the racial designation with excellence. Hughes argued, in contrast, that this sentiment was precisely what would prevent his peers from achieving artistic greatness.[72]

Hughes failed to elaborate or explain more fully what the "spiritual" dimension of his diagnosis entailed. What was clear is that Hughes observed Cullen's poetic ambitions as the cultural equivalent of attempting to "pass." The topic of passing was by no means novel, but it would take center stage in the Negro Renaissance two years later, with the publication of Nella Larsen's popular novel *Passing*.[73] Similar to Alain Locke,

Hughes drew upon a spiritual grammar to posit a cultural kinship to which Negro artists were heirs. To "run away spiritually" implied more treachery than transcendence. Once again, racial authenticity registered in spiritual tones.

Hughes was not alone in assigning spiritual significance to an emerging racial identity or in enlisting religious evidence in support of the New Negro. Unlike Locke, though, he felt no need to plumb the cultures of ancestral Africa. Hughes discerned the sources of a racial aesthetic on North American soil. Nurturing a tradition of Negro art did not require that black churches, or organized religion more generally, be displaced or harnessed, as Locke had suggested. Nor, as Schuyler argued, did it mean that Afro-Protestants were simply white Christians in blackface. There were indeed Negroes who did "not particularly care whether they are like white folks or anybody else." Large established black churches (i.e., "*the* Negro Church") might "worship the Lord correctly and quietly" like white Protestants, but other congregations were well equipped to birth truly great Negro artists.[74]

Langston Hughes suggested that some black churches were a valuable resource for racial aesthetics. More specifically, in looking to the churches of the Negro masses, Hughes turned Schuyler's argument on its head. First, he conceded that certain congregations were modeled after "Caucasian patterns." This phenomenon resulted in a bourgeois investment in respectability rather than a shared racial culture. Like Schuyler, Hughes described the mainline denominational churches of black elites as inclined toward an "aping of things white." That these churches held onto visions of an "Episcopal heaven" presented a significant obstacle to the development of a racial art.[75]

Hughes further clarified the classed nature of their disagreement by calling attention to the churches of the "low-down folks." Storefront churches, according to Hughes, were among the best sites to espy the stylings of a distinctive racial culture. In these congregations, Hughes explained:

> Their joy runs, bang! into ecstasy. Their religion soars to a shout. . . . They furnish a wealth of colorful, distinctive material for any artist because they still hold their own individuality in the face of American standardizations. And perhaps these common people will give to the world its truly great Negro artist, the one who is not afraid to be himself.[76]

With the aesthetics of a folk Afro-Protestantism as his model, Hughes both advanced racial particularism and resisted racial provincialism.[77]

Near the essay's end, he summed up his position as a defense for the new generation:

> We younger Negro artists who create now intend to express our individual dark-skinned selves without fear or shame. If white people are pleased we are glad. If they are not, it doesn't matter. We know we are beautiful. And ugly too. The tom-tom cries and the tom-tom laughs. If colored people are pleased we are glad. If they are not, their displeasure doesn't matter either. We build our temples for tomorrow, strong as we know how, and we stand on top of the mountain, free within ourselves.[78]

Here, the poet continued his critique of middle-class respectability. He also reasserted the spiritual significance of race. The distinctiveness of black folk culture was to be valorized rather than devalued. So he refused to relinquish a commitment to "the folk," even if it led to an art that was, at times, perceived to confirm a white public's plea for "the primitive." In doing so, Hughes both embraced the idea of a particular racial aesthetic and imagined an artistic plane that privileged individuality—wherein black people would be received as "Beautiful. And ugly too"—irrespective of racial difference or audience reception.

Hughes's analysis began with black folk churches as a distinct entity within a broader field of folk culture that included jazz and the blues. While he embraced the notion of a distinct tradition of black art, he objected to elitist or rigidly political norms. Efforts to portray the race exclusively in positive terms were at best incomplete. They conflated human freedom with social equality even as they exposed racial insecurities and a latent desire for white approval.[79] In the context of Hughes's obvious concern with race, his selection of the term "temple"—suggestive of a spiritual sanctuary but not necessarily a church—was telling. That is, Hughes's appeal to Afro-Protestantism in service to a racial aesthetic revealed a broader spiritual impulse that undergirded much of the political and cultural ambitions of the Harlem Renaissance.[80]

Certain race leaders might, understandably, feel shamed by the frenzied worship on display in Harlem's storefront churches. Respectability insisted that such religious practices impeded racial progress. Alain Locke had argued in *The New Negro* that a race-spirit was supplanting religious authority en route to political advancement. Now, in "The Negro Artist and the Racial Mountain," Hughes claimed that the churches of the Negro masses evinced a spirit of inner (racial) freedom that was not yet won in the wider society. In celebrating these particular churches, Hughes suggested that religious transcendence might precede social recognition.

What popular opinion considered "bad religion" was no less than the stuff of great art, Hughes argued. Paradoxically, he observed an aesthetic in those members of the race least likely to have access to the social privileges (or uplift anxieties) of Harlem's literary class. Moreover, rather than in tension or opposition, for Hughes, the church figured as the site and source of what others called a racial spirit.

As Hughes clarified in the essay's final paragraph, he claimed to speak specifically for a cadre of "younger Negro artists" who were willing to challenge the orthodoxies of an older generation.[81] The spirit(s) animating Haynes's modern church and Locke's ancestral Africa were two of the primary trajectories governing the politics of the New Negro. Both, Langston Hughes implied, were insufficient, and he sided with black folk culture in the present moment. At the same time, others called attention to such class tensions and the competing, yet inextricably tied, pulls of culture and politics. W. E. B. Du Bois, for instance, put forward a vision for Negro artists that also placed in conversation Hayne's church and Locke's racial spirit.

W. E. B. DU BOIS AND THE SPIRITUAL POLITICS OF NEGRO ART

In June 1926, W. E. B. Du Bois took to the stage at the NAACP's seventeenth national convention. He had been asked to speak at a ceremony awarding the organization's highest honor, the Spingarn Medal, to Carter G. Woodson, a fellow Harvard-trained historian who had founded Negro History Week in February of that year. Du Bois's decision to take the arts as his lecture subject at the convention was no spontaneous gesture. In addition to the dialogue on race and literature under way in the pages of *The Crisis*, George Schuyler and Langston Hughes's debate in *The Nation* had just taken place. In fact, Hughes's essay was printed on the same day that the NAACP's convention opened.

Du Bois's speech observed that the accomplishments of New Negro artists had created a whisper across society: "Here is the way out. Here is the real solution of the color problem."[82] But Du Bois was skeptical of the suggestion that the mere recognition of Negro artists was an adequate resolution. He intended to impose more specific criteria on racial aesthetics: Negro artists ought to represent the race in a positive light. From a historian's perspective, Du Bois explained that standing narratives of Africa and the United States portrayed black people as little more than the spoils of European conquest and the mules of American slavery, respectively. In light of this history, the recent memory of minstrelsy, and a marketplace ever willing to serve such popular imaginings, Du Bois called on Negro artists to provide images of black heroism.[83]

Documenting such heroism, as a historical intervention, was a theme of much of Du Bois's work. A decade later he would rewrite the history of Reconstruction, for example, highlighting the significant contributions made by newly freed black people to American democracy in the wake of emancipation. In this regard, *Black Reconstruction* (1934) provided a model of intellectual work that aimed to counter dominant narratives.[84] In 1926, Du Bois asserted that Negro artists should offset racist stereotypes with their creative work.[85] "I do not care a damn for any art that is not used for propaganda," Du Bois confessed. "But I do care when propaganda is confined to one side while the other is stripped and silent." Decrying those whom he described as "purists," he explained further, "I am one who tells the truth and exposes evil and seeks with Beauty and for Beauty to set the world right."[86] In his estimation, all art was necessarily implicated in a political order; all art was propaganda, either for or against the race.[87] So Du Bois self-consciously sought to direct the energies of Negro artists with the aims of race politics. With regard to the color line, racial aesthetics either supported change or endorsed the status quo. Du Bois cast his vote unequivocally with the former.

W. E. B. Du Bois's stature as a historian, sociologist, and social activist is well established. However, in addition to his preoccupation with social problems, he produced a significant corpus concerned specifically with religion. Even his classic work *The Souls of Black Folk* (1903) demonstrated his interest in both church and spirit. The book's first chapter began with a meditation on the Negro's "spiritual strivings" and ended with a prayer that Du Bois composed himself.[88] Du Bois began the book by framing the problem of the color line as a spiritual matter. Moreover, *Souls* extended an argument Du Bois had made six years earlier in his essay "Conservation of the Races." There he asserted that all ethnic groups possessed a "race-spirit" and that Negroes had not "yet given to civilization the full spiritual message which they are capable of giving."[89] Finally, *Souls* concluded with "The Sorrow Songs," which provided readers with a preliminary glimpse of what Du Bois took to be the content and form of that spiritual message. In his estimation, these songs were at once "the articulate message of the slave to the world," the "sole American music," and the "singular spiritual heritage of the nation."[90]

Just a couple of years before delivering his "Criteria of Negro Art" speech, Du Bois rehashed several of the arguments he had put forward in the final pages of *Souls*. In the final two chapters of his 1924 book *The*

Gift of Black Folk, he argued that the specific contributions of the Negro to American society were uniquely aesthetic and religious.[91] For one, he posited that "the Negro is primarily an artist." Yet Du Bois also insisted that

> above and beyond all that we have mentioned, perhaps least tangible but just as true is the peculiar spiritual quality which the Negro has injected into American life and civilization. It is hard to define or characterize it—a certain spiritual joyousness . . . an intense sensitiveness to spiritual values.[92]

To be sure, his claim that "the imprint of Africa" manifests itself primarily through art and religion adhered to common caricatures of "the Negro" as both overly emotive and naturally religious. However, his discussion of religion in "Criteria of Negro Art" two years later confirmed Du Bois to be more than simply a romantic racialist.[93] Religion was by no means a major theme in the speech. Yet he carried on the trope of church and spirit, offering yet another take on the implications of Afro-Protestantism for the Negro Renaissance of the 1920s.

Similar to Alain Locke, W. E. B. Du Bois described the most recent generation of Negro artists as "prophets." Against popular opinion, he insisted that the arts served a practical purpose that was not at odds with the NAACP's civil rights platform. Both were concerned with the creation of a more beautiful world. Du Bois explained that the demands of modern society made it nearly impossible for most people to appreciate the mundane beauty in everyday life, such as a sunset. This decline was akin to spiritual disenchantment, which by all accounts was a "universal failing." His prognosis and prescription again paired ethics (politics) and aesthetics (art). "We black folk may help for we have within us as a race new stirrings, stirrings of the beginning of a new appreciation of joy, of a new desire to create, of a new will to be," Du Bois told his audience. Enter here the New Negro artists: "The Negro Youth is a different kind of Youth, because in some new way it bears this mighty prophecy on its breast, with a new realization of itself, with new determination for all mankind." Like Locke, Du Bois observed in these novel "stirrings" the signs of a "new spirit" coming into sight.[94]

Although they seemed to agree on a basic spiritual assessment, Du Bois parted company with Locke in his interpretation of the conditions under which Negro art was produced as well as the direction it should take. Locke suggested that the emerging "race-spirit" apparent in the arts was rapidly supplanting religion's hold over black life. Du Bois, however, complicated this secularizing teleology of racial progress.[95] He also appeared to contradict his own insistence, earlier in the speech, concerning the necessarily political function of art. On one hand, "the white public" inter-preted all Negro art through a distorted "racial pre-judgment." On the other hand, Du Bois explained, the "black public still wants our prophets almost equally unfree." Racial aesthetics was constrained by race politics within and without, which made the "catholicity of temper" required for creative freedom a tall order.[96]

Given that he was addressing the NAACP, Du Bois devoted more time to the challenges imposed by black audiences. In this regard, he singled out religion as one source preventing the full development of a racial aesthetic:

> We are bound by all sorts of customs that have come down as second-hand soul clothes of white patrons. We are ashamed of sex and we lower our eyes when people talk of it. Our religion holds us in superstition. Our worst side has been so shamelessly emphasized that we are denying that we have or ever had a worst side. In all sorts of ways, we are hemmed in and our new young artists have got to fight their way to freedom.[97]

Although Du Bois started to disaggregate the problem into black and white, his reference to religion acknowledged the degree to which the two were always entangled. Sex was taboo and religion (presumably the Negro Church) was, in effect, a talisman. As these two things coalesced, the black public embraced what historian Evelyn Brooks Higginbotham has identified as a "politics of respectability."[98] However, while this politic was encoded within institutional Afro-Protestantism, it was, in fact, inher-ited—the "second-hand soul clothes" of whites. Indeed, the guiding logic of race politics had been formed in the likeness of American Christianity, specifically Puritanism. Du Bois explained that "still young black public" was, by default, both unreasoning and overly emotional and opposed to all forms of pleasure such as dancing, drinking, and sex.[99]

Interestingly, here Du Bois appeared to endorse artistic freedom rather than a program of racial propaganda. Negro artists ought to direct their efforts toward countering harmful racial stereotypes. Yet he also acknowledged that one side effect of a racist ideology that jus-tified slavery and segregation was that, in response, black people had begun to deny "that we have or ever had a worst side."[100] In the face of white supremacy, the Negro often overemphasized the positive, Du Bois observed. In this way the black public kept its "prophets"—that is, young Negro artists—"unfree."

This argument represented a departure for Du Bois. In both *The Souls of Black Folk* (1903) and *The Gift of Black Folk* (1924), he had lauded the cultural ingenuity apparent in black religious practices. In the first of these two books, he devoted an entire chapter to providing a historical account of the emergence of Afro-Protestantism. In "Of the Faith of the Fathers," Du Bois highlighted the "the preacher, the music, and the Frenzy" (i.e., ecstatic worship) as the pillars of the Negro Church. It was a celebrated, if complicated, first black institution on American soil.[101] In the latter, he referred more broadly to a capacious—vague yet generative—"gift of the spirit." Now, however, Du Bois singled out religion as impinging upon aesthetic freedom.[102] Whether or not Christianity alienated black people from an African past, as Alain Locke had argued in *The New Negro*, churches did limit the prospects for a racial aesthetic. Under the best of circumstances, religion might be overtaken by the rise of a racial spirit. At worst, religion would remain a repository of cultural superstitions that inhibited the creative flourishing of the race. On this count, both Du Bois and Locke seemed to agree.

For Du Bois and Locke alike, a nascent racial spirit presented the prospect of different political possibilities for black people, even if the sources and substance of that politics were debatable. For both, the arts might provide the occasion for spiritual rebirth, and vice versa. Their respective views illustrated the competing demands placed on Negro artists: the urgency of the "problem of the color line" (i.e., politics) and the presumably universal aspirations of true art (i.e., culture). This predicament would be inherited by generations of black artists and intellectuals to come. In many ways, Du Bois's "Criteria of Negro Art," delivered immediately in the wake of the debate between George Schuyler and Langston Hughes in *The Nation*, revisited and synthesized several of the main arguments that each of these young writers put forward.

The Negro Church—in all of its institutional and cultural diversity—at once harbored aspirations toward middle-class respectability, or whiteness, and was the marker of a distinct racial aesthetic. Afro-Protestantism, then, encapsulated the very complexities and contradictions that enlivened the idea of a racial spirit. For all the differences between their respective arguments, both Schuyler and Hughes provided evidence of the "new stirrings . . . of a new will to be." Each displayed an independence of mind and was developing the "catholicity of temper" required for creative freedom. They were clearly representative of the "different kind of Youth" W. E. B. Du Bois identified as "prophets."[103]

Indeed, Langston Hughes was by all accounts a leader of a rising generation of New Negroes. As much as it was a rebuttal to George Schuyler and a critique of Countee Cullen, his essay in *The Nation* was received as a credo, perhaps a confession of faith, for a cadre of "younger Negro artists" who were determined to scale the racial mountain on their own spiritual terms. Du Bois was no doubt taking cues from Hughes (and Schuyler) when he delivered his speech before the NAACP convention in June. Owing to a popular demand for the speech, *Crisis* printed it in its entirety in October of that year. Just one month later, Hughes and a group from the younger generation would seem to take Du Bois up on his call to "fight their way to freedom."[104]

NEW NEGRO PROPHETS

In November 1926, the first installment of *Fire!! A Quarterly Devoted to the Younger Negro Artists* was published, perhaps a preliminary effort in print to perform the kind of freedom Hughes had called for that summer. Although it folded after just one issue due to financial troubles, *Fire!!* was conceived by a cohort of Harlem's most promising younger artists. An editorial board of seven oversaw its development and publication, including Gwendolyn Bennett, John Davis, Aaron Douglas, Langston Hughes, Zora Neale Hurston, Richard Bruce (Nugent), and Wallace Thurman, who served as lead editor. As part of a commitment to more fully capture the complexities of black American life, the contributors to *Fire!!* took on a host of taboo topics including, most notably, black sexuality. Thurman's "Cordelia the Crude" explored the sexual desires of a young black woman; while Nugent's short story "Smoke, Lilies and Jade"—for which he assumed a pseudonym so as to not "disgrace the family name"—addressed his own homosexuality.[105]

The piece by Bruce Nugent, in particular, inflamed race leaders and leading Negro critics alike.[106] It did not help that *Fire!!* made them the subject of targeted scrutiny in the short essay titled "Intelligentsia" by Arthur Huff Fauset, a preacher's son who would, two decades later, go on to author the pathbreaking study *Black Gods of the Metropolis* (1944). With the exception of a few poets, Fauset was the only contributor to the journal who was not also a member of the editorial board. In *Fire!!*, Fauset poked fun at a group that, in his estimation, gave "art and artists a black eye with their snobbery and stupidity . . . false interpretations and hypocritical evaluations."[107] At least in part, the editorial team's vision for *Fire!!* was to fill in the deliberate silences and challenge the aesthetic orthodoxies of previous generations.

Indicative of the tensions between New Negro politics and aesthetics, race leaders had perceived differences associated with folk culture and the subject of sexuality as undermining the movement's uplift interests.[108]

The contributors to *Fire!!*, in contrast, saw such intersections as the currency of artistic autonomy. Wallace Thurman later acknowledged a direct connection between the publication's goals and Hughes's poetry:

> *Fire*, like Mr. Hughes' poetry, was experimental. It was not interested in socio-logical problems or propaganda. It was purely artistic in intent and conception. Its contributors went to the proletariat rather than to the bourgeoisie for characters and material. They were interested in people who still retained some individual race qualities and who were not totally white American in every respect save color of skin.[109]

Developing a distinct racial aesthetic rather than advancing race politics or addressing Negro problems was *Fire!!*'s foremost ambition. In this regard, the journal was representative of both a group of younger Negro "prophets," whom Du Bois declared was on the rise, and an apparently purist approach to art, which the elder statesman despised.

It was difficult for Du Bois, or anyone else, to anticipate what directions a newfound creative freedom might lead New Negro artists in. The range of perspectives to which the editorial board subscribed could not be reduced to any single ideology any more than their respective careers could be contained within one edition. However, like Langston Hughes's essay in *The Nation, Fire!!* effectively illumined a set of generational fissures concerning racial aesthetics.[110] The old guard often prized an aesthetic of instrumentality. They had valued art for what it could accomplish on behalf of the race. For many in the new guard, however, the goal shifted from the sociological to something "purely artistic." Although it was innovative in aesthetic terms, *Fire!!* certainly cut against the conventions of race politics at the time.

Issues such as sexuality, class, and skin color, all of which pressed upon intraracial divisions, featured prominently in the pages of *Fire!!* The publication was intended to be provocative, and it was generally received as profane. Yet the subject of religion was no less present, sparsely scattered across the periodical's forty-eight pages. Several of the poems selected drew upon biblical imagery and included allusions to God, and the first of Aaron Douglas's three sketches was of a Negro preacher. If these selections privileged the written and preached word, the sacred music of the Negro spirituals was important to the issue as a whole. Again affirming the centrality of Langston Hughes's work to the vision of *Fire!!*, the title had come from a spiritual written by the poet. His verse was put to music by the composer and violinist Hall Johnson, who later in the decade wrote the score to *The Green Pastures*. The Hughes–Johnson collaboration became the folk operetta *Fi-yer!*, which inspired the short-lived publication's name.[111]

In this way, the very name *Fire!!* put religion center stage and situated the text uniquely, if awkwardly, between a budding racial spirit and the aesthetic traditions of Afro-Protestantism. Moreover, the journal revealed the degree to which religion—and what specific kinds of religion—mediated generational tensions that surfaced during the 1920s. As suggested by the spiritual behind the journal's title, black sacred music was a primary source of inspiration for the brand of racial aesthetics celebrated by *Fire!!*'s team of editors.

Fire!!, in effect, enacted a creative synthesis between old-time religion and a modern racial aesthetic. The following year, theater critic Theophilus Lewis compared preachers and actors, as well as the respective stages on which they held court. With regard to both the church and theater, he concluded, "Each is strictly a spiritual institution." Yet in the novel context of the 1920s, Lewis also noted that the Negro theater was no longer simply an "appendage of the church." It was now disentangling itself from its past in "religious ritual, religious propaganda or religious orgy." For Lewis—a prominent writer during the Harlem Renaissance who would convert to Catholicism the following decade—the artist was "a spiritual pioneer," regardless of the medium in which s/he worked. Actors in particular were required to "raise the theatre above the plane of amusement and make it an instrument for the expression of the higher spiritual life of [the] people."[112] Lewis advanced a secularizing narrative for the theater that nonetheless maintained a spiritual purpose for the stage.

Lewis's essay appeared in the anthology *Ebony and Topaz: A Collectanea* (1927), edited by Charles S. Johnson, who was research director at the National Urban League for much of the decade. In 1926 Johnson had moved to Nashville to chair the Sociology Department at Fisk University. As editor of *Ebony and Topaz*, he struck a much more modest tone than Locke in *The New Negro*. Johnson observed a growing self-awareness and independence of mind in the younger generation. Yet what was evident among a new group of Negro writers was not emblematic of the race as a whole. He posited no one-to-one correlation between New Negro art and Negro life, nor did he claim that the new group was a sign of things soon to come. Johnson, however, did discern a growing willingness to reconsider the past, even the "memory of slavery," in ways that troubled the aspirational race politics of the Negro Renaissance.

Alain Locke had insisted that an emerging "common consciousness" was indicative of a liberating racial spirit taking shape in the urban North. Charles Johnson, in contrast, was already preparing to leave Harlem to return to his own southern roots. The only "spirit" he observed was of a growing white interest and investment in New Negro writers. However, Johnson did argue that "the return of the Negro writers to folk materials has proved a new emancipation."[113] At the same time, Theophilus Lewis's move to compare the church and theater through the language of spirit was entirely in keeping with a pattern of New Negro religious liberalism. Like Locke and Du Bois, Lewis identified in the arts a secularizing telos. The theater, in particular, would enable the race to achieve universal significance, escaping its provincial past as an adjunct of the church. Put another way, a presumably secular Negro theater would help inaugurate a modern racial spirit. Lewis seemed to suggest that New Negro actors would steal the show from the old-time Negro preacher.

NEW NEGROES AND THE AESTHETICS OF
THE OLD-TIME PREACHER

Aaron Douglas's first sketch on the pages of *Fire!!* featured a Negro preacher behind the pulpit, pointing to the centrality of an old religious figure and his form (the sermon). In doing so, he also suggested that these venerable traditions were instructive for a new spiritual vision. One year after this sketch was published in *Fire!!*, a series of Douglas's illustrations adorned the pages of a short book that canonized the archetypal figure of the "old-time Negro preacher." James Weldon Johnson's *God's Trombones: Seven Negro Sermons in Verse* (1927) returned to the contributions of the lead "actor" in the age-old theater that was the Negro Church. Just a year after George Schuyler and Langston Hughes's debate in *The Nation* singled out churches as a stage for debating racial aesthetics, Johnson celebrated the art of black preaching. Sermons were an "unnoticed" artifact of a rich cultural tradition. According to Johnson, "The old-time Negro preacher has not yet been given the niche in which he properly belongs."[114]

God's Trombones marked a key moment in Johnson's own evolving appreciation of the significance of Negro folk culture (e.g., dialect, "old-time religion," etc.) for racial aesthetics. Moreover, the book clarified the degree to which the forging of the modern and new was contingent upon "the old-time." Indeed, this entanglement of old and new in the racial aesthetics of the New Negro could best be described as a celebratory ambivalence toward the sources of Afro-Protestantism.

Near the start of the 1920s James Weldon Johnson had observed that despite "the undeniable creative genius of the Negro," it was still on "this side of prophecy" to anticipate a "distinctive and valuable contribution to American poetry."[115] These comments, of course, provided the author with an air of authority, as he offered them in the preface to his newly published anthology, *The Book of American Negro Poetry* (1922). In his 40-odd page introduction to the volume, Johnson provided a short history of all Negro contributions to American culture to date in order to make the case for what was to come. For now, he said, Negro music (e.g., spirituals, ragtime) best captured the ethos of "our national spirit."[116] In his estimation, success in "lower forms of art" such as music demonstrated that Negroes had the power to accomplish similar feats in "higher forms" like literature. Music became a model for race literature for many years to come.

Johnson also made two smaller claims that garnered significant attention. For one, he noted that "the final measure of the greatness of all peoples is the amount and standard of the literature and art they have produced."[117] The idea of "civil rights by copyright" was endorsed by one of the era's leading writers and activists. Second, in an age when Paul Laurence Dunbar was still the paragon of Negro poetry, Johnson all but declared that dialect was dead as a literary form.[118] Almost ten years later, in 1931, his anthology was reprinted and updated. With overwhelming evidence of a cultural renaissance in the intervening years, his prophecy appeared to have been fulfilled. That Negro writers contributed to the nation's "artistic, cultural, and spiritual values" was now generally an accepted fact, Johnson averred. Nonetheless, he felt the need to defend, revise, and clarify his position on dialect. Indeed, a discussion of dialect occupied almost the entirety of his new preface.

More than an outright elegy for or dismissal of dialect, Johnson both historicized and qualified it. On one hand, dialect was observed to be the product of the outside imposition of "minstrel traditions" that were not to be confused with "actual Negro life." That is, there was a particular history in which public performances of dialect served to maintain the social order of American slavery. However, dialect had also found new life in the "folk creations" of younger Negro writers— like Langston Hughes and Sterling Brown—who were both well-versed in its minstrel history and wrote verse, instead, "out of the common, racy, living, authentic speech of the Negro in certain phases of real life." Johnson even located himself within this group of writers, who worked in "the genuine folk stuff in contradistinction to the artificial stuff of the dialect school." Where Hughes drew inspiration on the streets of Harlem and Brown turned his eyes to southern roads, Johnson found "the unfailing sources of material for authentic poetry" in the pulpit of the Negro Church.[119]

By the time *God's Trombones* was published in 1927, James Weldon Johnson's thinking on racial aesthetics had begun to evolve. In the five years since he had penned the original preface to his anthology of poems, his appreciation for dialect (and folk culture, more generally) appeared to have grown. His analysis of its history and contexts was also more precise. Although Johnson recalled his experiences as a child, more recent observations in churches across the nation played an important role in shaping his shift. In his preface to *God's Trombones*, Johnson proffered that "*traditional* Negro dialect . . . is absolutely dead," even as he proclaimed that the aesthetics of Afro-Protestantism might provide poets with a "form that will express the racial spirit by symbols from within rather than by symbols from without." In their "fusion of Negro idioms with Bible English," the sermons of the "old-time Negro preacher" provided New Negro artists with a rich archive of source materials. Once again, the racial spirit invoked, contained, and required a persistent Afro-Protestantism.[120]

James Weldon Johnson hailed the sermons of the "old-time Negro preacher" as a resource for developing a novel racial aesthetic. However, his thoughts about religion were by no means limited to assessing the artistic merits of religious forms. Johnson identified as agnostic in his autobiography, *Along This Way* (1933).[121] Much of his writing, in fact, was often viewed as anti-religion. If Johnson's attempts to outline sources for Negro writers led him to celebrate a certain aesthetic brilliance in Negro churches, his recollections of religion in Harlem during the renaissance were more critical and circumspect. One such example could be seen in his 1930 book *Black Manhattan*, which provided a historical account of New York's Negro community.[122] Within this larger political narrative of race in the New World, Johnson privileged a different kind of Negro clergy than he had celebrated in *God's Trombones*.

According to Johnson, Harlem's significance as a race capital was in no small part a product of its location in New York City. Harlem became the "mecca" of the New Negro because of its place, Johnson argued, within "the greatest city of the New World."[123] More significantly, he also observed the centrality of religion to the cultural, political, and social worlds of black New Yorkers.[124] Without judgment, Johnson acknowledged the simple pleasures that various religious groups provided to the people of Harlem. With regard to neighborhood politics, he noted that Marcus Garvey's program was paramount. Yet by Johnson's account, the Universal Negro Improvement Association was "more than a movement, it became a *religion*."[125] As for the historic black Christian churches (namely, black Baptists and Methodists), he especially acknowledged their role in making possible a black press.[126] Across these various spheres, Johnson's analysis drew a familiar distinction between Negro churches as social institutions and a more capacious racial spirit.

As an elder statesman, James Weldon Johnson held to an instrumentalist account of the significance of churches. Reminiscent of the leading social scientific studies of the day, he observed that the upper Manhattan neighborhood was "overchurched."[127] Of the roughly 160 churches he estimated were in Harlem, Johnson concluded that over half of them could stand to be closed down. After all, the "little-church movement" of storefront churches had produced nothing more than "many cults and much occultism." They did little to advance the civil rights agenda of organizations like the NAACP, which he had helped to found and continued to support. If left to the devices of a "little church," the racial spirit might be reduced to spiritualism and superstition.

In contrast, Johnson praised the "integrating value" of large denominational churches. Like George Haynes, he concluded that these churches could appropriately direct the racial spirit, but only if they were held accountable. Instead of dismissing Negro churches wholesale, Johnson argued that this type of church ought to be encouraged to "live more fully up" to its obligation to organize the "spiritual forces" of the race.[128] Above all else, churches ought to function as agents of social service and racial uplift.[129] No other black institution, he surmised, had as much potential for "bettering the Negro's state in this world and in this country." Johnson hoped for an "element of the coloured clergy which realizes the potentialities of a modern Negro Churchman with sufficient wisdom to bring about a new Reformation."[130]

Although less optimistic than George Haynes, James Weldon Johnson acknowledged the potential that "the Negro Church" had to direct the Negro's "spiritual forces." Like Haynes, he failed to clarify the substance of what he meant by "spiritual." However, his critique of the "little-church movement" provided a clue. That is, the reformation Johnson envisaged would increase the number of clergy like Reverdy Ransom, a race man cut from the same socially engaged cloth as "secular" civil rights activists such as himself. If nothing else, Johnson's "modern Negro Churchman" was not the "old-time preacher" he celebrated in *God's Trombones*. Although a modern racial aesthetic required the form of the folk sermon, his normative vision of Afro-Protestantism hinged upon a nascent group of New Negro clergy. These preachers would discard "moss-back theology and obsolete dogmatics" for the practical demands of race politics. If such men occupied the pulpit, "the Negro church would not limit, but extend its spiritual forces." With the rise of a reformed New Negro ministry, the race would surely yield "higher spiritual returns."[131]

Johnson's account of the history of Negroes in New York City was published at the outset of the 1930s, a decade that would be defined by the Great Depression, which resulted in a dearth of opportunities for artists, black and white. While an optimism aided by migration and urbanization underwrote a forward-looking racial aesthetics during the Roaring Twenties, the stock market crash of 1929 set a decidedly different tone for the next decade. Indeed, by many accounts the New Negro was already a thing of the past.[132] Wallace Thurman's 1932 novel *Infants of the Spring* was received as a fictional elegy for the Harlem Renaissance. Two years later, the novelist, playwright, journalist, critic, and editor of *Fire!!* died at the age of thirty-two after an extended battle with tuberculosis.[133] Even if the New Negro movement was not entirely over, one of its most independent and brightest young stars was now dead, and all too soon.

From the early 1920s through the beginning of the next decade, the so-called Negro Renaissance had been fundamentally concerned with reforming the image of black Americans. As historian David Levering Lewis has noted, their vision for racial aesthetics was largely an effort at "civil rights by copyright," a literary and political project in which many black churches had long been invested.[134] During this time, the pairing of church and spirit provided black artists and intellectuals with a set of categories through which they engaged and interrogated the idea of "the Negro Church" even as it was just taking form. The 1920s was a decade defined by modernizing impulses in the grandest sense. Yet despite the anxieties that Benjamin Mays voiced in *The Negro's God*, the history of Afro-Protestantism was both secured and extended in African American literature in the years during and after the New Negro's decline.

For the New Negro, and in the years to come, the meanings attached to both church and spirit terms were never entirely stable or singular. Nonetheless, the spaces in between these two multivalent poles provided a staging ground for a range of more specific claims that touched upon issues such as class fissures within black communities, African religious traditions and their derivatives in the New World, trickster figures, folkloric heroes, messianic leaders, and much more. Indeed, the practice of invoking church and spirit in tandem (or by comparison) was constantly reconfigured, overturned, and reimagined, even as it remained a persistent pairing.

The 1920s was also the moment when systemized scholarship on African American religion was beginning to take shape—a development that grew in the 1930s, with the beginnings of ethnographic research, followed by the growth of sociological studies during the 1940s and 1950s. Such research blossomed still further in the 1960s with the creation of African American Studies programs on college and university campuses. The seismic shifts occasioned by migration and urbanization turned northern cities into laboratories with loads of data for the burgeoning social sciences. This scholarship spurred renewed interest in the rural South. Alongside the dramatic changes facilitated by the Great Migration, the law of racial segregation remained steady until the 1960s. Like racial aesthetics, scholarship on African American religion was as invested in advancing the cause of social equality as it was in dispassionate historical or social scientific inquiry.[135]

As well warranted as that agenda was, given the vicissitudes of Jim Crow, the dynamic of an activist scholarship led to an instrumentalist account of black churches as normative. Race politics provided the privileged criteria for assessing both literary and religious practices. Historians and social scientists had much to say concerning the emergence of eclectic and enigmatic religious leaders in the North and the diverse spiritual communities they founded, from Father Divine and Marcus Garvey in the 1920s and 1930s to the increased visibility of the Nation of Islam in postwar America. Scholars also observed the patterns of association among southern migrants, who maintained allegiance to black churches (e.g., Baptist, Methodist) in both elite and folk forms but who also created new ones (e.g., storefronts, Pentecostal and Holiness denominations) to address their varied this-worldly concerns.[136] The migration era was, as Eddie Glaude has noted, "an extraordinarily rich moment in which unanticipated ways of living in the world (and new kinds of black folk like the 'New Negro,' the Garveyite, and the black communist) emerged in the face of transforming social forces."[137]

Indeed, the novelty of the age of the New Negro was equally evident in the forms of intellectual ferment and aesthetic innovations and in the reimagining of religious identities. So much, it appeared, was up for grabs. Yet neither an aspirational New Negro subjectivity nor the novel "sects" and "cults" that took root within northern cities unseated the Christian consensus that had held sway in the rural South. An Afro-Protestant hegemony remained intact throughout the Negro Renaissance and would persist as a force to be reckoned with for years to come, despite accounts of differentiation and decline. However, a burgeoning race consciousness—a race-spirit, as some would call it—did emerge as a compelling organizing force alongside of (as well as within) the Negro Church.

Ultimately, efforts to theorize the aesthetics and politics of the New Negro illuminated how traditional notions of religion and an emerging racial sensibility competed for black people's loyalty. Similar concerns would limn the debate about racial aesthetics for decades to come. While institutional Afro-Protestantism did not come undone or lose its powers of persuasion, appeals to an ecumenical spirit—a marker of both a modern racial consciousness and an ancestral African past—were mobilized in service to racial aesthetics, but often also with the intent of orienting individual lives and organizing an increasingly heterogeneous black social life.[138]

CHAPTER 2

༄

Ancestral Spirits

The Negro is not a Christian, really.

Zora Neale Hurston

As evidenced by *God's Trombones* and *Black Manhattan*, James Weldon Johnson's engagement with the culture and politics of black churches reflected a defining tension in racial aesthetics during the 1920s. The Negro Church, politically, was often praised as a historic institutional symbol of racial striving even as it was critiqued in light of its perceived shortcomings in the present. At the same time, churches were endorsed for the possibilities they represented as instruments of racial uplift. Such a task, however, would require a thoroughly reformed New Negro clergy. In cultural terms, black churches were a frequently considered yet always contested site for aesthetic inspiration.

As the generosity of private patrons diminished and publishing opportunities declined and in some cases disappeared altogether during the Great Depression, a significant number of New Negro artists pressed on. They did, however, draw upon a different set of resources to advance new visions for a racial aesthetic. During the 1930s many black writers found work within the offices of the Federal Writers Project of the Works Progress Administration. Others found institutional support, intellectual camaraderie, and new publication prospects within the networks of a growing black institutional Left.[1] In the previous decade, literal movement added momentum to an ideology of racial uplift that tapped into that most American dream of economic mobility. Migration north to the "Promised Land" had fueled a range of ambitions, religious and social, encoded within the expansive rubric of a future-oriented racial spirit. Northern cities, of course, had quickly proven to be more complicated than they had been as an idealized promise. As the 1920s moved into the 1930s, artistic visions of modern racial spirits still remained dependent upon primitive pasts. West African and Afro-Caribbean cultures gained a more sustained and nuanced hearing via ethnographic study, folkloric research, and travel narratives. The American South also powerfully persisted in both experience and memory. During the 1930s, a number of black writers plumbed the meaning of this past in the making of a black cultural presence in modern North America.

One such writer was the poet and professor Sterling Brown. While Langston Hughes's poems and prose often captured the quotidian details of the urban streets that organized northern living, Sterling Brown's verse in *Southern Road* (1932) illuminated the everyday worlds of black folk in the American South. Precisely one decade after James Weldon Johnson declared the idiom of dialect all but dead and just two years since he had called for the "reformation" and rise of New Negro Churchmen, he penned a laudatory introduction to Brown's first book of poems. In it, Johnson conceded the staying power of Negro dialect. Brown did not replicate the "minstrel traditions." Instead he drew upon the "common, racy, living speech of the Negro in certain phases of *real* life." In doing so, Johnson noted, the poet had "absorbed the spirit of his material . . . truly re-expressed it with artistry and magnified power." Black southern "folk life" provided the substantive content of Sterling Brown's "distinctive contribution."[2]

Religious practices, as this chapter will show, remained especially significant as the ongoing effort to imagine a racial aesthetic enlisted a variety of ancestral spirits. For instance, in the monumental anthology *Negro* composed by British heiress Nancy Cunard, a revival service in Harlem provided the occasion for a debate between a primitive African past and Marxist propaganda. More pointedly, two of the leading black writers of the decade, Zora Neale Hurston and Richard Wright, agreed that a distinctive social and cultural world could be found in the southern Black Belt region of the United States, even if they fundamentally disagreed about the origins and the implications of this racial difference.[3] Yet the signs of a turn southward and the interpretive allure of Africa had already been apparent a decade earlier.

SOUTHERN ROADS, AFRICAN SPIRITS

The power of a folk past (and present) had never been entirely absent even in the heyday of the New Negro. After all, Jean Toomer's *Cane*, arguably the signal and most celebrated text by a black writer during the 1920s, was published two years before Alain Locke's *The New Negro*. Toomer's young northern narrator visited the South only to confess:

> I felt strange, as I always do in Georgia, particularly at dusk. I felt that things unseen to me were tangibly immediate. It would not have surprised me had I had a vision. People have them in Georgia more often than you would suppose. A black woman once saw the mother of Christ and drew her in charcoal on the courthouse wall.... When one is on the soil of one's ancestors, most anything can come to one.[4]

Inhabited by spirits and ghosts, the South was imagined as a region that still possessed the capacity to evoke visions and divine visitations that called to mind other much older worlds.[5]

Reverdy Ransom's poem "The New Negro," also published in 1923, assumed a liberal Negro Church located in the North with equal inheritances of literary and scientific reasoning. By contrast, *Cane* unveiled an emotional and spiritual vitality that was situated in the rural southern landscape. Indeed, Toomer's ancestral soils were the perfect foil to the Social Gospel spirit apparent in Ransom's Christian vision. While some identified black churches as being animated by a modern racial spirit, the South was often invoked as the site of the emotional, embodied, ecstatic, and expressive forms of black folk culture, a continued repository of an African religious past and the terrain of non-Protestant spiritual traditions.

Jean Toomer was himself a grandson of the South, a descendant of Blanche Bruce, the Reconstruction-era Senator from Mississippi. Yet he was raised comfortably within the trappings of black middle-class society in Washington, DC, situated at the crossroads of North and South. In *Cane*, Toomer invited readers to explore the segregated worlds of a rural South to which he was a distant heir and recurring visitor. In the popular imagination, the American South was still in possession of an Old World spirituality that was increasingly rare in modern America. This enchanted world, imagined or real, stood in stark contrast to the prospect of improved material conditions that had begun luring black people to the North since the immediate aftermath of Emancipation and during the decades that ensued. While the North was cast as the Promised Land, the migration narrative was also told as a story of secularization for which the South was the point of departure.[6]

Cane also illustrated the degree to which the fact and idea of black migration—a complex of tensions between South and North, old and new, primitive and modern, rural and urban, folk and elite—provided one plane on which ideas about religion exerted influence over the aesthetic visions of black writers and thinkers during the 1920s and 1930s. Migration—and the opposition of North and South—presented a source of creative possibilities as much as it posed a set of economic opportunities and social problems. In this regard, Jean Toomer's romantic, even mystical, depictions of the rural South captured the significance of an ancestral past for modern racial aesthetics.[7] More generally, in the face of rapid modernization and urbanization, the South gained significance in light of a search for an American spiritual identity and practice that drew upon the nation's indigenous artistic and cultural traditions.[8] For Jean Toomer, the turn South was the start of a spiritual quest. Yet Toomer's was by no means an isolated act or an exceptional religious expedition.

Reverdy Ransom's vision for an elite Protestant "New Negro" shared much with the 1920s political orthodoxy of Alain Locke's racial spirit. However, by the dawn of the next decade and as the Harlem Renaissance faded, the appeal of an ancestral, southern folk spirituality gained more traction. What had been an ambivalent attachment to Afro-Protestantism did not disappear during the 1930s, but it was reimagined under decidedly different terms. Increasingly, racial aesthetics required the spirits of ancestral pasts—located in the black South but also figured in relationship to Africa—for substantive content.

Jean Toomer's fiction a decade earlier had foregrounded a spiritual vitality apparent on southern soils. In contrast, Sterling Brown's poems told the mundane, and often profane, stories of folk heroes like Stagolee and John Henry. Indeed, sacred and secular were entangled, if imagined unevenly, in the New Negro's ancestral pasts. The same held true for the relationships, imagined and real, between New Negro writers and Africa. That is, a number of writers complicated the opposition that Alain Locke had set up in *The New Negro* between an inspiring, authentic African past and an alienating Christian present in the West. The old—whether below the Mason-Dixon Line or across the Atlantic Ocean—persisted as both problem and possibility for a racial aesthetic often assumed to privilege the North for the New Negro.

During the same year that Sterling Brown's debut book of poems was published, Wallace Thurman had staged a fictional, yet no less revealing, cross-generational conflict over the demands that "African traditions" placed upon racial aesthetics. In his telling, the generation of writers just emerging rejected the impositions of an inheritance necessarily tied to Africa. In *Infants of the Spring,* one of Thurman's young artists defiantly declared to an imposing elder, "I ain't got no African spirit."[9] If not a wholesale rejection, a number of New Negro writers tempered the impulse toward any natural or romantic attachment to Africa in light of the burdens and resources of American history.

Also in 1932, Claude McKay troubled facile connections to the continent in his essay "The Negro Writer and His Critics." Writing in the *New York Herald Tribune,* McKay noted that he was equally aware of both his "new-world birthright" and his "African origin." Moreover, he explained, modernity had made it such that neither place nor racial identity existed in a "pure state." Black artists had no inherent attachment to any continent. Nonetheless, McKay speculated, "The Aframerican may gain spiritual benefits by returning *in spirit* to his African origin, but as an artist he will remain a unique product of Western civilization."[10]

Two years later, in 1934, the visual artist Romare Bearden observed an inverse avenue of influence, stating that instead of Western civilization influencing the Negro artist, the legacy of black Africa had made a decisive impact on Western civilization. Bearden wrote matter-of-factly, "Modern art has borrowed heavily from Negro sculpture." In fact, the aesthetics of African art provided "one of the cardinal principles of the modern artist."[11] In these essays by McKay and Bearden, Africa figured as a concrete historical source rather than as an imagined racial ancestry or a romanticized past. These engagements with the African past complicated a mythical or mystical idea of Africa. Granted, mystical Africa was invoked to authorize black creative genius, while myths of the "dark continent" served to justify white supremacy. Yet Bearden and McKay were both informed by a close consideration of history, contemporary examples of contact and exchange, and extended observation, personal experience, and study. As McKay suggested, New Negro artists might forge spiritual ties to the African continent, but such connections were not to be assumed. And, whether they did so or not, a racial aesthetic would still be squarely a product of the West.

To be sure, fact-based histories are never told entirely apart from imagination, myth, or memory. Africa has always been a matter of both history and ideas, at least in the New World.[12] Both African pasts and American presents could "authentically" animate modern racial spirits in the present. To cement this connection, an increase in field research during the 1930s allowed for more detailed portraits of the cultures of the African diaspora, providing a richer historical record and novel resources for enunciating racial aesthetics.

A NEGRO REVIVAL IN REVIEW

In 1941, Columbia-trained anthropologist Melville Herskovits's book *The Myth of the Negro Past* made one of the strongest cases to date for cultural continuities across what would come to be known as the Afro-Atlantic world. However, several years before Herskovits's book, the British heiress and editor Nancy Cunard devoted a significant amount of her own resources to advancing similar arguments. The historian Ann Douglas has described Cunard as "one of the most formidable and eager members of the white welcoming committee that greeted the Negro in the Jazz age."[13] Clearly, if Cunard was any indication, the Negro remained in vogue well into the 1930s. Yet this particular investment in querying the links between African spirits and Afro-Protestantism was by no means exclusively the purview of white people. Even as Cunard carried on a conversation that often conflated primitivism with Negro culture, her edited collection, *Negro: An Anthology* (1934), provided an incredibly rich portrait of religion and culture in the African diaspora.

While Alain Locke's *The New Negro* was the most celebrated book of the day, Nancy Cunard's *Negro* was arguably the moment's most epic. Originally published in London, Cunard's massive volume included sections organized around each of the diaspora's Atlantic outposts: North America, the West Indies and South America, Europe, and Africa. Entries included essays, poems, portraits and photos, as well as sketches of African sculptures. With the exception of the section on Europe, religion occupied a central place throughout. Essays on the African origins of "Obeah" in Jamaica and "Candombe" [*sic*] in Uruguay appeared in the portion concerned with the Caribbean and South America, while the often-violent means through which missionaries converted colonized "natives" to Christianity figured prominently in several of the articles on Africa.[14]

The essays that focused on the United States both examined social problems attendant to race and illuminated the persistence of African cultural patterns in the black diaspora. True to the history of the New Negro, an interest in both aesthetics and politics extended across the respective sections. The perceived hypocrisy of Christianity as it was practiced and enforced across the asymmetrical lines of race and colonialism was also a recurring concern. The longest contribution by any author in *Negro* was a series of essays by Zora Neale Hurston about life in the Black Belt of the southern United States. In these essays, she portrayed the power of a folk tradition of Afro-Protestantism and indigenous conjuring practices that she attributed to African antecedents. In doing so, Hurston uniquely illustrated how the question of persisting African spirits was often entangled within efforts to discern the meaning and makeup of religion in the lives of American Negroes.[15]

The more than eight hundred pages that comprised Nancy Cunard's huge anthology did much to capture the diversity of religious expressions that animated the various locales of the African diaspora. However, one of Cunard's own essays once again confirmed the ways in which a trope of church and spirit effectively organized a vast array of cultural and social differences.[16] In "Harlem Reviewed," Cunard offered her take on the "so-called capital of the Negro world." Her analysis echoed one put forward by James Weldon Johnson in his 1930 book Black Manhattan, which she specifically cited. Within the space constraints of eight pages, Cunard noted such phenomena as residential crowding, intra-racial ethnic difference, and traditions of political organizing and cultural expression. Cunard's travel narrative also unveiled a practice of cultural tourism that called into question, apparently unwittingly, her own account of Harlem.[17]

Cunard observed a "jealous national spirit" that led to African American and Caribbean factions within Harlem, yet she also discerned a cultural unity across these ethnic and political divisions. This commonality resulted, in her estimation, from the perception that "the Negro is very real." Cunard concluded that the search for entertainment in Harlem was, in fact, a white quest for authenticity that was only to be found in "the other race." In response to the perceived sterility associated with modern (read white) society, black religion and culture—regardless of ethnic diversity—was imagined, as Ann Douglas has noted, as an "antidote" to the ruling logics of science and reason. In short, the racial other remained acutely real, a source of emotional and spiritual vitality in the face of a Western wasteland.[18]

However, although whites reveled in "the freedom of Harlem," such encounters did not translate to greater social freedom for black people. While whites received the fact of a black vivacity as a cultural balm, they also often made it the basis for continued political exclusion. As historian Curtis Evans has noted, black spiritual energies were often understood as at odds with the ends of American democracy.[19] Moreover, the authenticity that white people often attributed to Harlem, whether in the nightclub or at the political rally, was often read in religious terms. Indeed, the organizing center and stage for Cunard's essay was situated in the sanctuary of one of Harlem's churches.

After much encouragement and against her better judgment, Nancy Cunard explained, she ended up at a revival service in Salem Methodist Episcopal Church. Salem was then pastored by the Reverend Frederick Asbury Cullen, the adoptive father of the poet Countee Cullen. That night the guest preacher was none other than George Wilson Becton, a charismatic, albeit controversial minister who had acquired a significant following amid the seismic shifts occasioned by mass migration to northern cities. He was commonly known as the "Dancing Evangelist" for his histrionic presentation style. Becton, according to Cunard, "was a poet in speech and very graceful in all his movements . . . the personification of expressionism, a great dramatic actor."[20] Although an ardent secularist herself, she was nonetheless seduced by the drama of Afro-Protestantism.

Just two years earlier Langston Hughes had referred to Becton as the "big black Saint" of the "Consecrated Dime" in an infamous poem that derided the corrosive influence of capitalism on American Christianity.[21] Cunard, too, referred to a time in the service that was reserved for the "consecrated dime." Yet she summed up her time in Cullen's church as follows:

> One is transported, completely. It has nothing to do with God, but with life—a collective life for which I know no name. The people are entirely out of themselves . . . it seems positively another thing, not connected with Christ or bible, the pure outpouring of themselves, a nature-rite. In other words, it is the fervor, intensity, the stupendous rhythm and surge of singing that are so fine—the Christianity is only accidental, incidental to these. Not so for the assembly of course, for all of it is deeply, tenaciously religious.[22]

Cunard's encounter with Afro-Protestantism was defined by its sonic qualities, which were, by definition, spiritual. "The 'spirit' is coming with the volume of sound," she observed. However, she also noted a (normative) difference between the God of Christianity and the form of "collective life" she witnessed on display at the revival.

There were at least two key elements—a Christian church but something else as well, even if it was unclear exactly what that something else was—entangled in Nancy Cunard's portrait of the Harlem revival. Politically, Cunard herself was ensconced in the networks of an interracial and international Left, which most likely accounted for her reluctance to enter a church in the first place. She had entered a congregation governed by professed connections to a Christian God. Salem

Methodist Church was by all accounts part of Harlem's Afro-Protestant establishment. Yet for the discerning visitor, the service was no less than a "nature rite." That is, Afro-Protestantism was animated by a more powerful life force, Cunard noted, that was "not connected with Christ or bible." Aesthetically, the vestiges of an unnamed African animism exercised a "terrific hold" over the congregants in whose company Cunard found herself that evening. Under any other circumstances such an event would have been "utterly revolting." In the context of a Negro church, they were a "gorgeous manifestation of *the emotion* of a race."[23]

The portrait of religion provided in Nancy Cunard's *Negro* balanced images of an exotic and primitive Africa that persisted throughout the diaspora, on the one hand, with critiques of the colonial role of (white) Christianity in facilitating the conditions of violent dispersal, on the other. However, the "fetiches" of the Negro, although associated with a more pure, vital, and "real" spirituality, paled in comparison to what many contributors identified as the "true" religion of Christianity. Even when attention was paid to the American context (and the North, for that matter), the specter of Africa loomed large. The anthology, in general, provided a compelling critique of Christianity's key role in the spread of colonialism, although Cunard's review of Harlem revealed a lens into Afro-Protestantism that was ordered by a similar form of colonial reasoning.[24]

The familiar disorderly matrix of churches and racial spirits that animated the aesthetics of the New Negro was discernible in Nancy Cunard's *Negro*. Granted, Cunard deployed the trope of church and spirit to decidedly different ends that were not simply reducible to the race, class, or gender of the British heiress. Given the anticipated audience for her anthology and the radical circles in which she typically traveled, Cunard justified her detailed discussion of this particular Negro church:

> It may seem odd that one's thoughts stay so long with these black priests and their terrific hold over their large following. But religion amongst the Negroes, those that have it (for the younger generation is shaking off its weight, and replacing this by a desire for, an acquisition of, racial and economic facts), their reaction to religion cannot be disassociated in my mind from their past collective reaction to tribal ceremony and custom in Africa.[25]

Perhaps Cunard was unaware that she was the not the first white person to become enchanted by the charisma of black churches. Indeed, the primacy of religion in her review of Harlem was by no means exceptional.

Nor did it need any defense.[26] Nevertheless, she both identified an African spirit in the midst of an Afro-Protestant revival in Harlem and observed a secularizing impulse in the younger generation. Alain Locke had made similar arguments less than a decade earlier. Now, in 1934, Cunard clarified her own religious ambivalence and named her political commitments.

In this account, Africa was embraced only as the remnant of a primitive past. Yet this ancestral spirit needed to be directed in service to a more "real" form of authenticity. It was only the fact of this past that made Afro-Protestantism in the present allowable at all. Christianity, Cunard argued, more often than not inspired charlatanism, chicanery, and a crowd mentality. These mattered only insofar as they might be made to serve a modern spirit. "One longs for this collective force to be directed towards the right things," she confessed. More than predicting an inevitable triumph of modern materialism over an African animism—equally evident within institutional Afro-Protestantism, the song and dance of Negro nightclubs, and the speeches of Marcus Garvey—Cunard prescribed an additive secular presence to the mix of the standard Harlem revivalism.

Nancy Cunard's *Negro* simultaneously harked back to Alain Locke's vision in *The New Negro* and hailed her own future hopes for a growing black, and ultimately interracial, Left. In doing so, she extended an often-assumed narrative that the Negro Renaissance was secular and, more significantly, endorsed a Popular Front policy that was introduced the same year her anthology was published.[27] Specifically, Cunard allowed for something along the lines of Locke's racialism but then attempted to transcend it in favor of a class-based struggle. Indeed, as she moved toward her conclusion, the essay increasingly evolved into anti-imperialist polemic. Cunard took aim at the "super-brutality of American 'democracy'" and the institutions of the black middle class.[28] Churches, New Negro writers (save Claude McKay), and, especially, Negro newspapers were all in cahoots against the race's best interest. With the exception of the *Harlem Liberator*—"the only honest Negro paper in the States"—she announced that "the Negro race in America has no worse enemy than its own press."[29]

Nancy Cunard's critique of the "black bourgeoisie" coincided, unsurprisingly, with a celebration of "Negro workers." Indeed, race was but "a vicious lie." It was a strategy advanced by elites to create the false divisions required to sustain American capitalism. She took solace in the "growing volume of the Communist consciousness among the black workers, and in some of the Negro intellectuals." Cunard vested her hopes with Negro children, especially with young men. Black youth became the pliable and developing screen onto which Cunard projected her dream of "an all-Communist Harlem in an all-Communist United States."[30]

Nancy Cunard subtly wove a clear political vision into what was otherwise a cultural review of Harlem. Elsewhere, contributors to her anthology communicated Marxist propaganda more directly.[31] Such was the case in "Marxism and the American Negro," an essay by a young Jewish intellectual, William Herberg. Decades later he would become a prominent sociologist of religion with the now-classic book *Protestant, Catholic, Jew: An Essay in American Religious Sociology* (1955). In *Negro*, Herberg argued simply that "racial emancipation" was possible only through "the revolutionary overthrow of the capitalist system, of the victory of the proletariat."[32] What Herberg made explicit in his essay was inferred more subtly in Nancy Cunard's account of the spirit she discovered in the sanctuary of a Harlem church. A modern race consciousness might be superseding religion, but even this race-spirit would have to be shed en route to a Marxist revolution.

Ultimately, the politics at play in the portrait of Afro-Protestantism in "Harlem Reviewed" was indicative of an increasingly organized black Left that took shape during the Great Depression.[33] It also revealed one editor's agenda for an ambitious literary project that could not be contained even by her own vision. That is, Nancy Cunard's short essay by no means eclipsed the richly complicated portal into black culture across the diaspora provided by the anthology she compiled and independently published. It did, however, confirm the disciplining (and secularizing) power of the tropes of church and spirit to contain an African past, uplift ideologies, and Communist propaganda all at once.

ZORA NEALE HURSTON AND THE NATURE OF NEGRO EXPRESSION

Zora Neale Hurston was the only other contributor to the volume who covered close to as many pages as Cunard's, whose writing was interspersed throughout *Negro*.[34] Her writings, even if not by deliberate design, also constituted what was perhaps the strongest counter to the decade's dueling logics of church and spirit, on one hand, and Marxist materialism, on the other.

An ethnographer, folklorist, and novelist, Hurston would eventually become best known for her work in the last category. Her work in this genre included such novels as *Jonah's Gourd Vine* (1934), published the same year as Cunard's *Negro*, and what eventually became her most popular book, *Their Eyes Were Watching God* (1937). Before the 1930s were over, Hurston had also published a third novel, *Moses, Man of the Mountain* (1939), making for a trilogy of fiction that often featured plots driven by powerful black female protagonists. The characters of her novels, male and female, were distinctly chiseled deep within "the veil" of Negro life in the United States. In these worlds, by Hurston's telling, white people infrequently figured as major actors. Moreover, as her titles suggested, these stories were often sewn together along sacred plotlines, adopted from Christian scripture but adorned in the folk aesthetics of Afro-Protestantism (and its excesses) in the American South. As Hurston explained in her 1942 autobiography, *Dust Tracks on the Road*, as the daughter of a preacher she had "tumbled right into the Missionary Baptist Church" shortly after her birth.[35]

No less so than in her novels, religion figured prominently in Hurston's ethnographic writing. Moreover, it often did so in ways that frustrated efforts to map black culture into discrete religious traditions or make it serve neat political programs. Hurston was also difficult to place in terms of the generational camps that have been used to describe political factions within the Negro Renaissance. She was several years older than most of her collaborators when she joined the editorial team of *Fire!! A Quarterly for Younger Negro Artists*, which had unsettled the racial orthodoxies of older New Negroes. Hurston resisted the impositions of race leaders and elder statesmen like W. E. B. Du Bois, Alain Locke, and James Weldon Johnson. Yet she was also reluctant to assume the role of arbiter of artistic freedom, as Langston Hughes did in his apologia "The Negro Artist and the Racial Mountain." An independent-minded artist and intellectual, Zora Neale Hurston was as difficult to pin down politically as she was prolific.

Hurston's work appeared in *Negro: An Anthology* as two separate contributions. A short essay on "Spirituals and Neo-Spirituals" was printed in a section on American music. Here Hurston argued against Du Bois's singular presentation of the spirituals as "sorrow songs." She also critiqued the processes of commodification that determined their popular presentation and reception. The songs the wider world knew were actually "neo-spirituals," derivative tunes that were "distinctive adaptations" revised for the concert hall. They were not, however, the *real* thing. "Genuine Negro spirituals," Hurston opined, had never reached "any audience anywhere."[36] In the "America" section, alongside an essay on "Negro Folklore in North Carolina," Hurston authored the significantly longer essay "Characteristics of Negro Expression."[37] This article was broken up into several smaller parts, each of which called attention to specific religious practices (e.g., conversion, visions, shouting, and sermons) and practitioners (e.g., Mother Catherine, Uncle Monday).

Both selections would become the core of Hurston's body of folklore writings, which were reassembled decades later by Toni Cade Bambara under the popular title *The Sanctified Church*. When Bambara compiled this volume in the late 1970s, she separated the work into discrete categories of Christianity, Conjure, and Folklore.[38] While they also appeared in different sections of *Negro*, they were each part of Hurston's wider engagement with black folk cultures in the South as well as in the Caribbean. In "Characteristics of Negro Expression," Hurston provided a preliminary map of cultural life in the southern Black Belt states. "Spirituals and Neo-Spirituals" extended this inquiry and added to a provisional theory of racial aesthetics (i.e., Negro expression). Religion was the glue that held the two essays together.

In the second half of Hurston's treatment of spirituals, she located the music within a broader set of spiritual practices like conversion, sermons, and shouting. In the popular imagination, African American religion was often described as exceptional in its dramatic spontaneity.[39] On the contrary, she argued that "beneath the seeming informality of religious worship there is a set formality." Reading the selections in the order that they appeared in *Negro*, the specific practices of Afro-Protestantism illustrated the characteristics that Hurston first broadly outlined. The church, in effect, provides the concrete case for deciphering the cultural codes of Negro life. Ultimately, Hurston argued, "religious expression among Negroes is regarded as art."

Writing for *The Nation* almost a decade earlier, Langston Hughes had invoked the religion of the "low down folks" to support a vision of artistic and racial freedom.[40] Although a college dropout, Hughes observed Negro folk life in the North with a studied eye. Hurston, in contrast, had graduated from Barnard College and pursued advanced studies across the street at Columbia University under the noted anthropologist Franz Boas. Her account did not begin with a constructive task for racial aesthetics. Instead, she outlined a series of prominent features that she observed in Negro communities throughout the South during years of extensive field research. In this regard, Hurston's discussion of religion struck a balanced—although no less impassioned—tone; it departed from both Hughes's praise and Cunard's polemic.[41] Like Hughes, with whom she had recently parted ways while collaborating on the play *Mule Bone*, Hurston was fascinated with folk cultures.[42] For both, religion most readily marked racial difference.

Echoing Hughes in his 1926 debate with George Schuyler, Hurston observed a tendency among some Negroes to "slavishly imitate" whites. This was apparent in both fashion and beauty. It was also evident in a willingness to endure "a boresome church service," she joked.[43] Such mimicry, however, was not to be confused with the value ascribed to the practice of mimesis. An educated minority might conduct themselves as "apes of all the mediocrities of the white brother," Hurston conceded. However, for the vast majority—whom she described as the "Negro 'farthest down'. . . the man in the ditch"—mimicry was intrinsically rewarding. In this way, she confirmed the class claims implicitly at play in the debate between Schuyler and Hughes. Parody, in this view, was more than a high form of individual praise. It was a cultural performance with broader social meaning, one that provided intrinsic pleasures. "He mimics for the love of it," she explained. "He does it as the mockingbird does it, for the love of it, and not because he wishes to be like the one imitated."[44] Moving beyond journalistic observation and anecdotal evidence, Hurston outlined a system of linguistic and cultural norms to which Negro life in the South adhered.

Along with "Imitation," Hurston identified "Angularity," "Asymmetry," "Dialect," and the "Will to Adorn" as defining characteristics. Each of these specific qualities confirmed the "Drama" of southern Negro life more generally. Aside from portions of the essay that focused on particular spiritual practices, the subject of religion emerged most clearly in her treatment of "Negro Folklore" and "Culture Heroes." Contrary to popular opinion, "The Negro is not a Christian really," Hurston insisted. "The primitive gods are not deities of too subtle inner reflection; they are hard working bodies . . . Gods of physical violence, stopping at nothing to serve their followers."[45] Characters typically understood as divine in Christian doctrine were now part of a cast of embodied figures who acted concretely in human history. Continuing in this vein, she inverted the prevailing logic that privileged a Protestant account of American Negro life. "God and the Devil are paired, and are treated no more reverently than Rockefeller and Ford," Hurston explained. In this ensemble the Devil could be smarter than God, spiritual powers were assigned to animals, and—referencing the familiar African American folk hero High John the Conqueror—Hurston averred, "Jack beats them all."[46]

Instead of defining a distinct religious tradition or associating it with any particular institutional configuration, Hurston engaged what is typically understood as "religion" as part of a wider cultural and social experience. Negro expression was, however, a phenomenon distinct from a dominant American culture. If a sacred–secular binary did not hold, a break between black and white was more apparent. Although the institutions and expressive cultures of black Christianity, born in the New World, loomed large in both her critical and creative work, black religion involved more than independent Negro churches. Here Hurston attempted to address the question of origins, adding a historical dimension to her ethnographic details. For instance, she noted that the most powerful folk heroes bore strong resemblances to the trickster figures of West African societies. Paralleling arguments advanced by Melville Herskovits during the same decade, Hurston cited the American South as a repository of African cultural retentions.[47]

Nancy Cunard had made vague references to Africa in her essay "Harlem Reviewed." The fact of a primitive African past was the sole reason she made allowances for the overwhelming "collective life" that she witnessed at the Harlem revival. The frenzy of Afro-Protestantism exceeded the bounds of Christian doctrine. As Cunard put it, "it has nothing to do with God." Yet Cunard's ambivalent attraction to a Negro church reinscribed a Christian orthodoxy even as she affirmed "*the emotion* of the race" as persisting evidence of African animism. In light of this African past, Cunard's racial liberalism conceded that the Harlem revival was a practice of "honest," albeit misguided, religion. Afro-Protestantism—although a form of "false consciousness" and not "true" Christianity—was at least maintained in good faith.[48] Cunard's radical politics allowed her to take the material conditions and metaphysical claims of African spiritual worlds only so seriously.

In "Characteristics of Negro Expression," Hurston affirmed a pre-American history for the Negro. With the trained eye of a skilled ethnographer, she gave close attention to a range of specific practices. While Alain Locke had imagined a primitive African past as the authentic source of a racial spirit and Cunard had appealed to Africa to explain an undesirable, if enchanted, black America, Hurston's essay neither uncritically valorized African cultures nor devalued the culture of American Negroes. She resisted the impulse to look across the Atlantic for inspiration when the legacies of Africa were evident within the United States. Ancestral spirits had survived the trauma of the Middle Passage and now resided on the same southern soils that had hosted the institution of American slavery. A simultaneously ethnographic and insider gaze—not Christian orthodoxy, Marxist ideology, or European Romanticism—ordered her interpretation.[49]

Hurston's orientation privileged the experience of ordinary black folk.[50] Her academic training equipped her well to trace the connections between West African, Caribbean, and American cultures that illuminated how New World Negroes (re)made the West in their own image.[51] In Hurston's estimation, much like that of Langston Hughes, the Sanctified churches of the black masses were places where a distinctive culture had been forged. These congregations reflected an African heritage as much as, if not more than, the American context. They revealed an unfinished novelty that emerged in the entanglements between old and new worlds. Her analysis of shouting made this connection most forcefully. "There can be little doubt that shouting is a survival of African 'possession' by the gods," Hurston insisted. Ultimately, in the cultural practices of a southern Afro-Protestantism—which were not easily disentangled from the traditions of conjure/hoodoo or folklore—she readily discerned an African past at work in the making of a thoroughly modern Negro aesthetic.

Zora Neale Hurston's analysis did not downplay the significance of Christian churches in southern Negro life, but she did not privilege or romanticize Negro churches either. Afro-Protestantism—its songs, prayers, sermons, hums, chants, and shouts—was, on its own terms, an expressive and aesthetic form. "If anyone wishes to prove the truth of this let him step into some unfashionable Negro church and hear for himself," she exclaimed. "Some instances are unsurpassed anywhere in literature."[52] Inverting hierarchies between high and low, Hurston found in the expressive forms of Afro-Protestantism both the defining characteristics of Negro expression and the qualities of a distinctive aesthetic. "The truth is, that the religious service is a conscious art expression," she explained. "Sermons, prayers, moans, and testimonies have their definite forms."[53]

So while she did not avoid institutional religious life, Zora Neale Hurston departed from approaches that privileged politics over culture that had often worked to bolster the authority of Negro churches. Instead of a critique of Christianity, a constructive racial theory, or a Marxist critique, Hurston's argument required a simple yet profound observation. Negro culture in the New World was not entirely overdetermined by the colonial asymmetries that had ordered the arrival of enslaved Africans in the Americas. The character of Negro culture could not be adequately accounted for with the binaries of sacred/secular, African/American, or Christian/other. Afro-Protestantism, African spirits, and race politics were not zero-sum games. To put the matter differently, Hurston saw that the forms of American Negro culture had been encoded (incubated, expressed, extended, and revised) within the structures and forms of Afro-Protestantism.

REPLACING THE NEGRO PREACHER: RICHARD WRIGHT'S BLUEPRINT

While much of the financial support afforded the New Negro during the 1920s dried up after the stock market crash of 1929, Franklin Delano

Roosevelt's New Deal and its Works Progress Administration (WPA) provided resources for a number of black artists during the lean years of the
1930s. Zora Neale Hurston, for example, received funding for much of her
fieldwork from the WPA's Federal Writers' Project (FWP) in the middle
years of the decade before the publication of *Their Eyes Were Watching
God* (1937).[54] Another young writer who found support from the WPA
at this time was Richard Wright. After relocating from Chicago to New
York City in 1937, Wright was employed in the FWP's Manhattan office,
where research on "the Negro" was supervised by the Harlem-born and
bred journalist Roi Ottley.[55] The FWP was then in the process of working on a guidebook to New York City that would be published the following year. *New York Panorama* (1938) pieced together twenty-six articles on
New York on topics that ranged from architecture and education to labor
and literature.[56]

Richard Wright conducted research and authored the section devoted
to black Manhattan in *New York Panorama*. Although titled "Portrait of
Harlem," his essay provided a short, yet sweeping, account of Negro history in New York City from the colonial period (the slaves of Dutch settlers)
to the time of his writing, all in just twenty pages. Wright swiftly surveyed
topics ranging from abolitionism and slave insurrections to black elected
officials and civic organizations. About one-third of the essay offered a
historical narrative and the latter two-thirds were devoted to laying out
the contemporary landscape.

On the heels of the Negro Renaissance, it only made sense that Harlem's
contemporary art scene received the lion's share of his attention. However,
Wright did not overlook the community's religious life. "Playing the central role in the life of the Harlem Negro," he assessed, "is not the caba-
ret or café, as is commonly supposed, but the church." Wright noted that
"catering to the inner man is one of Harlem's chief industries."[57] Although
referring to the neighborhood's restaurants, he pointed out that fifteen of
Harlem's most notable eateries belonged to Father Divine's Peace Mission
movement. Wright's analysis playfully blurred the work of cafes, cabarets,
and churches, all of which were equally concerned with "the inner man."
Yet despite popular assumptions about Harlem's nightlife—and in contrast to a common secularizing narrative from writers such as Locke and
Cunard—Wright argued that churches were still most significant.

Richard Wright's "Portrait of Harlem" stopped short of James Weldon
Johnson's hierarchical ranking of large and "little" congregations. Yet he
too drew a distinction between established denominational churches and
the migration-fueled phenomenon of storefronts. The former were "conventional," while the latter were grouped with other, "unconventional

... tabernacles of 'prophets'" and the synagogues of black Jews. Calling attention to charismatic quasi-religious figures like Marcus Garvey and Sufi Abdul Hamid, Wright portrayed Harlem as home to "many diverse religions and cults." Afro-Protestantism abounded on large and small scales. Yet there was also a long list of less traditional congregations that arose in the wake of the migration to the North. Just a year earlier *The Crisis* had published Miles Mark Fisher's essay "Organized Religion and the Cults," which argued for the inclusion of these unorthodox groups within the Afro-Protestant mainstream.[58]

Although the FWP provided much-needed support to a number of black artists both in and beyond New York City, the WPA's publication *New York Panorama* allotted just a small fraction of its more than six hundred pages to the story of New York's "Negroes." Richard Wright's brief survey did not allow for a more detailed explanation of his allusions to the Negro's "inner man," which he described as being sustained by food, entertainment, and churches at once. Harlem, the mecca of Alain Locke's New Negro, was constituted, Wright wrote, by a heterodox set of spiritual communities that occupied the (sacred) space between the "two largest religious sects, the Baptists and the Divinists."[59] Wright's gesture toward interiority continued the popular pairing of inner and outer lives mapped onto a complicated cultural milieu of racial spirits and Negro churches. However, like both George Edmund Haynes and James Weldon Johnson before him, Wright acknowledged the primary role of institutional Afro-Protestantism not only in addressing the spiritual appetites of black Harlem but in tending to its corporeal needs as well.

The year 1938 was monumental for Richard Wright for other reasons. In December he learned that one of his short stories would be awarded the $500 first prize in the FWP-supported *Story* magazine's fiction-writing contest. Shortly after receiving the award and seeing his story in print, "Fire and Cloud" appeared again in book form along with three other tales.[60] Wright's first book, *Uncle Tom's Children* (1938), was published that year, weaving together the author's personal knowledge of both the southern black Christian experience and Communist propaganda. Although Wright was by no measure a practicing Christian, his criticism and creative writing both involved a critical performance of Afro-Protestantism. Christianity was readily apparent in *Uncle Tom's Children*, in which story titles like "Fire and Cloud" and "Bright and Morning Star" borrowed heavily from the Bible. Indeed, even as the book's title suggested a generational shift, its namesake (Uncle Tom) had entered the American literary canon through an act of Christian martyrdom.[61] By integrating Marxist politics with the cultural traditions of Negro life under Jim Crow, *Uncle Tom's*

Children modeled a literary aesthetic that Wright had announced just one year earlier.

Richard Wright, of course, is well known for his efforts to mobilize Leftist politics in literary form. In this regard, he was but one of many black artists and intellectuals whose vision of racial aesthetics was shaped by a constellation of Marxist ideas and organizations during the 1920s and 1930s. This list included W. E. B. Du Bois, Langston Hughes, Arthur Fauset, Claude McKay, Marian Minus, Louise Thompson, Paul Robeson, and Dorothy West, to name just a few.[62] Throughout much of the 1920s the radical journal *The New Masses* had raised criticisms of the racial politics of the Harlem Renaissance. During the 1930s, Dorothy West had founded *Challenge* and then *New Challenge* to provide a publishing platform for what was, in effect, a New Negro literary Left.[63]

During the same year that *New York Panorama* and *Uncle Tom's Children* appeared, the dean of Howard University's School of Divinity, Benjamin E. Mays, published his second book, *The Negro's God as Reflected in His Literature* (1938). *The Negro's God* represented a different kind of investment in religion than Richard Wright's. Five years earlier, the theologian and Christian minister had co-authored a seminal study of black churches, *The Negro's Church*, with the sociologist Joseph Nicholson.[64] Now Mays turned his attention to what he saw as a serious threat to institutional Afro-Protestantism. In the literature of the Harlem Renaissance, he identified the influence of Communism and an embrace of atheism on the part of several black writers. While Mays focused on recent literary innovations, he was more concerned with larger social developments. For example, in 1938 the two organizations most involved in efforts to institutionalize the race politics of the New Negro—the NAACP and National Urban League—dropped their anti-union stances.[65]

Indeed, by 1938 the New Negro movement was, by even the most generous accounts, a thing of the past.[66] Just one year earlier Richard Wright had offered an elegy for the Harlem Renaissance, although he had played a key role in a related black literary flourishing in Chicago before moving to New York. Wright's emergence on the New York scene did not reflect a sudden triumph of class consciousness over race politics. Rather, it reflected the maturation of a tradition of black literary and political radicalism that had been building momentum since the 1920s.[67] During the fall of 1937 Dorothy West published what would be the final edition of *New Challenge*. As much as the issue put forward a Leftist vision for Negro letters, it was also a collaborative effort between the Chicago and Harlem schools of the fading Negro Renaissance.

Dorothy West and Marian Minus, a friend of Wright's from Chicago, were listed as editors when *New Challenge* was printed in October of that year. Richard Wright was credited as associate editor. In addition to connecting writers from the Midwest with those living in the Northeast corridor, the issue assembled an intergenerational cast of Negro writers, old and new.[68] Margaret Walker, Sterling Brown, and Robert Hayden all contributed poetry and Langston Hughes translated a poem from French to English. Together these four poets constituted a tradition of American Negro verse by themselves.

The first published writing of Ralph Ellison, who had just arrived in Manhattan from Oklahoma City, a book review of Waters E. Turpin's *These Low Grounds*, appeared in the issue. So did Minus's assessment of Hurston's *Their Eyes Were Watching God*, which she described as "superbly done."[69] From the old guard, Alain Locke contributed a review of Claude McKay's autobiography and latest book, *A Long Way from Home*. It read more like an assessment of a career and a rehashing of old arguments. Locke argued that in the years since McKay's celebrated poem of 1919, "If We Must Die," the poet and novelist had vacillated between "erratically accepting and rejecting racial representatives." Such shifts were not evidence of a complicated writer or an independent and expanding intellect, according to the former dean of the Negro Renaissance. Instead, McKay's evolution amounted to a form of "spiritual truancy and social irresponsibility."[70]

Richard Wright's creative role in shaping the journal issue as a whole may have been understated on the masthead.[71] Still, the critical vision for racial aesthetics that he put forward in his own contribution would ultimately come to define *New Challenge* for future generations. Wright's essay "Blueprint for Negro Writing" was both an indictment of the New Negro of the past decade and an invitation to Negro writers, young and old, to reimagine their role. In his view, New Negro artists had accomplished little for at least two reasons. First, they tended to be more concerned with pleasing white audiences than with addressing issues that affected most Negroes. "The mere recognition of this places the whole question of Negro writing in a new light," Wright emphasized, "and raises a doubt as to the validity of its current direction."[72] His second criticism was closely related to the first. While New Negro writers functioned as objects of pride for educated blacks, they were little more than sideshows for the white audiences from whom they sought affirmation. They were the victims of their own racial insecurities and the pawns of white patronage. In sum, Wright likened the writers of the Negro Renaissance to "French poodles who do clever tricks."[73]

Moving beyond critique, Wright outlined a ten-point plan, synthesizing the Communist Party's Black Belt thesis with his own knowledge of black folk culture. In doing so, he advanced a class-based argument that had only been inferred by George Schuyler, Langston Hughes, and Zora Neale Hurston before him.[74] Hurston's Africanist reading derived from her anthropological training. By contrast, Wright's materialist account adhered to Marxist doctrine. He posited a vision of a national culture situated in the South, where most American Negroes still lived, despite years of migration north and west.

If the work of racial aesthetics was going to be of any benefit to significant numbers of black people, Wright argued, Negro writers should learn from workers organizing in the South. In the wake of Popular Front activism, he encouraged them to "take advantage of their unique minority position."[75] He elaborated:

> There is, however, a culture of the Negro which is his and has been addressed to him; a culture which has, for good or ill, helped to clarify his consciousness and create emotional attitudes which are conducive to action. This culture has stemmed mainly from two sources: 1) the Negro church, and 2) the folklore of the Negro people.[76]

Wright's Marxist commitments are well known and help explain the common perception of him as dismissively critical of religion.[77] Moreover, in *Black Boy: A Record of Childhood and Youth* (1945), he documented the personal pains of growing up in his grandmother's "fundamentalist" Christian home in Mississippi.[78] Yet Wright's budding vision of social realism required a deep engagement with religion.[79] His "Blueprint" put black churches at the center of a call for an insurgent literary aesthetic.

"It was through the portals of the church that the American Negro first entered the shrine of western culture," Richard Wright observed.[80] Disconnected from any "African heritage," the Negro's efforts to worship freely under the terms of antebellum slavery amounted to a "struggle for human rights." However, the ensuing history of "the Negro church" was one of decline, as it devolved from a "revolutionary struggle" into an "antidote for suffering and denial."[81] Now, according to Wright, the vast majority of Negroes in the United States were oriented by an "archaic morphology of Christian salvation" that left them ill equipped for the demands of modern society. Even as Wright's "Blueprint" largely endorsed a move beyond Christian beliefs, he identified the Negro church as one of the primary "channels through which racial wisdom flowed."[82]

Whereas most New Negroes appealed to racial spirits that were animated either by African pasts (Hurston), uplift futures (Haynes), or both

(Locke), for Richard Wright the church appeared as the institutional embodiment of a "nationalist spirit." That is, "the Negro church" was a formidable racial ancestor. According to Wright, the primary reality that Negro writers had to negotiate was the imposed nationalist disposition of black culture. As a result of enslavement and segregation, he explained, Negro communities developed separately from white society, complete with their own set of structural arrangements and cultural sensibilities. Churches, schools, social institutions, sports leagues, and an array of expressive practices all bore witness to a "Negro way of life in America" that was distinctive, unified, and comprehensive.[83]

Richard Wright clarified that this "way of life," as he understood it, was the product of slavery and Jim Crow. It did not, as Zora Neale Hurston had contended, result from African cultural retentions. He explained further: "The Negro people did not ask for this, and deep down, though they express themselves through their institutions and adhere to this special way of life, they do not want it now. This special existence was forced upon them from without by lynch rope, bayonet and mob rule."[84] Clearly, Wright parted ways with the sentimental celebrations of Negro folk life so central to the Negro Renaissance of the 1920s. While he agreed that a literature could indeed be developed out of the soils of folk culture, with Negro churches as the main institutional arbiter, Wright's analysis focused squarely on the issue of class. Regardless of the power of the cultural practices cultivated within segregated black communities, life behind the Du Boisian veil was never desired. It was a product of the "problem of the color-line."[85] A separate black social life had grown involuntarily out of and continued to be violently enforced by the material conditions of white supremacy.

There was a distinctive racial culture under Jim Crow, to be sure; but it was important only insofar as it could be utilized to counter racial (and ultimately economic) oppression. Richard Wright insisted that Negro writers had to negotiate, not celebrate, the distinctiveness of the terms under which their communities cohered. Ambivalent at best, he laid out the norms that guided his engagement with the culture of this black social world: "Negro writers must accept the nationalist implications of their lives, not in order to encourage them, but in order to change and transcend them. They must accept the concept of nationalism, because, in order to transcend it, they must *possess* and *understand* it."[86] Here Wright's analysis squared well with the strategies of Communist Party organizers who drew on folk culture, sacred and secular, as a resource for recruiting and mobilizing black workers in the South. Negro churches had to be understood and engaged because they were an organizing center, a tool to be utilized toward the end of class struggle.[87]

Although guided by a different set of concerns than positive representation, as Du Bois's "Criteria" essay was, in his "Blueprint," Richard Wright assigned writers to the role of race leaders. Negro writers were best situated to assume the mantle previously worn by the clergy, he asserted. Afro-Protestantism had at one time been defined by "revolutionary struggle." Now, however, Negro preachers were constrained by the social position attached to middle-class status. New leaders were needed to fill the void. The church's radical origins had been compromised. Wright explained at length:

> With the gradual decline of the moral authority of the Negro church, and with the increasing irresolution which is paralyzing Negro middle class leadership, a new role is devolving upon the Negro writer. He is being called upon to do no less than create values by which his race is to struggle, live and die. By his ability to fuse and make articulate the experiences of men, because his writing possesses the potential cunning to steal into the inmost recesses of the human heart, because he can create myths and symbols that inspire a faith in life, he may expect either to be consigned to oblivion, or to be recognized for the valued agent he is.[88]

In Wright's formulation, not only was a racial aesthetic possible, but writers were uniquely qualified to provide frameworks through which the masses could make sense of their deepest existential questions and reignite a revolutionary struggle once led by preachers. It was up to the Negro writer, in short, to "create the values by which his race is to struggle, live and die."

In keeping with Marxist doctrine, Richard Wright diagnosed the Negro middle class, namely preachers, as suffering from a form of "false-consciousness." In order to combat this problem, writers were needed to "create [new] myths and symbols that inspire a faith in life."[89] To accomplish this task, they had to draw upon the cultural ethos of the black masses, which Wright described disparagingly as "the ideologies and attitudes fostered in this warping way of life."[90] Only by mastering this "minority outlook" might Negro writing help transform and transcend the racist (and class) structures that so radically limited African Americans' life possibilities. By no means a Christian apologist, Wright maintained that black churches were a primary force sustaining a racial disposition. As such, they would have to be substantively engaged if either white supremacy or Western capitalism were to be overcome. "In order to transcend it, they must possess and understand it," Wright admonished.[91]

Written at the very moment when the majority of New Negroes were conceding the incapacity of the arts to conquer the color line, Richard Wright invited black writers to take up the burden of the preacher and become myth-makers for their communities. As a final word in New Negro debates concerning racial aesthetics, he synthesized a range of discourses that had defined the dialogue in the preceding decades. Wright linked the political sensibilities of the old guard, which had viewed art as activism, with the cultural forms to which creative freedom led "younger artists" like those associated with *Fire!!*—namely, the expressive cultures of the black churches. In this regard, Wright's "Blueprint for Negro Writing" signaled the end of the New Negro's universalizing ambitions. A masterful performance of the particulars of Afro-Protestantism was a necessary step toward advancing a radical politics. The black masses were in need, to paraphrase James Weldon Johnson, of new trombones.

While Richard Wright called attention to the constraints of class, his turn to the Negro Church also confirmed and helped encode a dynamic in African American letters that would persist in the years to come. Afro-Protestantism was presided over by a preacher class that was overwhelmingly male. The "Blueprint" made it incumbent upon Negro writers, perhaps unwittingly, to replace a masculinist model of race leadership and racial aesthetics. As much as this gendered logic prevailed by presumption among New Negroes in the North, Wright's formulation brought to the fore how the South was never too far from sight. Indeed, as the proximate site of an ancestral past, the South remained central to racial aesthetics even as the North provided access to new commercial networks and literary opportunities. Moreover, both Wright's "Blueprint" and Zora Neale Hurston's novels and folklore were reminders that the patterns of migration always flowed in at least two directions and that the black migrants who ended up in southern cities outnumbered those who made the pilgrimage to the North.[92]

Richard Wright's "Blueprint for Negro Writing" captured the complexities and contradictions of the ways religion animated racial aesthetics—torn between embracing a modern race-spirit and ancestral loyalties—during the period when the New Negro, to paraphrase Wright, "struggle[d], live[d] and die[d]."[93] In the following years Wright ascended to international renown and his social realist aesthetic developed into a literary orthodoxy to be undone. Although it was not until the 1960s that his essay became a call to action for a new generation, he would quickly develop into the looming literary ancestor. Richard Wright's rapid rise, in turn, cast a long shadow over all aspiring black writers in the intervening decades of the 1940s and 1950s.

CHAPTER 3

✧

Catholic Spirits

I cannot help but think that he consented because he was a Roman Catholic and felt a vague sympathy for Negroes.

Richard Wright

In 1940, Richard Wright's *Native Son* was published. Selected for the Book of the Month Club—the first by a black author—it quickly became a bestseller. That same year a new edition of *Uncle Tom's Children* was released, with the addition of one more story, "Bright and Morning Star," and an essay that became the book's introduction. The following year the novel inspired a Broadway play directed by Orson Welles and Wright was awarded the NAACP's Spingarn Medal. Four years later his autobiography, *Black Boy* (1945), came out to similar acclaim. The overwhelming fanfare immediately established Wright as the leading Negro writer of the day.

In 1946, Richard Wright left the United States for Paris, where he would reside for the rest of his life. Wright's presence remained prominent in American literary circles long after his departure for Europe. His writings also never left the United States behind, even as he incorporated a broader analysis of the colonial situation in the years to come. Although Wright's reach and vision were undeniably international, it is impossible to imagine his aesthetic without attention to the nation-state, specifically the United States. Early observations that *Native Son* displayed a "nationalist racial spirit" would continue to ring true for Richard Wright over the years. Communist reviewers, in particular, wrote derisively about what they took to be an undue investment in race and nation on the part of the rising star.[1]

Richard Wright was received by liberal readers as the leading voice of an emerging generation of black writers. His endorsement as such, at least among the Negro literary establishment, was implied when his autobiographical essay, "The Ethics of Living in Jim Crow," was selected for inclusion in *The Negro Caravan*, an ambitious anthology of African American literature that was published in 1941. In his searing portrait of the race politics that constrained the Jim Crow South, Wright credited a white Roman Catholic man in Memphis who borrowed books for him from a local library with making his early literary ambitions possible. The entangled webs of racial and religious oppression, according to Wright, made such an exchange possible. In ways that the anthology's editors did not imagine, Wright's suggestion that a shared set of experiences and sympathies connected black Americans and white Catholics anticipated a major development that would link religious history and racial aesthetics in the decade to come.

This chapter follows the rise of what is here referred to as racial catholicity, a formation that resulted from the convergence of a shift toward the universal in black writing and the marked expansion of an African American presence within the Roman Catholic Church. Attention is given, first, to two cases—one literary and one biographical—that help capture these respective developments: the publication of *The Negro Caravan* and the spiritual journey of Claude McKay that culminated with his conversion to Catholicism in 1944. Next, a close and comparative reading is given to two key texts of the moment—McKay's *Harlem: Negro Metropolis* (1940) and Roi Ottley's *New World A-Coming* (1943)—that reveal the tensions between the racial difference associated with Catholicism and black claims of catholicity. Ultimately, the plausibility of an assertion of racial catholicity remained connected to an Afro-Protestantism that, in this moment, was being expanded (at least by Ottley) to encompass a novel black Judeo-Christianity.

JOINING *THE NEGRO CARAVAN*

"'The Negro Caravan' comes as a long-awaited answer to the demand for a really representative anthology of American Negro literature," wrote Theodore Stanford in the *Philadelphia Tribune* in 1942. Stanford's review of the recently published book was so positive that he concluded by recommending it as a litmus test for democratic commitments and good race politics. In the journalist's estimation, *The Negro Caravan* "should occupy a conspicuous and favorite spot on the book shelf of every freedom-loving black and white man in America."[2] If Stanford's endorsement seems overstated, he was not alone in his praise. More than twice the size of Alain Locke's *The New Negro*, the Harlem Renaissance's definitive anthology, *The Negro Caravan* was a magisterial compilation of "Writings by American Negroes" (as the book's subtitle explained). Totaling more than one thousand pages, this volume aimed to chronicle "the entire period of Negro expression—from the writings of Phillis Wheatley and Jupiter Hammon to the current fiction of Richard Wright."[3]

Both anthologies spanned the genres of drama, poetry, prose, short story, and critical essays. Yet while *The New Negro* was largely organized around thematic concerns (e.g., "Negro Youth Speaks," "The New Scene") *The Negro Caravan* might better be described as encyclopedic. Each section of the book focused on a particular literary genre, organized chronologically and preceded by a critical introduction that contextualized the genre under discussion. Several reviewers noted the merits of these introductions as valuable contributions in their own right. Whereas Alain Locke sought to capture or make a claim about a new racial spirit in a specific historical moment, the editors of *The Negro Caravan* were less obviously guided by temporal concerns. Even if not intentionally, their comprehensive ambitions and the book's enthusiastic reception were no less representative of new developments in black literary aspirations.

The publication of *The Negro Caravan* was anticipated on the pages of the *New York Times*, announced between blurbs describing *Napoleon's Invasion of Russia* and Robert Frost's new book *A Witness Tree*, which would earn the poet his fourth Pulitzer Prize.[4] In addition to popular newspapers like the *Times* and *Tribune*, reviews of *The Negro Caravan* appeared in at least eight different academic journals, almost unanimously on positive terms. Read Bain, editor in chief of the *American Sociological Review*, was particularly effusive. "I am highly critical of 'literary materials' for sociological data," he confessed. Yet in the case of *The Negro Caravan*, Bain wrote, "I would be inclined to make exception." He continued: "Read it and you'll weep—and also laugh; you'll be proud and glad—and shamed and angry; you'll be a better American because you'll see that Negroes are Americans, too—human beings: artists and scholars."[5] In Bain's view, the collection captured the valuable contributions of black writers on both political and literary terms. It captured the significance of "the Negro" for American democracy.[6]

More than anything else, *The Negro Caravan* was intended by its editors and received by reviewers as a representative depiction of black life. In the words of Sterling Brown, Arthur Davis, and Ulysses Lee—who collaborated to bring the book to print—it was organized "to present a truthful mosaic of Negro character and experience in America."[7] Across reviews that appeared in both academic and popular outlets, words like "objective," "complete," and "comprehensive" were recurring accolades. As William Shands Meacham wrote in his review for the *New York Times*, "the whole epic of the Negro is stirringly written down in 'The Negro Caravan,' for the student and for the general reader."[8]

In addition to its comprehensiveness, a second common theme positioned the book as an argument against "the setting-apart of Negro writing as a special category"; at least that is what the Brooklyn College philosophy professor Howard Hintz asserted in his review essay for the journal *College English*.[9] The book's editors certainly seemed to agree. Their introduction averred, "The bonds of literary tradition seem to be stronger than race."[10] The book's most forthright criticism alluded to this point. Lorenzo Dow Turner, a historian who founded African Studies at Fisk University, complained that "so little information emerges from the book concerning the relationship that exists between certain aspects of the culture of the American Negro and that of West Africans."[11]

Black and white reviewers alike, for the most part, seemed to agree that "the Negro" (and thus literature written by Negroes), was decidedly a North American creation. Along with the book's editors, most reviewers reached a political conclusion: racial segregation was no more appropriate in literature than it was in social life. As Meacham wrote, "by their own objective attitude" Brown, Davis, and Lee had helped "prove that the cultural wall that has tended to isolate the Negro from the main currents of American culture is breaking down."[12] On intellectual and aesthetic grounds, at least according to the reviews, *The Negro Caravan* had effectively made the literary case against Jim Crow.

Arthur Davis, Ulysses Lee, and Sterling Brown insisted that, in short, the work of Negro writers was catholic. In this regard, *The Negro Caravan* was singular even as it was squarely in step with the spirit of the times. It received a stream of similar assessments—representative, comprehensive, objective, whole, complete, total. Years later one reviewer went so far as to elevate the anthology as possibly "the most important single volume of black writing ever published."[13] Indeed, the collection's perceived catholicity was the primary reason for its singularity. The anthology was taken to represent "the totality of black writing" and present "the whole epic of the Negro." Yet equally significant was how and what the volume argued concerning "the Negro" and the idea of Negro literature.

Although *The Negro Caravan*, in effect, established a canon of writing by Negroes in the United States, the editors argued that there was no

"Negro school of writing." Rather, they explained, "The Negro writes in the forms evolved in English and American literature." As such, their writing should not be placed "in an alcove apart."[14] Such a claim was by no means entirely novel among black writers. What was new, however, was the overwhelming response of reviewers across "the color line" who now affirmed the editors' fundamental premise. Black writing was American; moreover, it was universal.

During the 1940s and 1950s a catholic sensibility animated racial aspirations and religious ambitions alike—indeed, a racial catholicity—as black artists achieved new levels of American acclaim. Black writers accumulated an impressive list of "mainstream" honors during this period. Ann Petry won a Houghton Mifflin Literary Fellowship in 1946 for *The Street*, which sold over one million copies. Gwendolyn Brooks won the Pulitzer Prize for Poetry in 1950. Three years later, Ralph Ellison was honored with the National Book Award for *Invisible Man*. James Baldwin collected one fellowship after another between 1946 and 1956 (from the Eugene Saxton Trust and *Partisan Review* and from the Rosenwald, Guggenheim, and Rosenwald foundations), while Lorraine Hansberry received the New York Drama Critics Award in 1959. Although he won most of his awards later in life, Romare Bearden's evolving art and criticism during this period helped black people working in a variety of visual media gain a new hearing in "the Artworld."[15]

While it is certainly fair to attribute a catholicity to *The Negro Caravan*, it is perhaps more important to note that Brown, Davis, and Lee were themselves caught up in, and contributors to, an especially catholic moment in African American cultural and literary history. Interestingly, the development of a robust claim about the catholicity of black literature and culture and the lived experience that those forms attempted to represent coincided with a historical moment when black people began to join the Catholic Church in greater numbers than ever before. In the convergence of a catholic sentiment with an expansion of black participation in the formal traditions of American Catholicism, the beginning of the 1940s can be understood as the dawn of a uniquely catholic (and catholicizing) moment in African American culture.

RACIAL CATHOLICITY AND THE RISE OF BLACK CATHOLICISM

Just as black people were a numerical minority struggling for equality in the face of the white majority and the policies of Jim Crow, at the start of the 1940s Catholics remained largely at the social margins of a society presided over by a Protestant establishment.[16] The otherness mapped onto the bodies of immigrants who arrived in the United States from Europe through at least the first half of the twentieth century was attributed as much to their religious practices as to their race and ethnicity. Race, ethnicity, and religion were inextricably entangled in these immigrants' reception, setting the terms of existence for migrant Catholics as they forged lives in the United States. Anxieties about ethnic Catholicism were often articulated through a discourse on Romanism that dated back to the early nineteenth century, even as phenotype made accessible a potential, if idiosyncratic, passageway into a white identity.[17] Still, the adaptations that made possible access to the benefits and privileges attached to American citizenship were realized as much through mastery of the norms of good religion—which was equated with Protestantism—as they were through the achievement of whiteness.[18]

Popular perceptions of Catholicism evolved significantly between Alfred E. Smith's unsuccessful bid for the presidency in 1928 and the election of President John Fitzgerald Kennedy in 1960, both men being prominent politicians of Irish Catholic heritage. Certainly such shifts should, in part, be attributed to a gradually growing tolerance of Catholicism in American culture during the intervening years. Such changes were also aided by efforts to modernize the Catholic Church from within that, eventually took on more concrete form with the Second Vatican Council (1962–1965). These developments were also part of larger demographic changes that led to a concentration of political power in northern cities, the primary sites of Roman Catholicism in the United States, as the nation steadily experienced urbanization.[19]

Such developments—of migration and urbanization, especially— facilitated the conditions under which African Americans began to make significant inroads into the Catholic Church. As hundreds of thousands of black migrants made their way to such cities in the North as Boston, Chicago, Detroit, New York, and Philadelphia, they increasingly came into contact with the Catholic Church and its largely white membership. To be sure, ethnic Catholics made numerous attempts to draw clear boundaries between themselves and their new darker-skinned neighbors through policies of exclusion, patterns of flight, and rhetorical and physical acts of racial violence. Yet many white Catholics who stayed in the city attempted to engage with black migrants on more hospitable terms.[20]

Through the establishment of parochial schools and a range of programmatic efforts to reach young people in cities (e.g., Bishop Bernard Sheil's Catholic Youth Organization in Chicago), beginning in the 1940s the Catholic Church experienced a significant influx of African Americans into its rank and file.[21] All in all, in the three decades after the start of World War II, the number of black Catholics more than tripled from 296,988 to 916,854.[22] The contours of this Afro-Catholic moment also extended beyond the borders of the United States, as Catholicism facilitated key points of exchange between black artists and intellectuals in the United States and those within decolonizing Francophone African and Caribbean nations. For example, Negritude writers such as Aime Cesaire and Leopold Senghor emerged out of contexts in which Catholicism had been the religious rule rather than the exception, as was the case in the United States. However, these were not mutually exclusive phenomena. Both patterns signaled a black internationalist sensibility that became only more pronounced—in the United States and abroad—in the wake of World War II.[23]

To be clear, lest the claim of racial catholicity—a confluence between the increasing number of black Catholics and the rise of a catholic sensibility within black culture during the 1940s—outlined here be read too literally, Catholicism was but one religious tradition through which African American writers made a claim on the universal. Robert Hayden, for instance, pursued an entirely different path when he joined the American Baha'i community in 1943. For Hayden, the rubrics of a particular religious tradition—and, in Baha'i, a relatively new religion traced to the mid-nineteenth century that espoused a theology of unity in diversity—went hand in hand with a writer's desires to mount a universal claim for his aesthetic vision.[24] Although Hayden was reluctant to have his verse viewed through the lens or language of race, much of the content of his poetry remained rooted in the particulars of the black experience through epic poems like "Middle Passage," which detailed the arrival of enslaved Africans in the New World. With the adoption of this new faith, Hayden found himself on the margins of both religious orthodoxies and race politics.

Significantly, Hayden's conversion took place at precisely the same moment that an especially prominent black clergyperson, Howard Thurman, was preparing to vacate a prime post within the Afro-Protestant establishment. In 1944, Thurman left his position as dean of Howard University's Rankin Chapel to help found and co-pastor the Church for the Fellowship of All Peoples in San Francisco. Often considered the nation's first interracial and interfaith congregation, the church was established to embody "a religious fellowship that transcended artificial barriers of race, nation, culture, gender, and social distinctions."[25] In his leadership of this congregation, which refused to adopt existing nomenclature for almost every category of social difference in order to serve a vision of a universal church, Howard Thurman preached an ecumenical (if not inter-religious) faith. His pluralist and catholic version of Protestantism shared much in common with the racial catholicity apparent in the writings of Robert Hayden and the literary vision of the editors of *The Negro Caravan*.

While this rise in racial catholicity should not be conflated with the grow-ing turn to Roman Catholicism by African Americans, a number of promi-nent black artists did, in fact, join the church around this time. Included in these numbers was the children's book author Ellen Tarry, who converted during her teenage years at a Catholic boarding school in Virginia before she arrived in Harlem in pursuit of literary dreams. Theophilus Lewis, a writer and editor associated with the Harlem Renaissance who theorized a spiritual role for the Negro theater, also embraced Catholicism in the late 1930s.[26] Although Lewis was best known as a drama critic, he also wrote for a number of Catholic publications, including *America, Catholic World*, and *Commonweal* in the years that followed his conversion.[27] Perhaps the most famous of these Afro-Catholic converts was the renowned jazz pia-nist and vocalist Mary Lou Williams. Williams joined the church in the 1950s and began her own lay ministry of sorts, mainly to jazz musicians, from her apartment in Harlem.[28] Yet nobody was more emblematic of the coalescence between a racial catholicity and the expansion of Afro-Catholicism than Claude McKay.

CLAUDE MCKAY AND THE CATHOLIC TURN

Writing from Chicago during the fall of 1944, Claude McKay had news to share with his longtime friend and former literary collaborator, Max Eastman. They had first met in 1919, when Eastman was editor of the *Liberator* and published McKay's most famous poem, "If We Must Die." At the time the poem first appeared, McKay was already thirty years of age, significantly older than most of Harlem's rising literati. Yet his poem struck a tone that resonated with a new generation of black writers and the audiences they would reach. In the fifth stanza, the poet proclaimed:

> If we must die, O let us nobly die,
> So that our precious blood may not be shed
> In vain; then even the monsters we defy
> Shall be constrained to honor us though dead![29]

In the aftermath of the Red Summer of 1919, when white mobs had attacked black Americans in several dozen American cities, the poet's allusion to a noble death brought to mind the moral victory associated with martyrdom, the shedding of innocent blood on behalf of a righteous cause. McKay also tapped into a longer tradition of moral suasion. Such acts, even if deemed fruitless by the scales of war, might somehow prick the conscience of those oppressive "monsters."

If the Negro had to die, then he should do so "fighting back." The poem was reprinted in black newspapers across the nation and would eventually be hailed as an anthem of sorts for what came to be known as the Harlem Renaissance. In the wake of World War I, "If We Must Die" was taken as indicative of a newfound militancy associated with the cohort of New Negro writers emerging during the 1920s. Twenty-five years later, McKay wrote to Eastman in an entirely different voice, relaying the meaning he had found in a much older story of martyrdom. His October 16, 1944, letter began with a declaration of faith. "I must announce to you that on October 11, The Feast of the Maternity of the Blessed Virgin Mary, I was baptized into the Catholic (Roman) Faith," wrote McKay. After assuring Eastman that his decision to convert was not arrived at hastily, that he had been "preparing to take the final hurdle" for some time, he still felt compelled to give an account.[30] After all, he and Eastman had labored together on behalf of the radical Left. The two men had connected, at least in part, because of a shared faith in scientific rationalism.[31]

By embracing Catholicism, Claude McKay would appear to have abandoned his earlier ideals. For Eastman, it might also have seemed an outright betrayal of their common political struggles. In an earlier correspondence, Eastman had asked, "Why not just work with the Catholics?" McKay, in turn, explained that he "had always wanted to belong to some religion." Significantly, four years earlier, the native of Jamaica had become a U.S. citizen. Indeed, by the 1940s questions of belonging loomed large for the author and activist, as he now found himself outside the literary and political circles in which he traveled earlier in his life.[32] McKay's letters to Eastman at this time also suggest that he understood religion to address matters of association as much as belief or doctrine. Moreover, as he explained his conversion further, McKay claimed to be no less a man of reason now than he had been during his years on the Left.

In his letters to Eastman, McKay linked his embrace of Catholicism to a critique of reason's limits. Among other things, he cited World War I as evidence that even those in the West who identified as "agnostics or rationalists lost all sense of reason." For McKay, religion, like rationalism, had its contingencies. Faith did not erase doubt or the validity of competing truth claims. McKay was unshakably relativist in this regard: "After all, Max, what is truth?" he asked. Adherents of various religions and members of various ethnic and cultural groups all "think that [their] way is the right way." Ultimately, McKay confessed, "I prefer the Catholic church and its symbolic interpretation of the reality of the Christ Crucified." Catholic theology may have helped McKay resolve certain conundrums. He was, however, reluctant to make more specific theological statements.[33]

McKay did clarify that his conversion was not a rash decision, but the culmination—"the final hurdle"—of a long process of reflection. His faith was not to be reduced either to reason or irrationalism. Making use of the metaphor of romantic love, he explained, "It seems to me that to have a religion is very much like falling in love with a woman." And he was drawn to the Catholic Church because of "her color and the music and rhythm of her—for her Beauty, which cannot be defined."[34] Indeed, in his letters to Eastman, Claude McKay wove together aesthetics and religion in a way that was quite common among American writers at the time, as many found in the arts a new source of spiritual authority.[35] Still, McKay wanted his old friend to know that his religious romance made him "not the less a fighter." If Eastman was not enamored by McKay's new love, perhaps he might concede that the Catholic Church was "the greatest political organization in the world and a bulwark against the menace of Communism."[36]

Claude McKay had a long and fraught history with the institutional Left. During the 1920s and much of the 1930s he had been actively involved in Communist politics and had even traveled to the USSR. During those years he received both literary and personal support from a number of individuals and organizations within these networks. Max Eastman's *Liberator* magazine in New York was just one in a long line of radical associations that McKay kept (or observed and wrote about) over the course of his peripatetic journeys throughout the Atlantic world. McKay's letters to Eastman in the early 1940s unveiled the mind of not only a seasoned radical activist and writer but also that a new convert. The reasons he offered for his new faith were clear, if at times inconsistent. The rituals, symbols, and relationships that he found in the Catholic Church appeared to provide at least provisional answers to questions and mysteries that had confounded him for much of his life. Ultimately, by his own account, McKay's decision to convert defied easy explanations.

There is no doubt that for Claude McKay, race was among the most frustrating conundrums that he confronted. He frequently referred to the nature of human beings, and it may be that Catholic teachings on the human condition helped him finally come to understand the race problem as intractable.[37] At the same time, McKay's rendering of Catholic truth claims as imperfect yet reasonable alongside rationalist epistemologies was consistent with the brand of cultural pluralism that was being made popular by Franz Boas at Columbia University.[38] Perhaps he was never too doctrinaire a Marxist and perhaps he never became an entirely dogmatic Catholic. Claude McKay was a fervently independent thinker; and this was no less the case with his religious conversion or evolving political orientation. At least this is what McKay insisted during his final years.[39]

Metaphysical differences notwithstanding, there were continuities between McKay's years on the Left and his time within a circle of Catholic activists.[40] He encouraged Eastman "to remember that there is a formidable left wing within the Catholic church." As if to invite his old friend to join him, McKay continued, "because it can accommodate all, even you."[41] It is clear that a constellation of ideas and relationships—Communist and Catholic, but others as well—served to facilitate Claude McKay's evolving efforts to make sense of both his personal experiences and his literary and political ambitions.

Long before his conversion in 1944, Claude McKay was no stranger to the subject of religion. For a time he had fancied himself a "pagan." At other points, he was an avowed atheist. Early in his youth he had rejected his father's fundamentalist brand of Christian faith in favor of free thought. He briefly inquired into Islam as well. Yet in the early 1940s McKay converted to Catholicism in what would prove to be the final years of his life.[42] Certainly, sickbed conversion narratives are by no means exceptional occurrences. Accounts of individuals who find themselves down on their luck finding their way to religion are perhaps all too familiar. So arguing that McKay's conversion was the spiritual quest of an author whose literary light had waned would make for a convenient explanation. However, accepting this narrative too easily obscures a more complicated set of issues that McKay's spiritual evolution and literary oeuvre raised.

With both his literary prominence and physical health in decline near the end of the 1930s, Claude McKay slowly found sustenance in a new set of relationships that provided novel space for him to attempt to resolve long-standing religious questions. Instrumental here was his friendship with children's book author and social worker Ellen Tarry. McKay had first met Tarry in Harlem roughly a decade earlier, during the Harlem Renaissance. Although raised in a Congregationalist church in Birmingham, Alabama, Tarry had converted to Roman Catholicism while attending the St. Francis de Sales boarding school in Rock Castle, Virginia, as a teenager.[43] In 1941, she found McKay alone and sick in a Harlem rooming house. She aided him as his health failed and found him care through the Harlem branch of Friendship House, an agency

founded in 1937 by the Catholic social activist Catherine de Hueck
Doherty in Chicago.

Tarry (and Friendship House) introduced McKay to a network of
Catholic activists and intellectuals who became his primary community
during the last years of his life.[44] In 1944, upon the invitation of Bishop
Bernard Sheil, McKay moved to Chicago, where he would remain until his
death in 1948. There he found support from a new branch of Friendship
House and became more significantly immersed in Catholic life. In fact,
McKay worked alongside Bishop Sheil, advising him on matters per-
taining to race relations. In turn, the Bishop wrote several essays that
were published in *Negro Digest*.[45] McKay worked out of the offices of the
Catholic Youth Organization, an auxiliary of the Church established by
Sheil in 1930. As his health allowed, he taught in Sheil's new adult education program, which the bishop had started only a year before McKay
arrived.

Along with his affiliation with Friendship House and his work with
Bishop Sheil, McKay was also introduced to the woman best known as
the co-founder of the Catholic Worker Movement: Dorothy Day. McKay
and Day corresponded for some time, and he visited her retreat center in
Easton, Pennsylvania, at least once.[46] Even though McKay wrote a second
autobiography and enough new poems for another book of verse, very little that he wrote at this time was published before his death. During these
years he found little success in either mainstream (white) or black publications. However, Dorothy Day's *Catholic Worker* printed several of McKay's
later poems. In the estimation of most critics, the artistic merits of his
Catholic poems pale in comparison to those written prior to his conversion.[47] Some invoke religious themes and reflect his newfound faith, while
others reveal a desire to reconcile himself to the course his life had taken.

One poem written in 1943 reveals a defensive McKay attempting to
clarify the cause of his literary decline:

> They say in Harlem that I'm pretty washed up . . .
> I'd rather clean the sewers of New York,
> And be washed up against a long cold bar,
> Rather than be a Harlem commissar.[48]

It was true that he had fallen out of favor in Harlem. McKay conceded
as much, but he explained that it was because he refused to align himself with the Communist establishment. Here the author cast himself as a
martyr for creative freedom. Other poems capture McKay weighing in on
pressing social issues. In a poem published in January 1945, he explored

the relationship between domestic civil rights and international military affairs. The first four lines played with the imagery of prayer:

> Lord, let me not be silent while we fight
> In Europe Germans, Asia Japanese
> For setting up a Fascist way of might
> While fifteen million Negroes on their knees
> Pray for salvation from the Fascist yoke.[49]

McKay had never been known for much formal innovation, and these later poems illustrated his continued preference for the classic English sonnet. Their content revealed him to be in step with a major black political campaign associated with World War II. By linking Jim Crow segregation at home to the fight against fascism overseas, McKay's verse was consistent with the Double Victory (or "Double V") platform.

In 1941, A. Philip Randolph helped organize the Double V campaign as part of the March on Washington movement orchestrated primarily by black leaders, activists, and organizers—including Randolph, Bayard Rustin, and others. This movement identified fascism abroad and racial segregation in the United States as a single enemy to be undone. The campaign was advanced through public forums and political pressure and on the pages of the black press and on the radio. As Farah Jasmine Griffin has noted, many black artists also weighed in on the campaign. For instance, dancer Pearl Primus was quoted in a 1943 *Daily Worker* story as stating, "I know we must all do our part in this war to beat Fascism and I consider the battle against Jim Crow in America part of that fight. . . . Each one of us can wield a weapon against Jim Crow and Fascism and my special one is dancing."[50] McKay's poem was another instance of an aesthetic performance of "the double political consciousness . . . embodied in the Double V campaign," as historian Barbara Savage described the agenda, wherein black and American identities and struggles were fused.[51]

The title given to McKay's poem on the pages of the *Catholic Worker*— "Look Within"—added another layer of meaning to the verse. Here social critique and spiritual concerns were framed as necessarily connected. The newspaper was started by Day and Peter Maurin in 1933 in association with the Catholic Worker movement. Through the *Catholic Worker,* they intended to make the Catholic Church's progressive social teachings more accessible while also highlighting the plight of the worker, much like its secular predecessor the *Daily Worker*. Whether McKay chose the title or the editors assigned it to the poem, it invited a religious reading from an audience that was both American and Catholic. McKay's poem required readers to reconsider their patriotism and their faith at once. As with the Double V campaign, McKay's poem argued that waging war with fascism on an international plane demanded that Americans also face up to racism within the borders of the United States.

"Look Within" also encouraged individual readers—as citizens and as Christians—to turn their eyes inward, shifting their focus from external appearances to their own internal condition. Moreover, McKay's allusion to "fifteen million Negroes on their knees" can be read as pointing out the paradoxes of faith and patriotism by recasting the submissive posture of prayer as something enforced, at least for black people, by the law and the lynch mob. The poem's multiple layers tapped into a long history in which slavery was diagnosed as the nation's original sin and its active legacy under de jure segregation left the soul of the country with a gaping racial wound for the world to see.

Claude McKay's turn to Catholicism in the early 1940s provided a glimpse of religion and race coalescing in ways that were both unorthodox and indicative of the times. Even in the finding of faith, a phenomenon that has been overly associated with black people in the United States, McKay's experience proved contrary to the normative traditions of Afro-Protestantism. His conversion did not take place on evangelical, outwardly expressive, or ecstatic terms. It was not a return to his father's fundamentalism, nor did it happen in the churches—whether storefronts or established denominations—that moved to Harlem during the days of the Negro Renaissance.

Studies of "the Negro Church" had developed a burgeoning historiography during the decade preceding McKay's conversion, helping establish Afro-Protestantism as a familiar fixture in American culture. In contrast, in the words of historian Albert Raboteau, the story of black Catholics in the United States was one of a "minority within a minority" that was largely untold in the early 1940s.[52] However, McKay's conversion to Catholicism was more than the isolated act of a down-on-his-luck writer with a track record of challenging convention. Rather, as we have seen, his Catholic turn was characteristic of a broader trajectory in which African Americans joined the Roman Catholic Church in much greater numbers than ever before, even as it was emblematic of a catholic spirit taking new shape within black cultural expression more generally. McKay embodied both dimensions of the kind of racial catholicity that was on the rise.

Alongside the numerical advances that the tradition of Afro-Catholicism experienced beginning in the 1940s, the culmination of Claude McKay's spiritual journey in Catholicism coincided with the rise of a wider catholic spirit apparent in the racial discourse at the time. The degree to which

McKay's evolution anticipated broader black aspirations in the wake of World War II is at least as interesting as his individual conversion narrative. From this perspective, McKay's embrace of Catholicism was in line with his long-standing insistence on what can be identified as a certain racial catholicity—that is, an assumption of the universality of the quotidian black experience. In addition to the network of social activists it furnished, the Catholic Church may have also offered McKay fresh intellectual space and rhetorical resources with which to mount a novel attempt to reconcile the universal/particular conundrum, especially as it continued to haunt black writers. If such a perspective was contradictory, it was nonetheless consistent with the broader racial catholicity that animated the ambitions of the generation of artists, intellectuals, and leaders emerging during the 1940s.

Akin to Alain Locke's introduction to *The New Negro* (1925), which pointed optimistically to artists as evidence of a "new cultural and spiritual awakening," new literary voices once again insisted, to paraphrase the journalist Roi Ottley, that a "New World" was soon coming at the dawn of the 1940s. If the category of spirit proved singular in its ability to simultaneously mark race as particular and universal for New Negroes, then McKay's embrace of Catholicism was entangled in a similar logic. His conversion to Catholicism was the culmination of an abiding insistence on the catholicity of the most mundane, even profane, dimensions of black life. Yet this Catholic turn also suggested that such reconciliation might require theology as much as the leftist social theories to which he had once subscribed. In this case, a Catholic sense of mystery—more than historical materialism—might allow for the unresolved irrationalism of America's original sin of slavery and racism's persistence during the segregation era: the perennial paradox in the face of modern progress.

Although his 1922 poem "If We Must Die" had been hailed as an anthem for the New Negro in Harlem, McKay was an outlier in the literary movement in which he is most often located. Not only was he not present in Harlem much of the time that, in Langston Hughes's words, "the negro was in vogue" but McKay refused, if inconsistently, to abide by the racial orthodoxies of New Negro politics.[53] At times he both refuted and embraced a reading of his most celebrated poem, and of his writing in general, as racially representative.[54] Even as he was being claimed by the race, McKay was often reluctant if not outright unwilling, to have his writings read as such. The demands of race politics often worked to "emasculate the colored literary aspirant," he had argued—on obviously gendered terms—on the pages of the *New York Herald Tribune* in 1932.[55]

On the one hand, his prose and especially his poetry were taken as indicative of a strident radicalism within New Negro literary circles. Yet on the other, over the course of his literary career Claude McKay maintained a range of complicated, if not contradictory, perspectives on race questions—a fact that often did not endear him to race leaders or literary gatekeepers. Indeed, in a *New Challenge* review of his autobiography, *A Long Way from Home* (1937), Alain Locke diagnosed McKay with a bad case of "spiritual truancy."[56] Claude McKay has been made to fit, begrudgingly, within the rubrics of the Negro Renaissance, so perhaps there is good cause to claim him for the next generation. If McKay is the New Negro's spiritual truant, then maybe the Jamaican-born, world-traveling critic, poet, novelist, and provocateur—and then repentant pagan and Catholic convert—might also be a patron saint of sorts for what literary historian Lawrence Jackson has identified as an "indignant generation" of black writers who came to the fore during the 1940s and 1950s.[57]

Claude McKay's conversion, in this view, was less a rejection of the leftist politics of his past and an embrace of something even more passé (i.e., religion) than it was a harbinger of something new. For it took place precisely during a moment when black artists were becoming, as art historian Richard Powell notes, "conspicuous, cosmopolitan, and candid about their universality and growing political importance in world affairs."[58] By all accounts, for years McKay had embodied all three of the qualities Powell attributes to a generation of black artists on the rise at the time of McKay's decline. He had long been "conspicuous, cosmopolitan, and candid" about his claims on the world stage.

Claude McKay's 1944 conversion to Catholicism was by no means at odds with the ethos of racial catholicity, which took the form of a wider insistence on the universality of black literature and culture in the years during and after World War II. Within the United States, McKay was part of the larger movement of black people into the Catholic Church during the 1940s. At the same time, owing to the histories of colonialism and missionary activism, Catholicism was a common denominator among many black writers outside the United States, a point of distinction from the Protestant churches that provided the religious norms for black American culture. Negritude writers such as Aimé Césaire and Léopold Senghor were part of an Afro-Catholic diaspora, and they both often cited the significance of McKay's writings to their literary and political aspirations. As Brent Hayes Edwards has persuasively argued, McKay bequeathed an aesthetics of vagabondism to Negritude. In return, he became heir to the primary Christian idiom of the Francophone black world. Ironically, his conversion to Catholicism amounted to opting out of an Afro-Protestant establishment just a few years after he had embraced American citizenship. Yet, in effect, it also meant casting his lot—although perhaps inadvertently—with an international black literary network in which his work remained vital.[59]

A TEXT BETWEEN THE TIMES: CLAUDE MCKAY'S
HARLEM: NEGRO METROPOLIS

Just about midway between the publication of his autobiography, *A Long Way from Home* (1937), and his conversion in October 1944, Claude McKay's final book was published. Combining previously published essays with new writing, McKay had high hopes that *Harlem: Negro Metropolis* (1940) would help revive his once bright literary career. In *A Long Way from Home* he had engaged the subject of religion sparingly and, more often than not, on rather disparaging terms. Although his earlier novels were often criticized for blurring the lines between fact and fiction, *Harlem* was actually his first book-length work in the genre of nonfiction.[60] In this regard, the text can be read as an extension of McKay's earlier work—primarily prose and poetry written in political adjacency to the radical Left—as it evolved into an analysis organized around the intersecting categories of race, class, nation, and religion. More specifically, the book reflected his most substantive and sustained critical treatment of "the religion of the Negro" even as it was framed more explicitly through the discourses of race and nation mapped onto the historic Manhattan neighborhood.

Harlem contained a circumspect assessment of the role of religion within black social life. In his earlier writing McKay made a name for himself with favorable portraits of black folk cultures that avoided the social science discourse of pathology or the Marxist discourse of false consciousness. As the 1930s ended, he was even less persuaded by uncritical dismissals of cultural and religious practices within the various radical circles he formerly frequented. Here his writing reflected sympathies with the spiritual worlds that occupied Harlem's cultural landscape during the interwar years. In this regard, *Harlem: Negro Metropolis* was a transitional text in the same way that the author's Catholic turn anticipated the catholicity that would define black literature and culture for much of the next two decades. Something about an emboldened assertion of universality allowed for an even deeper delving into the particular forms of black life, including—and perhaps especially—its religious dimensions.

In the decade that preceded the publication of *Harlem: Negro Metropolis*, a number of writers had penned essays on the neighborhood that hosted the Negro Renaissance. While religion was an unavoidable topic, for them it was not the focus of analysis. Given the circulating social science terminology of the day, it was almost pro forma to mention an overabundance of churches in Harlem and distinguish between large, established churches and less conventional "sects" and "cults."[61] There was *the* Negro Church and then there was a range of other black spiritual communities that failed to meet the orthodoxies of either race politics or Christian doctrine. McKay, too, acknowledged such distinctions, but he went further to highlight a number of more specific differences among religious leaders, institutions, and practices. Thus, his book lent itself to a portrayal of Harlem in which religion occupied a fundamental place in the overall portrait.[62] His analysis showed a sympathetic eye for the unusual primacy of Harlem's religious personality. Perhaps it was McKay's own circuitous spiritual pilgrimage that provided him with the insight required to render a more complicated, if ultimately conflicted, portrait of black religion.

Claude McKay devoted an entire chapter to both "occultists" and "cultists," each of which fell outside the umbrella of the Afro-Protestant establishment. Most formative to his understanding of the occult was that it evinced an "animism" associated with African cultures. "The cruder the magic," wrote McKay, "the greater its influence in Africa." Although black people converted to Christianity and Islam, he suggested that even black Protestants and Muslims still practiced their faiths "on pagan terms." The magical influence of Africa was manifest in "music and wild dancing and shouting" and in "vari-colored jugs of oils with euphemistic labels such as: Jupiter, King Solomon, Felicity, Love-charm, Commander" and more.[63] This litany of "ritualistic paraphernalia" separated occultists from cultists, who were otherwise similar in their "primitive emotionalism."[64]

Cultists, McKay explained, distinctively wed religious performances to political platforms or financial profit, cultivating a "spiritual excitement to compete with the ungodly distractions of the time." Preeminent among these figures was George Wilson Becton—affectionately known as "Saint Becton / Of the Consecrated Dime"[65]—whom McKay playfully deemed the "prestidigitator of primitive piety." Ultimately, cultists and occultists alike confirmed his observation that "the church is no adequate outlet for the burning religious energy of the black masses."[66] Although sociologists diagnosed newly black metropoles as "overchurched," McKay argued that there was no way that churches could contain the Negro's spiritual energies.[67] For McKay, this was evidence of a modern people still possessed by an African past.

In addition to his proto-Africanist reading of Harlem's occult communities, Claude McKay devoted even more substantial chapters to three of the neighborhood's most heralded leaders—Father Divine, Marcus Garvey, and Sufi Abdul Hamid—all of whom were cut from a charismatic religious cloth. After providing a general historical context for contemporary Harlem in chapters 1 and 2, the book's first focused chapter homed in on Father Divine, who was "Hailed as God by his followers [and] . . . stands on a pinnacle above them all."[68] And it was the "African Zionism" of Marcus Garvey to which McKay credited Harlem's emergence as "the Negro capital of the world."[69] Other chapters addressed such entities as local businesses (legal and extra-legal) and electoral politics. In each instance, McKay appeared particularly interested in what might be called the clerical (or working) class, including elected officials, civil servants, bosses, and entrepreneurs. For McKay, black people invested even the allegedly secular trades with an overtly spiritual ethos. "Harlem is haunted by numbers," he wrote, referring to the lottery as the community's oldest "clandestine industry."[70]

Divine, Garvey, and Hamid stood out because each of their personal narratives and leadership styles were deeply infused with religious sensibilities: race, religion, and politics, sacred and secular, were all so compellingly entangled. Many reviewers were critical of the book because McKay refused to dismiss these unorthodox religious leaders as charlatans who achieved celebrity during a period of perpetual motion in and out of northern cities and who preyed on the easily duped.[71] Consistent with his earlier novels, here McKay's nonfiction was more about the regular people who provided these ostentatious religious personalities with their platforms. Grasping the allure of these commanding spiritual figures offered a clue into the minds and meaning(s) of the black masses. Despite what the rationalist orthodoxy of the Left would argue, allegiance to a religious leader such as Father Divine did not correlate with a lack of intellectual capacity.[72]

Claude McKay's portrait of Harlem offered an inroad into the politics of religion in black American culture in the interwar period. Although he invoked an African past to explain "the religious heart of the Negro," McKay presented black religion as a New World—and thus modern—phenomenon. *Harlem*, as such, squared well with scholarship on African American religion emerging at the time. Alongside texts that focused on the singularity of the historic "Negro Church," McKay's analysis reflected a keen ethnographic sensibility that engaged black life outside the familiar frame of "Negro problems." And it was published four years before Arthur Huff Fauset's classic text, *Black Gods of the Metropolis* (1944), one of the earliest academic works to examine black religion beyond Protestant denominationalism. Even as Harlem became legible to the world as an exceptional racial enclave, McKay showed the spiritual pulse of its people to be part of the mainstream. Father Divine extended a New Thought tradition that had begun in nineteenth-century North America. Marcus Mosiah Garvey adapted the aesthetics of the Afro-Protestant establishment to sacralize a black nation. And Sufi Abdul Hamid built a black labor platform in partnership with a racialized Islam that had recently taken root on the soils of American cities.[73] In all three cases, black religion was a quintessential iteration of American modernity even as each marked black life as distinct.

With regard to New Thought, McKay captured connections between Father Divine's theology and this native brand of metaphysical thinking.[74] In McKay's estimation, the Peace Mission's adherence to a practice of spiritual confession to transcend physical and material differences placed its proponents in the company of such prominent clergy as Norman Vincent Peale. While Peale is best known for his bestselling book *The Power of Positive Thinking* (1952), he first rose to popularity in New York City during the same decade that Father Divine gained a following in Harlem.[75] McKay concluded his discussion of Divine by comparing the Peace Mission movement to Mary Baker Eddy's Christian Science church, which remains America's most prominent New Thought denomination.[76] Father Divine and the Peace Mission have typically been relegated to the margins of American religion. In truth, they held much in common with mainline religious (read Protestant) celebrities like Peale and his Marble Collegiate Church.

Claude McKay was by no means alone in highlighting the religious presentation of Marcus Garvey and his Universal Negro Improvement Association (UNIA). Garvey himself was born into Methodism and later became a Catholic convert.[77] While the UNIA maintained no denominational affiliation, it owed much to Protestant creeds, hymnody, and liturgy. Garvey was inspired by the oldest independent black denomination, the African Methodist Episcopal Church (AME), its founder Richard Allen, and Bishop Henry McNeal Turner, who preached a pan-African theology while extending the AME Church's reach in the South.[78] The Christian Bible, of course, was crucial to Garvey's rhetoric, and Psalm 68:31—"Princes shall come out of Egypt; Ethiopia shall soon stretch out her hands unto God"—served as the UNIA's unofficial mantra.

Claude McKay also noted that Garvey helped establish the African Orthodox Church as an auxiliary to the UNIA's work. He enlisted a highly regarded black Episcopal priest, George Alexander McGuire, to serve as UNIA chaplain-general and to lead the new denomination.[79] Additionally, the UNIA's music director and "band master" was Arnold Josiah Ford, a migrant from Barbados who is generally considered the first black rabbi in the United States. Ford designed the UNIA's *Universal Ethiopian Hymnal* and composed its anthem, "Ethiopia, Land of Our Fathers."[80] While the UNIA revised black church rituals to reflect its pan-African philosophy, such liturgies connected Garvey to the body of Methodist churches in the Atlantic World—what historian David Hempton has described as an "Empire of the Spirit."[81] Indeed, Garvey mastered the Protestant logics of American pluralism in service to an institutional manifestation of intra-racial ecumenism.[82] The UNIA was by all counts, as one scholar put it, "a black civil religion." In McKay's account, it was "African Zionism."[83]

The final and longest chapter in *Harlem: Negro Metropolis* focused on a charismatic figure who now receives far less attention than either Divine or Garvey in popular accounts of migration-era Harlem. Sufi Hamid also fused religion and race politics to build a following in the urban North. However, as McKay noted, Hamid's labor activism put him squarely at odds with the organized Left, including black people within its ranks. Hamid was tough to pin down, owing both to his inability to institutional-ize his political program and his knack for reinvention. He morphed from mystical teacher into radical organizer, only to transform once again into religious sage. Observing his return from politics to mysticism, McKay attributed Hamid's transformations to opportunism. Hamid himself had told McKay that "there was so much religion and regalia in the soul of the Negroes one could do nothing with them without some show of it."[84]

In this regard, the former "Bishop of Conshankin," who was known for donning a turban and European military attire, was both unique and strangely familiar. As McKay put it, Hamid was "an unusually strange mix-ture of opposing elements." He possessed the requisite mysterious personal narrative, migrant backstory, and spiritual transformation that were com-mon features in the biographies of many black religious leaders at the time. Several "prophets" created iconic names for themselves, including Divine, Noble Drew Ali, and Elijah Muhammad. Indeed, the city provided the con-ditions that made possible such reinvention. New names meant that novel identities, and thus fresh possibilities, were accessible to almost anyone. In this modern iteration of religion—facilitated by migration and urbaniza-tion—anonymity was often a precondition for achieving iconicity.

Claude McKay's portrait of the brand of proto-Islamic union activism of Sufi Adbul Hamid (born Eugene Brown) served larger purposes than the writing of biography. Hamid was part of a wider pattern of mixing "modern" political ideologies with "primitive" religious ideas—a practice that was certainly not unique to Harlem.[85] In addition to his extrava-gant religious performance, Hamid had also proven rather effective in galvanizing a movement for black workers in Harlem. In this regard, he provided McKay with a platform to discuss more than a strange case of Afro-modern mysticism. Hamid offered entrée into the "long neglected bootleg labor jungle of Harlem."[86]

In this culminating chapter of the book, Claude McKay's tone shifted dramatically from description to prescription. While his depictions of Divine, Garvey, and the cultists and occultists were by no means celebratory, they challenged the Marxist orthodoxies that guided social scientific critiques of black religion and culture. Such interpretations more often than not appealed to variations on the themes of false consciousness and manipulative fakery. Now McKay, too, seemed to join the chorus, moving from sensitive portraiture to strident polemic. His primary target was the Left, especially the Communist Party, but only to the extent that it exploited "the Negro." In fact, McKay staged an almost cosmic struggle between an established and racially privileged white Left and an under-resourced, idiosyncratic, and internally fractured black race struggling for economic autonomy—all on the streets of Harlem.

Setting up the book's final chapter, McKay opined that "religious, political and industrial factors are intricately jumbled in Negro life and the indiscriminate mix-up is not only appalling, but also paralyzing to Negro progress."[87] Communist forces without and cultural factors and political factions within together frustrated efforts to achieve an equitable entrance into modernity. It was only after Hamid's activism was undermined by claims of anti-Semitism that he retreated to "the mumbo jumbo of African-fetishism [*sic*] and Oriental philosophy." Still, McKay argued, "the new spirit that the Sufi had kindled in Harlem remained alive."[88] Communist efforts to graft race politics to class struggle had produced a long line of leaders, like W. E. B. Du Bois and A. Philip Randolph, who ultimately left the party "disillusioned, cynical, bitter."[89] Hamid, for McKay, represented an autonomous effort to represent the economic interests of black workers.

In contrast, the organization that A. Philip Randolph later founded— "the Brotherhood of Pullman Porters . . . a national negro union of negro works"—figured as the institutionalization of the sort that Hamid's spirit inspired.[90] McKay elevated Randolph's personal evolution from intellectual (socialist theorist, writer, and speaker) to organizer as an exemplary model for black leadership. "The mainspring of the Negro minority lies within itself," he concluded, not within a Left riddled with white supremacy and whose primary interests were outside the United States. Perhaps most interestingly, McKay ultimately rendered Communism a crude form of religious fundamentalism that "promoted Russia as the sacred, the holy land." The Communist Party functioned like "a sacrosanct state with an infallible government." Members of the Communist Party of the United States of America in Harlem were "the bigoted disciples of Marx [who] transferred their heritage of faith from the domain of religion to that of social science and soon became a universal menace."[91]

Ultimately, *Harlem: Negro Metropolis* was its own "strange mixture of opposing elements." On one hand, the book's conclusions had much in common with Richard Wright's essay "Blueprint for Negro Writing," which three years before had recommended that writers step up to play the role of race leaders.[92] Given his background, Randolph was exemplary in this regard. The vision Claude McKay put forward of racial self-determination tied to an autonomous political economy showed that his analysis was indebted to the Left even as he criticized the influence of Communism on black life. On the other hand, the call for an independent radicalism seemed to undermine an otherwise empathic portrait of black religion.

Wright's "Blueprint" also highlighted the necessity of an intimate knowledge of black culture for the specific purpose of aiding racial transcendence in favor of class struggle. McKay, too, insisted on the reality of a distinctive black culture that was most apparent in religion. However, he posited an African origin of such difference, much like Zora Neale Hurston. Although McKay did not believe that the roots of black difference were to be found in racial oppression the social fact of racism ensured that such differences persisted. Even if transcending race was desirable, McKay was less optimistic about the prospects for unraveling what he referred to as a "tangle of race problems."[93] Claude McKay, once the New Negro's poet of pugnacity, now appeared resigned to the dim prospects for racial inclusion, either within the Communist Party or within the U.S. body politic. As the book drew to a close, class seemed to cede to race as an organizing idea. The cultural politics of religion in black life figured, for McKay, as a key point of unresolved tension. That religion suffused all of black life was a source of cultural distinctiveness, but it was also a marker of social difference that was "paralyzing to Negro progress."[94]

Harlem: Negro Metropolis revealed Claude McKay to be a quintessentially modern thinker concerning religion, to the point that he challenged the nature of the very category. Under the aegis of modern progress, religion was something to be disciplined as autonomous from the world of politics and industry. Yet in his telling, Father Divine, Marcus Garvey, and Sufi Hamid, as well as the occultists, cultists, and number-runners, all appeared as fascinating foils to such claims. At least in part, the racial difference of the Negro metropolis rested upon an apparent disregard for the disciplining logics of modernity. The Peace Mission was proto-Communist and the mundane activity of running numbers was a novel form of "mysticism." Even black Protestants, who did not receive much attention at all in the book, were deemed to be inescapably pagan. Ultimately, each example was portrayed as its own complex evidence of an alternative (or black) modernity. Each represented a religious attempt to reorder the material conditions of black people's lived experience under the rule of a presumptively secular white order.[95]

Harlem's damning critique of Communism followed the same logic: this professedly secular organization was, in effect, a modern religion whose social practices had much in common with the racial politics of segregation. Notably, Claude McKay's nuanced treatment of black religion did not prompt him to join the first autonomous black institution with its own economic base—namely, "the Negro Church." Rather, McKay's Catholic turn suggested that he maintained a commitment to the universal while conceding that the material and economic conditions that constrained black life might be fully achieved only on spiritual terms. Put another way, the relationships and resources that McKay accessed through the Catholic Church provided a set of ideas and practices that squared well with his long-standing activist commitments.

Although Claude McKay never managed to organize these ideas into a coherent political program and systemic theology, they might have coexisted fairly comfortably with the idea of mystery embraced in Catholic teachings, especially after the arenas of literature, science, and radical politics and the social reality of the United States had proved such unwelcoming homes for them. As much as *Harlem: Negro Metropolis* was a retrospective account of Harlem during its cultural heyday, the text is very much an artifact of the transitional moment in which it was first published. Reviewers were not generous. That it was reviewed at all in such outlets as the *New York Times* and the *New Republic* revealed that the author's reputation was not fully diminished. That it was panned by prominent young black journalists like Ted Poston and Roi Ottley as out of touch with the times clarified that a generational shift was occurring. Ottley, in particular, would become a leading voice on race matters in the 1940s. In contrast to Claude McKay, Ottley's interpretation of black life in the wake of World War II was a future-oriented and decidedly hopeful call for something "new."

NEW WORLD A-COMING: ROI OTTLEY AND THE AFRO-PROTESTANT AESTHETICS OF RACIAL CATHOLICITY

Although Claude McKay was critiqued as old hat, his detailed attention to religion reveal him to be a more astute analyst of black life than reviews of *Harlem: Negro Metropolis* acknowledged. The ways charismatic black religious leaders captivated loyal followers and fascinated a larger public during the 1940s and 1950s confirmed that religion still suffused black life. This proved, for McKay, that "black folks' religion is not the same as . . . white folks' religion."[96] In religious difference he found the strongest evidence of racial distinctiveness that confounded prospects for social inclusion under the terms of liberal optimism. Journalist Roi Ottley may have disagreed with the implications of such difference, but much about Ottley's first book resembled Claude McKay's last.

Similarly posed as a local project about Harlem, Ottley's *New World A-Coming* (1943) examined a range of prominent individuals and organizations in order to make a claim about the collective life of "the race." The familiar figures of Father Divine, Sufi Hamid, and Marcus Garvey received no less attention than McKay had given them, as did politics (both labor and electoral), the intra-racial negotiations of skin color, and the Harlem riot of 1935. Ottley also penned chapters on the boxer Joe Lewis, the black press, FDR's "Black Cabinet," the white Jewish presence in Harlem, and "The Lost Tribe of Black Jews." He gave specific treatment to intellectuals such as Alain Locke, J. A. Rogers, and Arturo Schomburg, whom he identified as the "Apostles of Race." And, like McKay, Ottley singled out A. Philip Randolph as exemplary among contemporary black leaders. Randolph was emblematic of "the trend of Negro thinking." Although Ottley confirmed McKay's observation of a preponderance of racial sentiment in the wake of World War II, the conclusions he drew concerning its meaning were quite different. Where McKay accented the ongoing influence of an African past, Ottley saw evidence of an increasing "militancy" in the thrust toward full integration in the United States. If preachers held sway in a previous era, organizers and politicians with a professorial tone, like Randolph, would win the new day.

The crux of Roi Ottley's argument hinged upon the idea that black people were "the barometer of democracy."[97] In this regard, *New World A-Coming* can be read as a literary missive in support of the Double Victory campaign being waged at the time. Summing up the book's argument, Ottley explained, "He [the Negro] is against fascism, finally and inexorably, both at home and abroad."[98] Many of his chapter epigraphs subtly signaled a black claim on American culture and citizenship. Each chapter, in this way, gestured toward the end of integration. Ottley's long history of New York cast black people as the "first successful cultivators of the wilds of America," for example. Black Jews shared much in common with their "[white] co-religionists." Harlem was emblematic of American poverty writ large, the equivalent of "a hundred delta cabins" within just a few city blocks. Black elite society mirrored "the same social illusions that feed the vanity of white men." Joe Lewis's success was not a confirmation of the black male's mythic physical prowess. Instead, he embodied the "desirable traits in any race or any nation." Racial distinctiveness was not so much dismissed as it was repositioned as both an instance of the universal and a particular example of a larger American phenomenon. Each assertion of Americanness countered white racism and an undesirable rise in racial chauvinism among black people that Ottley had observed.

The very title of the book—*New World A-Coming*—was indicative of Roi Ottley's resistance to a totalizing racial narrative, even as the book evinced a familiar racial catholicity. It was about both black America and something novel, something not reducible to race that was still in the making. The subtitle—"Inside Black America"—framed the book's substantive contents as evidence of the inability of race to fully capture the historical record and, especially, what stood on the horizon. What was once undisputedly a black world was becoming something new, something not as neatly defined on racial terms.

A bona fide Harlem native, Ottley began the book by challenging the famous narrative of the neighborhood as a special black enclave. As an insider, he knew better than to cast Harlem as wholly black. To do so, he provided a longer history of black life in New York that began downtown in 1626, precisely three centuries before the familiar tale that focused on the 1920s. In following migration patterns to northern Manhattan, he also highlighted the community's current ethnic diversity. Ottley explained, "Here live hundreds of different peoples, subdivided into a bewildering array of clan, tribes, races, cultures, and colors—of red, brown, yellow, whites, and black, and unimaginable shades in between."[99] Harlem was always more than a "mecca of the New Negro." Yet this was how the neighborhood was etched in the imaginations of Americans and of people around the globe.

In Roi Ottley's telling, Harlem was as much the product of the cultural and religious pluralism that distinguished American democracy as it was of the migration patterns and racial narratives that fed its rise as a black metropolis and race capital. Yet his analysis was in keeping with a formula wherein appeals to plurality—ethnic, religious, or otherwise—were enabled by adhering to Protestant logics. The combination of Ottley's emphasis on cultural diversity in Harlem and a larger argument for racial integration, advanced a racial vision that bore the marks of what Ann Pellegrini and Janet Jakobsen have described as a "Protestant secularism."[100] Moreover, the journalist's interpretation of postwar black life via a close reading of the most storied of modern black communities was also emblematic of a Judeo-Christian sensibility that was emerging during the Second World War.[101]

In all these ways, Roi Ottley's critique of racial particularism coincided with normative assumptions about the progressive role that religion should play in modern society. Racial identity and religious practice, in Ottley's view, were both to be ordered by the democratizing norms associated with American liberalism. Chauvinism of any sort had no place. Good religion was that which served the interest of black people's full claims on U.S. citizenship and of democracy generally. In the context of World War II, bad religion was the enemy of reason and racial democracy. In turn, authentic blackness was tantamount to a reasonable wartime patriotism. At their worst, racial and religious identities and ideologies promoted "fanaticism" and fascism.[102]

Throughout *New World A-Coming*, Ottley's assessments conformed to these criteria. For instance, he conceded that Marcus Garvey's "creation of a Black Religion with a Black God" added a liturgical dimension to the UNIA that enabled the movement to attract the black masses. Garvey's spiritual appeal was dangerous, however. In the hands of a Garvey, race functioned akin to a religious fundamentalism in ordering—better yet, for Ottley, deforming—modern black life. His creation of the African Orthodox Church—"the true church of the black man," according to Garvey—was the source of "much constructive belligerency today," Ottley noted.[103] In short, the UNIA's earlier prominence was to blame for the rising wave of "racial chauvinism" during the 1940s.

Roi Ottley's discussion of religion took its fullest form in a chapter devoted to a figure who rejected the very category of race. Surprisingly, Ottley argued that Garvey's assertion of a black God made it possible for Father Divine, a black man, to claim that he was God. In Ottley's telling, Father Divine capitalized on the racial utopianism that the UNIA had cultivated and stepped into the leadership vacuum in Harlem created by Garvey's decline, deportation, and death. While "Garvey rode in on the wild currents of post-war national and racial hatreds," Ottley explained, "Divine emerged from the ashes of the Depression."[104] In this way, Father Divine was a synthesis of Harlem's diverse spiritual landscape and the economic constraints of the 1930s.

Consistent with classical deprivation theories of the day, Ottley argued that the pronounced lack of material resources at the time made spirituality "flourish in a big way." The financial crisis was to be credited with sustaining the "mystics," "cultists," and "fakirs and charlatans of every brand" that lined Harlem streets with "much mumbo-jumbo." Yet they were just "small-fry practitioners" compared to "the grandiose sweep and the magnificent scale of operations" of Father Divine.[105] Ottley assigned a menacing quality to all of these figures, who might otherwise have been characterized more benignly as primitive holdovers from a bygone era. According to Ottley, the key to the effectiveness of Garvey, Divine, and the "herb doctors, clairvoyents [sic] and 'jackleg' preachers" was "mass hypnotism."[106]

Ottley's chapter epigraph gave away his argument at the outset. Enlisting V. F. Calverton's recent book *Where Angels Dared to Tread* (1941), he drew a straight line between a variety of American utopian movements and fascism on the global stage. In Calverton's words, Father Divine and other religious leaders represented a "kind of lunacy, embodied in higher but more sinister form in a person like Hitler."[107] This quote provided more than a clue into Roi Ottley's critique of leaders such as Garvey, Divine, and others. It also revealed his perspective on the role of religion in the new world he envisioned. In these cases, religion often worked against black people's interests and bad religion was an enemy of modern democracy. Lest they grow anxious, Ottley assured his readers that Father Divine's "influence will hardly extend beyond the span of his lifetime." Again, by his estimation, the growth of the Peace Mission movement was the result of a moment of economic scarcity. World War II now presented new opportunities. Even still, Ottley's conclusion concerning the failure of other black messianic figures to gain mass followings—"they came in periods when Negroes were in no mood to listen"—read more like a naïve hope for the future than a descriptive assessment of the past.

Terms like fanaticism, fundamentalism, and fascism set the critical tone of Roi Ottley's treatment of the new gods and their spokespersons who emerged in migration-era Harlem. Not coincidentally, these "bad" forms of religious practice were decidedly not "true" Christianity. Yet Ottley's unfavorable accounts of Garvey, Divine, and other unnamed actors was not the only attention he gave to religion. Chapters on black Jews and Adam Clayton Powell Jr. rounded out the book's coverage of the topic and clarified the author's commitments. Insofar as Ottley understood black religions as connected to economic deprivation domestically or as consistent with a climate of anti-Semitism internationally, he relegated them to a bygone era. Yet with the war against fascism as a backdrop, new space emerged for the formation of a shared spiritual (and American) alliance between Afro-Protestants and black Jews on the side of democracy.[108]

In this way, *New World A-Coming* implied a Judeo-Christian agenda for black America. In contrast to Ottley's strident criticism of Garvey and

Divine, black Jews and Powell received balanced, if not gracious, reviews. Both were observed as evidence of a religious sensibility that was at once rational, interracial, and oriented toward democracy. The difference between Father Divine and his ilk, on the one hand, and black Jews and Protestants, on the other, was made clear: Roi Ottley marked a difference between bad and good religion that, above all, secured a privileged place for a secularized Afro-Protestantism aligned with racial equality and American democracy.

Much of the early journalistic literature on Harlem's black Jewish community explicitly cast the movement as one of several new "sects and cults." Black Jews were viewed as a variant of black nationalism, and they were certainly not viewed as a species of orthodox Judaism.[109] It is striking then that Ottley opted not to join the chorus that dismissed the group as a "truckload of nonsense" or "yet another religious freak."[110] Instead, he told two distinct histories of black Jews that coalesced in the formation of Rabbi Wentworth Matthew's Commandment Keepers community in Harlem. First, Ottley provided a complex story of non-white Jews that gave primary attention to Ethiopia's Falashas and identified three other tribes: "the Sudanese Jews, the Black Jews of Cochin, and the Beni Israel Jews of India." At the center of this story were the "unmistakable traces of Hebraic influence among the various African tribes" that had led to a diaspora across Africa, China, and South Asia.[111] Second, he narrated a history of "Black Abyssinian Jews" who early in the nineteenth century "immigrated to the U.S. as free men to escape anti-Semitism abroad and opened a synagogue in lower Manhattan." Although this community had since disappeared, Ottley cited "considerable speculation" about the relationship between these black Jews and Harlem's Abyssinian Baptist Church, which was founded at precisely the same time and place.[112]

Abyssinian Baptist Church, to which Ottley belonged, was the subject of a separate chapter in *New World A-Coming*, which will be discussed in a moment. However, Ottley's history of black Hebrews anticipated—or, more aptly, adhered to—his analysis of Afro-Protestantism, as embodied by Adam Clayton Powell Jr. That is, Roi Ottley presented Rabbi Wentworth Matthew and Harlem's Commandment Keepers Congregation as a model of the "politics of respectability" that a church like Abyssinian Baptist was typically taken to represent.[113] Although "Negro characteristics curiously enough thread through their practice of Judaism," black Jews were "rational and law-abiding." "They do not drink, fight, or quarrel among themselves," Ottley explained. Black Jews cultivated a distinctive, if familiar, racial discourse. They opted to be called "*Ethiopian*, an *African*, or even an *Afro-American*," rather than Negro. Although black and white Jews rarely shared intimate space, Ottley affirmed, "in [black people's] practices of Judaism, there is little difference from white Jews."[114]

While Roi Ottley's account of black and white Jews was generally a story of similarity in support of human universality, he playfully noted several minor differences. Attendance at a Yom Kippur service in Harlem's Commandment Keepers congregation afforded an interesting case. Upon entering, Ottley found the temple possessed by a "quiet, subdued air," which he deemed "decidedly rare for Negro worship." Yet before long it became clear that one might as well be in "the black church," as the congregation quickly "threw their hands up in supplication."[115] On spiritual matters, black Jews were cut from the same theological cloth as their white "co-religionists"; however, on matters of liturgical expression and political affinity, a racial difference was clear. At the end of the day, he surmised, "The Black Jews, it appears, are more intensely Negro than Jew." Still, Ottley cast black Jews as models of religious orthodoxy and racial respectability years before respect or recognition was granted by major white Jewish denominations (e.g., Reform, Conservative, and Orthodox) or major black religious and civil organizations like the NAACP and the Urban League.[116] In fact, Ottley's book appeared at a moment when white Jews were themselves just being incorporated into the U.S. body politic.[117]

In Roi Ottley's presentation, black Jews had much in common with white Jews. Yet their commitment to a shared race politics and consciousness was in keeping with that of their black Protestant co-racialists. Similarly, where politics (i.e., segregation and racial identification) and culture (i.e., music and worship style) made for a distinctive black church experience, most black Christians took for granted the theological doctrines and denominational structures of their white counterparts. Without naming it explicitly, New World A-Coming posited an emerging "Judeo-Christian tradition"—one that formed in opposition to fascism and in favor of democracy—within black life during World War II.[118] At the same time, Ottley's affirmation of black Jews clarified his own investment in an Afro-Protestant vision of modern black life that provided the norms for his presentation of a black Judeo-Christianity.

To be clear, Roi Ottley neither explicitly endorsed nor offered an apology for the "Negro Church." Rather, while New World A-Coming critiqued other expressions of African American religious experience as antimodern forms of "chauvinism" and "mass hypnotism," and recognized black Judaism via various rubrics of religious orthodoxy and racial respectability (i.e., it was "rational" and "law abiding"), it affirmed a generative space for Afro-Protestantism within a Judeo-Christian vision of American democracy. Tellingly, Ottley's only sustained discussion of black churches appeared between chapters on electoral politics and leadership.

As Ottley clarified in the latter chapter, black organizational life was now animated by a "militant racial sentiment, and thus of racial solidarity" that was directed toward achieving "constitutional revolution" through "orderly democratic processes."[119] Ottley subjected Afro-Protestants subjected to similar assessments. If religion was to have any place moving forward it would have to be aligned with civil rights in the United States and with democracy around the globe. Ottley's discussion of Adam Clayton Powell Jr. confirmed these expectations. Black churches should be oriented outward into American public life. Institutional Afro-Protestantism needed to be in service to racial integration and democratic politics.

The title that Roi Ottley assigned to his chapter on Powell, "Glamour Boy," was somewhat misleading, even as it aptly highlighted the personality of a man known as a preacher, a politician, and an avid participant in New York City nightlife. His characterization called to mind W. E. B. Du Bois's classic interpretation of the Negro preacher—he was a "leader, a politician, an orator, a 'boss,' an intriguer, an idealist."[120] In comparable fashion, Powell was "at once a Salvationist and a politician, an economic messiah and a super opportunist, an important mass leader and a lighthearted playboy." He was a prime example of "the new and different kind of preacher that the Negro church has produced."[121] Referencing the classic black sermon, Ottley noted that this Baptist pastor "preaches no Valley-and-Dry Bones sermons, but salts down his speeches with nicely chosen Negro idioms about everyday issues."[122] Capturing the manner in which he viewed Powell as a bridge figure—a bit of the old, but also a sign of something new—he blithely summed up the preacher's style as being "as modern as jive talk." Powell, in short, was the archetypal New Negro clergyman. For Ottley, he was simultaneously more than the Negro preacher of old but still not quite enough for a new day.

If Adam Clayton Powell Jr. did not represent the most effective model of racial leadership, his ministry was emblematic of a new breed of preachers who were pointing their pulpits toward direct political engagement. Ottley highlighted a cohort of clergy that included Chicago Baptist clergyman J. C. Austin; Harlem's Unitarian preacher Ethelred Brown; and AME bishops R. R. Wright and Reverdy Ransom, all of whom had been part of an Afro-Protestant establishment in the North in the preceding decades. He also noted Elder Solomon Lightfoot Michaux, who wielded spiritual authority more through the media than through traditional denominational structures. For Ottley, Powell was evidence that "new types of leaders are taking over—men who are trained, socially conscious, and forward-looking, with their fingers on the pulse of the Negro."[123]

In addition to an orientation toward political advocacy, Roi Ottley considered Powell novel in terms of his willingness to open his pulpit to guests outside the boundaries of racial orthodoxy or Christian confession. He noted that under Powell's leadership Abyssinian Baptist Church had hosted a diverse group of speakers, including the Communist agitator James W. Ford, birth control activist Margaret Sanger, Evangeline Booth of the Salvation Army, and Stephen S. Wise, the Reform rabbi who started the free synagogue movement. Powell's ministry and life provided the sort of drama that made for compelling preaching and politics and for great journalism. Yet at the end of the day, Ottley's assessment of the preacher-politician-playboy was ambivalent at best. "Actually," he concluded, "Negroes are more dazzled than lifted by him—which indeed makes him a tough man to beat."[124] Even if he failed to lead them forward, Powell was in touch with the times as much as any black leader of the day.

Roi Ottley's arguments concerning Adam Clayton Powell Jr. were about more than one man or a singular historic church. In addition, Ottley's attention to Powell's biography failed to acknowledge—or even obscured—the connection between the pastor's story and his own. Ottley was not simply a dispassionate observer. He had personal ties to the charismatic preacher who would head to Congress just two years after the publication of *New World A-Coming*. Ottley was a longtime member of Abyssinian Baptist Church and had played for its basketball team as a youth. During the Depression, he had worked in the church's relief program at the same time that he was forging a career in journalism with the *Amsterdam News*. As adults, Powell and Ottley were, in fact, known to be good friends.[125]

Although Roi Ottley had a personal stake in presenting Powell and Abyssinian in a particular fashion, the preacher and the institution he led served a larger point of interpretation. "The church . . . is one of the most important tools the Negro has in his struggle for status," Ottley explained. He then provided a brief history of black Christianity. As was common practice, "Negro Methodists" and "Negro Baptists" were foregrounded. The latter were identified as most popular because, Ottley opined, they lacked "hierarchy and formal ritualism." He also acknowledged recent gains made by Catholic missionary work in cities. Otherwise, he gave little attention to denominational differences, let alone matters of theology or dogma. Religious questions aside, the "Negro Church" was a social institution. Afro-Protestantism was significant if for no other reason than its role in "fostering race-consciousness."[126]

For Roi Ottley and many others, churches were a key barometer of black life. "What is happening to the church is a reflection of what is happening to Negroes," he insisted. In this regard, his analysis was consistent with early historiography that positioned black churches largely on political terms.[127] Ottley also advanced a familiar narrative of decline in which black churches emerged under slavery as agents of freedom then retreated from social engagement around the turn of the twentieth century. Ottley conceded that "the Negro church of today does not approximate the vigorous instrument it was in the antislavery period." Yet he insisted that there were contemporary black clergy who "have spoken out clearly and have frequently mobilized forces for aggressive action in the Negro's cause."[128] Powell and a cohort of rising clergy suggested to Ottley that "the Negro Church is attempting to recapture its former place in the secular life of the black man."[129]

Roi Ottley's chapter on Adam Clayton Powell Jr. ostensibly offered a descriptive account of the political career of a rising minister. At the same time, it confirmed the author's investment in the long-standing normative logic of the Protestant-inflected vision of racial democracy that organized the book's core claims. Institutional Afro-Protestantism—in the form of black Baptist and Methodist churches—provided a rich history even as it remained an important organizing base. Ottley had conducted much of the research for New World A-Coming during his time with the WPA's Federal Writers Project, the same project that led to Richard Wright's New York Panorama (1938) essay. Moreover, his arguments concerning Powell resembled James Weldon Johnson's call for a reformed (i.e., educated, rational, and politically engaged) black clergy in Black Manhattan (1930).[130]

The Negro Church was necessary "so long as the race is discriminated against," Ottley conceded. Adam Powell was a bridge figure, at best, with one foot firmly rooted in the religious history, the other planted in electoral politics for a better way forward. Ultimately, he affirmed, "Men and institutions beyond church doors, and without political labels, lead the race today." As if to suggest the trajectory from religion to reason he envisioned for black leadership, Ottley ended his discussion of Powell with the preacher's campaign in the New York City Council on behalf of black professors.[131]

Although Roi Ottley had vehemently criticized Claude McKay's portrait of Harlem in his review in the New York Times, his book seconded McKay's conclusion that intellectual leaders like A. Philip Randolph best represented the future of the race.[132] Alongside figures like Randolph, Mary McLeod Bethune, Alain Locke, Walter White, and Roy Wilkins— each of whom occupied leadership positions in major black educational and civic organizations—Ottley claimed that "Negro writers and artists" were a part of this group.[133] Across genres and media, artists such as Marian Anderson, Langston Hughes, Paul Robeson, and Richard Wright "have articulated the Negro's aspirations" and "by their acts, inspire the masses to greater racial solidarity." Wright had called for his literary peers to function in this way just six years earlier.

Published in the pages of *New Challenge*, Richard Wright's "Blueprint" essay had appealed to a narrative of religious decline, much like Roi Ottley's first book. In 1937 Wright had called upon writers to embrace a role as race leaders. In his estimation, black preachers had vacated this role.[134] Ottley reasserted Wright's call to literary leadership under the authoritative guise of journalistic observation. Similarly, here he examined the black religious past through the lens of a rationalist—if still racialized—present, shifting the focus from clergy to artists and intellectuals. Black people still possessed "an abiding faith," but it was placed in the "eventual rightness of things" rather than in the Christian God. There was "nothing mystical about the Negro's aggressive attitude."[135]

To illustrate his claim, Roi Ottley extended this secularizing logic to a rereading of the popular Christian hymn "My Hope Is Built on Nothing Less." "When they sing '. . . on solid rock I stand!' this is no illusion," he argued, "for the foundation of their aspirations comes directly from the nation's great promise contained in its Constitution."[136] No longer was Jesus the "solid rock," in Ottley's rendition. A liberal Judeo-Christianity was now gaining ground. In turn, Afro-Protestantism was being remade in the likeness of American civil religion. And he encoded modern blackness in Christian hymnody even as he conveniently dropped "Christ" from the equation. "Inside Black America," to borrow the author's subtitle, the Christian God was being supplanted by the surer foundation of the god of democracy. And, as Roi Ottley declared with apocalyptic fervor in the book's final sentence, "a new world is a-coming with the sweep and fury of the Resurrection."[137]

Claude McKay and Roi Ottley offered competing takes on Harlem—and black life at large—at the beginning of the 1940s that simultaneously had much in common. Having already experienced what happened during World War I and after, when racial optimism about military service was crushed by the persistence of white supremacy in Jim Crow America, Claude McKay was arguably justified in being cynical about the prospects for full inclusion. This was clear on the pages of his *Harlem: Negro Metropolis*, though the book went to print just before the United States entered World War II in 1941.

At the time *New World A-Coming* was published, Roi Ottley was riding a hopeful wave of the renewed tide of racial activism as African Americans once again served in the military. His journalistic career was also on a rapid ascent. Indeed, America's first black war correspondent proclaimed his faith in the virtues of democracy in the United States and abroad. Although the reviews for *New World A-Coming* were more generous than those McKay's last book received, reviewers stopped short of endorsing Ottley's optimism. Even though Ottley's analysis was deemed objective, the sociologist Guy Johnson noted that "one may have to disagree with his poetic premise that 'a new world is a-coming.'"[138]

Perhaps the greatest praise for Roi Ottley came in the form of a musical composition by the great Edward "Duke" Ellington. Ellington borrowed Ottley's title, *New World A-Coming*, for a symphony that he premiered at Carnegie Hall on December 11, 1943. Ellington was known to resist being categorized as a jazz musician, at least in part because of the provincial race politics that surrounded efforts to define the form.[139] However, his memory of the inspiration for the symphony even better captured the catholic, if fleeting, ambitions of the period. As Ellington recalled in his biography, almost apocalyptically, "I visualized this new world as a place in the distant future where there would be no war, no greed, no categorization, no nonbelievers, where love was unconditional, and no pronoun was good enough for God."[140]

The respective assessments that McKay and Ottley made regarding the plausibility of equality and inclusion were informed by deep engagements with religion in black life. For both, religion marked racial similarity and/or distinctiveness across "the color line." The real difference, however, was to be found in their arguments about the meaning of the religious details (i.e., which and what kinds of religion). For McKay, "the religion of the Negro people stirs and wells and rises riotously over the confines of the Negro church." This was evidence of a uniquely black religion and culture, and such pronounced racial difference tested the limits of democratic inclusion. For the poet, more personally, at least, a different kind of religious institution—perhaps the Roman Catholic Church—was required. Better yet, McKay's black Harlem might be understood as marked by something similar to a Catholic difference animated by a surplus of religious practices that did not readily fit within the Protestant rule of the United States. Indeed, at the time, Catholicism was still often perceived as too parochial and particular, still on the margins of an American religious mainstream, to make a legitimate claim on catholicity or democracy. Instead, the familiar form of Afro-Protestantism—now with a novel Judeo-Christian cast—continued to represent a better chance at achieving the universal.

In congregations like the Commandment Keepers and Abyssinian Baptist Church, Roi Ottley noted a nascent Judeo-Christian sensibility in the growing race consciousness of the day. These congregations addressed the particular needs of black Americans under the regime of segregation even as they functioned as transitional entities in a longer narrative of secularization that was under way in America. Ottley maintained that black people were animated by the same religious and political aspirations as their "white co-religionists," Christians and Jews alike. In this formulation, again, good black religion was American and anti-fascist, modern and democratic, liberal and Protestant, catholic and Catholic, and, now, Jewish too. When religion—black or white, in the United States or abroad—failed to adhere to these norms, as it did with Father Divine and Marcus Garvey's movements, it was not really religion at all. Or at least it was "good" for no one. According to Ottley, such religious communities were sects or cults at best. They were, at worst, forms of "mass hypnotism." In the battle between democracy and fascism, religion was an arbiter of black America's future. If a preaching activist and politician like Adam Clayton Powell Jr. could not entirely inaugurate a new world, then perhaps artists and intellectuals might.

Despite their different takes on "the problem of the color line," both Claude McKay and Roi Ottley called on black writers to produce works of literary and political value. Racial aesthetics, in short, would help build a better world. In this regard, they echoed a familiar refrain within a much longer history in African American letters that assessed art through its instrumentalist aims. To paraphrase W. E. B. Du Bois, race politics provided the criteria for Negro art. Such a claim concerning the utility of black art and culture had been advanced more recently in Richard Wright's "Blueprint." By now this configuration of race, art, and politics was less a presumed position than a site of rich contestation. Indeed, this had been the case for several decades, at least since the debates over New Negro art and culture of the 1920s.

This evolving dialogue about the shape and value of racial aesthetics continued throughout the 1940s and 1950s. For other writers, like James Baldwin, Gwendolyn Brooks, Ann Petry, and others, religion continued to figure as a key variable in their efforts to outline an aesthetic vision. In ways that were consistent with the larger catholic claims of the era, many of these writers attempted to understand and imagine a role for black artists outside the constraints of racial categorization. Indeed, the ethos of racial catholicity emphasized artistic craft and creative experimentation even more robustly in these decades as black writers attempted to scale the "racial mountain" that Langston Hughes had identified as their shared dilemma in 1926.[141]

CHAPTER 4

∽

As the Spirit Moves

We believe in the oneness of mankind and the importance of the arts in the struggle for peace and unity.

Robert Hayden

When Roi Ottley declared that a "new world" was on the horizon, his optimism was by no means novel. The newfound militancy that he both observed and asserted in the 1940s had been associated with the group of writers who came of age in Harlem after World War I. In fact, Claude McKay—the object of Ottley's criticism—had been considered one of the poets who best embodied the new "race-spirit" that animated the aesthetics of Harlem's Negro Renaissance during the 1920s.[1] Yet even if Ottley's arguments were familiar, reviewers were right to question whether there was empirical evidence to support his claim that change was "a-coming with the sweep and fury of the Resurrection."[2] On the contrary, journalists' observations and the authority of the objectivity they claimed confirmed the degree to which Jim Crow inequality persisted in the wake of World War II.

Ottley seemed to admit as much in his next book. *Black Odyssey: The Story of the Negro in America* (1948) claimed to present a complete history of black life in America from 1619 to 1945. As one reviewer described it, *Black Odyssey* provided "one of the most comprehensive descriptions of the discrimination technique, undertaken to date."[3] "Mr. Ottley notes each successive development in the art of keeping the Negro in his place," a blurb in *The New Yorker* announced. "It's not a pleasant story, but the author tells it well and manages to control his temper in the process, even while recalling some of our fanciest lynchings."[4] Instead of a chronicle of black contributions to American history, Ottley's second book impressed readers as a compelling account of the persistence of racial oppression. *Black Odyssey*, in this regard, was more in keeping with a tradition of activist journalism that laid bare the terror employed to sustain slavery and segregation. If not as bloody as Ida B. Wells's *Red Record* and *Southern Horrors*, Ottley's resurrection hopes were certainly sobered and his aims were more strategic as the end of the 1940s approached. Registering a shift in tone, *Black Odyssey* was markedly less aspirational than *New World A-Coming*.

After the end of World War II, literature and sociology became entangled anew in ways that reflected the impositions of the color line and the immeasurable efforts it inspired in black artists to undo and overcome its constraints. As was noted in the reception of *The Negro Caravan*, during the early 1940s black literature was viewed as significant both in terms of what it contributed to literary debates and for what it revealed sociologically. In its universality, black literature would underwrite the assertion of black humanity on the global stage and help secure the host of rights and protections afforded to U.S. citizens.

Individual authors and artists, however, took many different positions on the tensions between race politics and American literature. Claude McKay and Roi Ottley represented more than just two different individual interpretations of Harlem. They constituted two competing answers to the question of racial difference, each with implications for the prospect of eradicating the color line. For both McKay and Ottley, something about black religion(s)—ordered either by a distinct African sensibility or a shared Judeo-Christian ethos—contained the key to understanding the prospects for black life in modern America. Yet despite their different takes, both men agreed that artists and intellectuals, more than preachers and prophets, should lead the way in forging a future for the race.

In examining a number of key essays written by black artists and intellectuals from the late 1940s through the late 1950s, this chapter chronicles an uptick in literary claims consistent with the racial catholicity identified in chapter 3. This shift, as seen in the evolving effort to theorize racial aesthetics, had implications for the way religion was valued. Writers such as James Baldwin, Gwendolyn Brooks, Ralph Ellison, Robert Hayden, and Ann Petry all offered different perspectives on the role of individual writers and the relationship between race (specifically black culture) and American literature.

Instead of simply narrating universalism's triumph, these artists and intellectuals displayed a concern with digging more deeply into the specific details of black life—including, albeit not especially, its religious traditions—to support an assertion of racial catholicity. They also erred on the side of valuing aesthetic craft and cultivating the specific forms most capable of achieving such universality. Here the particularities of religion figured as key to arguments that racial aesthetics, and thus black people, were by definition American. Here, African American religion, as a number of prominent black writers imagined it, was claimed as the stuff of American culture.

DEBATING THE NEGRO ARTIST'S ROLE
IN POSTWAR AMERICA

In 1946, in his regular column "Here to Yonder" in the *Chicago Defender*, Langston Hughes wryly observed that while "art crosses color lines," artists themselves experienced no such transcendence. Whether it was the music of Duke Ellington and Dorothy Maynor, the novels of Ann Petry, or his own popular poems, the work of black artists was received in places "where Negroes are not served."[5] Hughes recounted a time when he was denied the services of a "colored shoe shine boy," even as a poster for a poetry reading in which he was featured was displayed in the window of the shoeshine parlor. Black people were allowed to serve in the military and perform for the troops, but neither black soldiers nor "Negro USO talent" could expect a decent place to lay their heads. Similarly, Hughes related an anecdote about the jazz great Fletcher Henderson's orchestra, which had been forced to "sleep all night in a bus after playing an air base because the field had accommodations for whites only."[6]

In light of this entanglement of embrace (of black literature and music) and exclusion (of black people), Hughes concluded, "ART MUST BE like religion." Both were able to "cross physical color lines with ease" without appearing to "have much effect on most white people's hearts and souls." He elaborated, "I am really puzzled about this, ours being a Christian country, but with so many people who are not Christ-like toward their darker brothers."[7] Hughes's polemic left little room for confusion. In terms of performance and consumption, both art and religion were capable of crossing racial lines. Yet at the level of social equality and intimacy, they shared an indifference toward, or incapacity to address, Jim Crow. Neither great art nor good religion was able to undo the policies or personal dispositions that sustained segregation. In the face of beautiful literature and music,

Hughes concluded, "Richard Wright, Marian Anderson, Muriel Smith, or Duke Ellington, had just as well be dogs."

Despite Hughes's poignant observations, black artists and intellectuals continued to publicly debate the role of the arts in advancing social change. The visual artist and critic Romare Bearden was one such participant. His criticism illustrated how debates about the content and form of racial aesthetics were understood to have implications across the genres and mediums in which black artists worked (i.e., literature, music, visual art). During the mid-1930s, writing for the National Urban League's *Opportunity*, Bearden had placed the burden of developing a "social philosophy" primarily in the hands of black artists. "The Negro is possessed of remarkable gifts of imagination and intuition," he argued. However, "We need some standard of criticism then, not only to stimulate the artist, but to raise the cultural level of the people." Black artists were not to blame, but, he insisted that it is time for the Negro artist to stop making excuses for his work."[8] In the mid-1940s Bearden revisited similar themes in his essay "The Negro Artist's Dilemma," while emphasizing the social context that made forging a critical tradition so difficult. In November 1946, Bearden addressed a primarily white audience on the pages of *Critique: A Review of Contemporary Art*.

According to Bearden, race politics, within and without, placed an undue burden on black artists. They suffered from several structural constraints, including limited funding sources and, when funded, the imposition of sociological criteria. During the same decade that the NAACP mounted successful legal campaigns against segregation, Bearden litigated his own case against the art world's practice of holding racially segregated exhibits. Black artists, in general, suffered from a "disharmony between practice and ideals," he explained. Yet this dissonance was a product "not only of complex economic and social forces, but also of the distortions that years of oppression have ingrafted [sic] in the minority consciousness." This history inhibited the maturation of black artists. Still, Bearden insisted that a "reorientation of values and ideals" was required of all parties.[9]

Despite the definitive break of the Middle Passage and historical constraints imposed by slavery and Jim Crow, Romare Bearden identified a tradition of black art that in its earliest form was substantively religious: namely, the theological lyricism of spirituals. Yet his assessments in this regard were by no means celebratory. Black people were latecomers in the world of visual arts in part because of the "pseudoscientific" arguments of white Christian ministers regarding black inhumanity. This lag was also attributable to Negro leaders who "looked to Jehovah and the benevolence of their white friends as instruments of advancement."[10]

Early generations of black artists were undermined by faulty intellectual claims, limited by economic resources, and bombarded by "false standards," Bearden argued. Their creative gifts had little chance to flourish. "It was not until the twenties that the Negro entered the various fields of art in any substantial numbers," he continued.[11] Slightly more hopefully, he outlined a new cohort of younger artists who had emerged since the "dog days of the depression and the WPA art project" that included Charles Alston, Elizabeth Catlett, Ernest Crichlow, and, of course, Jacob Lawrence, who by then had already experienced wide acclaim. Despite Lawrence's celebrity, which included a featured 1943 exhibit at the Museum of Modern Art, most black artists remained on the outside of a racially segregated art world. Indeed, Bearden's central critique—that segregated art exhibits subjected black artists to "artificial and arbitrary artistic standards"—was indicative of a wider argument against the impositions of sociology on art at the time.[12]

Romare Bearden summed up the Negro artist's dilemma as threefold. First, black artists were expected to build upon African art traditions. Second, they were required to "attempt a unique, nationalistic expression." Third, and finally, they were supposed to articulate black "political and social aspirations." As George Schuyler had pointed out in his 1926 essay "The Negro-Art Hokum," Bearden noted that black people were thoroughly ensconced in American society and shared little with the cultural worlds of West Africa. As evidence, he invoked a religious example that highlighted the lines between aesthetic and social concerns. With more than a hint of sarcasm, Bearden quipped, "Few Negroes believe that a statue can banish demons, else Negro artists would be over worked carving fetishes to keep landlords away from their people's doors."[13]

The work of Negro artists ought to reflect the artistic sensibilities of the period in which they lived, Bearden countered, instead of the ritualized context in which African sculpture was produced. While myriad social forces lumped all black artists together, no artistic criteria justified such practices. These impositions only clouded the artists' judgment and censored their vision—both requirements for any artist of merit. Like the editors of *The Negro Caravan*, Bearden insisted that "the Negro is part of the amalgam of American life, and his aims and aspirations are in common with the rest of the American people." After all, weren't the bonds of national tradition stronger than the construct of race? "The true artist feels that there is only one art—and it belongs to all mankind," he maintained. While he embraced the racial particulars, Bearden felt that to assert Americanness was to assume their universality. He concluded, "The Negro artist must come to think of himself not primarily as a Negro artist, but as an artist. Only in this way will he acquire the stature which is the component of every good artist."[14]

The poet Robert Hayden presented a similar view in the introduction to the Counterpoise Series, which he co-edited with Myron O'Higgins in 1948. Hayden was ardently opposed to their work being received, "as the custom is, entirely in the light of sociology and politics."[15] Describing Hayden and O'Higgins's new work as a "manifesto," one critic anticipated that it would become "regarded as the entering wedge in the 'emancipation' of Negro poetry in America."[16] While the series failed to achieve this lofty goal, it certainly marked a transition in Hayden's aesthetic vision and career trajectory. Hayden had developed significantly as a poet while working as a writer for Detroit's WPA Federal Writers Project during the 1930s. He then honed his craft further at the University of Michigan in the early 1940s, where he pursued his master's degree under the tutelage of W. H. Auden.

Also in the 1940s, along with his wife, Erma, Robert Hayden embraced the teaching of the Persian prophet Baha'u'llah and joined the American Baha'i community. Much later he would confess to struggling with his faith, but during the mid-1940s the Baha'i emphasis on religious and racial unity paired well with Auden's push for Hayden to move beyond the particulars of racial themes.[17] Indeed, although it was not precisely Protestant, Hayden's poetry wed literary and religious modernisms to great effect.[18] Before the end of his distinguished career, Robert Hayden would be appointed as both the first poet laureate of Senegal (1966) and the first *black* poet laureate of the United States (1976–1978), among other honors. However, when the first Counterpoise leaflet was released, he had just finished his studies at the University of Michigan and was still settling into a faculty position at Fisk University. Hayden had moved to Nashville in 1946 somewhat reluctantly. Up to that point, the Jim Crow South had been more familiar to him as a history lesson and literary theme than it was as a lived reality.

Despite receiving a Rosenwald Fellowship and another fellowship from the Ford Foundation in 1954, it was not until the 1960s that Hayden gained a wider hearing. In fact, his first publication with a commercial press, *Selected Poems*, was not until 1966, by which point a new generation of artists was deeming him passé because he refused to identify as a "black poet."[19] During the 1940s, however, Hayden's simultaneous emphasis upon the particulars of everyday black life and appeal to the universal made perfect sense. Although a review in the *New York Times* suggested that he represented something new for "Negro poetry," Hayden's vision was entirely in step with the times. Thus, the Counterpoise Series was emblematic of a larger (and long-standing) trajectory within racial aesthetics even as it marked a major shift in Hayden's own journey as a poet.[20]

Although Robert Hayden and Myron O'Higgins were part of a broader development among black writers during the 1940s, the two men intended their collaboration to signal, if not create, a novel independence. While their manifesto made no direct mention of race matters, it is clear that they were speaking to several audiences at once, addressing orthodoxies on both sides of the color line. In ways that anticipated Hayden's confrontation with Black Arts poets during the 1960s, the Counterpoise Series rejected any particular status or category for writers who were also "so-called" minorities. In language similar to that employed by the journalist and race man Roi Ottley, Hayden was "opposed to *the chauvinistic*, the cultish, to special pleading."[21] While the richness of the African American experience offered unique resources, Hayden and O'Higgins would not allow race politics "to limit and restrict creative expression." Nor would they provide the sort of racial propaganda often called for by race leaders. Irrespective of artistic medium (i.e., "writing, music and the graphic arts"), openness to "the experimental and the unconventional" was paramount.[22]

Echoing Romare Bearden's assessment, Robert Hayden contended that uncritical celebrations of underdeveloped work by black artists—by a liberal, largely white art world—were equally undesirable. Neither "a conscience to salve" nor a political "axe to grind" were due cause for anybody to be "overpraised." Hayden was not suggesting that mainstream presses were indiscriminately underwriting black mediocrity. After all, he would not receive a contract from a commercial publishing house for another two decades. To the point, those who presided over publication opportunities—"editors, reviewers, anthologists"—were not to be granted the power of life and death over an artist's vision. Black leaders and the literary establishment were both served notice. The poet would not be bought, either by affirmation or exclusion.[23]

Robert Hayden's poetry plumbed the particulars of his own experience. He witnessed an evolution of literary acts in which first the New Negro and then Black Arts prevailed, although he did not identify himself with either movement. Instead of an elision of race politics, Hayden's refusal of the modifiers "negro" or "black" was born, at least in part, out of religious commitment. As he later explained, "I believe in the essential oneness of all people and I believe in the basic unity of all religions. I don't believe that races are important. ... These are all Bahá'í points of view, and my work grows out of this vision."[24] Indeed, the Baha'i faith encouraged in its adherents an "abandonment of archaic systems and attitudes, the attendant loss of identity, and the acquisition of insecurity and trepidation."[25] For believers, relinquishing racial identification was part of a process of achieving spiritual maturity. In this view, the Counterpoise Series announcement can be read as both an artist's credo and a confession of faith.

Structured something like a hybrid of poetry and prose, yet not quite either genre, the introduction to the Counterpoise Series appeared devoid of any definitive beginnings or endings. Its lack of any periods or capitalized letters revealed a modernist emphasis on experimentation in form. The piece perhaps most resembled a religious litany. It read as a call to action to be recited by a congregation of believers. The word "believe" appeared three times: once early on to affirm "experimentation" and then again in each of the manifesto's last two lines. Here Hayden's religious ambitions were subtly unveiled. His insistence that "poetry has humanistic and spiritual values not to be ignored without impunity" may have also grown out of his studies with W. H. Auden, who by the time Hayden arrived at the University of Michigan had begun to think of poetry as a "religious vocation."[26] Yet Hayden asserted his own spiritual identity as he invoked the most fundamental Baha'i principle. Announcing a vision that was simultaneously religious and literary, Hayden professed, "We believe in the oneness of mankind and the importance of the arts in the struggle for peace and unity."[27]

The quintessentially modern religion's first principle, "The Oneness of Mankind," had been articulated in the United States in a series of public talks given by Abdul Baha in 1912 and was later codified in *The Promulgation of Universal Peace*. Before World War I, Abdul Baha had spoken to many African American audiences, including the NAACP, Howard University, and the Bethel Literary Society at the historic Metropolitan African Methodist Episcopal (AME) Church. Similar talks were also given in homes and at civic organizations, synagogues, theosophical societies, and liberal churches of diverse denominational ties. The Baha'i message of racial equality and religious unity found an audience with many black Americans, whether Baptist, AME or otherwise affiliated.[28]

Three decades later, and on the heels of World War II, such ideas sounded anew on both religious and political registers. Statements endorsing the "oneness of mankind" had taken on new institutional life with the formation of the United Nations in 1945. Hayden's manifesto appeared the same year that the General Assembly of the UN adopted the Universal Declaration of Human Rights (1948). Indeed, one secularizing trajectory Christian theology followed throughout the twentieth century was the discourse of human rights. By no means isolated from the history of human rights, racial aesthetics paved a parallel afterlife for Protestantism—a path no less traveled, if not as familiar, and just as religious.[29]

Robert Hayden's long-held position on the outskirts of the African American canon was a by-product, at least in part, of the fact that his aesthetic was so deeply Baha'i. Although his poetry drew heavily on the Bible, his version of Afro-modernism was post-Protestant—it was neither a disavowal nor a declaration of Christian faith. It was ultra-modern, to the point of misrecognition. Because of this, he was relegated to the margins of black cultural life even as he was welcomed into the annals of American poetry. The following year, another black writer mounted a theological critique of literature that was much more legible to the (liberal) American and (black) Protestant mainstream. And it would make the young James Baldwin almost an immediate literary celebrity.

JAMES BALDWIN'S LITERARY VISION: BEYOND PROTEST THEOLOGY AND RACE POLITICS

No artist has better captured and conjured the aesthetic genius of Afro-Protestantism than James Baldwin. The cultural and spiritual imaginary of "the black church"—the power of its music, the poetry of its sermons, and the pathos of what Du Bois once called "the frenzy"—all flowed from Baldwin's pen. He was raised in Harlem and for a short time was a teenaged preacher in a Pentecostal church there. His literary vision remained indebted to the drama of black religion long after he had fled to Greenwich Village and let go of its theological claims.[30] Baldwin was both nurtured and traumatized by the sanctified, storefront, and southern congregations that appeared in his writing. These were the same churches that Langston Hughes and Zora Neale Hurston had described as the spiritual home of the black masses and the source of a racial aesthetic.[31] Much of Robert Hayden's marginality may be attributed to his embrace of an unfamiliar form of utopian, post-Christian, religious modernism in the Baha'i faith, which also rendered him racially other. In turn, Baldwin's rapid ascent was at least partially a product of his refusal to forsake (or inability to shake) the primitive spirits of his religious roots in the evangelical cultural worlds of Afro-Protestantism.

Go Tell It on the Mountain (1953), James Baldwin's first book, began with a portrait of these religious worlds as they were being reconstituted in the urban North.[32] In this autobiographical coming-of-age story, Baldwin mapped a deeply personal intergenerational struggle onto one of the nation's largest demographic shifts, the Great Migration, which was still under way. The tradition of black sacred music provided the book's soundtrack and inspired its title. Baldwin's debut novel announced his promise to the American literary scene, yet by that time he had already made a name for himself in nonfiction. His second book, *Notes of a Native Son*, garnered significant critical and popular attention when it went to press in 1955. As a collection of essays, much of the writing had been published over the course of the preceding six years. Along with *Go Tell It on the Mountain* and an unpublished play that had a decent run in Europe (*Amen Corner*, 1954), *Notes* established Baldwin as a versatile writer of significance. Moreover, his analyses of race therein made him, albeit reluctantly, "the representative black voice of his generation."[33]

The first two essays in the volume, "Everybody's Protest Novel" and "Many Thousands Gone," had originally appeared on the pages of *Partisan Review* in 1949 and 1951—one and three years, respectively, after the first leaflet in the Counterpoise Series. Where Robert Hayden's manifesto prioritized the experimental, Baldwin's essay took issue with a familiar literary form that was especially in fashion. He did so by making a target of his mentor, Richard Wright, the most prominent black writer at that time. While the essays revealed a personal "anxiety of influence," Baldwin was also pursuing larger artistic goals.[34] In "Everybody's Protest Novel," he took issue with protest literature, outlining a tradition of texts from *Uncle Tom's Cabin* (1853) that extended to the present, with Wright's *Native Son*.

James Baldwin conceded the "good intentions" of the genre as a whole. After all, he noted, "the avowed aim of the American protest novel is to bring greater freedom to the oppressed."[35] Yet while authors in this tradition professed a "devotion to Humanity," they were, in fact, animated by a "terror of the human being." Such texts relied upon rigid racial ideologies rather than the rich texture of human experience. Although such texts attempted to explain the present situation, Baldwin argued that they actually "boomeranged us into chaos." Protest literature reinscribed the very dynamics it set out to oppose and undo. Baldwin observed a peculiar and ancient form of fear masquerading as Christian faith that preceded Uncle Tom by centuries. Protest literature, then, was part of a long-standing impulse that once burned witches at the stake and now motivated lynch mobs. "The spirit that breathes" in this genre, he wrote, was "activated by what might be called a theological terror."[36] The racial binary (i.e., white over black) upon which the literary formula depended was persuasive to the degree that it was organized by a familiar yet inadequate religious world view that Baldwin knew all too well.[37]

James Baldwin's vocation as a writer was inseparable from his own particular Afro-Protestant past. He simultaneously engaged and critiqued all of the forces that had forged that peculiar religious tradition. Given the definitive role churches had played in colonizing the Americas and creating a New World, Christianity was not so much a matter of belief, in his account, as it was the birthright of U.S. citizenship. With regard to protest literature, *Uncle Tom's Cabin* was a formative literary moment in a dishonest American dialogue that continued after the legal end of racial slavery. It was no less bankrupt when black people were telling the story. Black protest writers, in particular, were complicit in a religious imaginary that continued to render them less than human.

Baldwin argued that black engagement with Christianity was a quintessential example of the paradox that was the American experiment. *Uncle Tom's Cabin* codified a social and theological hierarchy in which skin color directly correlated with salvation and damnation. "Here, black equates with evil and white with grace," Baldwin explained.[38] He further alleged that protest writers, black and white alike, carried forward theological categories that cast characters as problems rather than as real people. The binaries of black and white, demon and angel, or saved and damned did not accurately map human experience or American history. By clinging to such dualities, he asserted, "we are diminished and we perish." In *Native Son*, Bigger's damnation resulted not from the power of white supremacy but rather because he—and protest literature, more generally—"accepted a theology that denies him life."[39] "It must be remembered that the oppressed and oppressor are bound together ... share the same beliefs ... depend on the same reality," he argued. "Only within this web of ambiguity, paradox, this hunger, danger, darkness," Baldwin insisted, "can we find at once ourselves and the power that will free us from ourselves."[40] Only by coming to terms with the terror of history and the paradox of the human condition, he claimed, could writers help create the circumstances necessary for transformation.

Once again, in "Everybody's Protest Novel," the tenuous relationship between sociology and art emerged forcefully. "Literature and sociology are not one and the same," Baldwin announced.[41] More precisely, this socio-literary tradition was constrained by a specific theology. Protest literature made do with Christian myths and avoided the messiness of the human condition. Providing new myths, as Richard Wright had proposed in his "Blueprint for Negro Writing" (1937), was not the business of black writers. The fundamental duty of all artists was to reveal "the disquieting complexity of ourselves." This was all the more the case in a society content to forget its past, one more comfortable with noble causes than with such complexity. In Baldwin's estimation, protest writers embraced social "responsibility" when "revelation" was their real task.[42]

Although the idea of a racial aesthetic appeared nowhere in the essay, Baldwin's argument assumed a direct link between protest literature's origins and aims and the nation's religious and racial formation. In the introduction to *Notes of a Native Son*, which was tellingly titled "Autobiographical Notes," Baldwin reckoned with race by considering the implications of "the negro problem" for black writers. Like Robert Hayden, he explained that they deserved no "special pleading." "One writes out of one thing only—one's own experience," he noted. "Being a Negro" was, then, his only subject matter. Making art out of the chaos of one's own experience was "the only real concern of the artist."[43] To accomplish this as a black writer, to render truthfully and beautifully an American story, one had to grapple with the fires of religion (Christianity) and race (blackness).

Literary caricatures like "Aunt Jemima and Uncle Tom" only confirmed "the dehumanization of the Negro" and affirmed on theological terms that "black is the color of damnation."[44] *Native Son*—"the most powerful and celebrated statement we have yet had on what it means to be a Negro in America"—was emblematic of the protest tradition. Yet it did nothing to challenge social myths. On the contrary, Bigger found his "significance as the incarnation of a myth" rather than as a human being. Again, Baldwin's engagement with Wright's first novel in these two essays entailed more than an instance of aesthetic patricide. Both the significance of "the color line" and the substance of "Negro life" were at stake.[45] Protest literature, he argued, denied the latter possibility because it gave too much authority to the former problem.

James Baldwin observed that *Native Son* had depicted black life as set apart from the American reality by Jim Crow—"the isolation of the Negro within his own group"—even as it failed to "convey any sense of Negro life as a continuing and complex group reality." Protest literature reduced black people to "the Negro problem," the perpetual other, seen only as through a glass darkly. Insistence upon a rigid otherness rendered black life opaque, leading (white) Americans to "believe that in Negro life there exists no tradition, no field of manners, no possibility of ritual or intercourse." This was not the case, Baldwin argued. Wright missed a crucial dimension of the Negro's story. *Native Son* did not capture "the relationship that Negroes bear to one another, that depth of involvement and unspoken recognition of shared experience which creates a way of life." It was not the case that "the Negro has no tradition," he insisted. However, "there has as yet arrived no sensibility sufficiently profound and tough to make this tradition articulate."[46]

This literary inarticulateness, in Baldwin's estimation, was a by-product of confusing the idea of a distinct cultural tradition with the legal reality of racial segregation. "For a tradition expresses, after all," he explained, "nothing more than the long and painful experience of a people; it comes out of . . . their struggle to survive." What the law called for had not, in fact, ever held as social fact. Despite what the policies of segregation sought to enforce, the lives of black and white Americans were intimately, if tragically, intertwined. Indeed, "The story of the Negro in America is the story of America—or, more precisely, it is the story of Americans."[47] The bond between black people and the nation was "literally and morally, a *blood* relationship."[48]

By insisting that literature and sociology were altogether different matters, James Baldwin's criticism wove together a prevailing set of parallel discourses that were prominent at the time. On one hand, he appealed to the idea of religion as an art form. On the other, he captured religion's power as a sociological phenomenon and a marker of social difference. Baldwin further demonstrated that these were related observations. Although primarily a critique of a specific literary form, "Everybody's Protest Novel" and "Many Thousands Gone" demonstrated that American racial discourse was, in fact, a religious practice. Protest literature, if it did nothing else, performed a theology of race. In doing so, it helped maintain the racial order. Recalling the social rituals that often surrounded lynchings, Baldwin argued that America's faith was "made perfect" when Wright's Bigger was executed with the "mystical ferocity of joy."[49] The same Christian theology that sanctioned participation in racial violence (i.e., lynching) had underwritten the cultural phenomenon of protest literature.

Many of the arguments put forward in *Notes of a Native Son* anticipated the sweeping critique that James Baldwin would levy against Christianity in his later nonfiction writings on colonialism. Simultaneously autobiography and American history, his 1953 novel, *Go Tell It on the Mountain*, which garnered a National Book Award nomination, suggested that Baldwin himself had begun the work of articulating the American story of the "negro's struggle to survive" in literary form. That same year, the National Book Award was presented to another black writer, the first to win the prize. Two years later, in the introduction to *Notes*, Baldwin identified that awardee, Ralph Ellison, as "the first Negro novelist . . . to utilize in language, and brilliantly, some of the ambiguity and irony of Negro life." As Baldwin had attempted to do with his own debut, Ellison refused to render black life as "a thing apart." *Invisible Man* (1953) was evidence of a "more genuinely penetrating search." It aimed to do more than explain the "negro problem." Instead, it examined "the general social fabric"—the paradoxes, contradictions, and brute power—of the American experience.[50]

James Baldwin's critique of Richard Wright helped him stake out a space distinct from his mentor in the postwar literary scene. His choice to foreground the fundamental Americanness of "the American Negro's story" was in keeping with what a number of other black writers were doing at the time—most notably Ralph Ellison. Moreover, it was consistent with a burgeoning civil rights movement that was making significant, and increasingly successful, claims on American citizenship in the early 1950s. Yet Wright, Baldwin's target, was still the most prominent black writer of the day; his literary aesthetic was anything but unpopular. The task would fall to others to parse the more subtle distinctions between Baldwin's wholesale damning of protest literature and the genres in which Wright primarily wrote, namely naturalism and social realism.

THE AESTHETICS OF ANN PETRY: COMMUNISM, CHRISTIANITY, AND AMERICAN LITERATURE

In 1950—sandwiched between the publication of "Everybody's Protest Novel" and "Many Thousands Gone"—Ann Petry asserted an abiding significance for the "novel of social criticism." Petry, born Anna Lane, belonged to one of the few black families who called Old Saybrook, Connecticut, home. A promising student throughout her youth, Lane dropped out of college after one year at Hampton Institute in Virginia. She returned home in the early 1930s, earned a degree in pharmacology, and joined the staff of the family pharmacy. She also began making regular trips to New York City to take part in its arts scene. There she met George David Petry, and the two aspiring writers secretly married in 1936.

Two years later they moved to New York, making Harlem their home. Although they would live there for less than a decade, these were busy years.[51] Petry took a position as a reporter for Adam Clayton Powell's publication *People's Voice*, which was a gathering space for prominent black radicals.[52] She worked there for several years, becoming deeply enmeshed in the activism that surrounded the paper and Powell's People's Committee. In 1941 Petry became the paper's "women's editor." Eventually she authored a regular column, "The Lighter Side," which focused on the cultural and political lives of Harlem's black elite.

During the 1940s Petry was equally busy in the worlds of art and politics. She studied at Columbia under Mabel Louise Robinson and took classes at the WPA-supported Harlem Community Art Center, which claimed the visual artists Romare Bearden and Aaron Douglas, among others. Petry also began to write short stories and found support for her writing from several popular black publications, including older mainstays like *The Crisis* and *Opportunity*. Her work also appeared in newer outlets like *Negro Digest* (later *Black World*), the fledgling publication of what would grow into the Chicago-based media empire Johnson Publishing.[53]

With the help of a fellowship from Houghton-Mifflin, Petry became a full-time writer in 1943, and her first book was published in 1946. She left Harlem the next year and went on to write two other novels, each based in New England. Only *The Street*, which was written and set in Harlem, became a commercial success. It eventually sold over one million copies, a first for a black woman, and achieved for Petry a certain measure of literary fame. The novel was written in a style similar to the social realism of Richard Wright's *Native Son*, which had also been wildly popular.[54] In this regard, as Farah Jasmine Griffin has noted, Petry was part of a cohort of black social realist artists that, along with Wright, included the painters John Biggers and Elizabeth Catlett and poets like Sterling Brown and Langston Hughes. Although her later novels did not sell nearly as well as *The Street*, Petry remained attentive to race and gender and continued to put forward a leftist political critique. She, Wright, and others "saw fiction as the form that could best serve to educate and reform society."[55]

Ann Petry's commitments in this regard were made clear in her essay "The Novel as Social Criticism," which was published in the 1950 anthology, *The Writer's Book*. Edited by Helen R. Hull, a Columbia professor of creative writing, the book's table of contents reads like a who's who in postwar letters. Contributors included the British-born poet W. H. Auden; Pearl Buck, the first American woman to win both the Nobel and the Pulitzer; Thomas Mann, the German Nobel Laureate; Leonora Speyer, the Pulitzer-winning poet and violinist; and literary critic and Columbia faculty member Lionel Trilling. As the tag line on its cover stated, *The Writer's Book* was intended to provide "practical advice by the top experts in every field of writing."[56] Each author was tasked with commenting on the challenges associated with a specific genre of literature.

Unsurprisingly, Petry's article was the only contribution by a black writer. Her tone was more personal than practical. Petry's essay was largely a defense of the "novel of social criticism," including her own writing. More precisely, it can be read as a response to criticism that her first book, *The Street*, had received in several leftist publications in the preceding years. Petry also offered an apologia for social realism at the moment when the form was being overshadowed by the rise of the black modernist novel.[57] However, her arguments hinged less on a claim for any racial aesthetic or leftist literary agenda than it did upon an appeal to the significance of religious sources for all American writers and the Western tradition more generally.

Ann Petry, to be clear, was neither an advocate for black churches nor a Christian apologist in any form. Perhaps this was so, at least in part, because her husband, George, rarely attended church after experiencing the racism of a Roman Catholic priest.[58] Petry herself voiced ambivalence toward Christianity. Following the overwhelming popularity of *The Street*, Earl Conrad from *The Chicago Defender*'s New York Bureau interviewed her for the paper's "American Viewpoint" column. Petry posited labor unions as the strongest advocates for "the Negro's interest." Her sense of the support churches provided paled in comparison. "I don't think that church groups even touch the surface of the question," she shared. "If Christianity were a living thing, it would be all right, but it does not live," Petry continued. "The bulk of the population gives only lip service to the thoughts of Christianity."[59] Conrad's presentation of Petry's assessment of American Christians in the *Defender* did, however, suggest that she held onto a sense of Christian ideals.

In "The Novel as Social Criticism," the author and activist had more to say concerning the "thoughts of Christianity" and how they implicated the American literary canon. Calling attention to inconsistencies between the principles and practices of those who espoused Christianity was an age-old tradition in American letters. Indeed, some of the earliest and most strident calls to end slavery in the Atlantic World were carried out on Christian terms.[60] Here, Ann Petry did more than craft a Christian critique of racism; she theorized that Western literature was indebted to Christianity's sacred texts. In her estimation, novels with a social message dated as "far back as the history of man." Over time they had been "cut from the same bolt of cloth" as folk and fairy tales, biblical parables and morality plays, and the most ancient of tragedies.[61]

According to Petry, despite the intellectual chasm occasioned by the Enlightenment, "the basic theme . . . is essentially the same: And the Lord said unto Cain, 'Where is Abel thy brother?' And he said, 'I know not: Am I my brother's keeper?'" It was this passage that provided the core idea that enlivened the work of the "socially conscious novelist," Petry maintained. Modern literary conventions drew a false dichotomy between art and politics while delineating an abundance of distinctive styles (e.g., naturalism vs. realism). In her estimation, this elaborate "professional pattern" was, in truth, "confused patter." In words that closely resembled W. E. B. Du Bois's speech at the NAACP's 1926 convention in Chicago, Petry shared, "It seems to me that all truly great art is propaganda. . . . The novel, like all other forms of great art, will always reflect the political, economic, and social structure of the period in which it was created."[62]

By the beginning of the 1950s, the United States had entered the Cold War and Senator Joseph McCarthy's anti-Communist campaign was under way. Under this heightened scrutiny, leftist literary circles had diminished considerably by the time Ann Petry's essay appeared. In her estimation, a preoccupation with the "perfidious influence of Karl Marx" meant that a wide range of political novels had been "lumped together" and had fallen out of fashion. Indeed, she noted, "the ghost of Marx" haunted the aspirations and expectations of the current literary scene. More than Marxist dogma, Petry argued that a "fictional emphasis on social problems" could more accurately be credited to "the Old Testament idea that man is his brother's keeper." This biblical idea had been corrupted under many names. Socialism and Communism were two modern efforts to apply this idea, she contended. This was to be expected because Christianity, after all, "was part of the cultural heritage of the West." Regardless of whether individuals identified as Marxist or Christian (or neither), Petry argued that "a larger portion" of the American cultural inheritance "stems from the Bible."[63]

By attempting to shift attention from Karl Marx to the story of Cain and Abel, Ann Petry called attention to how Marxist ideology and Christian theology provided competing sources for (and interpretations of) American literature. In the United States, however, Christianity rarely operated on mutually exclusive terms with Marxist ideologies. The same could be said for Afro-Protestantism. Christian practice, black and white, was often an organic or strategic amalgam of the presumed poles of politics and spirituality, sacred and secular, radicalism and religion. Ironically, Petry's assessment—that American critics overestimated the influence of Marx at the expense of obscuring the greater significance of Christian scripture—anticipated a critique that the esteemed black political theorist Harold Cruse would later levy against Richard Wright in the 1960s.[64] For the time being, though, en route to endorsing Wright's stylistic acumen, Ann Petry astutely noted a historical connection between the literary trends of her day and the reasonable fear that McCarthyism fomented among American writers.

The aesthetic and political merits of the modernist fiction of black writers like Baldwin and Ellison, who grew increasingly popular in the early 1950s, require no defense. Yet Petry's account of current literary leanings revealed that it was possible to boldly embrace formal innovations and at the same time anxiously eschew one kind of politics in favor of another.[65] More pointedly, her critique suggested that the triumph of liberal (over leftist) politics, rather than any "objective" aesthetic criteria, provided the social context for these literary shifts. Social realism had fallen out of fashion, and Richard Wright had departed for France just four years earlier. Within a climate of Communist witch-hunts, perhaps Petry thought that shifting attention from Marx to the socially acceptable influence of Christian scripture might allow for a more generous assessment of "the sociological novel."[66]

"The craftsmanship" apparent in such books was "of a high order," Ann Petry asserted. As with all novels, success depended upon an author's ability to delicately balance thematic concerns with other qualities, like character development and dialogue.[67] For evil to have literary power it had to be made apparent as both the "social system," and as a "thing of the spirit." Novels had to reveal the human struggle within and without. Celebrating and comparing *Native Son* with Shakespeare's *Othello*, Petry argued that in both, "dialogue advances the action, characterizes the speaker and yet at no point smacks of the pulpit or of the soapbox." Novels that addressed the topic of race relations no more required a specific literary category than, as the experimentalists insisted, black people required a "special pleading." "The Negro problem" was "the very stuff of fiction, sometimes comic, more often tragic, always ironic, endlessly dramatic."[68]

All literature had a politics, Ann Petry explained, from social realism to sentimental fiction. All books also ran the risk of failure on artistic terms. No less than other genres, social criticism novels solicited emotional responses from readers. Yet, she concluded, they also encouraged social reforms. At their best, they "influenced the passage of the civil rights bills."[69] Petry was, in part, responding to criticisms that *The Street* failed to provide solutions to the problems it portrayed. Although this may have been true, she insisted that realistic portraits of social evils, in themselves, did "do a lot of good." Novels disturbed readers and, in doing so, called them to account. In this way, literature was often the "original impetus" for social reform.

Having cited *Uncle Tom's Cabin*, Ann Petry was no doubt well familiar with a popular legend associated with the end of slavery. In 1862, as the story goes, President Lincoln had addressed Harriet Beecher Stowe as "the little woman who wrote the book that started this great war." Whether Petry intended to imply that there was a direct causal relationship between literature and legislation was no more or less important than the veracity of such Civil War literary lore. What was more significant was that Petry affirmed the novel's value as a mode of social criticism. To do so was to privilege a literary "blueprint"—most prominently associated with Richard Wright—of art and politics as necessarily enmeshed just as such a mode was becoming unpopular. Black writers were increasingly moving to reimagine, if not wholly undo, such entanglements.[70]

GWENDOLYN BROOKS AND THE REAL BRONZEVILLE

Despite the fact that both Ann Petry and her contemporary, Gwendolyn Brooks, had few direct ties to Richard Wright, neither woman could entirely avoid the shadow cast by his commercial success. The same, to be sure, was true for most black writers in the postwar era. For Petry, who resented such connections, this resulted mostly from their shared medium of social realism.[71] Brooks's poetry was often grouped within this genre as well, but the differences between her and Petry became apparent when both wrote for the relatively new but popular travel monthly *Holiday* magazine.

In April 1949, Ann Petry's photographic essay "Harlem" was published in *Holiday*, providing a prose account of the precariousness of Harlem's streets. Two years later the magazine devoted an issue to the midwestern metropolis of Chicago, enlisting Gwendolyn Brooks to write a section on the city's "Negro thousands."[72] When Brooks penned "They Call It Bronzeville" for *Holiday*'s October 1951 edition, Petry's essay may have been a model. Both of their contributions to *Holiday* reflected the influence of social realism, although Brooks emphasized a bit more of the beauty of quotidian black life on Chicago's South Side than Petry did with the upper Manhattan black enclave.[73]

Although Ann Petry's piece fit within a burgeoning "Harlem as Ghetto" literature, Gwendolyn Brooks struck a slightly more sanguine note. Both authors ultimately indicted the racial segregation that produced the social geography and subjects of their stories. Petry was already a regular editorialist for several black periodicals before her first novel went to press. In contrast, "They Call It Bronzeville" was one of Gwendolyn Brooks's early forays into nonfiction. Langston Hughes noted this novelty in *The Chicago Defender*, describing her essay with superlatives. It is "one of the finest pieces of reportage I have seen in a long time," Hughes gushed. "The girl's prose is going to be as good as her poetry, and her poetry is excellent."[74]

Coming from Langston Hughes, who may well have been the most celebrated black poet since the days of Harlem's Renaissance and was a popular essayist, this was high praise.[75] Gwendolyn Brooks's star was in the process of a rapid rise. Beginning in the mid-1930s, she regularly contributed poems to *The Chicago Defender*.[76] In the years leading up to the publication of her first book of poems, *A Street in Bronzeville* (1945), she participated in a WPA-supported workshop at the South Side Community Arts Center, and she won prizes from the Midwest Writers Conference in three consecutive years (1943–1945). In 1945 three of her poems appeared in *Poetry Magazine*.[77] By the end of the 1940s, Gwendolyn Brooks had acquired several of the nation's most prestigious prizes, including fellowships from the Guggenheim Foundation (1946) and the American Academy of Arts and Letters (1946). Then, in 1950, she received the Pulitzer Prize for her 1949 collection of poems, *Annie Allen*, which made her the first black person to win this award. With ample supporting evidence at his disposal, Hughes declared her to be "one of the most important literature talents in America."[78]

Although she never pursued the promise that Langston Hughes saw in her reportage, Gwendolyn Brooks did write prose to complement her poetry. The same year that she won the Pulitzer, she offered her take on the task required of black poets. In *Phylon*, an Atlanta University–based quarterly publication devoted to questions of race and culture, Brooks published "Poets Who Are Negroes." Her contribution was significantly shorter than the others in a special themed issue on "The Negro in Literature." Perhaps a reflection of the poet's precision, it was less than three hundred words, not quite enough to fill an entire page. Despite a literary career that now spanned two decades, the statement was one of her first efforts at criticism, albeit not a fully formed articulation of her aesthetic vision.

At the outset, as if to short-circuit the idea of a "special pleading" for black writers, Brooks wryly asserted that "the Negro poet has some impressive advantages." In fact, others often envied black bards their experience. After all, they had easy access to the sort of "major indignities" that made "the pen run wild." The raw material of racial oppression provided the black artist with "ready made subjects." For Brooks, for instance, there was a realpolitik to discern in everyday performances of black physicality.[79] "His mere body, for that matter, is an eloquence," she explained. "His quiet walk down the street is a speech to the people." Sure, Brooks conceded, "Every Negro poet has 'something to say.'" Yet "no real artist" should be satisfied with merely having access to good source material. Brooks declared that "the Negro poet's most urgent duty, at present, is to polish his technique."[80]

Much less of a manifesto for aesthetic freedom—the sort offered by Langston Hughes in "The Negro Artist and the Racial Mountain" (1926) or in Robert Hayden's Counterpoise Series (1943)—than a matter-of-fact observation, this brief statement suggested that black poets had the same burdens as all other writers. The cultivation of craft should be their highest priority.[81] Gwendolyn Brooks received praise on the pages of the same issue of *Phylon* from Margaret Walker, a fellow Chicago-based poet who viewed Brooks's Pulitzer Prize as a sign that "the Negro has finally achieved full status in the literary world as an American poet." If not entirely accurate, Walker's ebullience was not uncommon amid a climate of postwar optimism within black communities.

Although the Double V campaign could not yet declare complete victory, the international dimensions of the battle against segregation in the United States were increasingly evident. In this vein, Walker predicted that the "future of Negro writing" rested in the hands of young poets who comprehended the "spiritual problems" that world wars had posed for Western culture. Citing several renowned white writers such as T. S. Eliot, W. H. Auden, and Robert Lowell, she noted their renewed interest in a "religious revival." Overlooking (or perhaps unaware of) Robert Hayden's Baha'i commitments or Claude McKay's Catholicism—Walker mentioned both writers elsewhere in the article and both had embraced a new faith during the preceding decade—Walker observed no similar spiritual renewal among her black peers. While a comparable spiritual awakening might still bloom for Negro poets, it was more important that the rising generation be both "technically aware and intellectually worthy."[82]

As for discernible trends within racial aesthetics, Margaret Walker argued that Gwendolyn Brooks's poems evinced a movement away from social protest. Black poets were now "less preoccupied with race" and addressed it more as a "point of departure toward a global point of view." Indeed, "the tendency is toward internationalism rather than toward nationalism and racism," Walker concluded.[83] Although she pointed to Brooks's Pulitzer as a sign that black poets had attained their Americanness, the broader shift she observed—from a provincial concern with race and nation to an expansive global view—was perhaps better evidence. It was also another example of the racial catholicity that was identified in chapter 3.

The onset of the Cold War brought together domestic and international concerns in ways that shaped both the political culture and cultural politics in the United States. Black writers were significantly influenced by these developments.[84] *Holiday*, which was founded in 1946, was very much a product of this period. The magazine was informed by both liberal optimism and the opposition to the Soviet Union that fed American exceptionalism after the end of World War II. One reader later recalled the cultural sensibility of the magazine by saying, "It was the beginning of the glamour of flying. It was just long enough after the end of the war, and everybody had money again, and you had guys who had been to Europe and were now anxious to go back under different circumstances."[85] In addition to the experience of war, new technology made possible mobility in the form of transatlantic flights and expanded what even ordinary Americans imagined could be possible. *Holiday* brought these international aspirations to American living rooms, presenting readers with "an ideal of travel as enrichment, a literal path to intellectual and spiritual betterment."[86]

Black Americans, including "Negro poets," were no exception to these developments. Of course, the scars of military service, magnified by the social wounds of Jim Crow's welcome home, were more pressing for most black people than the prospect of international air travel. Yet *Ebony* magazine, which Johnson Publishing began distributing in 1945, sold similar dreams of travel and leisure to its readership, often through images of black celebrity and achievements that were unattainable for most readers.[87] Ironically, given *Ebony*'s headquarters in Brooks's hometown of Chicago, her writing appeared in *Holiday* before it appeared in *Ebony*.[88] However, her account of black life in Chicago was even more at odds with *Holiday*'s cultural tourism than with *Ebony*'s celebration of black success. If *Holiday* trafficked in high art and dreams of travel to exotic destinations, Gwendolyn Brooks invited the magazine's readership to view a more sobering reality across Chicago's South Side.

"They Call It Bronzeville" was adorned with beautiful photographs taken by the Bermuda native Richard Saunders, who had worked in the photo labs at *Life*.[89] Saunders's images, both black and white and color, focused largely upon the cultural and social lives of the city's African American elite. He captured teenagers in formal attire at a cotillion, a house party of "artist-writer friends," a painter with his masked—but otherwise nude—subject, and "sepia show girls" performing for a "mixed audience." Bronzeville was bohemian and bourgeois, but it was also blighted. As if to confirm the neighborhood's neglect—lest readers think all was well in the black metropolis—the article's final photograph presented a young "Bronzeville waif." The child, described as orphaned by his deceased mother and absent father, was caught gazing "wistfully at life from the window of his foster home."[90]

Appearing on eight different pages, the story was spread across the issue. Brooks began, unapologetically, with an indictment: "BRONZEVILLE . . . is something that should not exist—an area set aside for the halting use of

a single race." Yet, she continued, "since a Bronzeville does exist, it is satis-
fying to demonstrate that here resides essentially only what is ordinary."[91]
Brooks established her argument immediately: segregation was an inhu-
mane and condemnable offense. Still, evidence of humanity abounded.
The story of Chicago's black South Side was one of racial oppression and
exclusion, but it was also a tale of ceaseless "fighting to improve conditions." In her conclusion, Brooks described Bronzeville as simply "a place
where People live."[92] On the pages in between, she imagined leading an
unfamiliar "white Stranger" on a tour of a community whose residents had
embraced the "set-aside" space as a place "where God and God's grace are
more truly with him."

Racial segregation's insidious power was that it maintained its hold not
only by external logics (i.e., exclusion under the law) but also from within
"the race." Nothing was singular in Brooks's account of Bronzeville. Its
people evidenced differences in culture, class, and skin color among other
things. Brooks brought the neighborhood to life by introducing a character that would be more fully developed two years later in *Maud Martha*. A
latchkey kid before the term existed, "little Clement Hewy" was the son of
a single mother who, deserted by her husband, toiled long hours as a house-
maid. Clement was a "spirited" child and a good student who occupied
himself in her absence and was always excited upon his mother's arrival
at home. She "would be proud of him if she had the time," Brooks opined.

The long hours and labor associated with the weekdays might have been
balanced by the weekend, but Brooks did not show the Stranger the fictional Hewy household on Saturday. Instead, she turned her attention to
a party at the home of real-life characters, the sculptor Marion Perkins
and his wife, Eva. In the Perkins home, readers encountered a creative
elite that included photographers, scientists, teachers, and writers.[93]
Unsurprisingly, Brooks noted next that on the following morning "the
Stranger might go to church." Sunday morning provided the perfect occasion for Brooks to illustrate class distinctions. First, she depicted a service
at the historic Coppin Chapel AME, then pastored by the Reverend Joseph
L. Roberts Sr.[94] Rev. Roberts and his church were cast as the epitome of
austerity, authority, and order within the wider ecology of the community's social hierarchy.

Sunday evening provided an entirely different picture of what Brooks
termed "Bronzeville religion." An unmarked "'store-front' church," led
by an unnamed pastor who preached after the testimony of an anonymous "large lady in white," provided the perfect foil to Coppin Chapel's
seriousness and scripted service. Hymns and chants were countered by
"Hallelujahs" and "Fast, jazzy music." Spontaneity, participation, and

"spirited prayer" in which "everyone plays a part" were the rule of order here.[95] Despite the denominational variety, Brooks conceded that the Stranger might not be in the mood for more church. So she suggested, as an alternative, a return to Saturday's artistic fare with a show at the historic Regal Theatre. Instead of a church performance of "jazzy music," the Regal was frequented by some of jazz music's greats. Louis Armstrong, Duke Ellington, and Ella Fitzgerald were just a few of the names that Brooks cited.

The poet next visited the George Cleveland Hall branch of the library, which offered "one thousand volumes by and about negroes." Here visitors might see local black stars such as Edith Sampson, a lawyer who had become the first black UN delegate the previous year, or *Ebony* editor Era Bell Thompson, who was Brooks's friend. The home of *The Chicago Defender*, "the militant Bronzeville newspaper," was close by, as were the headquarters of Johnson Publishing. Its flagship publication, *Ebony*, was the first "to furnish the truth . . . about the Negro" by presenting the good, the bad, and the ugly of Black America. According to Brooks, *Ebony* both affirmed black humanity to white readers and instilled a deeper self-respect among black people. Other revered community institutions, like the South Side Community Arts Center, Parkway Community House, and Providence Hospital, were all close. If not entirely a boast about the neighborhood she called home, this litany of storied institutions and celebrated individuals provided evidence of Bronzeville's contributions to American history.

Even so, Gwendolyn Brooks refused to end her account on such a celebratory note. Moreover, the article's conclusion cemented the sense that internal divisions of class, color, or culture paled in comparison to the ubiquitous color line. Throughout the essay Brooks identified members of the black elite and middle class by name even as she maintained the privacy of poor and working-class black people under terms of anonymity or the invention of a fictional identity, as with Clement Hewy and his mother. Whether out of respect for their vulnerability or to better engender empathy, the strategy effectively decreased the distance between "the Stranger" (who stood in for the presumably white reader) and Brooks's anonymous beleaguered subjects. The practice also highlighted the exceptional individuality of those who were named.

Even if such class differences were less rigid than the essay suggested, the distinction nonetheless inferred that the unnamed or invented characters represented the majority. They were, ultimately, the true citizens, as Brooks put it, of "Bronzeville proper."[96] Yet embedded within "They Call It Bronzeville" was a deeper reflection on, and critique of, social valuations that granted individuals of a particular social status the authority to define and determine "the real." At the end of her litany of "Who's Who" in black Chicago, Brooks took her Stranger to the 111 Club, which she acknowledged was a "pseudonym for one of many cocktail lounges" in the neighborhood. There she introduced the story's final fictional figure, Howie Joe Brown.[97]

Gwendolyn Brooks created Howie Joe Brown as a young man in his twenties who, like "many of his contemporaries," exchanged his educational aspirations for a job so that, as a teenager, he could earn the paycheck his family desperately needed. He was not interested in "'higher' things" such as the arts or the library. Instead of books, Brown preferred "poolrooms and the movies, where he tries to forget his anonymity." Unhappy with his life and disappointed with his marriage, home, and work, Brown became preoccupied with "the people he would like to impress." Brown was an invisible man, unable to capture the attention of the "Real people" he enviously observed adorned in all the latest fashions. Although he gained entrée to the 111 Club, "Real people" were its true clientele.

Howie Brown's isolation was only magnified by an apparent "unspoken agreement" between the "Real people" and the club's staff, who "want you to know that they are as good as you are and maybe a lot better."[98] While highlighting the different types in the club, through her attention to his interior life—his desire "not to know that, to him, almost nothing at all will happen"—Brooks collapsed the distinctions between Howie Brown and those he so badly desired to be. The narrative attended to the subtleties of Brown's plight. Yet the larger message—that he was destined to "merely live from day to day" until he died—indicted everyone present in the 111 Club, including "the Stranger" and Brooks's unwitting *Holiday* readers.

At the time Gwendolyn Brooks's *Holiday* article went to press, St. Clair Drake and Horace Cayton's magisterial study of Chicago, *Black Metropolis*, was but five years old. E. Franklin Frazier had been elected "the first Negro president" of the American Sociological Association in 1948, and a Marxist orthodoxy held interpretive sway in the field. Although Frazier's strident critique of the black middle class, *Black Bourgeoisie*, would not be published until 1956, Brooks seemed to levy a literary claim of false consciousness. And the distinction she drew between the South Side's "stars" and those who were just struggling was not simply an essentialist argument for authenticity. "They Call It Bronzeville" stopped short of conflating race and poverty with the goal of uncritically celebrating "the folk." One senses that she privileged the storefront church over the well-heeled Coppin Chapel AME Church. Yet class asymmetries were placed in a new light at the 111 Club. Brooks may have also had a subtle bone to pick with Chicago's Negro society. The black elite celebrated her accomplishments, but theirs was a club into which she had not been born and may have never felt fully at home. At the same time, her criticism of class relations held true for the elite readership of *Holiday*, irrespective of race. Everyone was implicated in the questions of what was "the real," who were "Real people," and who had the authority to say so.

Finally, as a tale that trekked across Chicago's segregated cityscape— "up and down, and across and back"—"They Call It Bronzeville" captured intra-racial differences and divisions even as it attempted to bring them into fuller relief on an American, and even a human, scale. Although its population was never a monolith, Bronzeville was set apart by a single variable: race. In this regard, Brooks's real and, especially, her imagined characters represented all black people to white readers, most of whom saw "the Negro" only as Howie Joe Brown saw himself: "isolated, strange and unimportant."[99] Instead of relaying a story of a "true" Bronzeville that was so often imagined, the Pulitzer-winning poet-turned-reporter hoped that "the Stranger" would simply tell the truth about Bronzeville. Brooks invited readers to share a strangely novel discovery: real people lived in Bronzeville.

For Gwendolyn Brooks, black churches and nightclubs proved most effective at illustrating class differences and authenticating competing definitions of racial aesthetics. In this regard, she carried on a commonly drawn comparison between churches and nightclubs as incubators of black identity and cultural expression that dated back to the 1920s. Brooks's *Holiday* essay can also be read as a transitional text. In some measure it signaled a diminishing of the social realist tradition's stranglehold on the political expectations of African American literature. Richard Wright's singular prominence was subsiding because of his sustained absence (now five years) from the United States. More space was opening up for black writers who experimented with high modernist forms.

Within the next two years, Ralph Ellison's *Invisible Man* (1952) and James Baldwin's *Go Tell It on the Mountain* (1953) were both nominated for the National Book Award; Ellison won in 1953. Such novels were consistent with Brooks's insistence on quotidian humanity—the daily struggle to survive without radically opposing or overturning the social orders of race and class—of the people who lived in Bronzeville. If Brooks's essay did not help achieve the goal of recognition or equality, it certainly coincided with several significant political and social developments in the United States that seemed to affirm the humanity of black people.

RALPH ELLISON AND THE AFRO-PROTESTANT SOURCES
OF AMERICAN CULTURE

By the 1950s, when Gwendolyn Brooks was challenging readers' precon-
ceptions in *Holiday*, Oklahoma native Ralph Ellison had established a
track record of writing poignant political and cultural criticism, primarily
for several radical publications. More significantly, he had become one of
the most eloquent voices to insist upon the inseparable and entirely equal
virtues of black contributions to American culture. Upon accepting the
National Book Award for his debut novel, *Invisible Man*, Ellison remarked,
"We are fortunate as American writers in that with our variety of racial
and national traditions, idioms and manners, we are yet one. On its pro-
foundest level American experience is of a whole. Its truth lies in its diversity and its swiftness of change."[100]

The ruling of the U.S. Supreme Court the following year in *Brown v.
Board of Education* for once affirmed in the law what Ellison (and countless
others before him) had uttered in speech. Ralph Ellison, of course, was not
a seer predicting the imminent fall of racial segregation. Yet his speech—
and his aesthetic vision more generally—did signal a shift in black letters
that was more substantive than the affirmation provided by the award.
Indeed, Ellison's nod to diversity and swift change may have been a subtle
dig at his friend Richard Wright and at the naturalist aesthetic that read
black life as "set apart" by the conditions of Jim Crow.[101]

When Richard Wright had first arrived in Manhattan in May 1937,
fresh from a falling out with Chicago's Communist Party, it was a young
Ralph Ellison who had helped him learn the city. Langston Hughes had
introduced the two men by way of a letter to Wright when he was still in
Chicago. Ellison had moved to New York only a year earlier. Although he
had come searching for a summer job after completing his junior year at
Alabama's Tuskegee Institute, Ellison would never return to complete
his degree.[102] However, it was Wright who, in his late twenties, was
already a published author and an activist with access to local political
and cultural networks. He quickly began work for Benjamin Davis in
the Harlem Office of the Communist Party's *Daily Worker*. There, Davis,
a Harvard Law School graduate and soon-to-be city councilor, encouraged Wright to help renew the vision of the well-regarded, albeit short-
lived, radical magazine *Challenge*, which Dorothy West had founded in
1934.[103]

A few months after Wright and Ellison met and became fast friends,
Wright invited Ellison to contribute to *New Challenge*, although Ellison
had yet to set his mind on becoming a writer.[104] Ellison's review of

Waters Turpin's novel *These Low Grounds* was printed that fall.[105] Not insignificantly, Ellison's first published essay shared the stage with Richard Wright's manifesto, "Blueprint for Negro Writing," on the pages of what would be the final issue of *New Challenge*. The two men remained close friends for several years. In 1938, Ellison joined the New York office of the Federal Writers' Project, where he worked as a researcher and writer for the next four years. Roi Ottley supervised the office's writing on black culture. As was discussed in chapter 2, Wright was on staff at the FWP and authored, among other things, a chapter on Harlem in *New York Panorama* (1937). Unlike James Baldwin, Ellison found much to praise in Wright's *Native Son* and he held Wright in high regard as a writer. He discovered his own literary voice writing for radical papers like *New Challenge* and *New Masses*, although it was not long before he departed from a leftist approach to literature.[106]

In 1942, Ellison added the title of managing editor to his growing literary résumé when he was recruited to join the staff at *Negro Quarterly*. There he worked alongside Angelo Herndon, who had gained renown in 1932 after being arrested and jailed for organizing workers in Atlanta.[107] Herndon served two years of a twenty-year sentence before the Supreme Court overturned his conviction in 1937. In the early 1940s he founded the Negro Publication Society and launched several radical outlets, including *Negro Quarterly*, where he hired Ellison. Herndon remained tied to the Left as a publisher. Ralph Ellison, by contrast, later recalled 1942 as the year in which his own aesthetic vision evolved from being grounded in radicalism into one that emphasized radical individualism.[108]

If Ralph Ellison's politics were in flux during his time at *Negro Quarterly*, while there he began to articulate his own complicated theory of black culture. Early in 1943, in an oft-cited editorial, he called for readers to engage in "group self-examination" and then initiated his own provisional inquiry by outlining three common attitudes. Two dispositions—an "unqualified acceptance" of racial inequality, on one hand, and an "unqualified rejection" of any claim to full citizenship for black people, on the other—tended to predominate, according to Ellison.[109] The former posture was indicative of persons who were "comfortable only when taking orders" and "happy only when being kicked." In his estimation, this was an attitude maintained by too many Negro leaders. The second outlook, Ellison observed, was defined by "Negro cynicism" and despair even as it often masked itself in the kind of "courageous display of manhood" associated with folktales about figures such as John Henry. While occasionally heroic, individuals of this outlook, at worst, were known to "resort to a primitive form of magic to solve the whole problem by simply abolishing the word *Negro* from the American language."[110] Ellison was no doubt referring to Father Divine, who had risen to celebrity in Harlem a decade earlier. The man formerly known as George Baker claimed divinity for himself and rejected the standing nomenclatures of race and gender, insisting that his followers refer to themselves only as "angels."[111]

These two stances were actually two sides of the same coin, animated by inverse logics yet equally "impotent before the complex problems of the Negro situation." "Fortunately, there is a third attitude," Ellison exclaimed.[112] He asserted that an attitude of "critical participation, based upon a sharp sense of the Negro people's group personality" was able to take seriously a commitment to the ideals of American democracy without obscuring the fact that they were rarely, if ever, attained in practice.[113] Such an approach required "Negroes to come to terms with their own group"—not as though they existed in a vacuum but rather "through a consideration of the major problems of our revolutionary times." Race leaders needed to study "new concepts, new techniques and new trends among other peoples and nations." Yet they should only adopt ideas that addressed "the reality of Negro life."[114]

An engagement with world problems was the only way to address racial inequality. In turn, solving the latter was essential to addressing the former. Ellison called for close attention to developments in technology, economics, and politics. Yet he insisted that culture was as critical as material conditions. "Perhaps the zoot suit conceals profound political meaning; perhaps the Lindy-hop conceals clues to great potential power," he conjectured. Though not to be conflated, culture and politics were inseparably connected. "Learning the meaning of the myths and symbols which abound among the Negro masses" was necessary to any viable political program.

Lest the materialist reader be confused, "This is not to make the problem simply one of words," Ellison qualified. Rather, it was a call "to recognize that words have their own vital importance." He concluded his editorial by admitting that all politics should be assessed according to deeds rather than words. In the following years Ellison increasingly withdrew himself from politics in general and the Left in particular.[115] Language and literature were to become the primary terrain for his own battles, and he would harshly critique writers whom he felt confused politics with culture.[116]

Over the next several years Ellison's literary reputation grew. Meanwhile, his relationships with a number of prominent black writers, like Langston Hughes and Richard Wright, either waned or became strained. In 1952, Random House released *Invisible Man*, and the following year Ralph Ellison became the first Negro novelist to win the National

Book Award. His address at the award presentation was as much a meditation on the meaning of America as it was a reflection on the sources and
inspiration he drew upon for his novel. In the decade since he had served
on the editorial staff at *Negro Quarterly*, Ellison's vocabulary had shifted
from identifying an attitude of "critical participation" to advocating for
a "return to the mood of personal moral responsibility for democracy."[117]

In writing *Invisible Man*, Ellison explained, he was both discovering his
own voice and searching for a form that could express and "confront the
broad complexities of American life" in the twentieth century. His novel
would need to engage the nation's racial history if it was to say something
new about its "rich diversity and its almost magical fluidity and freedom."[118] He had availed himself of "the rich babel" of more than three
centuries of history, drawing upon "a mixture of the folk, the Biblical, the
scientific and the political."[119] Committed to "leaving sociology to the scientists," Ellison was determined to capture a truth that transcended modern social—and academic disciplinary—distinctions. He wrote with the
conviction that black people were not a special case but rather "the gauge
of the human condition."[120]

How better to begin this task, in *Invisible Man*, than with a blues sermon
embedded in a jazz song. Not long after introducing himself to the reader,
Ellison's unnamed and invisible narrator recalled an instance in which he
fell into "the breaks" of science and reason. In modernity's break, he "not
only entered into the music, but descended, like Dante, into its depths."
There, in the lower depths, he "*heard* an old woman singing a spiritual."
Then, on a "still lower level," he "*saw* a beautiful girl the color of ivory"
standing "before a group of slaveowners who bid for her naked body."
Finally, he descended to yet a "lower level," below the spectacle of the auc-
tion block in which an apparently white woman was the prized commod-
ity. Here, this invisible man "*heard* someone shout: 'Brothers and sisters,
my text this morning is the 'Blackness of Blackness.'" Indeed, beneath the
music—amidst a mystifying daze of sight and sound and time and space—
in the bottom rungs, "'there was blackness' . . . the preacher shouted."[121]

In Ralph Ellison's effort to arrive at the truth of the human condition
through "the gauge" that was "the Negro," he took his readers to church.
There, among a "congregation of voices," a shouting preacher delivered a
babbling sermon on the "Blackness of Blackness." This shouted blues sermon haunted the hearer (and Ellison's readers), if for no other reason than
it confounded any obvious meaning. Blackness, as indicative of the human
condition, was not to be bound by the social markers that defined modern
society, even as the making of the modern was premised upon the bind-
ing of black bodies. What better way to illustrate this paradox—indeed,

the human paradox—than to stage an encounter between the sight of an invisible man and the sound of the hypervisible and incessant (pre?) modern performance (i.e., the expressive culture of the Negro church), which was often made to stand in for all that was wrong with "the race." There was also the fact that the entire encounter was staged as a modern mediation, through a phonograph record. Moreover, it was enhanced by the influence of marijuana, which had been criminalized one year before the novel's publication. Ellison could hardly have woven a more complicated and layered web of contradictions.[122]

Two years after *Invisible Man* received the National Book Award, Ellison was honored with the Prix de Rome fellowship at the American Academy of Rome. He remained in residence there from 1955 through 1957 with his wife, Fanny. Upon returning to the United States he accepted a position on the faculty of Bard College, just an hour north of New York City in Annandale-on-Hudson. Beyond Bard's base salary, Ellison supplemented his income as a somewhat reluctant jazz critic. At least this is how he described himself (or claimed that others described him) in a letter he wrote to close friend and fellow writer Albert Murray in 1958. Given the enthusiasm he and Murray shared for the art form—and which occupied so much space in their letters to one another—and the profits such writing provided, surely Ellison was poking fun at himself.[123]

Just the day before he wrote this letter to Murray, one of Ellison's jazz essays was published in the *Saturday Review of Literature*. In the missive, Ellison ignored his most recent publication, but he made mention of an essay he was writing for a special jazz issue of *Esquire* magazine.[124] The substance of his letter to Murray was about his attendance at the fifth annual Newport Jazz Festival, which had taken place in early July. Recalling his experience at Newport, he vented about a white "critic-composer" who had denied any relationship between jazz music and black culture. Ellison proudly confessed to having told the man "who his *black* daddy was" while also reaffirming his position on race politics. "I don't fight the race problem in matters of culture anymore," he explained, "but anyone should know the source of their tradition before they start shooting off their mouth about where jazz comes from."[125] Responding to his confidant, Murray turned the topic of their exchange to his friend's most recent writing.

That essay, published in *Saturday Review*, dealt with Mahalia Jackson, whom Duke Ellington had finally persuaded to grace the secular stage at Newport with his orchestra. While their collaboration is now the stuff of legend, Ellison and Murray (and much of the audience, apparently) agreed that Jackson's performance was a failure.[126] Ellison's account of the 1958 festival, "As the Spirit Moves Mahalia," focused on this failed experiment. Although his letter to Murray voiced frustration with the race politics surrounding jazz music, the essay on Mahalia Jackson more pointedly addressed the occasion of her Newport performance.[127] His study of the revered gospel singer took readers to school regarding the music's sacred (and racial) sources, even as he insisted that the two genres, gospel and jazz, were very distinct tributaries.[128] Jackson was the embodied evidence of the connections among the music the market named "jazz," gospel, and black life.

This was not entirely new territory for Ralph Ellison, although most of his writing focused on what were presumed to be secular subjects.[129] Inspired early on by T. S. Eliot, Ellison's terrain was the spiritual wasteland of modern literature and culture. More than fifteen years before, he had argued that black popular expressions (e.g., dress and dance), though often a "mystery," contained "profound political meaning."[130] Yet when his invisible man was plunged into the depths of a Louis Armstrong phonograph recording, Ellison unearthed the sacred sounds of a woman singing spirituals followed by, at the deepest register, a preacher's shout and an echoing chorus from the congregation.

First in the novel and now in his nonfiction, Ellison argued, perhaps unintentionally, that some of those deepest, most complex meanings were encoded within the paradigmatic performances of song and sermon in black churches.[131] Additionally, and surprisingly for Ellison, echoes of a racially exclusive, insider/outsider logic were also apparent, if subtle, in the essay. Part of the reason people often misread the meaning of Mahalia Jackson's music was because they had "come upon it outside of the context of the Negro community." With language that recalled his earlier critique of an unnamed Father Divine, Ellison observed that many people believed she was "really a blues singer who refuses, out of religious superstitions," to sing "secular" music in any form or setting.[132] In truth, Ellison argued, "Miss Jackson is the master of an art of singing which is as complex and of an even older origin than that of jazz." It may be "all joy and exultation and swing," he continued, "but it is nonetheless religious music."[133] With a celebratory nod to the singer, Ellison once again took his readers to church.

In his estimation, the singer had fallen flat at Newport for the very reason that she was, in truth, a "high priestess in the religious ceremony of her church." To be fair, Ellison claimed—at least in the confidence of private correspondence with Albert Murray—that just about every musician at Newport in 1958 had failed, except for a 39-year-old Thelonius Monk, who "outplayed most of the modern boys and was gracious and pleasant while doing so."[134] Ever the fierce critic, Ellison afforded Ms. Jackson what was for him a rare gesture of deference. His analysis took the singer at her word. "I'm used to singing in church, where they don't stop me until the Lord comes," Ellison quoted Jackson as saying. To see Mahalia "at her best"—as had, he claimed, the lucky few who traveled to Newport's Mt. Zion AME Church on Sunday, July 6, 1958—one had to "venture into the strangeness of the Negro church."[135]

There was good reason to respect the specific context in which Mahalia Jackson's sound had been cultivated and sustained. By not taking seriously "the spiritual reality which infuses her song," one might "fail to see the frame within which she moves" and thus miss her meaning. Yet Ellison had never been one to argue for just one reading of a single source, even if he was convinced his interpretation was best. Multiplicity and complexity were his signatures.

There is no doubt that certain strands of American Christianity, including a broad swath of Afro-Protestantism, have rigidly policed the perceived lines between things sacred and secular. A rejection of "modern" ideas, music, media, and science has been a familiar religious position. Yet religious actors have just as commonly embraced the modern—seemingly blurring or blending sacred and secular—to make things new. In truth, these categories have never been fixed or stable. Rather, they are constantly reconstructed, porous, and fluid and are always being made fresh and imagined anew.

Through personal experience and sustained "critical participation" in American culture, Ellison knew this all too well. Yet his insistence that "the church and not the concert hall" was the right context for Mahalia and his argument that her music predated the twentieth-century advent of jazz embraced a rigid distinction between sacred and secular that he had sought to trouble, if not collapse, in *Invisible Man* and elsewhere. Trying his hand at religious criticism, Ralph Ellison read Mahalia Jackson's performance in a way that engaged with modern religious tropes that he had elsewhere eschewed and that circled around the problem of the color line in subtle ways. His criticism of Jackson's performance put him at odds with the common observance that there was continuity between the church and the nightclub. It also suggested that he still might be wading in the waters of a cultural analysis unable to ward off race politics.

To note this paradox does not amount to calling the modernist Ralph Ellison a fundamentalist when it came to Mahalia Jackson and gospel music. Nor does it mean that his assessment of the singer and her self-identified context of the Christian church was not accurate. It does, however, call attention to the challenges involved in articulating Ellison's entangled definitions of the human condition, the American nation, and "the Negro" as a barometer of both.[136] Caught up in a complex web of contradictions, Ellison's arguments about Mahalia Jackson evinced a deeply modern and American, even Protestant, logic.[137] Still, Ellison was also a Negro. And, in this instance, he appeared to engage with a form of racial apologetics—reluctant yet proud, fighting "the race problem in matters of culture"—after being provoked by the white "critic-composer" at Newport.[138] Although he set the record straight on the black (and, surprisingly, black church) sources of jazz, Ellison in no way reneged on his complicated American vision.

Invoking a very specific, albeit not exclusive, racial and religious history for Mahalia Jackson's music, Ralph Ellison still claimed universality for the singer. As a human being, she was a product of the particularities of her own history. Yet because of her singular gifts it was only to be expected that Mahalia would be "claimed by the world as its own."[139] Ironic but nonetheless celebratory, "As the Spirit Moves Mahalia" brought together the racial and the sociological, and the aesthetic and the experimental, in a compelling piece of prose that insisted on the Americanness of the black Christian church and its music. According to Ralph Ellison, jazz—that most modern and most black of American art forms—was undeniably Afro-Protestant.

In accounting for the sacred artistry of Mahalia Jackson, Ralph Ellison's interpretation disentangled religion and aesthetics even as he declared her aesthetic to be religious. More simply, he argued that her musicianship did not make sense in the nightclub or on the concert stage. Ms. Jackson's music found its real meaning only in the context of ministry in the Christian church. In contrast, in her Bronzeville essay Gwendolyn Brooks had suggested that black churches and nightclubs alike were the organizing cultural centers of black social life. Sacred and secular were entangled in her rendition of Chicago's South Side neighborhood, although this took distinctive forms in different institutional settings. Brooks and Ellison posited different religious meanings even as they both affirmed the centrality of Afro-Protestantism to the making of racial aesthetics.

Gwendolyn Brooks and Ralph Ellison, at least in these instances, each implied that a distinct cultural logic held for black life. Yet both authors also advanced a larger argument about the Americanness (and universality) of black culture that was in keeping with a wider ethos of racial catholicity in African American literature during the 1940s and 1950s. Albeit in different ways, writers like Brooks and Ellison—and Robert Hayden and James Baldwin and the artist and critic Romare Bearden—wrote against the orthodoxy of infusing racial aesthetics with an instrumentalist and oppositional race politics. An investment in a complicated definition of American culture that valued the particular place of racial difference was increasing in importance. This vision privileged complexity, contradiction, and openness and prioritized artistic craft and formal experimentation. Such an interpretation evaded easy definition but in doing so constituted its own interpretive claim.

Literature and sociology, aesthetics and politics, black and white, religion and radicalism, Christian theology and Communist ideology: none of these binaries were to be taken for granted as mutually exclusive. Yet neither were they to be uncritically accepted as necessarily entangled. Even Ann Petry, who endorsed the politics of social realism and the protest tradition as they were falling out of style, did so on terms that did not forthrightly affirm a racial aesthetic. If Petry's leftist account of literature did not foreground race, it did bring religious sources to the fore. The protest tradition was part of American culture and modern literature, and as such, it bore the marks of the New World's primary religious heritage, Christianity. More than Karl Marx, Petry explained, the Christian Bible had shaped the contours of the literary canon to which black writers were making a novel claim.

Perhaps the United States was on the eve of witnessing the end of racial aesthetics, the parochial giving way to the catholic. Perhaps, as Ralph Ellison speculated, America's "rich diversity and its almost magical fluidity and freedom" might finally be realized.[140] Perhaps, as the editors of *The Negro Caravan* had suggested and as Roi Ottley had vehemently argued, a new world was coming; one in which the racial, the American, and the international would exist on equal terms. Perhaps a universal acceptance of black literature and culture was actually on the horizon and racial catholicity would be recognized as such.

Or maybe not. As the decade of the 1960s dawned, the growing emphasis on experimentation and universality and the catholicity of craft that had prevailed in the postwar years began to subside and a renewed emphasis on racial uniqueness—black life, as set apart—was increasingly on the rise.

CHAPTER 5

cⅣɔ

An International Spirit

The customs of the colonized people, their traditions, their myths—above all, their myths—are the very sign of that poverty of spirit and of their constitutional depravity.... The Church in the colonies is the white people's Church, the foreigner's Church. She does not call the native to God's ways but to the ways of the white man, of the master, of the oppressor. And as we know, in this matter many are called but few chosen.

Frantz Fanon

In the seven years that transpired between Gwendolyn Brooks's 1951 *Holiday* tour of Bronzeville and Ralph Ellison's 1958 essay on Mahalia Jackson, a great deal about the United States had changed. Even black America's most famous exile at the time, Richard Wright, seemed to be reconsidering things. As the end of the 1950s approached, Wright noted that the predominance of lofty sentiments in literature and politics were the product of a decade in which racial integration appeared imminent. "Naturally this effort on the part of the American nation to assimilate the Negro has had its effect upon Negro literary expression," he observed. Noting the 1954 Supreme Court decision on school desegregation, Wright suggested that if this pattern of integration continued, America might actually witness "a disappearance of Negro literature as such." Sounding almost hopeful, he concluded, "At long last, maybe a merging of Negro expression and American expression will take place." If, however, black writing "should take a sharp turn toward strictly racial themes," then it would be evidence that the promise of equality was not quite fulfilled.[1]

Instead of the end of racial literature in the United States, the pendulum had already begun to swing in the opposite direction, warding off any overstated racial optimism. Although the *Brown* decision had raised expectations by winning the ultimate legal victory for a new generation of black children, a year later images of Emmett Till's marred body loomed just as large. The brutality of Jim Crow crystallized on the cover of *Jet* magazine when it printed a picture of the face—bludgeoned beyond recognition—of the fifteen-year-old black boy from Chicago who was murdered in Mississippi. Media coverage of Till's funeral service and the trial and eventual acquittal of his alleged murderers put a human face on the persistence of racial injustice after the legal end of school segregation. In this way, the black press helped foment a national racial consciousness.[2]

Black writers did their part as well, including Gwendolyn Brooks. In 1960, the year Richard Wright died, Brooks composed a pair of poems that paid tribute to mother and son Mamie and Emmett Till. Brooks, Wright, and the Till family had all at one time called Bronzeville their home.[3] By the end of the 1950s, writers such as Brooks, Wright, Lorraine Hansberry, and James Baldwin had made it increasingly clear that a concern with racial catholicity was on the wane and an "age of blackness" was beginning to dawn.[4]

As was the case in the preceding decades, domestic upheaval remained tied to international developments as the 1950s progressed. Richard Wright's remarks on the evolution and current state, of "Negro literature in the United States" began as one of several speeches that he delivered in Europe over the course of the 1950s. His reporting on the social revolution on West Africa's Gold Coast (now Ghana) had led to *Black Power* (1954). The following year he traveled to Bandung, Indonesia, to attend the first Afro-Asian Conference, and based on that experience he wrote *The Color Curtain* (1955). The next year, back in Paris at the Sorbonne, Wright spoke at the First International Conference of Negro Writers and Artists (sponsored by the International Society of African Culture). There he debated the cultural and political prospects of the African diaspora with other leading black artists, intellectuals, and statesmen from around the world.

A contingent of American attendees carried these conversations back home with them, and in 1957 they formed the American Society of African Culture. Two years later the new organization, in effect a U.S. branch of the international society, announced its work at an inaugural meeting in New York City. Richard Wright did not attend this event and less than three years later he was dead, having never returned to his native land for any extended period of time. Even though Wright ultimately cast his lot with Europe and died as a citizen of France, in many ways his heart, if broken, was always back home. Richard Wright's final writings also reflected a deep knowledge of the global context of colonialism, of which the U.S. Black Belt into which he was born was one specific social formation. Indeed, the man who mapped a "blueprint" for American Negro writers in 1937 often returned to the topic of the United States to examine the problems its particular history of slavery and segregation posed.

Given all that was transpiring around the world, the 1960s promised to be a period of intense social ferment for black communities in the United States. Dramatic changes would be put on full display through political organizing and rhetoric and through artistic expression.[5] The most obvious transition—at least in emphasis, as these two ideologies had been coterminous for several decades—would come in the shifting of public attention from the rhetoric of civil rights to the rhetoric of Black Power. While the aesthetics and politics of Black Power were vigorously debated, at least one almost informal consensus was discernible across much of the period's writing.

Despite the fact that most of the artists did not think of themselves as religious, per se, the various media associated with the Black Arts (e.g., criticism, literature, music, and visual culture) were understood to serve a spiritual purpose. In certain respects, the history of racial aesthetics— as a genealogy of spirit—reached a denouement with the idea of a black aesthetic. Yet *the black aesthetic*, as a singular organizing theoretical term for a nascent Black Arts movement during the late 1960s and early 1970s, remained the topic of a robust debate with a range of perspectives. This particular racial aesthetic was primarily concerned with making art that would take artistic cues from black life, would be created for black people, and would be judged by black critics.[6] From this perspective, the Black Arts would illustrate and illuminate but also order and organize, black social life.

Chapter 5 tracks the transition from the ethos of racial catholicity of the 1940s and 1950s to the increase in nationalist sentiments that would come to define racial aesthetics—indeed, the black aesthetic—of the 1960s. Beginning with the first Negro Writers' Conference and then James Baldwin's *The Fire Next Time*, this chapter highlights the political tone that was present at the outset of the decade. The Black Arts grew out of a historical moment in which the emergence of postcolonial Africa converged with the gains of the civil rights movement in the United States to foment an international racial (and religious) consciousness and to both frustrate and inspire a nascent movement of black artists and intellectuals just a few years later. James Baldwin's essay illustrated the explicit connections that were being made between the black aesthetic, Christianity, and a critique of colonialism at this moment. All of these elements were essential to the social analysis and spiritual diagnosis that shaped the Black Arts of the 1960s on much broader terms.

CHALLENGING AMERICAN EXCEPTIONALISM
ON THE EVE OF THE 1960S

In 1959, a year before Richard Wright's death, the American Society of African Culture held the first Conference of Negro Writers at New York City's Hudson Hotel. Despite the absence of several prominent black writers and intellectuals (including Wright), the showing of academics, activists, and artists was still strong.[7] Although the event took place in New York and was particularly concerned with the plight of black writers in the United States—the conference's theme was "The American Negro Writer and His Roots"—Africa remained at the forefront of the conversation in ways that would not have been the case even a decade before. Gatherings around the globe in the preceding years, like the 1957 conference at the Sorbonne, had renewed and strengthened long-standing networks of black writers across the African diaspora.[8] Moreover, a series of independence movements during the 1950s in places like Algeria, Ghana, Guinea, and Kenya created a climate in which the struggles against segregation within the United States and anticolonial activism in Africa (and elsewhere) were increasingly seen as part of one international political horizon.[9]

Horace Cayton, a sociologist who had coauthored the landmark study *Black Metropolis* (1945), was one of the academics in attendance at the Hudson Hotel. Writing about the conference for the *Pittsburgh Courier*, Cayton credited it with introducing him to "one new concept," in particular: "Negritude."[10] While it was not a new term, Cayton defined it for *Courier* readers as "the feeling that the Negro's universal experience at the hands of the white world has given him a psychological unity wherever he may live."[11] Cayton sympathized with this affective "kinship between all people of color," even as he took pains to clarify that the goals of independence in African nation-states and integration within the United States were contingent upon entirely different historical developments. Even if Africans and "American Negroes" were connected by a "color line" that cut across the globe, their respective geographic contexts required different political strategies and remedies.

Despite his interest in this feeling of kinship and his hopes that the conference would prove black writers to be "consumed with these momentous movements," Cayton noted that "this feeling is limited." He was disheartened by what he took to be an overwhelmingly "sentimental interest in Africa." In his assessment, the conference failed to provide any substantive engagement with "the very roots of European imperialist civilization."[12] Participants appeared to be more interested in establishing emotional connections with black people on the continent and with how the American Negro writer "could make a buck."[13] While Cayton's assessment of the first Negro Writers' Conference may have been fair, commercial success and critiques of colonialism were not mutually exclusive. Such concerns were coming together in ways that would take on new forms in the Black Arts movement during the following decade, and future gatherings of the Negro Writers' Conference would prove instrumental in cultivating the artistic wing of Black Power.

At least one participant in this inaugural convening offered a compelling colonial analysis even as she was in the midst of a commercial breakthrough. Lorraine Hansberry, another Chicago native, delivered a paper titled, "The Negro Writer and His Roots: Toward a New Romanticism" on the second day of the conference, ten days before her award-winning play *A Raisin in the Sun* premiered on Broadway.[14] Hansberry had been closely following the development of African independence movements and penned several articles on the subject in the early 1950s for the journal *Freedom*, published by Paul Robeson.[15] In May 1959, Hansberry communicated her sense of an urgent connection to ongoing anticolonial struggles in an interview with Mike Wallace that was never broadcast.[16] Two months before that interview, she expressed similar ideas to the audience of black writers at the Hudson Hotel.

Lorraine Hansberry's 1959 paper located "The Negro Writer" squarely within the American literary tradition, even as she outlined a clear international vision. Black writers were obliged to engage with "the intellectual affairs of all men, everywhere," she argued.[17] It was of paramount importance that black writers expose "the illusions of one's time and culture." To this end, she cataloged a litany of illusory images that inundated consumers of American popular culture, including television programs, movies, and theatrical events. Despite a public preoccupation with radical politics, she pointed out that popular culture was no less implicated in the spread of "social statements." In a statement that recalled Ann Petry's claim that all literature was political, Hansberry argued that black writers had the power—and thus, the responsibility—to determine "*what* the(ir) statement will say."[18] Hansberry singled out the myth of American exceptionalism as "the last great illusion." The idea of "the equality of man," codified in the U.S. Constitution, may very well be dead, she suggested, at least in terms of its potential realization for black people. The truth was that "the ultimate destiny and aspirations of the African people and twenty million American Negroes are inextricably and magnificently wound up together."[19] Hansberry held that an anticolonial internationalism rather than integration and American liberalism presented the most viable prospect for black political organizing.[20]

Perhaps he missed her lecture, but Horace Cayton certainly did not have Lorraine Hansberry in mind when he claimed that the First Negro Writers' Conference was characterized by a merely "sentimental interest" in Africa. Although she outlined the basis for an attack against "White Supremacy" in the realm of "cultural values" at the conference of writers, her own literary agenda was inseparable from a record of activism. It was also increasingly rooted in the political struggles of black people around the world. Her paper was something of an outlier, and when the American Society of African Culture selected papers for a publication of conference proceedings in 1960, hers was not included. John Davis, the society's executive director, indirectly acknowledged this oversight. Davis awkwardly noted that she had presented at the conference's final session in the last paragraph of his preface to the volume. Without mentioning the substance of her talk, he described *A Raisin in the Sun* as both "social protest" and a "consummate work of art."[21]

Cayton's sense of black authors' growing fascination with Africa as "sentimental ground" was far from baseless. In fact, it presaged how, in the coming decade, the "dark continent" would be discovered anew around the world. This was an especially important development within black communities, but it was significant for American society more generally. One sign of this growing interest was *Holiday* magazine's April 1959 issue, "An Entire Issue Devoted to Africa," a first for the high-culture travel magazine. Even though the magazine's jet-age interest in transporting readers to foreign new lands lent the issue an emphasis on the exotic, it also offered commentary on colonialism and the color line. Known for enlisting novelists as travel writers, the magazine featured an interracial pair of politically engaged South African writers. Peter Abrahams provided an essay, "The Blacks," as did a thirty-six-year-old Nadine Gordimer, whose contribution was titled "Apartheid."[22] In 1959, not even *Holiday* could reduce the continent to simply a vacation.

Ralph Ellison had twice agreed to write an essay for *Holiday* during the 1950s, invitations that came not long after he won the National Book Award for *Invisible Man*. Although neither assignment made it into print, his literary modernism was pitch perfect for the magazine's visual aesthetic—and a reminder that not all black writers were equally enamored with Africa's literary or political potential.[23] Arguably the Negro writer most prized by the white liberal establishment, Ellison did not attend the 1959 Negro Writers' Conference. In the years that followed, he remained committed to his complicated vision of America, where "the Negro" figured as a key component of, and critical lens on, the nation's political and cultural landscape. He held firmly to this position well after Negro literature took a dramatic nationalist turn and was made over as black.

Even so, in claiming the black religious "sources" of jazz music, Ralph Ellison's argument about Mahalia Jackson was not entirely at odds with the 1957 Newport Jazz Festival's billing of gospel music as the roots of the popular American music. Nor was he, on at least that occasion, entirely opposed to the Black Arts idea of an aesthetic tradition. As was noted in the previous chapter, Ellison took great pleasure in privately boasting to his buddy, Albert Murray, about schooling a white critic on the black roots of jazz. "I didn't bite my tongue in telling this guy where he came from and who his daddy was—who his *black* daddy was," he bragged to his friend. Yet Ellison could not have imagined, and would certainly bemoan, how literally an emerging generation of black writers would come to understand their sources. Nor could he have anticipated how much further back in history (indeed, to an imagined pre-history) they would go to discover them.

FORECASTING THE FIRE: RELIGION, RACE, AND LITERATURE IN THE EARLY 1960S

If Ralph Ellison did a decent job of resisting the pull to "fight the race problem in matters of culture," James Baldwin was less successful.[24] Baldwin had begun to sound a different note by the dawn of the 1960s. The retreat of European colonial rule abroad, the recent civil rights gains in the United States, and the emergence of black studies programs on campuses around the nation contributed to a renewed cultural and political interest in Africa. Although he held fast to a position that resembled Ellison's early idea of "critical participation" in the American project, Baldwin was perhaps more influenced by the global critiques of colonial power that Richard Wright had made in his most recent books and that had galvanized Lorraine Hansberry in her 1959 Negro Writers' Conference speech. His now-classic book *The Fire Next Time* offered an apocalyptic portrait of America and predicted that the nation was facing a racial crossroads.

Thirteen years after he launched his attack on the protest novel, James Baldwin revised his theological reading of race and literature in light of the recent revolutionary events overseas. Whereas his earlier essays had argued that sociology and literature ought not be intertwined, now he provided a lengthy polemic that was undeniably attuned to pressing social developments. Early in the decade Baldwin offered one of the most compelling critiques to date of Christianity's central role in justifying the regimes of colonialism and chattel slavery that made the Americas. In his estimation, this insidious entanglement of racist ideology, religious institutions, and ritualized violence put the lie to the moral telos associated with American democracy and Enlightenment reason.

The Fire Next Time foreshadowed the religious character of the racial and cultural transformations that unfolded during the 1960s and the aesthetic innovations of a new group of black writers. Moreover, Baldwin's theological framing of the moment anticipated how a number of Black Arts writers and thinkers came to understand their movement in spiritual terms. With *Go Tell It on the Mountain* (1952), the novelist had illustrated in fiction how the Great Migration facilitated several related schisms (age, class, color, gender, religion, etc.) within black communities. A decade later, Baldwin was thrust into the spotlight as a racial spokesperson. While reluctant about taking on this role earlier, now he delivered on the assignment.

On the national stage, the competing worldviews of South and North and of civil rights versus Black Power were understood in relationship to the disparate responses to Martin Luther King Jr. and the Southern Christian Leadership Conference's (SCLC) activism. This stark difference was evident in how events unfolded in Selma and Chicago. In Selma, Alabama, in 1965, police used violence to quell protests, prompting media coverage that helped the modern civil rights movement turn a corner. In contrast, during the SCLC's Chicago Campaign in the summer of 1966, protestors were greeted not only by police but also by angry white mobs throwing rocks. Such hostilities were taken as an indication that the southern movement of nonviolent "Christian" struggle was less viable in the North.[25]

The increasing appeal of more radical religious idioms like the Nation of Islam (NOI) suggested that a new black world might be on the horizon.[26] In April 1961, James Baldwin participated in a televised conversation with NOI spokesman Malcolm X, and later that year he met with the group's founder and prophet, the Honorable Elijah Muhammad, during a visit to Chicago. Baldwin reflected on these experiences in an extended essay that was originally intended as an article for the Jewish publication *Commentary*. Eventually the piece was published in *The New Yorker* on November 17, 1962, under the title, "Letter from a Region in My Mind."

Because of the incredible reception the article received, it was released in book form the following year, with a new lead title, "Down at the Cross." The book was named *The Fire Next Time*, and it also included a shorter letter Baldwin addressed to his brother's son, "My Dungeon Shook: Letter to My Nephew on the One Hundredth Anniversary of the Emancipation."[27] In addition to commenting on his encounters with the NOI's two most prominent ministers, Baldwin offered a sweeping interpretation of the relationship between religion and race in the modern world.

Deeply personal yet profoundly political, "Down at the Cross," began with a detailed description of the circumstances that precipitated the author's childhood conversion to Christianity. The book culminated with a theological critique of white supremacy that appealed to apocalyptic imagery. Borrowing from the biblical story of Noah as distilled through the Negro spirituals, Baldwin summed up the contemporary situation: "God gave Noah the rainbow sign, No more water, the fire next time!"[28] A shift in James Baldwin's literary priorities away from art and toward politics could clearly be discerned at the outset of the 1960s. The public platform that he assumed that decade was made possible, at least in part, by the overwhelming popularity of *The Fire Next Time*.[29]

The book was a synthesis of two trajectories—that of the artist and that of the activist—that had long been present in Baldwin's writings. On one hand, he had conjured with great mastery the black Christian vernacular in his novels and plays, such as *Go Tell It on the Mountain* and *Amen Corner*. On the other hand, his essays had proven him to be a masterful critic in the tradition of the American jeremiad.[30] In *The Fire Next Time*, Baldwin's writing took on an increasingly urgent tone. The author no longer seemed content to relay the story of Christianity's colonizing past and present. Toward the end of the book, he began to prophesy doom. America's history of church-sponsored white supremacy had run its course. Now, Baldwin predicted, "cosmic vengeance" loomed on the horizon.[31]

James Baldwin's words reflected the tenor of the times: As early as 1962, before the passage of civil rights legislation and the subsequent murders of Malcolm X and Martin Luther King Jr., he saw signs that America's ever-brewing cauldron of racial hostilities was beginning to bubble over.

Images of burning streets would soon become a mainstay in the media as racially motivated uprisings overwhelmed cities across the United States in the period 1964–1969.[32] Yet the race problem extended beyond the scope of domestic politics. Across the Atlantic Ocean, anticolonial struggles in Africa also indicted the Christian Church. Illuminating the inseparability of Christian theology, white supremacy, and colonial rule in the modern world, Baldwin explained the implications of the revolutions under way in Africa:

> The Africans put it another way: When the white man came to Africa, the white man had the Bible and the African had the land, but now it is the white man who is being, reluctantly and bloodily, separated from the land, and the African who is still attempting to digest or to vomit up the Bible. The struggle, therefore, that now begins in the world is extremely complex, involving the historical role of Christianity in the realm of power—that is, politics—and in the realm of morals.[33]

Any discussion of Christianity disconnected from the politics of colonialism in both Africa and Asia was dishonest, Baldwin argued.

To call into question the racial order of the day, as domestic civil rights struggles and the emergence of postcolonial nations abroad did, was to challenge the authority of Christianity—both its theological claims and its institutional practices. Citizens of the West would have to "reexamine themselves and release themselves from many things that are now taken to be sacred."[34] The historical record of racism (i.e., slavery, colonization, and the continued reality of segregation) had proven the Christian church to be morally bankrupt. Baldwin's earlier religious reading of American literature developed here into a historical critique of Christianity and a theological critique of white supremacy. If any "concept of God" were to survive, freedom would have to be its currency. "If God cannot do this, then it is time we got rid of Him," Baldwin stated.[35] As *The Fire Next Time* forecasted, religion—and Christianity in particular—would be an essential dimension of the transformations in black political and cultural life during the tumultuous decade of the 1960s. If the racial ethos of the era was increasingly secular, then it was simultaneously, and explicitly, spiritual.

As a primary source from the early 1960s, *The Fire Next Time* helped locate the desire to instantiate the Black Arts as part of a broader spiritual impulse in American culture. In the context of racial aesthetics during the 1960s, Baldwin's gay identity and universalizing commitments have often led to his exclusion from conversations about the Black

Arts. In short, Baldwin's sexual and artistic bona fides were not "black" enough. To be sure, his ability to simultaneously conjure and critique the persistent powers of Afro-Protestantism in shaping black life was uncanny. In this regard, he knew more about the religious imaginings of Black Power art and politics than the Black Arts movement might admit. Moreover, Baldwin's analysis of race and gender anticipated the critiques black feminists would levy against the Black Arts' normative masculinity—which was itself mediated by religion—by the end of the decade.[36]

As a rule, those involved in Black Power politics and arts have been cast as the youthful, radical, separatist, and secular critics of the clergy and churchgoers who constituted the public face of civil rights integrationist activism.[37] However, the story of religion's role in the black freedom struggle has been much more complicated than such an account allows. For one thing, black Christians of various political stripes had advocated a politics akin to Black Power for some time.[38] Yet the religious dimensions of Black Power's art and politics and the place of spirituality in the broader field of black literature and culture during the 1960s more generally still requires a more complete telling.[39]

NEW GODS, NATIONALIST VISIONS: RELIGION AND BLACK POWER ART AND POLITICS

Religion played a vital role in both the political and aesthetic articulations of Black Power.[40] More precisely, within the context of racial aesthetics during the 1960s the value ascribed to any particular religious idiom—ideas, individuals, institutions, practices, etc.—often corresponded to a perceived ability to evoke Black Power. As James Baldwin suggested, racial injustices around the globe clarified that Christianity was found wanting. Although this assessment may not have been unanimous, the ideology of Black Power did dramatically renew a long-standing debate about the role of Christian churches in addressing the concerns of black communities.[41] In reimagining religion through the prism of blackness, the Black Arts took up Baldwin's provocative assessment of what he understood to be the Nation of Islam's fundamental premise. Since, "the white God has not delivered them; perhaps the Black God will."[42]

Presumably "secular" artists were not the only ones, however, who reimagined the gods. Black Christians also developed theologies of Black Power that insisted that God sided with the oppressed.[43] The examples of two popular preachers based in Detroit during the 1960s—Albert Cleage and Clarence LaVaughn Franklin—illustrate two different trajectories followed by black clergy who were contending for the direction of black churches (and the communities they claimed to serve) during the age of Black Power. Cleage developed a tradition of Black Christian Nationalism. He eventually left the overwhelmingly white denominations (Presbyterian and Congregationalist) in which he had entered the ministry to found the Shrine of the Black Madonna and the Pan African Orthodox Church.[44] The visual arts most auspiciously helped inaugurate a new era in his ministry, as Cleage enlisted local artists to paint a huge mural of a Black Madonna for the wall of his church's sanctuary.

In contrast to Cleage's nationalist orientation, C. L. Franklin blended a more traditional biblical theology with his own version of black consciousness. He was known to be Dr. Martin Luther King Jr.'s favorite preacher and was sought after in black Baptist circles and beyond. Franklin would ultimately become better known as the father of "the queen of soul." Aretha Franklin grew up singing by C. L.'s side in church but followed her musical gifts to fame in the secular industry. However, many of the songs that she recorded—especially during the 1960s—imparted a sense of spiritual dignity to black Americans in ways that were not that different from what her father's sermons did.[45]

Black music, secular and sacred, proved paramount to C. L. Franklin's everyday theology of Black Power. In February 1969, during the first Negro History Month after King's assassination, Franklin preached a sermon series that provided a glimpse of his sense of the term. Celebrating Detroit as the city that had birthed the Motown sound, Franklin's first two sermons explored how two of the era's most popular soul singers, James Brown and Marvin Gaye, referenced black literature and history. In the first sermon, Franklin traced a tradition of artists beginning with the New Negro movement of the 1920s who had proclaimed, like Brown (aka the Godfather of Soul), "I'm black and I'm proud!" In the second, Franklin once again looked back to the same decade, but this time he lauded Carter G. Woodson's founding of Negro History Week in 1926. As he understood it, both Woodson and Marvin Gaye revealed "the grapevine of history, authentic history" by bearing witness to black humanity in their research and recordings.[46]

Franklin and Cleage, both as men and as ministers, were dramatically different. Yet both gave the arts an instrumental role in their ministries. Detroit's vibrant Black Arts scene at the time could surely claim at least some of the credit in this regard.[47] In distinctive ways their respective ministries illustrated the importance of the arts to black life and within black Christian communities, more specifically, during these years.

Christian responses to Black Power by Afro-Protestants but also by black Catholics often included an engagement with the arts.[48] Perhaps for this reason, several leading theorists of the black aesthetic took note. For instance, Larry Neal, a Black Arts luminary who will feature prominently in the next chapter, challenged his colleagues to reconsider the possibility that Christianity might be a resource in the liberation struggle. Indicative of this openness, Neal noted in 1970 that national-ists who advocated for a black aesthetic needed to "reassess their atti-tudes toward the church."[49] It was perhaps unsurprising that Neal cited Cleage as an example of the kind of revolutionary Afro-Protestantism upon which artists might draw. That a preacher such as Cleage figured as exemplary also provided some clue to the sources of the masculinity often enshrined in the Black Arts.

But the wrestlings of the Black Arts with "the church" were only one part of the story of how religion intersected with racial aesthetics as the 1960s progressed. A whole host of new gods was arising, their arrival alternatively heralded and worried over by various players. When the his-torian and civil rights activist Vincent Harding penned the preface to a thirtieth anniversary edition of Benjamin Elijah Mays's classic text, *The Negro's God as Reflected in His Literature,* he reflected on this change. When the first edition was published in 1938, Mays had argued that the New Negro movement of the 1920s and 1930s revealed "the first stages of pub-lic doubt and questioning of God by black folk."[50] Now, Harding suggested, a current version of *The Negro's God* would "move us into an explosive black world where Gods are dying and being resurrected at every turn." He continued:

> It would tell of how significant elements of the black community have joined the rest of society in its movement toward a practical agnosticism, but it would also include the arrival of new Gods: The Allah of the Nation of Islam, the new-old Gods of Yoruba and Housa [sic] peoples, the nameless, still anticipated Gods of profoundly searching young revolutionaries.[51]

Here Harding acknowledged the presence of several "new Gods," perhaps as a nod to the figures first put forward in Arthur Huff Fauset's *Black Gods of the Metropolis* (1944). Black religious diversity was becoming increas-ingly visible, especially in American cities, as a result of the dual forces of urbanization in the United States and immigration from Africa and the Caribbean.

As a historian, Harding had a clear sense of the long history of black migration patterns across the Americas. Yet he may also have had in mind

recent changes made possible by new legislation, as just three years earlier Congress had passed the Immigration and Nationality Act of 1965.[52]
This legislation abolished quotas that limited immigration to the United
States from various African, Caribbean, and Latin American countries.
The "new-old Gods" of this new wave of black and brown immigrants were
certain to be traveling with them. Harding also anticipated that the "profoundly searching young revolutionaries" of the 1960s would give birth to
entirely new black gods that were consonant with their insurgent political
claims. In doing so, he implicitly refuted the common assumption that the
younger advocates of Black Power were a secular alternative to the brand
of Christian activism embodied by Martin Luther King, Benjamin Mays,
and others—including Harding himself. As different as Albert Cleage and
C. L. Franklin's platforms may have been, they were each examples of how
black Christians were both influenced by and engaged in Black Power art
and politics.

Similarly, there was a religious dimension to the Black Arts, even
if it had not yet been explicitly named. The larger platforms of civil
rights and Black Power shared an interwoven history that dated back at
least to the formation of independent black churches in the nineteenth
century. Churches had provided social and intellectual resources that
were central to the formation of a collective (i.e., nationalist) black
identity in the United States.[53] Race and religion had been intertwined
throughout American history. Rarely, if ever, had they been easily
disentangled. Just as appeals to the "spiritual" might mark a specific
racial identity, so too was blackness invested with varying degrees of
spiritual significance.[54] Religion had long been a fixture in formulations of racial identity. During the 1960s, blackness itself developed
more forcefully as a category vested with spiritual significance. [55] For
many activists, artists, and intellectuals, the very word "spiritual"
came to be synonymous with "black."[56]

The revolution, as envisaged in Black Power art and politics, was often
premised upon an ideology that ascribed religious significance to race. Just
as Afro-Protestantism aligned itself with American citizenship to enliven
the social aspirations of King and the Southern Christian Leadership
Conference, racialized visions of selfhood and social life animated a spiritual sensibility among the advocates of Black Power.[57] At least since the
New Negro movement of the 1920s, black writers and intellectuals had
posited that race was supplanting the authority typically attributed to
religion, especially black churches. Amid the revolutionary fervor of the
1960s, Maulana Karenga captured well the ethos of the era when he proclaimed: "Blackness is our ultimate reality."[58]

The version of blackness gaining currency in the 1960s might be understood as the racial equivalent of religious fundamentalism. That is, the
authority granted to race worked to make "blackness . . . a shorthand for
the complexities of black conditions of living."[59] In so doing, appeals to
an almost metaphysical blackness glossed over a host of differences that
informed black people's lived experiences. Although some understood
Christianity to be inherently antagonistic to the aims of the Black Arts,
for many others blackness provided an overarching rubric through which
to reimagine a range of religious ideas. By all accounts, the Black Arts
constituted a set of spiritual practices that was intended to sustain black
life.

The prevalence of a racialized critique of Christianity has commonly
been associated with the politics of Black Power and this has informed
an assumption of the movement's secularism. However, the religious sensibilities that suffused black artistic expressions during the 1960s were
much more complex than such an account suggests, even if they were
also at times contradictory.[60] In order to conjure a spirituality commensurate with the claims of Black Power—a "holy, holy black," to borrow one
participant's words—black artists and intellectuals frequently advanced
one (or more) of three lines of thought. First, they commonly reimagined
Christian theology through a politics of radical blackness, as with Albert
Cleage's Black Christian Nationalism. Second, they appealed to Islam as
the black man's true religion—the course prescribed by Malcolm X and
Elijah Muhammad. Or third, they embraced a romanticized view of Africa
and African diasporic religious practices. In each case, an allegiance to—
and ability to creatively imagine—blackness was prioritized over fidelity
to doctrinal orthodoxy or historical veracity.

In keeping with the third pattern, the poet and activist Amiri Baraka
(formerly known as LeRoi Jones) later admitted to a rather naïve fascination with Baba Oserjeman's Yoruba Temple in Harlem.[61] Remembering the
Yoruba Temple in 1984, he acknowledged:

> It was to us the essence of Blackness. The authentic historical presence of our
> African history and culture. It is not unimportant that all of these groups had
> distinct and ultimately oppressive roles for women. Particularly their adher-
> ents. Whether the veils and segregation of Islam or the polygamy of their tra-
> dition and the common practice of Yoruba. And we were also influenced by
> these ideas and practices as legitimate forms of *Blackness*.[62]

Baraka's comments revealed that religious ideas and traditions were valued insofar as they were perceived to authorize a particular kind of black

self and social life.[63] The gender implications in this equation will be discussed more fully in the following chapter. For now it is important to note that, more so than fidelity to the orthodoxies of specific religions, what united an otherwise heterodox array of ideas and practices was an imagined ability to conjure blackness. That is, theorists and practitioners of the Black Arts prioritized the pragmatic goal of social change over a concern with the systematic. Still, as the definitive signifier in opposition to whiteness, an abstract blackness functioned as an ordering Urtext that disciplined an embrace of black religious diversity. In this way, the Black Arts sought to conjure "by any means necessary" a new black spirit.[64]

Indeed, the term "conjure" is particularly germane for thinking about religion in relationship to the Black Arts of the 1960s. An indigenous conjuring that was rooted in slavery and had links to West African cultures had been apparent in African American literature for over a century. In the *Narrative of the Life of Frederick Douglass, An American Slave* (1845), Douglass received crucial advice from a conjurer who provided him with a "root" that proved pivotal in helping him secure his freedom.[65] In his 1899 collection of short stories *The Conjure Woman*, Charles Chesnutt portrayed the powers attributed to the conjuring tradition as a form of cultural and spiritual authority that existed alongside churches in the South.

Roughly thirty years later, conjure figured centrally in the work of one of the Harlem Renaissance's most celebrated writers. Zora Neale Hurston's novels and folklore writings chronicled black life, especially in the American South and the Caribbean. In both genres Hurston included ethnographic and fictional depictions of Hoodoo (another name for Conjure) and Voodoo, the indigenous and African-derived Haitian spiritual tradition. Although Hurston's literary star faded during the 1940s and she died in relative obscurity in 1960, her legacy and literary canon were resurrected a little more than a decade later, as black (and African) cultures garnered renewed interest in the "Age of Blackness." Her work also became something of a sacred canon for a growing black feminist community that found a new platform during the late 1960s. The longstanding conjuring tradition and Hurston's Hoodoo gained a new literary hearing in the Black Arts.

Given the concern with developing autonomous standards for assessing the arts, conjure is perhaps the most fitting category through which to sort through the religious sensibilities of the Black Arts. At the most basic level, conjure has been defined as the ability "to summon (a devil or spirit) by magical or supernatural power."[66] The meaning of conjure, commonly referred to as a form of black magic, has been overdetermined by its perceived opposition to a normative Christianity, which came to define "religion" for the modern world. In this view, conjure was irrational, magical, and superstitious. Conjure was part of the primitive past. It was not religion—or if it was, then it was certainly not "good" or "true."[67] Conjure was bad, the occult; black magic. Yet the logics of the Black Arts inverted such reasoning. In effect, bad religion was hailed as the good.

Black Arts practitioners embraced conjure as a technology of the spirit capable of transforming individual lives and reorganizing social worlds. It was a form of black reasoning. Appeals to conjure could both exorcise evil (i.e., whiteness, the West) and invoke good (i.e., blackness, Africa). In this way, artists and intellectuals attempted to transform and reconstitute—that is, to conjure—black social life by both theorizing and performing the Black Arts. The Black Arts, in short, constituted a form of conjuring. Moreover, conjure (or Hoodoo) figured as the sign and source of an alternative spiritual and cultural world. In this regard, "blackness" served as both the prescriptive measure and the desired product of Black Arts theorists' conjurings. Blackness could and would save you by making you black.

"WE WANTED AN ART THAT WAS REVOLUTIONARY": SOLIDIFYING THE BLACK ARTS MOVEMENT IN THE LATE 1960S

In *The Fire Next Time* James Baldwin observed the desire to conjure a black god and anticipated the rise of a black spirit. Writing of his encounter with Elijah Muhammad and the Nation of Islam, he empathized with their logic and with their frustration at the moral failures of a God that appeared to endorse white supremacy. Timing, he explained, was responsible for the fact that "suddenly, people who have never before been able to hear this message hear it, and believe it, and are changed."[68] Baldwin identified a family resemblance between the Nation's spiritual power, the increasing cultural salience of the cry that "Black is Beautiful," and the broader recognition of the threat posed by a "black man who refuses to accept the white world's standards."[69] While the Nation of Islam most fervently preached the good news of a Black God, the key to its appeal was not attributable to any specific Islamic theology. Rather, it was the blackness, defined in opposition to "whiteness," that the Nation was taken to represent that resonated deeply and widely with the spirit of the times.

Although seduced for a moment, ultimately James Baldwin was not won over by the NOI's vision of Black Power. Yet along with many of the individuals who comprised the Black Arts movement, he was deeply shaped by the style and substance of the NOI's most prolific minister. For many black artists, the assassination of Malcolm X on February 21, 1965, in effect, provided an impetus for inaugurating the Black Arts. In the months following that event, several young black artists who had been immersed in downtown Manhattan's bohemian art scene began to extricate themselves from interracial arts circles.[70] The years from 1965 to 1970 proved most pivotal in the formation of the Black Arts movement.

Increasingly influenced by the black nationalist posture that Malcolm X represented, LeRoi Jones soon found a new identity in Islam and changed his name to Amiri Baraka. In 1965, Jones, Larry Neal, and several others moved up to Harlem, which had remained a spiritual home—indeed, a "Mecca"—for black artists since the renaissance of the 1920s. Together they formed the Black Arts Repertory Theater/School (BARTS) as part of an effort to institutionalize a commitment to creating black art for black people. Recounting the movement's formative moments and aspirations, Baraka explained:

> We wanted an art that was revolutionary. We wanted a Malcolm art, a by-any-means-necessary poetry. A Ballot or Bullet verse. We wanted, ultimately, to create a poetry, a literature, a dance, a theater, a painting, that would help bring revolution.... That was what it *all* was about. That's what the whole movement and essence of the Black Arts was raised and forwarded by, the desire by Black youth to make revolution in the U.S.[71]

At least in his recollection, the importance of Malcolm X as a cultural, political, and religious symbol—indeed, an icon of blackness—could not be overstated. As a testimony to his significance, Detroit's Black Arts entrepreneur Dudley Randall edited an anthology in his honor not long after his death, compiling poems by many of the Black Arts rising stars. As one scholar of the movement noted, *For Malcolm* was "a tributary volume to the presiding spirit of the new radical African American nationalism."[72]

BARTS itself was short-lived, and the fledgling theater company survived less than a year. However, it was just one of many new organizations that formed in the late 1960s to provide institutional support for the Black Arts. Similar entities were founded in cities across the country over the next few years. Some developed deeper roots, lasting well beyond the decade's end. Although Baraka left Harlem not long after founding BARTS, he soon started another new organization with similar aims, Spirit House, in his native city of Newark. Also in 1965, Dudley Randall began Broadside Press in Detroit and Maulana Karenga helped found U.S. in Los Angeles.[73] The following year constituted a calling together of black artists. The first Black Writers' Conference was hosted in Nashville at Fisk University, where the poet Robert Hayden had once taught. In many respects, the origins of this event were to be found in the first Negro Writers' Conference that had convened in New York City in 1959. While in Nashville, Gwendolyn Brooks underwent a conversion-like experience and was remade into a "Black" artist, much like the conference itself was renamed to signal a new era in racial aesthetics.[74]

In Detroit, also in 1966, a first Black Arts Convention was held. The Black Writers' Conference and the Black Arts Convention each met once again in 1967. That same year, Third World Press and the Organization of Black American Culture (OBAC) were founded in Chicago. Additionally, a group of OBAC's visual artists painted the city's "Wall of Respect," paying homage to a constellation of black icons. The mural included images of leaders like Marcus Garvey and Malcolm X and jazz musicians such as Sarah Vaughan and Ornette Coleman. In Harlem, the Negro Ensemble Company—which would go on to shape African American actors such as Samuel L. Jackson, Angela Bassett, and Denzel Washington—and the New Lafayette Theatre were formed.[75] Also in Harlem, one of the most respected nationalist thinkers, Harold Cruse, published his tome *The Crisis of the Negro Intellectual* (1967), which confirmed the continued role of the historic New York City neighborhood as a center for black cultural, intellectual, and political life.

By 1968, the Black Arts was also establishing a presence in the South, as both BLKARTSOUTH and Nkombo were founded in New Orleans.[76] Local groups such as these helped announce the Black Arts as a national phenomenon. The spread of Black Arts organizations was indicative of a shared emphasis on creating independent black institutions, which in turn helped facilitate the exchange of ideas between black artists and intellectuals across the country.[77] The year 1968 proved to be pivotal for several reasons. Paralleling the institution-building efforts of a burgeoning Black Arts movement, the nation had witnessed a series of urban black uprisings during the preceding four years. Television media helped make a permanent fixture of burning streets and bloodied American cities.[78] Additionally, the assassination of Martin Luther King on April 4 of that year followed more than a decade of highly publicized killings of black people: the teenaged Emmett Till in 1955, the Congo freedom fighter Patrice Lumumba in 1961, the Mississippi civil rights activist Medgar Evers in 1963, four little girls in Birmingham that same year, and Malcolm X in 1965, to cite just a few. These murders shaped the political consciousness and aesthetic visions of the Black Arts' leading voices.[79]

The ubiquity of black blood in the media helped galvanize the modern civil rights movement. By the latter half of the 1960s the bloodshed had also served to radicalize a younger generation of black activists for whom the Christian rhetoric of redemptive suffering proved unpersuasive. The very meaning of the shedding of black blood became an area of contestation. Preaching in Detroit the Sunday after King's assassination, Albert Cleage offered an interpretation of black life and death during the years since Emmett Till's murder:

> Dr. King was still talking every night about redemptive suffering. He was still saying, "If blood must flow in the streets, let it be our blood and not the blood of our white brothers." . . . Dr. King was saying one thing and they [black people] were learning another. . . . White folks remember what he said, his words. But we remember where we were thirteen years ago, and where we are today. . . . But he created the confrontation situation in which we could learn, in which we could work, and which Brother Malcolm could interpret. Everything was working together.[80]

As Cleage observed, King and his cohort of nonviolent civil rights activists had tried in earnest to draw upon the Judeo-Christian imagery of the sacrificial lamb and suffering servant in order to move the moral conscience of white America. Instead, he argued, in spite of King's activism and now because of his death, "a whole new black world has come into being, a Black Nation now exists."[81] Cleage preached that it was King's shed blood that stirred a nationalist consciousness and inspired urban rebellions. If in life King had organized peaceful protests, then the taking of his life worked to different ends. His assassination, in effect, helped conjure the spirit of Black Power in the black masses.

That same year Larry Neal took notice of Reverend Cleage. In doing so, he called attention to both the content and form of Black Christian Nationalism. "He [Cleage] now preaches a new gospel—the gospel of the gun, an eye for an eye," Neal explained. "The gospel is preached in the rhythmic cadences of the old black church. But the content is radical."[82] Neal encouraged his Black Arts colleagues to take black churches, or at least the idea of a "new" black church, more seriously. Cleage, Neal suggested, was a harbinger of a new spirituality. Neal also noted parallels between Cleage's ministry and the recent work by young black playwrights. For instance, he wrote, "[Ben] Caldwell twists the rhythms of the Uncle Tom preacher into the language of the new militancy."[83] Here

Neal was referring to the short play, *Prayer Meeting; or, The First Militant Minister*, written by the Los Angeles–based dramatist Ben Caldwell. Neal and Baraka were so impressed by Caldwell's one-act play that they included it in their anthology *Black Fire*, which was published that year.

Prayer Meeting staged the story of a black preacher whose late-night prayers were interrupted by an angry burglar. The preacher, who was described as a "hustler" at the opening of the play, mistook the burglar for the voice of God and unwittingly accorded the thief divine authority. With his newfound power, the burglar decided to persuade the preacher that he was called to lead a black uprising. Indebted to a Marxist analysis, Caldwell used the scene of a home invasion to exorcise the middle-class preacher of his "false consciousness," even as the burglar freed the minister of his material possessions.[84] The play portrayed a black preacher as the familiar caricature of the charlatan who perpetuates the status quo for his own purposes. The burglar, on the other hand, stood in for a call to black class consciousness. Ultimately, Caldwell invited his audience to imagine a radical black religious identity in the style of the slave preacher, Nat Turner, who discerned a call from God to lead a rebellion in early nineteenth-century Virginia.[85]

In the plays of Ben Caldwell and the preaching of Albert Cleage, Larry Neal identified signs of a "new Spirituality . . . from the concise point of view of the colonialized."[86] Neal's treatment of religion affirmed an argument that Harold Cruse had recently advanced. In *The Crisis of the Negro Intellectual*, Cruse recalled Richard Wright's 1937 essay, "Blueprint for Negro Writing," only to claim that Wright's Marxism limited his analysis of black culture. "He had swallowed whole the Communist Party's dogma about proletarian literature," Cruse claimed. Given Wright's Mississippi roots, he "should have known that the Holy Bible was the most popular literary work among Negroes."[87]

Cruse's analysis resembled Ann Petry's observation, in 1950, that the Christian Bible, more than Karl Marx, was the primary source for all American literature. Cruse concurred with regard to black culture even as he overlooked Richard Wright's assertion that "the Negro church" remained a key conduit of "racial wisdom."[88] Wright's naturalism had fallen out of favor amid the liberal optimism (and the Red Scare) that had moved so many black writers during the 1940s and 1950s.[89] Modernism's emphasis on the individual, the experimental, and the universal had trumped the particular form of social responsibility that Wright demanded of Negro writers. However, not long after his death in 1960, the Black Arts breathed new life into Richard Wright's "Blueprint."

Larry Neal conceded that most black churches were still beholden to an "Old Spirituality" that held sway in black communities. Yet he, and others, insisted upon the need to develop a "New Spirituality" that would require a deeper engagement with Afro-Protestantism—a combination of the Christian Bible, independent black churches, and cultural traditions. Despite their different readings of his work, both Neal and Cruse cited Richard Wright to posit the relevance of Afro-Protestantism for the spiritual revolution that the Black Arts hoped to inaugurate. The invocations of Wright here were telling, as his "Blueprint" essay offered a compelling model for many black artists during the 1960s.[90] In his 1937 elegy for the Harlem Renaissance, as discussed in chapter 2, Wright had argued that writers should assume a new role in relationship to the black masses. He explained:

> He [the black writer] is being called upon to do no less than create values by which his race is to love, struggle and die ... because his writing possesses the potential cunning to steal into the inmost recesses of the human heart, because he can create myths and symbols that inspire a faith in life.[91]

In short, black writers were to replace religious leaders, taking hold of the spiritual authority once exercised by Christian preachers. Roughly three decades later, Larry Neal appeared to agree as he resurrected Wright's claim. "The writer must accept the responsibility of guiding the spiritual and cultural life of his people," Neal insisted.[92] Indeed, a concern with inspiring a new "faith in life" among the black masses enlivened efforts to delineate a black aesthetic.

During the 1960s, theorists of the Black Arts took up Richard Wright's call to construct "new myths and symbols," consistently appealing to religion (e.g., specific traditions, ideas, practices, leaders) and spirituality more broadly. They argued that black culture was essentially spiritual and celebrated black spirituality as an oppositional resource and source of authenticity (i.e., "soul").[93] Moreover, they often engaged black religious traditions with the aim of conjuring a novel black spirituality. That is, they aimed to exorcise the Christian content from black forms of spirituality or to reimagine the former to bring it in keeping with their view of the latter. A particular kind of imagined black church was a key source for the spirituality the Black Arts announced. In Neal's words, this "New Spirituality" issued forth "from the concise point of view of the colonialized" and was thus a buffer against (and counter to) the influences of white Western culture and values.

Ultimately, the Black Arts were envisaged as fundamentally spiritual, capable of conjuring new lives and social worlds for black people. One of the primary means through which theorists and practitioners of the Black Arts would seek to execute Richard Wright's blueprint—to conjure this new spirituality—was through the creation of a new canon. Just after the end of the long 1960s, one of the movement's leading conjurors argued as much in a key anthology of the era. In the penultimate chapter of Addison Gayle's *The Black Aesthetic*, Ishmael Reed—Hoodoo historian and prophet par excellence of the Neo-HooDoo church—explained that "words (nommo) were the rappings of not one but thousands of Spirits." In contrast to the formulas of Western art and religion, the Black Arts, or what Reed named as "literary Neo-HooDooism," would "summon a God."[94] In this regard, the practice of making anthologies would also prove paramount for establishing the Black Arts during the latter half of the 1960s. Words carried the social currency and spiritual capital to make a new world for black people.

CHAPTER 6

༄

That Spirit Is Black

Black poets will waste their words if they do not give articulation to the spirit . . .
Ron Welburn

The timing was no doubt auspicious when, in 1968, Atheneum Press opted to republish Benjamin Elijah Mays's classic text *The Negro's God as Reflected in His Literature*, which was originally published in 1937. Vincent Harding was the perfect person to write a preface to the new edition. As a historian, Harding despaired that no one had updated Mays's work in order to explore the spiritual dimensions of African American literature since the 1920s. As a civil rights activist and an observer of contemporary affairs, he also speculated about what a religious reading of black literature might reveal concerning the present "Age of Blackness," as he named the moment.[1]

A second edition of *The Negro's God* could not have appeared at a more appropriate moment in American literary history. That same year Atheneum also released a new edition of Alain Locke's classic anthology, *The New Negro* (1925), which had been significantly more popular than Benjamin Mays's book. Robert Hayden, the recent recipient of the Grand Prize for Poetry at the first World Festival of Negro Arts in Dakar, Senegal, added a new introduction. Recalling the era when Locke's volume was originally published and perhaps reflecting Hayden's own religious sensibilities, he observed, "The New Negro movement had no formal organization, and it was more aesthetic and philosophical—more metaphysical, let us say—than political."[2] Seemingly with reluctance, Hayden suggested that the organizing impulses of the Negro Renaissance were perhaps more spiritual than they were social or material. Moving forward to the 1960s, Hayden contrasted the integrationist aims of the New Negro with the nationalist fervor associated with the Black Arts and the "profoundly searching young revolutionaries" to whom Vincent Harding now pointed.

The following year, Sterling Brown, Arthur Davis, and Ulysses Lee's 1940 anthology *The Negro Caravan* was also reprinted. Julius Lester wrote a new introduction that ran as a review—of the moment as much as of the republished book—in the *New York Times*.[3] Lester took aim at what he took to be the creative constraints of a nationalist aesthetic. "The present romanticization of blackness," according to Lester, made it difficult for "the black American writer spiritually to do that which only he can do." Recalling the ethos of racial catholicity in which *The Negro Caravan* first appeared, he insisted that the responsibility of black writers was to "illuminate the consciousness of Man through the specifics of his own particular black experience."[4] As the Black Arts overwhelmed racial aesthetics, appeals to the universal by "Negro" writers like Hayden and Lester became increasingly rare.

Artifacts of earlier generations of black writing, each of these anthologies had at one time helped authorize a general claim that there was a tradition of African American letters. Each of these reissued volumes also underscored a shared kinship between the cultural renaissance of the 1920s and the artistic formations taking shape during the 1960s. Both *The Negro's God* and *The New Negro*, in effect, implied a literary history by positing a narrative of continuity across these respective moments even as the new introductions revealed their competing racial ideologies and aesthetic visions. In contrast, *The Negro Caravan* was a kind of bridge text that brought together the distinctive integrationist aspirations of the New Negro with the nationalist particularism of the Black Arts. Most significantly, the new introductory framings Harding, Hayden, and Lester provided each called attention to the often overlooked, yet consistent religious ambitions on display in many of the representative anthologies of black literature of the preceding decades. Such spiritual aspirations were no less apparent during the decade of the 1960s and in the emerging Black Arts movement.

In addition to forming new organizations, Black Arts theorists aimed to institutionalize and evangelize on behalf of the black aesthetic by editing anthologies. These new collections were, by all accounts, efforts to make a new black canon, in the fullest theological sense. To be sure, this revolution in racial aesthetics challenged the leadership and laity of black churches to rethink their own doctrinal claims, ritual practices, and iconography in light of an insurgent blackness. Yet to observe the 1960s was to witness an attempt to fundamentally rethink the spiritual terms of black existence.

Both black artists, intellectuals preachers, and laypersons grappled with a range of religious ideas and practices, and they did so in manifold ways that were at once creative and contradictory. Some reimagined a radically black Christianity (Protestant and Catholic) in order to reverse the logics of white supremacy. Some embraced Islam, both Sunni and the Nation, as a "true" black religion. And still others invoked a range of African-derived religious practices (from Yoruba to Voodoo and Hoodoo) as the essence of black identity and history. In each case, the idea of a radical blackness was the animating principle. All together, the Black Arts involved a comprehensive effort to conjure a new black world by any means necessary.

A new canon was one such means. The enterprise of anthologizing, at this moment, might be understood as an effort to produce representative texts—even, it can be argued, sacred texts—that would inaugurate a new vision of blackness and conjure a new spirit within black readers.[5] To mediate this new spirituality to the masses, scores of Black Arts anthologies were produced during the second half of the 1960s, many of them published by black presses and a majority of them focused on poetry. In his introduction to *The New Black Poetry* (1969), Clarence Major invoked the legacy of W. E. B. Du Bois to suggest that the contribution of these new black poets was singularly spiritual. Major predicted that a stream of anthologies would soon come to embody an "international spirit."[6] Acknowledging the surplus of poetry that both preceded and followed Major's work, Dudley Randall surmised, "Now ... there are so many anthologies of black poetry that each editor must justify the publication of a new one."[7]

In addition to the abundance of poetry anthologies that appeared toward the end of the decade, from 1968 to 1971—what Sylvia Winter identifies as the "apogee years"[8] of the Black Arts—three of the period's most comprehensive and representative anthologies were published: Amiri Baraka and Larry Neal's *Black Fire* (1968), Toni Cade Bambara's *The Black Woman* (1970), and Addison Gayle's *The Black Aesthetic* (1971). Much like *The New Negro* and *The Negro Caravan*, these collections aimed to counter antiquated ideas about black people and provide narratives appropriate for a new day.[9] Yet as much as they countered white supremacy, the competing black voices in each of these volumes revealed the robust debate within the Black Arts and unveiled the religious imagery and "New Spirituality" that defined the burgeoning movement.

This chapter offers a close reading of the ways that religion circulated throughout each of these anthologies and gives special attention to how gender figured as a key fault line, both complicating and clarifying a masculinist orthodoxy at work in the overtly spiritual aspirations of the Black Arts.

CANONIZING THE SACRED WORDS

Larry Neal and Amiri Baraka's collection of critical essays, poetry, and excerpts from recent plays, *Black Fire: An Anthology of Afro-American Writing* (1968), was the Black Arts movement's seminal anthology. The book's title bore witness to the impact recent urban uprisings had on the political vision of the young writers who contributed to the volume. The title borrowed the biblical symbol of fire—simultaneously an apocalyptic sign of judgment, refining, and rebirth—that James Baldwin had popularized in 1962 with his landmark work *The Fire Next Time*. In the turbulent years since Baldwin's work, the jazz composer and pianist Andrew Hill (with Joe Henderson, Richard Davis, and Roy Haynes) had released a record of the same title, *Black Fire*, with the Blue Note label. The popular poet and music critic A. B. Spellman wrote the album's liner notes. He also contributed an essay and three poems to Baraka and Neal's book. In addition to foregrounding the theme of revolutionary fires, Hill's record and Baldwin's essay captured well the cross-pollination between black writing and music during the decade.

Black Fire also gestured to an earlier moment in African American literary history in which black (sacred) music offered inspiration. One of the most celebrated and short-lived publications of the Harlem Renaissance had taken a similar title much earlier than Baraka and Neal. As discussed in chapter 1, *Fire!! A Quarterly Devoted to the Young Negro Artists* published just one issue during the fall of 1926. Including writing by Countee Cullen, Langston Hughes, Zora Neale Hurston, and Richard Bruce Nugent and visual art by Aaron Douglass, *Fire!!* featured the best of a younger generation of New Negroes who gladly challenged the class, gender, and sexual mores of their elders.[10] While Amiri Baraka and Larry Neal announced the Black Arts as a novel development and a new generation in racial aesthetics, their anthology was very much in keeping with a longer tradition.

Black Fire broadcast the Black Arts as a national movement. The editors imagined their book to be a watershed publication at least in part because they hoped it would serve as a source of spiritual regeneration for readers.

Just a quick glimpse at the book's foreword and afterword, written by Baraka and Neal, respectively, illustrates the anthology's religious vision. In the foreword, Baraka announced that the publication of *Black Fire* was divine provision for black people. He also confirmed his and Neal's canon-making ambitions. "These will be the standards black men make reference to for the next thousand years," Baraka proclaimed. "These the sources, and the constant striving (jihad) of a nation coming back into focus." He continued in verse:

> Throw off the blinds from your eyes
> the metal pillar of Shaitan from your minds
> Find the will of the creator yourself where it was
> Sun being eating of the good things[11]

Linking the artist ("the bards") and the cleric ("the babalawo") in spiritual warfare against the Shaitan (Arabic for "devil"), Baraka penned simply: "The black artist. The black man. The holy holy black man. The man you seek. . . . We are whom you seek. . . . We are presenting. Your various selves. We are presenting, from God, a tone, your own. Go on. Now."[12] Although work by a few women was included in *Black Fire*, the contributors were overwhelmingly male. The book's foreword once again illustrated how an entanglement of religion, race, and masculinity appeared as an ordering principle in the Black Arts.

Much of Baraka's writing at this time drew on the apocalypticism in the Nation of Islam's mythology.[13] Moreover, he was at the height of his "poet-priest" phase, defining faith in poetry as a form of divine activity and referring to himself as Imamu Amiri Baraka.[14] Although he often identified as a Muslim cleric in this way, the foreword to *Black Fire* did not invoke Islam exclusively. Baraka also referenced "the wizards, the bards, the babalawo, the *shaikhs*, of Weusi Mchoro," bringing together Yoruba, Arabic, and Swahili all at once. This interreligious and African cast of holy black men were the conjurers of a "Black Design."[15] Baraka's metaphysics marked the writings in *Black Fire* as scripture, divine utterances, and anticipated a question he himself would pose in the poem, "Ka 'Ba," published the following year. There he concluded by asking simply:

> . . . What will be
> The sacred words?

As a sacred canon, the anthology inaugurated a divinely inspired "holy holy black" identity and social order. If undefined and not entirely clear to the contemporary reader, in 1968 *Black Fire* was intended to make plain "the will of the creator" to the black masses.[16]

Continuing in this vein, Larry Neal's afterword more explicitly articulated a spiritual task for black artists. As Harold Cruse had done in *The Crisis of the Negro Intellectual*, Larry Neal invoked Richard Wright to advance his vision. Using the title "And Shine Swam On," a reference to the black trickster figure Shine, Neal explained that *Black Fire* was meant to provide a "critical re-examination of Western political, social and artistic values."[17] Instead of remaining torn by the tension of existing as "both a Negro and an American," Neal understood the Black Arts to be concerned with offering black people a new identity rooted in their own lived experience. While wedded to the social struggle for Black Power in the West, the roots of such concerns ran deeper than politics, in Larry Neal's estimation. He assessed the relationship between aesthetics, politics, and spirituality accordingly. "The artist and the political activist are one," Neal observed. "They are both shapers of the future reality. Both understand and manipulate the collective myths of the race."[18]

Yet for Larry Neal, more was at stake for artists and activists alike. He continued, "Both are warriors, priests, lovers and destroyers. For the first violence will be internal—the destruction of a weak spiritual self for a more perfect self. But it will be a necessary violence. It is the only thing that will destroy the double-consciousness—the tension that is in the souls of black folk."[19] Here Neal synthesized his dual attraction to modernism, on one hand, and the revolutionary ethos of the era, on the other. At the same time he suggested a resolution to the problem posed in W. E. B. Du Bois's classic text, *The Souls of Black Folk* (1903) and he answered Richard Wright's call for writers to function as myth-makers.[20] In his assessment, black activists and artists still struggled with a "general lack of clarity." Accordingly, Neal argued that the leadership styles of Malcolm X and Marcus Garvey were "more emotionally cohesive . . . not as intellectually fragmented."[21] He invoked Garvey and Malcolm X as models of spiritual—and thus, black—wholeness. Both of these men were rare individuals who had managed to do away with the demon within—what Du Bois termed "double-consciousness."[22]

Citing Du Bois, Wright and, most recently, Frantz Fanon, Larry Neal explained that the impulses guiding young black artists during the 1960s coalesced around a commitment to destroy that double-consciousness. Instead of addressing white supremacy by social protest or moral suasion, Neal argued that the West would not be rid of racism until "certain political, social and spiritual truths are understood by the oppressed themselves—inwardly understood."[23] Although secularism and materialism were increasingly perceived to be winning the day, the Black Arts required "not merely integration of the flesh, but also integration of the spirit."[24] Directing black artists to "the spirit," Neal adopted Richard Wright's nationalist interpretation of black culture but did away with its Marxist materialist teleology. As Stephen Henderson has noted, for Neal the "true spirit of the revolution lay in *the forms* of black culture."[25] This led him to the music and culture of black churches, topics to which theorists of the Black Arts repeatedly returned.

As bookends, Baraka's and Neal's essays clarified their editorial vision: the Black Arts would probe black interiority and cultivate spiritual integrity. *Black Fire*, in this regard, was a pivotal effort on the part of black writers during the 1960s to both call for and model—indeed to conjure—a new spirituality for black America.[26] In addition to Baraka and Neal's anthology, Addison Gayle's collection of criticism, *The Black Aesthetic* (1971), helped map out the content and form of racial aesthetics as imagined by practitioners of the Black Arts. Gayle claimed that his anthology was the first of its kind. He also explained that its contents confirmed no consensus but instead indicated that the substance of the black aesthetic was still up for grabs.[27]

Whereas the authors published in *Black Fire* consisted of a "who's who" in the 1960s Black Arts scene, *The Black Aesthetic* featured a significant number of new black writers plus a historical review. Several of the contributions had been published during the latter half of the 1960s in periodicals or as stand-alone essays. Also included were a few older pieces by New Negro luminaries like Alain Locke and Langston Hughes and, again, Du Bois and Wright. The content of these respective compilations captured even more clearly how a variety of religious ideas animated the movement's spiritual quest for a black aesthetic.

In his introduction to *The Black Aesthetic*, Addison Gayle extended the nationalist claim to its fullest conclusion. He argued that black people, in effect, constituted a separate nation within the United States. As such, it was in the best interest of black artists to concern themselves solely with black people, both as their intended audience and as their critics.[28] Gayle summed up the ethos of his generation:

> Speaking honestly is a fundamental principle of today's black artist. He has given up the practice of speaking to whites, and has begun to speak to his brothers. . . . His purpose is not to convert the liberals . . . but instead to point out to black people the true extent of the control exercised upon them by the American society, in the hope that a process of de-Americanization will occur in every black community in the nation.[29]

Gayle's essay also took clear cues from Wright's "Blueprint." In this view, New Negro artists were predestined to fail because they were concerned with white approval and controlled by white patronage. The lessons of the Harlem Renaissance, in Gayle's opinion, were intended to provide readers—and more specifically the Black Arts—with a usable past.[30]

The principle of "speaking honestly" meant something quite precise to the Black Arts, at least according to Addison Gayle. The persistence of racial oppression in the United States meant that black artists were, by definition, at war with the larger white nation. Exclusion, he argued, had produced a distinctive black culture that was animated by a justified rage. These were the only honest conclusions one could draw from the historical record, Gayle argued. The Black Arts, as a logical extension of this history, would advance a form of cultural practice that was equally opposed to the aesthetics of the American mainstream. Of course, neither black anger nor Black Nationalism was new. But whereas the anger of previous generations was directed toward integrating into the nation-state, Gayle asserted that the rage of Black Arts activists signaled a war of secession. They were intent on securing their own nation. Honesty about this desire to secede, in short, was what made the Black Arts of the 1960s novel. Perhaps most significantly, the black aesthetic aimed not just to illustrate or describe "the beautiful"; it would both prescribe and make possible the "transformation from ugliness to beauty."[31] Ultimately, at least in Addison Gayle's view, *The Black Aesthetic* was animated by the utopian hope that it might help give birth to a new black new world.[32] The Black Arts would make black life over and anew.

The Black Aesthetic included a previously published essay by Amiri Baraka that illuminated the political ambitions, aesthetic visions, and racial ironies of the volume as a whole. In 1963, LeRoi Jones had published his landmark book-length interpretation of black life in America, *Blues People*.[33] In 1966, he published the essay "The Changing Same: R & B and the New Black Music." Consistent with many of his arguments in *Blues People*, the essay provided a more concise theory of black music. In doing so, Baraka both located contemporary black music in relation to its cultural antecedents and interpreted black music in the climate of the revolutionary 1960s. In connecting the past and the present, he posited a spiritual core as the essence (i.e., "the changing same") of a black musical tradition.

In *Blues People*, LeRoi Jones narrated a history of black people in the United States—from Africa through the Middle Passage and slavery up through freedom—organized around their music(s). In "The Changing Same," Jones (soon to become Baraka) theorized an essence of black music that was pliable enough to include, in the present moment, popular rhythm and blues, soul music, and avant-garde jazz. He referred to the last genre as the "New Black Music" and included as its practitioners musicians such as John Coltrane, Archie Shepp, and Sun-Ra.[34] His central claim was that the blues best embodied black experience. "The Blues, its 'kinds' and diversity, its identifying parent styles," he explained, created a continuum that included a wide range of black music as well as certain "European" appropriations. The blues, for Baraka, constituted a "central body of cultural experience" across time and space.[35]

Baraka further posited that the range of innovations in black music, literature, and the arts during the 1960s were variations of the blues. Moreover, the blues was both the musical equivalent of and a model for the Black Arts. Much in the same way that Baraka appealed to African religions as a sign of blackness, he and many other artists of the era understood black music to be a primary "site of authentic artistic 'blackness.'"[36] Where some cast the blues as a secular (and profane) tradition running parallel to the (sacred) spirituals, for Baraka both were religious, inseparable, and of a kind. That is, religion was the essential ingredient in both the roots of the blues and the routes this tradition continued to travel.[37]

All black music began with "the worship of spirit," making the blues an inherently spiritual form. Concerning the origins of the blues, Baraka explained: "Indeed, to go back in any historical (or emotional) line of ascent in Black music leads us inevitably to religion, i.e., spirit worship. This phenomenon is always at the root in Black art—the worship of spirit—or at least the summoning of or by such force."[38] Beginning with an originating moment of "spirit worship," he traced two entangled narratives of decline across all black music. A set of processes, which he described as "gradual erosion," had begun with the Middle Passage. Black communities in the United States were engaged in an ongoing struggle against the forces of Americanization, and, closely related, Western society was experiencing the effects of a larger historical arc toward secularization. While distinguishing between these two forces, Baraka wove both processes together into a single religious history but did not go so far as to argue that black people were immune to secularizing forces and the West's "loss of religiosity." Instead, Baraka offered a rather nuanced interpretation of the role of religion (and secularism) in American history.[39]

Recalling, yet again, Richard Wright's "Blueprint for Negro Writing," Baraka suggested that for black people, secularization and Americanization were inextricably tied.[40] In this narrative, Christianity and American culture shared a family resemblance in that they were both of the West.

Christianity had forcibly replaced "Black pre-American religious forms" under the coercive terms of chattel slavery. This spiritual transformation, the result of conquest and colonization, facilitated the development of a syncretic Christianity in North America, but only en route to secularity. In this way, Afro-Protestantism (although that was not the terminology he used), the spiritual sign of New World identity, provided Baraka with the earliest historical referent in a philosophy of black culture.

A historical teleology—from African origins through the bowels of black Christian churches and beyond—organized Baraka's interpretation of the significance of religion to contemporary black music. He explained further: "Black Music is African in origin. African-American in its total-ity, and its various forms (especially the vocal) show just how African impulses were redistributed in its expression, and the expression itself became Christianized and post-Christianized."[41] As Americanization and secularization came together in the 1960s, Baraka asserted that the "church continues, but not the devotion."[42] In his view, black popular music (i.e., R&B and soul) and the "New Black Music" (i.e., avant-garde jazz) were tributaries from a common source. Both, he reasoned, bore wit-ness to a shared religious beginning and remained religious at their core.[43]

To further explain cultural developments during the 1960s, Amiri Baraka deployed the familiar adage that all black musicians had their beginnings in "the church." If, Baraka described secularization as a story of decline, now it became a tale at once tragic and triumphant of the commercial music marketplace. Black music, in its secular perfor-mances, maintained a "churchified" sound. In crossing over from sacred to secular, music was emptied of its Christian theological content even as it retained its emotional and spiritual core. James Brown, for Baraka, was the embodiment of this tradition, an exemplar of "the most deeply religious people on the continent." Motivated by materialism, Brown left God and the church behind to "slide into the slicker scene, where the dough was."[44] Even still, his music remained faithful to the "spirit" of its original sacred form.

The possibility of financial profits drew "R&B people" like James Brown out of churches, Baraka contended. In contrast, he claimed that a more explicitly religious concern guided the aspirations of the avant-garde. What animated the ambitions of black music at the time was "the rise to spirit . . . expanding the consciousness," something that sometimes even bordered on mysticism.[45] Whereas R&B musicians sang often of unre-quited love, New Black musicians sought freedom in musical form. Their hearts had been broken, Baraka suggested, by a nation-state that aligned itself with white supremacy. They sang and played out of pain caused by the continued social and political exclusion of black people in the United States. For these artists, "to play strong would be the cry and the worshipful purpose of life ... a way into God. The absolute open expression of everything."[46]

According to Baraka, musicians such as John Coltrane, Albert Ayler, and Pharoah Sanders possessed the power to transform tools of classical Western music, such as the saxophone, into "howling spirit summoners." They were comparable to the ministers of music in a "Sanctified or Holy Roller church (the blacker churches)."[47] These musicians rejected the doctrinal orthodoxies of institutional Afro-Protestantism (i.e., theological content), yet they remained true to the performative qualities of black churches, which provided the formal qualities of blackness in his theory. Drawing clear lines between content and form, Amiri Baraka privileged the latter (spiritual/black forms) over the former (Christian/white content). In doing so, he highlighted the contributions that black people made both to American Christianity and jazz music. Moreover, in making this distinction he identified in black music a unique religious tradition that neither began nor ended with Western Christianity or the United States.

The logic of Amiri Baraka's religious and racial schema also involved a critique of the American cultural marketplace, which made black music both lucrative and popular. Baraka presented the efforts of white artists and music companies to appropriate and profit from black (necessarily sacred) music as acts of bad faith. The mainstream popularity of gospel music, in his view, was fueled by people so focused on financial gain that they were willing "to make them bux off another people's *ultimate concern*." Ironically, Baraka mobilized the liberal Protestant (read white) language of the German theologian Paul Tillich to present his racial critique and affirm black religion. Tillich's definition of religion as "ultimate concern" had gained popular currency in a Supreme Court hearing on religious freedom just one year before Baraka's essay was published.[48]

Amiri Baraka's notion of the "changing same" provided a theoretical framing expansive enough to identify an artistic tradition that was apparent in the music of both James Brown and John Coltrane, two of the most popular black musicians in their respective genres during the 1960s. Along this continuum Baraka maintained a racial logic wherein black artists were continually wrestling with the threat of having their blackness watered down by the influence of the West, a result of the forces of capitalism and Christianity. Consistent with the Black Arts more generally, blackness again figured as radical opposition to all things "white."

Cultural expressions that were perceived to maintain the closest connection to Africa were celebrated above all.

The musical paths Baraka outlined—grounded in U.S. ghettos, black churches, and Africa and evolving out into the market—played a pivotal role for black artists and intellectuals who sought to delineate a racial aesthetic during the 1960s.[49] Moreover, the move to disentangle the form(s) of blackness from the content of Christian theology was mirrored throughout the contributions to Gayle's *The Black Aesthetic*. A number of writers included in the collection both described and prescribed an aesthetic vision in which black religious practices figured prominently. While the Black Arts intended to conjure a new spirituality, its content and form remained definitively shaped by the aesthetics of Christian faith.

Yet while this new spirituality rested on that traditional, "old-time" Afro-Protestant foundation, Black Arts theorists significantly broadened its base. James Stewart's lead essay in *Black Fire*, "The Development of the Black Revolutionary Artist," punctuated this point powerfully.[50] Stewart, a musician, painter, and writer from Philadelphia, clarified that the Black Arts were fundamentally concerned with constructing a "Cosmology" that "correspond[s] to the realities of black existence."[51] Perhaps unsurprisingly, Africa proved crucial for Stewart's aesthetic vision, but so did ancient India and Japan. Each of these civilizations, in his account, understood that art, culture, and knowledge were necessarily unfixed, improvisational, and enmeshed in their natural environments. Each of these societies maintained an entirely different system of valuation from that of the Western art world. "Art is change, like music, poetry and writing are, when conceived. They must move (swing)," Stewart explained.[52] Stewart called for "a methodology affirmed by the spirit," and shifted from prose to verse:

> That spirit is black.
> That spirit is non-white.
> That spirit is patois.
> That spirit is Samba.
> Voodoo.
> The black Baptist church in the South.[53]

Stewart's litany revealed much, even though he never quite explained the specifics of his spiritual method. His methodology is perhaps best understood as an anti-method. Stewart's appeal to the spirit entailed a refusal of fixed forms, an embrace of improvisation, and the ability to respond creatively to the demands of any historical moment. In this view, the revolutionary black artist was like a jazz musician, seeking and finding freedom in formal experimentation.

Stewart's litany did, however, provide readers with a series of exemplary clues. First, he identified spirit as both black and nonwhite, suggesting an oppositional race politics. Next, he outlined a trio of syncretic forms: patois, Samba, and Voodoo, respectively. All three of these examples were drawn geographically from the Caribbean, reflecting hybrid practices that emerged out of the asymmetrical encounters facilitated by colonial contact. Each also appeared to build sequentially in intensity from language to dance to worship. Stewart then juxtaposed the spiritual traditions of Haiti with those of the American South—"Voodoo. The black Baptist church in the South."—before returning from verse to prose. In one swoop he reimagined the normative distinction that held between Christianity and Voodoo (the Caribbean equivalent of Hoodoo), all while affirming the official religion of the first independent black nation—Haiti—in the Western Hemisphere. Afro-Protestantism and the Black Arts, Stewart suggested, were indeed of a kind.

James Stewart's larger argument followed the logic that Baraka had effectively established in the anthology's foreword. Religious difference mattered little as long as the different religions being invoked were made to serve the spiritual authority of a revolutionary blackness. What united these diverse manifestations of "spirit" was their common marginality in relationship to the American mainstream and their perceived proximity to Africa. As Stewart explained, black artists were bound together by the fact that they were all equally "historically and sociologically . . . rejected." As such, they were to be held accountable by the shared standard of "revolutionary art."[54] While "the white West . . . denies change, defies change . . . resists change," the responsibility of the black revolutionary artist was to "emancipate our [black people's] minds from Western values and standards."[55] "The task of the Negro writer is revolutionary by definition," he noted. While Stewart valorized an open aesthetic of improvisation, fluidity, and change, this statement was the closest he came to defining his "methodology of spirit."[56] Fortunately, the task of putting flesh on the bones of this spiritual method was taken up more directly by others during the decade.

In addition to his duties as co-editor of *Black Fire*, Larry Neal was one of the foremost theoreticians of the Black Arts. He was also one of a very few writers to author more than one selection in Addison Gayle's anthology.[57] Arguably more than any other artist of the period, Neal offered the most sustained effort to theorize the significance of religion (and the church, in particular) for racial aesthetics during the 1960s. Indeed, he both called for a new spirituality and identified revolutionary developments within black churches. It was Neal who identified the Black Arts as Black Power's "spiritual sister" in his signal essay on the movement, which was also included in *The Black Aesthetic*. Additionally, he contributed "Some Reflections on the Black Aesthetic," which was precisely what the title suggested.

Together these two works provided a fuller glimpse of Larry Neal's sense of the religious significance of the Black Arts. In the first essay he called for the development of a "separate symbolism, mythology, critique, and iconology."[58] The second was more of an outline draft than a fully developed essay. Here Neal sketched out a series of "categories and elements"—perhaps in response to his own call or as a preliminary step toward constructing the cosmology that James Stewart had invited.[59] Organized in the form of a chart, Neal's categories established a historical continuum in which religion remained a fixture. In addition to its "radical opposition" to whiteness, his vision for "the Black Aesthetic" was based on an appeal to Africa as the spiritual source.

References to Spirit worship, Orishas, ancestors, African Gods, the Holy Ghost, Jesus, Shamans, and Preachers were held up alongside blues singers, musicians, mackdaddies (recalling his celebration of Shine in the afterword to *Black Fire*), and politicians. Neal's pairings exemplified the Black Arts practice of partnering sacred and profane in service to an oppositional aesthetic and based on an idea of Africa where such divisions did not hold.[60] In both respects, Neal echoed and expanded upon Stewart's call for a spiritual method and Baraka's theory of "the changing same." At the end of the journey from Africa through the Middle Passage and into an American synthesis, Neal envisioned a "Blues God" who was prone to "mixing up the blues with hymns" and confounded traditional divisions between good and evil.

Like Baraka, Larry Neal's "Blues God" privileged the forms of the black church over its content; cadence and rhythm were more important than doctrine or theology.[61] He was much "more concerned with the vibrations of the Word, than with the Word itself."[62] Neal reflected further on the relationship between Africa, Afro-Protestantism, and the Blues God:

> The Black Church ... represents and embodies the transplanted African memory. The Black Church is the keeper ... the spiritual banks of our most forgotten visions of the Homeland. The Black Church was the institutionalized form that Black people used to protect themselves from the spiritual and psychological brutality of the slavemaster. ... The blues are the spiritual and ritual energy of the church thrust into the eyes of life's raw realities ... extensions

of the deepest, most pragmatic spiritual and moral realities. Even though they primarily deal with the world as flesh, *they are essentially religious.*[63]

That Neal's provisional theory failed to draw fixed boundaries around black churches and the raw "spiritual and ritual energy" he observed on display in black life was very much in keeping with the moment. As with the blues, the church was a conduit of the African past and a cultural resource for the black present, and both were "essentially religious" and equally indicative of a larger spiritual vision for the Black Arts.

In this way, Neal's formulation was strikingly similar to the relationship George Edmund Haynes had posited between "The Church and the Negro Spirit" (1925), albeit updated and amplified by the politics of Black Power.[64] As discussed in chapter 1, in the 1920s Haynes imagined the "Negro Spirit" in the form of the respectable race man as New Negro clergy. Haynes's racial spirit was imbued with an uplift ethic, institutionalized within the church, and directed toward inclusion within American democracy. Now, in the 1960s, Neal's Blues God was more akin to a jazzman styled after (yet set up to replace) the Negro preacher. Although the congregation was now an emerging black nation, this new spirituality still took aesthetic cues from the church. After all, it was through the "Black Church," Neal suggested, that an "African memory" had been maintained. Here, in a reversal of sorts, Larry Neal valorized the blues—a musical form typically cast as secular, if not profane—as "essentially religious." The spiritual energy associated with the Black Arts was defined both by its African origins and its opposition to the West. At least in Neal's telling, black churches best exemplified the persistence of this spirit on American soil, and its presiding preacher class—à la Richard Wright's "Blueprint"— provided the model for a new cast who were taking stage to conjure the Black Arts.

GENDER TROUBLES AND THE NEW SPIRITUALITY OF THE BLACK ARTS

For all their revolutionary rhetoric, both *The Black Aesthetic* and *Black Fire* remained staunchly traditional in at least one key way. *The Black Aesthetic* consisted of thirty-three essays by some thirty authors, but only two selections were written by women. The proportion of women contributors in *Black Fire* was not much better.[65] If Black Power arts and politics appeared to amplify the racial ambitions of the freedom struggle with its nationalist sensibility, it also magnified the long-standing assumption that securing black freedom would be achieved as an enactment of man-hood.[66] Indeed, an epigraph borrowed from the poet Margaret Walker was made to authorize this gendered order in the front matter to *The Black Aesthetic*. The Black Arts, in Walker's words, was a call to, "Let the martial songs be written, let the dirges disappear. Let a race of men now rise and take control."[67]

The spiritual subjectivity and social life announced in the Black Arts assumed and often explicitly privileged a male and masculinist organiz-ing logic. This became especially clear in the appeals of Black Arts men to Islam and Christianity, which were often taken to authorize this gen-der order as natural or necessary. In their representative ambitions, both *Black Fire* and *The Black Aesthetic* revealed how the Black Arts instanti-ated a particular alignment of gender, race, and religion. Ironically, and emblematic of the problem, this configuration took shape even as Larry Neal announced that the Black Arts movement was the "spiritual sister" of Black Power.[68]

That Black Arts men could be radical on all things racial and often uncrit-ically conventional in support of a heteronormative hyper-masculinity has been well documented.[69] In the age of Black Power politics, Larry Neal argued that the arts should serve the purpose of "spiritual integration."[70] However, the Black Arts involved "an evocation of spirit" that simultane-ously obscured and reinforced gender asymmetries. To be sure, the reli-gious performances of Neal and other Black Arts men both invited and received a gender critique. Black Arts women by no means let this spiritu-alized masculinity go unquestioned.[71] Black women were by all accounts active in the ranks of Black Power art and politics, and religion provided an important pivot around which they were able to assent to and dissent from a dominant gender discourse.[72] To this end, Toni Cade Bambara's volume *The Black Woman: An Anthology* (1970) revealed how a number of black women called attention to and complicated the gender dynamics on display in *Black Fire* and *The Black Aesthetic*.

By the very act of editing *The Black Woman*, Bambara, a writer, film-maker, and teacher, helped ensure that the contributions of Black Arts women would not be erased or overlooked. Importantly, as Farah Jasmine Griffin has observed, the book brought into conversation two discourses commonly considered to be at odds with one another—black nationalism and feminism.[73] At the same time, the anthology did not entirely overcome the gender troubles of the Black Arts movement. The very publication of *The Black Woman* made visible, and prominently so, the contributions of black women to both the aesthetics and politics of Black Power. While many of the selections attended to asymmetrical gender relations in black

culture, the volume also put on display the investment, albeit an ambivalent one, of many black women in the cult of black masculinity.

The Black Woman was not quite the constructive or systemic claim for
black feminism of the likes of the soon-to-be-written Combahee River
Collective Statement. Ultimately, the anthology complicated and crystallized the power of Black Arts masculinity even as it offered evidence
that a more explicit black feminism was in the making. *The Black Woman*
included offerings from such prominent artists as Nikki Giovanni,
Abbey Lincoln, and Audre Lorde, each of whom had prior track records
of engaging black spiritual traditions in their work.[74] Lorde also would
play a role in developing the Combahee River Collective Statement four
years later.

Where Larry Neal's afterword to *Black Fire* advocated a black integrity
styled after the male preacher (à la Malcolm X and Marcus Garvey), Toni
Cade Bambara called attention to the shortcomings of that model. Her
own essay in the volume, "On the Issue of Roles," took up the topic of religion both to illustrate the problem and propose some provisional alternatives. In doing so, she appealed to Africa only to assert that Christianity
was to blame for the gender crisis of the West (including black people).
Bambara wrote:

> I am convinced, at least in my reading of African societies, that prior . . . to the
> introduction of Christianity, a religion fraught with male anxiety and vilifica-
> tion of women, communities were more egalitarian and cooperative. . . . There
> were no hard and fixed assignments based on gender, no rigid and hysterical
> separation based on sexual taboo.[75]

Bambara's argument was in keeping with a romanticized reading of pre-
colonial African societies that was popular at the time: that the continent
had fallen from an Eden-like state at the precise moment when European
colonizers and missionaries reached it with the Christian gospel. The gender problem of the Black Arts was just part of the collateral damage.

Bambara argued that black communities in the United States remained
deeply shaped by the colonial legacies of Christianity. Black Arts masculinity was, in this view, an effort to overcome the original trauma of colonization. Even still, it was not to be left unquestioned. She encouraged
readers to "submerge all breezy definitions of manhood/womanhood . . .
until realistic definitions emerge through a commitment to Blackhood."[76]
Although the "metalanguage of race" at times served the interests of
male privilege, here Bambara advocated abandoning gender talk in favor
of a shared blackness.[77] In the face of limited options, the appearance of

gender neutrality was to be preferred over distorted definitions of man-hood or womanhood.

In some respects, Cade Bambara's concern with a generalized "Blackhood" rather than a specifically feminist program echoed an essay in *The Black Aesthetic* that had proposed "spiritual oneness" as a strategy for confronting racial oppression. Carolyn Gerald's essay was tellingly titled, "The Black Writer and His Role." In it, the Philadelphia-based writer staged a spiritual confrontation in the arts that assumed a masculine sub-ject. Gerald explored the idea of "image-making" as emblematic of human efforts to construct a self and society. The images writers and artists created reflected their self-perception and their view of the world. Most importantly, she argued, "the image we have of ourselves controls what we are capable of doing."[78]

For Carolyn Gerald, image making was a high-stakes contest that was fundamentally concerned with spiritual matters. She explained further:

> For the black writer, the only possibility for spiritual oneness has been non-race or religious literature. But non-race or religious literature takes on insidi-ously the image projected by what is called the larger culture, and so takes on a white image. Black writers have attempted to reflect spiritual oneness by writing within a totally black framework. But white images are implanted at the core of black life, the most obvious example being that of the Church, where God is white.[79]

In her estimation, the Black Arts were necessarily spiritual. "Spiritual oneness" would be accomplished by working within a "totally black frame-work" as a counter to a religious literature that was, by default, white. Interestingly, Gerald neglected to address the degree to which American gender norms were also encoded in Christian imagery. In doing so, she left unchecked an ethos in which a male subject was presumed as constitutive of "the core of black life." Instead, Gerald directed black writers to imagine a generalized "spiritual oneness" even as her languages assumed a male identity for the artist.

Like many of the contributors to *The Black Aesthetic*, Carolyn Gerald identified religion—specifically, Christianity—as a primary terrain on which racial images and myths were constructed and contested, identi-ties and communities were formed, and possibilities were determined. Religion was the means through which racial difference was marked in ways that both constrained and inspired black life. Gerald's argument recalled Richard Wright's "Blueprint"—an essay frequently alluded to, directly and indirectly, in both *Black Fire* and *The Black Aesthetic*. As Wright had, she insisted, "The artist then, is the guardian of image; the writer is the myth-maker of his people."[80] At the end of her essay, Gerald began to model her imagistic method, breaking old myths and creating new ones as she moved from prose to poetry.

This genre-blending performance was part of a broader effort in the Black Arts to blur the boundaries between literary forms, to write orality and aurality into the literary, and to perform the black aesthetic that was being theorized.[81] Here Gerald also appeared to at least ambivalently account for gender, as the subject of her stanzas was figured as female:

> Make it hot. . .
>> Make it hate.
> Clap and stomp round the fire
>> And shout the spirit out of her.
>>> And draw your circle close
>>>> For we'll kill us a devil tonight.
> Come on away, now!
>> Now!
>>> We'll find our own saint
>>>> (or another name for her)
> No need for hell's fire now
> The fire's weak
>> And burned out
>>> The universe is black again.[82]

In short verse, Gerald imagined a fiery scene in which the muse of Greek mythology was exorcised of white "spirit," murdered or martyred, or maybe just renamed. A woman (or a group of women) stood at the center of the action, but only as a transitory figure. Devils are destroyed, new saints are sought after, and the universe is returned to its primordial blackness—the condition and color of "spiritual oneness." Gerald's own literary transition from prose to poetry brought her essay to its close as she conjured a new black world into being through verse.

Carolyn Gerald's essay illustrated how religion figured as a site of struggle over the question of race for a number of other black women writers at the time. Better yet, racial aesthetics constituted a site of religious contestation. However, Gerald mostly ignored gender as a distinct issue that mediated both religious and racial imagery. Similarly, the other essay by a woman writer in *The Black Aesthetic* did very little to trouble the gender norms presumed and performed in the Black Arts. Whereas Gerald theorized the power (and pairing) of religious and racial

imagery, Sarah Webster Fabio relayed a religious history that acknowledged gender, or the role of women, only by inference or association.

If Gerald's poetry aimed to conjure a black universe, then Fabio's
"Tripping with Black Writing" unveiled a "hoodoo" history of the Black
Arts. A poet and critic, Fabio taught black studies at Oakland's Merritt
College during the mid-1960s and was part of the Bay Area's Black Arts
scene. Her essay referenced jazz music (Duke Ellington's "A Train") to
put a modern spin on the black freedom struggle while also recalling the
iconic Underground Railroad. During the 1970s, according to Fabio, black
writers would "Take the A-Train to Black liberation."[83] Her brief essay
also paired Black Power politics with the aesthetics of black religion—
specifically Sanctified worship (i.e., stomping and speaking in tongues) and
conjure, specifically. In this regard, Fabio participated in a longer literary
history of Hoodoo that included Zora Neale Hurston, Charles Chesnutt,
and others. This conjuring tradition was being powerfully performed and
theorized in the present by another writer, Ishmael Reed, who also made
the Bay Area his home around this time.[84]

Indeed, Sarah Webster Fabio was very much in step with the times;
Larry Neal, Ishmael Reed, and others invoked a pluralistic pantheon
of black gods, conjurers, and spirits during the 1960s. For the Black
Arts, a continuum of spiritual entities—from the ecstatic forms of
Afro-Protestantism to Hoodoo, Islam, and a host of African spirits—
served to authenticate and authorize an oppositional order. The Black
Arts' bottom line was that, in short, as James Stewart put it, "That
spirit is black."[85] Unfortunately, such spiritual invocations often autho-
rized a kind of blackness that obscured, ignored, or reinscribed gender
imbalances.

In *The Black Woman*, several selections did undertake a line of questioning that placed increased scrutiny on the ways appeals to religion
were made to endorse a male-centered vision of power in the Black
Arts. For instance, expanding upon a familiar theme in her essay
"Black Romanticism," Joyce Green advanced a postcolonial appraisal
of Christianity not unlike that of James Baldwin in *The Fire Next Time*.
Green acknowledged the plausibility of theories of secularization that
had gained traction in the United States during the 1960s. She also noted
that owing to its role in sustaining white supremacy, Christianity's normative authority was increasingly being recognized as illegitimate. If
America was actually becoming secular, it was at least partly due to the
racial failings of white Christians.

Causal connections aside, Green surmised that these developments
communicated a single message: "He Who Never Prays Has the Power."

Atheism was now equated with authority, and this presented black people with a problem. Because "the Black man is innately spiritual, with religion rooted in his life style," Joyce Green explained, "it becomes a constant task to renounce it."[86] The goal of social inclusion demanded that black people disavow their "true" spiritual selves. To pass as secular, for that matter, was the exact antithesis of the religious vision prescribed by the Black Arts. At the same time, via an engagement with Eldridge Cleaver's *Soul on Ice*, Green averred that in the United States freedom and full citizenship were both equated with access to white women. Black men were thus torn between the spiritual values of their communities and the seductive belief that white women were the symbol of American social life. At first glance, it appeared that Green, too, was overly invested in a spiritualized black masculinity that kept concerns specific to black women secondary.

In Joyce Green's peculiar equation, W. E. B. Du Bois's notion of "double-consciousness," wherein black people were torn between being "Negro and . . . American," was revised (or intensified) by her attention to gender.[87] The precarious nature of black men's social position—which was exacerbated by irreconcilable interracial sexual desires—only made matters worse for black women, who found themselves silenced by the fear that in speaking out, they might "emasculate the black man."[88] According to Green, this quandary of race and gender—here always already entangled—was, in fact, a modern extension of an older religious idea. American freedom, as embodied in white women, made contemporary the venerated myth of the Virgin Mary.

Green read black male sexual desire as indicative of a spiritual predicament. The well-being of the black woman—"first as a person, secondly as a Black woman"—was contingent upon black men freeing themselves from a "Black/White myth" that seamlessly wed religion, race, and male sexual desire. It was the burden of black men to resist the allure of white women, which amounted, for Green, to the call of Mary, the mother of God. Only then would they be able to also "create a new system of values . . . a new aesthetic, based on their blackness."[89] Christian myths and symbols, as much as colonial asymmetries, were to blame for the masculinist politics of the Black Arts. Black women, Joyce Green seemed to confirm, largely remained an afterthought, their concerns made marginal to those of black men.

Toni Cade Bambara, as suggested earlier, affirmed Joyce Green's assessment. Black gender anxieties were overdetermined by a "Black/White myth" that presumed male privilege. In "On the Issue of Roles," Bambara eventually clarified her call to prioritize a general "Blackhood" over manhood and womanhood. New myths, made for all black people, might help resolve gender divisions. Yet myths engendered problems as well as possibilities, she suggested. Where Green critiqued Christian mythology and Bambara called for new myths, Ann Cook suggested that new myths might not be enough.

In her essay, "Black Pride? Some Contradictions," Cook interrogated Islam's growing appeal as part of the popular Afrocentric discourse emerging alongside Black Power. An educator and linguist who had traveled extensively in Africa, Cook challenged Afrocentricity's selective investment in the continent. She also questioned the motivations behind black Americans' attraction to Islam: "My question is, why really do we embrace Islam? As a reaction to Christianity? Because of the religious tenets? . . . Because it can unify Africans?" Cook balked at this last idea especially, before she offered her own provisional answer. "I wonder if in addition to our choosing Islam as a rejection of Christianity and for its tenets, we are not also accepting it because of its legitimacy."[90] Here Cook brought into focus the biases inherent in the idealized and customized view of both Africa and Islam many black artists and activists had at the time. Such appeals were extremely selective, Cook noted. They privileged the continent's literate societies and ignored Africa's expansive oral traditions. Despite what Black Arts activists intended by affiliating with Islam, they actually reinforced European ideals and colonial authority.

Ann Cook speculated that the attraction to African Islamic societies was attributable to their association with literacy, rather than something particular to Islam as a religion. This prioritization of the literary, for Cook, exposed an inferiority complex among African Americans, who still sought recognition as equals in the West, where literacy (as evidence of reason) was the rule.[91] In no small dose of irony, she observed that Black Power art and politics had adopted the West's normative definition of religion even when claiming to privilege African perspectives in opposition to Europe. Cook called such reasoning into question and proposed something different for the Black Arts. She invited a closer engagement with the "traditional African religions" of "'pagan' Africa," from where, she also noted, the ancestors of most black Americans had been taken.[92]

If the aesthetics of Black Power were to prove fruitful in orienting black lives in the New World, Cook suggested, they might require a more accurate retracing of the routes of the slave trade. A more faithful account of geography and history could lead practitioners of the Black Arts to the true spiritual source. West African religious worlds—paganisms, according to Enlightenment reason—might actually better facilitate a truly black aesthetic to oppose the West. In this way, Ann Cook both called attention to the contradictions apparent in "black pride" and shed light on the larger racial logics embedded in the moral and religious geographies of modernity.

As perceptive as it was, Ann Cook's analysis left gender relatively unquestioned. Yet her own social position as a black woman clearly contributed to her skepticism toward any romantic appeal Islam may have offered men in Black Power art and politics. Cook's impulse to question the religious veneration of a mythological Africa was indicative of an implicit gender critique if not a forthright feminist analysis. As noted in chapter 5, the attraction to an idea of Islam or the imagining of a particular kind of Africa were significant because they imbued claims of racial authenticity with spiritual authority. However, as Cook's critique revealed, these religious visions also underwrote a specific gender order.

Indeed, one of the Black Arts' leading priests, Amiri Baraka, eventually admitted as much. Writing in 1984, Baraka conceded that African religions were often embraced as "the essence of Blackness." He then observed:

> It is not unimportant that all of these groups had distinct and ultimately oppressive roles for women. Particularly their adherents. Whether the veils and segregation of Islam or the polygamy of their tradition and the common practice of Yoruba.[93]

Africa was significant as a marker of both raced and gendered difference. Although Ann Cook's claim that enslaved Africans and their descendants had stronger historical ties to traditional African religions, such as Yoruba, than they did to Islam may have been sound, in some ways her argument missed the point. The differences between these respective religious traditions were often blurred or insignificant in the quest for true blackness, as Baraka observed. How Africa (or Islam) was imagined was less a question about historical or geographic accuracy than it was about identifying (or creating) cultural resources for contending with an American context in which citizenship had long been understood as synonymous with both whiteness and manhood. The difference between imagining Africa as matrilineal utopia or patriarchal pathology was, at least in part, to be found in the United States' own long-standing investment in (black) masculinity.

In bringing together a wide range of voices in a single volume, Toni Cade Bambara's editorial debut made a singular intervention. *The Black Woman* directed focused attention to the perspectives of black women, which were all too often undervalued in Black Power art and politics. In this way, the volume was not entirely out of step with the attachment—albeit an ambivalent one—to black masculinity that provided the normative gender politics of the Black Arts. At the same time, Bambara's anthology largely affirmed the means (i.e., images, myths, symbols) and substance of the revolution, social and spiritual, called for by Black Arts men. In advocating a turn inward, Bambara had much in common with the editors of both *Black Fire* and *The Black Aesthetic*. "Revolution begins with the self, in the self," she insisted. "The individual, the basic revolutionary unit, must be purged of poison and lies that assault the ego and threaten the heart."[94] The kind of inward work called for in the Black Arts movement was a new spirituality that sought to address the intramural dynamics of black life on its own terms.

Yet Bambara's heightened interest in myth making found unexpected source material in a controversial figure from the recent past: Father Divine. Bambara reminded her readers about this charismatic, albeit unorthodox, religious leader who claimed an audience—all the while claiming that he was God—during the same moment that a Negro Renaissance was in bloom. Recalling the massive following he acquired, she speculated: "When Father Divine launched his program, the Peace Mission Movement, the first thing he insisted upon from the novitiate was a shifting from male-hood and female-hood to Angelhood. If the program owed its success to anything, it owed it to this kind of shift in priorities."[95] Father Divine was distinguished, among other things, by his theology of racial transcendence and the Peace Mission movement's interracial composition. Given the nationalist politics of the 1960s, highlighting Divine—who refused to use the word "Negro" and called for the end of racial classifications[96]— was a surprising move, to say the least. Harlem's "God" preached nothing that resembled the brand of black consciousness proclaimed by the likes of the Muslim minister Malcolm X or Albert Cleage, C. L. Franklin, and the scores of other clergy who took on the topic of Black Power during the 1960s.[97]

Father Divine was certainly different from most of the models of spiritual integrity (i.e., Marcus Garvey, Malcolm X) celebrated during the 1960s. It must have been odd for readers to find Father Divine on the pages of *The Black Woman* in 1970, the same year that Toni Cade took the additional name Bambara as an homage to her African heritage.[98] He was not, by any measure, the kind of racial messiah typically conjured by the Black Arts. Yet it was there, in her essay "On the Issue of Roles," that Bambara invoked the positive-thinking preacher as a potential resource for her pioneering black feminist writers and readers.

This unexpected connection may have been made possible because Bambara had access to local knowledge of Divine's legacy. As a native of Harlem, she had grown up in proximity to remnants of the Peace Mission business empire. She fondly recalled trips with her father and brother to the Peace Barber Shop, which remained in Harlem long after "God" had left the neighborhood.[99] Fond familial memories aside, Toni Cade Bambara and Father Divine were still a strange spiritual and political pairing. Yet Bambara drew upon Divine's ministry in a way that was consistent with the larger themes of her anthology. She appealed to Divine to make a case for the equality of the black woman. In the face of Black Power's masculinist performance, his notion of a gender-neutral "Angelhood" might help heal rifts between black women and men or at least temporarily hold them at bay.

In this way, the Peace Mission movement represented an intriguing alternative to the gender binaries apparent in African pasts, the American present, and, of course, Black Arts mythology. Divine's turn to a gender-neutral nomenclature to reconstitute community offered an intriguing counter to "hard and fixed gender assignments," Bambara suggested.[100] Such a shift would be a welcome improvement over the gender troubles that resulted from Western Christianity and the colonial encounter and those that continued to frustrate black social life. Toni Cade Bambara encouraged the construction of new myths and the cultivation of a revolution within the self as important methods for dismantling both racism and sexism. In the midst of a "by any means necessary" moment like that of the late 1960s, the allegedly unmarked idea of "Angelhood" made even the unlikely figure of Father Divine a potentially fecund spiritual resource for the Black Arts.

Ultimately, a preoccupation with the power of religious and racial myths was evident across all three of these seminal anthologies. All three volumes both reflected and articulated the aspirations of the Black Arts. *Black Fire, The Black Aesthetic,* and *The Black Woman* called attention to the different ways that American mythologies constrained black life, and the editors and authors conjured new myths that affirmed the religious ethos of the "Age of Blackness." Yet this heightened interest in myth and in enlisting black writers as myth-makers for "the people," was not entirely new in the 1960s. Richard Wright, so often cited by theorists of the black aesthetic, had argued in 1937 that writers should "create the myths and symbols that inspire a faith in life."[101] And more than a decade before Wright, at the dawn of the Harlem Renaissance, Alain Locke had observed that a "New Negro" was replacing the "Old Negro," who even in the 1920s was stilled viewed as "more of a myth than a man."[102] Indeed, the acts of creating and destroying myths had long been central to the history of racial aesthetics.

The Black Arts extended, renewed, and amplified this religious history. However, not all black writers in the late 1960s agreed with the strategy of resurrecting Richard Wright's agenda of making black writers into myth-makers or with the position that literature and art were to be utilized as political tools for black liberation. Indeed, even in the midst of a moment when nationalist politics provided the norm for racial aesthetics, several writers—both familiar faces and fresh voices—challenged the orthodoxies of the Black Arts. These contrarians challenged both facile notions of racial identity and Christianity's complicated legacy in black life and American history.

CHAPTER 7

✧

Contrary Spirits

American culture, even in its most segregated precincts, is patently and irrevocably composite. It is, regardless of all the hysterical protestations of those who would have it otherwise, incontestably mulatto. Indeed, for all their traditional antagonisms and obvious differences, the so-called black and so-called white people of the United States resemble nobody else in the world so much as they resemble each other.

Albert Murray

By the time Toni Cade Bambara invoked Father Divine's angelic vision in *The Black Woman*, the history of racial aesthetics had come a long way. During the Harlem Renaissance, Alain Locke had announced the prophetic race spirit of the New Negro and denounced Claude McKay as a spiritual truant. Not long after W. E. B. Du Bois valorized the Negro's singular gifts of art and spirit, Wallace Thurman issued a denial in his fiction that any "African spirit" could place demands on Negro writers. In the early 1940s, the editorial vision of Sterling Brown, Ulysses Lee, and Arthur Davis in *The Negro Caravan* evidenced a catholicity of spirit that was affirmed by the book's reviewers. Later that decade the poet Margaret Walker diagnosed the "spiritual problems" that defined a new generation of Negro poets. Not too long after that, Ralph Ellison observed in Mahalia Jackson the power of a "spiritual reality" that was rich with aesthetic possibilities. To be sure, much had changed in the years since 1927, when the Catholic drama critic Theophilus Lewis described the Negro theater as a "spiritual institution." By 1968, when Larry Neal called for a "theater of the spirit" to stage the Black Arts, the substance of that spirit was anything but a single story. In particular, the spiritual grammar that animated racial aesthetics had been reinvented countless times even as it was sustained across several decades.

Yet in many other ways, racial aesthetics remained loyal to their original spiritual form. Religious ambitions, albeit articulated in dramatically different registers, were no less apparent as the revolutionary 1960s came to a close than they were during the 1920s, when the New Negro was all the rage. There were still efforts to announce the black writer's triumph over traditional religion (i.e., the Negro Church), as was the case in Richard Wright's 1937 "Blueprint for Negro Writing." There were also ceaseless attempts—à la Amiri Baraka and Larry Neal—to disentangle the spiritual forms of blackness from the content of Christian theology. Racial aesthetics never suffered from any lack of proposed religious alternatives. From Zora Neale Hurston's Hoodoo to Robert Hayden's Baha'i faith, Toni Cade Bambara's appeal to the teachings of Father Divine, and Amiri Baraka's invocation of a "holy holy black man," racial aesthetics remained a special site of religious alterity across the years. And soon Ishmael Reed would hail the birth of a Neo-HooDoo church.

Yet for every Hurston, who claimed "the negro is not a Christian really," there was a George Haynes to argue that the church represented the best of "the negro spirit." Claude McKay's pagan spirit eventually made its way through the doors of the Catholic Church. Even Ralph Ellison—never one to toe the line of orthodoxy—conceded that in certain cases, one had to step into a black church to see the true spirit of the blues really move. Racial aesthetics continued to bear the peculiar markings—the constraints and possibilities—of American Christianity specifically. In the face of repeated allusions to a rising racial spirit and despite recurring declarations of religious decline, the Negro's church still seemed omnipresent. Although some artists and intellectuals had doggedly envisioned an end to the reign of black churches, Afro-Protestantism had not come undone. Indeed, when theorizing the new spirituality, Larry Neal clarified that, rather than the death of God, it was "the reconstruction of Christianity by the black man that interests us here."[1]

In revisiting and synthesizing the strands of a knotted debated that was, by the end of the 1960s, at least five decades old, this chapter engages four writers—Ishmael Reed, Alice Walker, Ralph Ellison, and Albert Murray—who varied greatly in their literary visions and political positions and in how the public received them. Yet each of these authors wrote in interesting ways against the orthodoxy of an oppositional art and culture that dominated the debate about racial aesthetics during the 1960s. Each of these authors challenged the idea of black culture as set apart from (or necessarily opposed to) the larger American cultural scene, and they complicated facile ideas that conflated art and politics, especially in the work of black writers. Finally, in their efforts to rethink relationships between race (i.e., blackness) and nation (i.e., America) and between literature and politics, Reed, Walker, Ellison, and Murray also invited a more compelling account of the entangled actualities of religion and aesthetics in American life.

ISHMAEL REED AND THE NEO-HOODOO CHURCH REVIVAL

Although Ishmael Reed positioned himself on the periphery of the Black Arts movement, the Chattanooga-born, Buffalo-raised poet, novelist, and critic traveled in the circles of a New York literary scene that produced many of the figures who came to define the Black Arts.[2] A parodist and provocateur par excellence, Reed announced his own artistic vision through a coded invocation of race. His Neo-HooDoo aesthetic clearly harked back to Zora Neale Hurston, but it also extended the long-standing African American conjuring tradition that was discussed in chapter 5. In this way, Reed's aesthetic arguably bested the Black Arts in terms of its radical alterity. Reed's Neo-HooDoo vision clarified, obscured, and conjured the period's spiritual sensibilities all at once.[3] In addition to a penchant for provocation (he engaged in an extended public disagreement with black feminists), he made a name for himself by challenging the canonical authority of Western art and literature on issues that ranged from its claims of universalism to its classificatory genres.[4] Ultimately, Reed offered an alternative view of America (and "the West") that included taking sharp aim at Anglo-Christianity in general and particular forms of Afro-Protestantism.

Ishmael Reed's "Neo-HooDoo Manifesto," first published in the *Los Angeles Free Press* in September 1969, enunciated a religious aesthetic that included subversive symbols, figures, and cultural forms.[5] The following year he published a series of poems that illustrated his aesthetic in a pamphlet titled *catechism of d neoamerican hoodoo church*. In 1972, he spelled out his vision further with his book *Conjure*, which compiled poems that he had written during the 1960s. Ostensibly an essay, "Neo-HooDoo Manifesto" defied the conventions of any single genre. It combined poetry and prose, theory and performance, satire and sober reportage. It also playfully troubled perceived divisions between sacred and secular and presented a profoundly entangled religious history. Although the history of racial aesthetics charted a genealogy of spirit that dated back to the 1920s, Reed offered a much longer chronology of the hoodoo church.

Ishmael Reed's form-confounding efforts were intentional. By shifting from prose to verse in "Neo-HooDoo Manifesto," he was, in effect, enacting the Neo-HooDoo Church's commitments to fluidity and freedom. Part Pentecostal revival, part performance poetry, part jam session, and all spirit conjuration, Reed's essay mirrored the strategies of a black sermon as it approached its climax:

> Neo-HooDoo is a litany seeking its text
>> Neo-HooDoo is a Dance and Music closing in on its words
>> Neo-HooDoo is a Church finding it lyrics . . .
>
> Neo HooDoo signs are everywhere . . .
>
> Almost 100 years ago HooDoo was forced to say
> Goodbye to America. Now HooDoo is
> back as Neo-HooDoo[6]

Similar to Amiri Baraka's "Changing Same" and Larry Neal's "Blues God," Reed narrated Neo-HooDoo as an explicitly religious story with African origins. In this regard, his manifesto was less a novelty than it was a revival of a primordial tradition. Ishmael Reed celebrated the renewal of the conjuring tradition that had been forced to hide in the darkened shadows of a de facto Christian nation.

This black religion was coming back above ground to shine in the bright light of a new day. Yet Neo-HooDoo was woven into the wider fabric of the vibrant counterculture movement of the 1960s, which was not exclusively black. From the "House of Candles and Talismans" on Manhattan's Lower East Side, to East Harlem's "botanical gardens" (i.e., Afro-Latino "botanicas"), and out west to "Min and Mom" on East Haight Street in San Francisco, Reed linked together an elaborate network of "underground centers" of spiritual authority (and alterity) across the United States and he named it Neo-HooDoo. By contrast, Christians—better known as "Jehovah revisionists"—represented the history of Western colonialism, from the conquest of Africa and the Americas to militaristic imperialism in Vietnam during the 1960s.

Christianity had provided the constitutive spirit that animated the ascendance of European colonial power, the emergence of American empire, and the rise of the United States as a superpower during the Cold War. In effect, Ishmael Reed remapped the normative orders of the

West and repositioned Eastern cultures (Asian and Indian) and African and indigenous American spiritual traditions as norms. He declared a "rematch" of a colonial encounter that had baptized the New World (and old Africa) in the image of Enlightenment reason and installed the social order of chattel slavery under the sign of Christian salvation and white supremacy. By all accounts, Reed's "Neo-HooDoo Manifesto" staged a full-scale hoodoo resurrection and, thus, a cultural revolution.

In its opposition to all things associated with the American mainstream, Reed's "Neo-HooDoo Manifesto" erected the blackest church imaginable.[7] Yet he clarified that the enemy was not exclusively white or Christian. Poking fun at Islam—in both its orthodox and nationalist forms—and its widespread influence on black cultural life during the 1960s, Reed joked that "Neo-HooDoo never turns down pork." Neo-HooDoo was nothing if not eclectic and unorthodox in its appetites. It was styled in the image of a true "heathen"; it was a heretic in its valorization of excess and heterodoxy. In this regard, Reed's manifesto was one of the most robust attempts to take up James Stewart's call for a "methodology affirmed by the Spirit." Reed offered blackness as fluid, dynamic, and changing, an excessive, ecstatic, and embodied amalgam of oppositions. Neo-HooDoo was radically black in its political orientation even as it eschewed racial essentialism. It celebrated its multiethnic and polycultural composition, the impurity and porousness of black cultures in the New World.[8]

With his invocation of multiple, seemingly opposed sources simultaneously, Ishmael Reed staged a contest over the meaning of America itself. Blackness was a complicated matrix of Americana in which the African diaspora was constitutive. In Neo-HooDoo, multiple competing and colliding cultural worlds were entangled rather than separate or mutually exclusive. Racial purity, black or white, was demythologized, and the white-over-black racial logic of colonial contact was inverted and aestheticized. Recalling the form of religious reasoning prominent in Protestant America, "Neo-HooDoo Manifesto" mapped an alternate geography of native spiritual authorities that linked "Haiti, Africa, [and] South America." Here the fragmented margins of modernity were (re)imagined as a single moral community. For Reed, the American center itself was black.

A CHURCH FINDING ITS LYRICS

Neo-HooDoo was the truest kind of American church; it embraced "the black influence" that had been repeatedly obscured in efforts to craft a national culture.[9] Clarifying his claim by way of critiquing Christianity, Ishmael Reed announced:

> In Neo-HooDoo, Christ the landlord deity ("render unto Caesar") is on probation.
>   This includes "The Black Christ" and "The Hippie Christ." Neo-HooDoo tells Christ to get lost.[10]

Reed made his point clear: No version of Christ would survive, nor would the church's clergy class. Confirming what James Baldwin suggested might be the case in *The Fire Next Time*, Reed asserted that Christianity was beyond redemption, despite the revolutionary efforts of Albert Cleage and others. In the Neo-HooDoo church, "every man is an artist and every artist a priest."

Reed's Neo-HooDoo reasoning remade the margins as the center and refigured the outside as the organizing core. Neo-HooDoo was fundamentally at odds with the literary rules of organized elite black churches, even when the institution of the Black Church was reimagined in the form of a pan-Africanist liturgy and iconography. As much as Reed's reading of Christianity critiqued the middle class, Neo-HooDoo argued that Christian churches were implicated in the commercial milieu of American capitalism. Neo-HooDoo rejected the political economies of Christian churches. For example, although Reed affirmed Amiri Baraka's assertion that James Brown's music was an extension of an ancient spirituality, the Neo-HooDoo Church was not willing to claim Brown unless he shed "the lyrics and ads for Black Capitalism." It was not enough to relinquish Christian theology or class aspirations; Neo-HooDoo renounced Western capital, writ large. "Christ" was capitalism's God.

In a reversal of Christianity's founding story, Reed celebrated Judas Iscariot as the favored disciple. Consistent with Neo-HooDoo's oppositional logics, it remade the man who betrayed the messiah as the most beloved. Christianity—whether black or white—was a "Cop Religion." It imprisoned rather than liberated adherents and seized every opportunity to keep Neo-HooDoo "underground." Despite this history of suppression, Neo-HooDoo had managed to thrive—out of sight and beneath the surface—in the environs of "black ghettos" across the United States. On the heels of the 1960s, Reed explained, Neo-HooDoo was finally reappearing to issue "warrants for a god arrest."[11] At the same time that he put the proverbial nail in Christianity's coffin, Ishmael Reed hailed the resurgence of a different kind of spiritual tradition, even though he availed himself of the language of institutional Christianity.

According to Reed, a true "church" was coming out from behind the darkened veil of Christian pretense. Neo-HooDoo, Reed suggested, could be found in the ecstatic and frenzied spiritual energies of black Pentecostal, Baptist, and holiness congregations. These were the same kinds of congregations that Amiri Baraka considered "blacker." They harked back to the Harlem "holy roller" church Baldwin's protagonist attended in *Go Tell It on the Mountain* and to the spirited prayer of the congregation of the Chicago storefront church in Gwendolyn Brooks's portrait of Bronzeville. Reed's appeal to the storefront recalled the churches of the "low down folks" Langston Hughes and Zora Neale Hurston had celebrated during the 1920s and 1930s. As Hughes put it in *The Nation* in 1926, "Their religion soars to a shout."[12] Neo-Hoodoo was made in the image of what Hurston had referred to as "the Sanctified Church." Reed's church would be free from the intellectual constraints of doctrinal orthodoxy and the emotional and expressive constrictions bourgeois respectability enforced.

In Neo-HooDoo, hierarchical distinctions between clergy and lay were discarded. In keeping with Neo-HooDoo's outsider status, the main characters in Reed's manifesto were cut from the same cloth as the trickster figures of African mythologies and black American folklore.[13] Images associated with Africa, such as drums and ankhs, replaced Christian symbols like crosses, graves, and church organs. At the organizational level, Haitian Voodoo and American Hoodoo (or Conjure) were the most fitting models for the Neo-HooDoo Church. Both eschewed any semblance of a hierarchy, according to Reed. Yet unlike much of the Black Arts vision, Neo-HooDoo called on America to acknowledge its black influences even as it valorized its own interracial and multicultural makeup. "Neo-HooDoos are Black Red . . . and occasionally White," Reed observed. The Indian leader "Black Hawk" and the white "Madamemoiselle [*sic*] Charlotte" were cited as HooDoo philosopher and Haitian *loa* (Voodoo spirit), respectively.[14]

In narrating the Neo-HooDoo Church's past and theorizing its present, Ishmael Reed's aesthetic aligned well with the determination in the Black Arts to reclaim history and create new myths. At the same time, his aesthetic implied a more inclusive order across the lines of both race and gender. While instances of white practitioners or spirits were rare, his manifesto demonstrated a far greater degree of gender equality in its elevation of women, at least in terms of representation. These included the renowned HooDoo/Voodoo priestesses Julia Jackson and Marie Laveau, the famed culinary expert and author of *Vibration Cooking* Vertamae Smart-Grosvenor, and vocal artists like Aretha Franklin, Etta James, Nellie Lutcher, Ma Rainey, Bessie Smith, and Tina Turner. Tituba, the slave girl accused of witchcraft in seventeenth-century Salem, and the once-celebrated (and soon to be revived) folklorist and novelist Zora Neale Hurston were all a part of the tradition. Each of these women was an exemplar of Neo-HooDoo.[15]

Men were by no means absent in Reed's religious history. However, a "pantheon" of black women—from "arm-waving ecstatic females" to the "Mambo" in Haitian Voodoo—were especially inclined to possess, or be possessed by, the powers of Neo-HooDoo. Women, even more than men, would preside over Neo-HooDoo's ascent back above ground. Allowing for racial fluidity and gender parity, Neo-HooDoo presented a group of black men and women who together imaged and embodied cultural, political, racial, and religious alterity in relation to the American mainstream.

Reed accomplished this feat by coding his aesthetic as an appeal to Hoodoo, a spiritual tradition understood as indigenous to black communities in North America. In effect, Neo-HooDoo called to life—indeed, conjured—a set of new (and old) black gods, spirits, and saints. While not a literal "church," Neo-HooDoo was an extension and revival of a black cultural tradition that had long been figured as the site of an alternative and oppositional spiritual authority in the face of an overwhelmingly Christian order.[16] African culture would be exorcised of the demons of American imperialism. Any Christian theology in Afro-Protestantism would be cast aside. Most simply, what modernity classified as "bad religion" Ishmael Reed celebrated as the good.[17]

Nevertheless, jettisoning Christianity was not so easy, as Reed's work revealed. Indicative of his ambivalent, if evolving, relationship to organized Christianity, Reed dedicated his 1970 volume of poems, *catechism of d neoamerican hoodoo church*, to Father Ted Cunningham. Not long before writing the poems in *catechism*, Reed had met Cunningham in Omaha, where the priest was a professor of black studies at Creighton University. That year Cunningham had left his order to get married, an event that made its way into *Jet* magazine.[18] In his acknowledgments in *catechism*, Reed listed the former Jesuit simply—perhaps because of Cunningham's recent decision to leave the priesthood—as a "member of the loyal opposition." Years later Reed explained that while he had once thought the church was "monolithic," he credited Cunningham with persuading him "that there was probably more rebellion within the church than any coming from without."[19]

catechism of d neoamerican hoodoo church consisted of ten poems. The first, "Black power poem," announced that the "specter of neo-hoodooism" haunted the nation, and that "old America" had formed a "holy alliance to exorcise this specter." Among the ranks of the evil empire, Reed included

Allen Ginsberg, Billy Graham, the *New York Review of Books*, and Richard Nixon. Literature, the nation-state, and church powers had all aligned themselves in opposition to Neo-HooDoo. "May the best church win," Reed declared.[20] In the title poem, he explained that "d neoamerican hoo-doo church of free spirits" intended to institutionalize an anti-aesthetic. "DO YR ART D WAY U WANT ANYWAY U WANT," he proclaimed.[21] In "Sermonette" Reed put this spiritual arsenal to verse. Here the poet played witness to a spell that was placed upon a corrupt judge. He stood by to witness the havoc that "black powder" wreaked on "his honah" and his family. Reed testified to the ancient powers of such spells while poking fun at popular church tunes:

> gimmie dat ol time
> religion
> it's good enough
> for me!

As he quoted the lyrics of a familiar spiritual, Ishmael Reed reimagined a staple of Afro-Protestantism as a song in praise of black magic.

   catechism ended with a poem that consisted of a simple inventory of Neo-HooDoo "Gris Gris" (i.e., a talisman) that included "Goddess of Love," "Good Luck Powder," and "Goofer Dust." Reed's Neo-HooDoo church was, in short, against all hierarchies. Fluidity and freedom offered their own kind of (un)holy order. What was elsewhere considered super-stitious, Reed rendered as systematic theology. In both the "Manifesto" and *catechism* for his Neo-HooDoo church, Ishmael Reed played the role of theorist and practitioner, preacher and professor, cleric and conjurer, all at once. Yet as compelling as his poetry may have been, the radical revaluation that Reed claimed would create the conditions for a HooDoo revival was not to be fully realized in real time. Christianity would not be so easily unseated. Reed unwittingly acknowledged this irresolu-tion when he declared that "Neo-HooDoo is a 'Lost American Church' updated."[22]

   Afro-Protestantism, even in the face of opposition, was not to be undone. The central irony of Ishmael Reed's Neo-HooDoo aesthetic is that even as he elevated the black spiritual form of Conjure/HooDoo, he imag-ined it in the form of a "church." Reed resisted one kind of church only to install another. His conjurations were a literary reformation, or better yet, an artistic attempt at a "Black Revival."[23] Perhaps what was distinc-tive, in this instance, is that Reed reversed the more familiar narrative of a Protestant Reformation. Whether a product of independent study, a nod to New Orleanian Catholicism and carnival, or a result of conversations with Father Ted Cunningham, Reed's Neo-HooDoo Church had much in common with the traditions of Catholicism, which was a marginal black Christian presence compared to the standing narrative of the Protestant "Negro Church."

Scholars have long noted Catholicism's capacity to serve as a receptacle for religious practices tied to the African past. Indeed, it was under Catholic colonial orders that Black Atlantic religions such as Vodun, Santería, and Candomblé thrived in French and Spanish (Caribbean and South) American nations.[24] The ritual practices of Roman Catholicism were seen to be more capable than Protestantism of sustaining black religious difference, or at least they absorbed that difference in a more porous manner than the literary and disciplinary constraints enforced by the Protestant rule of early North America. Moreover, African religions and ethnic Catholicism were each marked as sites of racial difference by virtue of their reception, and exclusion, by an Anglo-Protestant establishment. Ishmael Reed mounted an aesthetic that was, in effect, a performance of Catholic alterity—a black Catholicism, in its hybrid fusion of Christian and African content and forms—from the universalizing assumptions of American Protestantism.[25] Ultimately, through literature Reed sought to conjure up a new/old church that would stand in opposition to all that was hallowed in the West.[26]

ACCENTUATING THE ORDINARY AESTHETICS
OF EVERYDAY BLACK LIFE

The aesthetics of the Neo-HooDoo Church was very much a product of the radical ethos of the Black Arts. Yet Ishmael Reed was never entirely in the movement or of it. His politics were radically opposed to all things Western, including capitalism, Christianity, and colonialism. Yet he also drew upon and valorized a repertoire of source materials that confounded simplistic distinctions like "East versus West" and "black versus white" even as such categories required binaries to maintain their meaning. In this way, Reed both politically embraced and culturally confounded the racial binary that was taken as orthodoxy for racial aesthetics during the 1960s. While the increasing prominence of the Black Arts and its entrepreneurial anthologies and institution building represented the most dramatic shift in black cultural expression during that decade, there was a diversity of thought within its ranks. The black aesthetic was always more of a bundle of questions than a position of consensus. There were also

critics who derided the nationalist political sensibilities that were taken
to organize its expressive forms. Racial aesthetics during the 1960s consisted of more than just the Black Arts.

One writer who argued against an all-consuming race politics was Alice
Walker. In February 1970, the same year that Ishmael Reed's *catechism of
d neoamerican hoodoo church* was published, a twenty-six-year-old Walker
returned to speak at her alma mater after spending a few years teaching
in her home state of Mississippi. Her first book of poems, *The Third Life of
Grange Copeland*, was slated for publication later that year. This was three
years before Walker discovered Zora Neale Hurston's unmarked grave in
Eatonville, Florida, wrote about it in *Ms.* Magazine, and thus began to res-
urrect Hurston's literary legacy.[27] It was more than a full decade before
she would engage the writings of the black Shaker visionary Rebecca Cox
Jackson in a review for *The Black Scholar*.[28] And it was thirteen years before
she would win the Pulitzer Prize for her novel *The Color Purple*, which
would make her both a cause célèbre and the target of Ishmael Reed's
caustic criticism.

At Sarah Lawrence College in 1970, a young Alice Walker had been
invited to speak to the school's Black Students' Association. The arguments in her presentation ran in two different directions. The first took
aim at the exclusion of black writers from the American literary canon.
Black artists and intellectuals had been altogether absent on her under-
graduate syllabi, so now Walker was complementing her formal schooling with "simply a college of books." Such a re-education was required if
she were to be a "black poet, writer and teacher."[29] Her second concern
was about the many assumptions attached to "the role of the revolutionary black writer." The first half of Walker's title, "The Unglamorous but
Worthwhile Duties of the Black Revolutionary Artist," recalled the title of
James Stewart's lead essay in *Black Fire*.[30] However, her presentation's subtitle—"or of the Black Writer Who Simply Works and Writes"—suggested
that she understood the terms of revolution differently.

Alice Walker did not deny the fiery urgency of the 1960s or the racial
responsibilities associated with the Black Arts. Here, however, the logic
of her argument about black representation was inverted. She took issue
with the unwillingness of many black writers to even engage the American
canon. Specifically, Walker singled out a "young man (bearded, good looking), a Muslim," who "refused to read Faulkner." In her estimation, such
a posture was emblematic of a cult of "black perfection," which in many
ways resembled the myopic form of "Black Pride" that Joyce Green took
issue with in *The Black Woman*. Walker argued that such a position not only
assigned all imperfections to white people, it also was intellectually lazy.[31]

She did not linger much on the topic of the young man's Muslim identity, but her comments implicitly highlighted the ways that, in recent years, rigid racial orthodoxies had often been reinforced by appeals to religion.

Alice Walker saw things differently. The work of the revolutionary black artist, for her, was to attend to the experience of ordinary black life. It was to engage in the regular work of reading and learning each day of one's life. The task was to see and put into written words the complexity of "man *as he is*" (italics in the original) rather than to fit literary characters into the political categories of black and white. She singled out the main character in the text that had come to represent all of sociological literature: Richard Wright's *Native Son*.[32] According to Walker, Wright's Bigger Thomas was "many great and curious things, but he was neither good nor beautiful. He was real, and that is sufficient."[33] Reed's Neo-HooDoo was animated by an oppositional politics based on cultural hybridity. In contrast, Walker's arguments refused the political binary altogether and engaged anew with the everyday sources of black American life.

Alice Walker's 1970 critique of the Black Arts came relatively late, as the movement's most vital period was already beginning to wane. However, she would become a prominent voice in a growing movement of black feminists that emerged in the wake of the publication of Toni Cade Bambara's *The Black Woman* that same year. Perhaps the most public troubling of the racial orthodoxies that ordered black cultural production during the 1960s came even before a Black Arts movement was formally announced. When Ralph Ellison wrote a scathing critique of *Blues People* in 1964, LeRoi Jones had yet to change his name to Amiri Baraka, co-found the Black Arts Repertory Theater, or move back to Newark to create Spirit House. *Blues People* was the versatile thirty-year-old writer's earliest work of book-length prose and it provided a historical survey of what Jones would later theorize as "the changing same."[34] Ellison had spent the preceding decades making a claim that jazz and the blues were quintessentially American and universally significant aesthetic forms. Jones argued, in contrast, that this music narrated the particular story of oppression and exclusion that was the black experience.

It was only fitting that Ralph Ellison's review appeared in the *New York Review of Books*. Just a few years later Ishmael Reed's *catechism* would identify that publication as the literary arm of the American empire.[35] A number of black writers, like James Baldwin and Gwendolyn Brooks, were to varying degrees swept up in the radical ethos of racial aesthetics during the 1960s. Ellison, however, remained true to his pre–Black Arts era form. He held fast to what he had once articulated as a vision of "critical participation" in which "the Negro was the gauge of the human condition."

Roughly a decade before he reviewed Jones's book, Ellison had determined that he would leave "sociology to the scientists."[36]

The crux of Ralph Ellison's criticisms of *Blues People* was that in his estimation, LeRoi Jones allowed the urgencies of race politics to overdetermine his engagement with what was first and foremost an artistic form. "Jones attempts to impose an ideology upon this cultural complexity," Ellison explained. "But his version of the blues lacks a sense of the excitement and surprise of men living in the world." The political burden that Jones placed on the blues extinguished the very creative fires that had fueled the musical form. Ultimately, Ellison concluded, "The tremendous burden of sociology which Jones would place upon this body of music is enough to give even the blues the blues."[37]

As was discussed in chapter 4, just short of a decade earlier Ralph Ellison had been equally unkind to a white "critic-composer" at the Newport Jazz Festival, whom he railed against for trying to eviscerate the music of its racial history.[38] In resolving this earlier argument, Ellison had resorted to taking his readers, with Mahalia Jackson, to church as the original source and continued site of a living blues (and black) aesthetic. Such a move would not work now, however. After all, like Ellison, Jones had spent his youth regularly attending a black church.[39] Here Ellison could not claim the status of insider vis-à-vis Jones, on either religious or racial grounds. So he kept his undressing of Jones within a secular register. Instead, Ellison made a universalizing claim that the blues offered an aesthetic vision that was more convincing than religion or race politics. Acerbic in its tone, Ellison's review could reasonably be read, on more personal terms, as an effort to undermine an imposing competitor (and his competing aesthetic vision) who was on the rise. Indeed, just one year later Jones would change his name to Amiri Baraka and emerge as a leading voice of the Black Arts.

Ralph Ellison's clash with the young LeRoi Jones illustrated how the former, a consummate American insider, could become a racial outsider in the radical black days of the 1960s. Robert Hayden had suffered a similar fate during this time, as had James Baldwin, because of their adherence to art and refusal to embrace sociology.[40] The Black Arts politicized the literary conversation in ways that frustrated such writers—including Ellison and his comrade Albert Murray. Ellison and Murray had been close friends since the 1930s, when they had met at Tuskegee Institute. Their friendship blossomed in the ensuing decades, although their respective careers as writers developed unevenly. *Invisible Man* skyrocketed Ellison to immediate literary fame in the early 1950s, while Murray was sidetracked by the demands of military service and other responsibilities. His first book finally appeared in 1970. Eventually Murray outproduced Ellison as a novelist, but none of his fiction surpassed the acclaim accorded to his friend's single masterpiece. Not unlike Ellison, Albert Murray emphasized the complexity of the cultural traditions of black people in the United States and the fundamental Americanness of "the Negro idiom."[41]

In 1970, just as the decade of Black Power was coming to an end, Murray's *The Omni-Americans* was published. Subtitled *Some Alternatives to the Fakelore of White Supremacy*, some of what was printed in Albert Murray's debut monograph had already appeared as essays elsewhere. They were no less part of a single argument that riffed against the orthodoxy of the oppositional race politics that dominated racial aesthetics during the 1960s. Rather than demolish the Du Boisian "double-consciousness," as Black Arts theorists like Larry Neal had advocated, Murray celebrated black people's heterodox and contradictory cultural inheritance. Instead of tracing a continuum that linked black people directly to an ancestral home in Africa, he highlighted the power black people displayed by creating an expressive tradition in the midst of a society predicated on systematic racial exclusion. He refused to conflate blackness with a folk or ghetto culture in opposition to the larger society, insisting instead that black people were "Omni-Americans." The "black dimensions" for Albert Murray, were both inextricable from and definitive of American culture.[42]

Drawing on the blues as a test case for his theory, Murray argued that framing the blues tradition simply as oppositional totalized it. It constructed a "Blues God," as Black Arts leader Larry Neal had done. Such a perspective, Murray objected, actually limited the "infinite potential of the black dimensions of the American tradition."[43] As an indigenously American black expressive form, the blues was "the product of the most complicated culture, and therefore the most complicated sensibility in the modern world."[44] The paradox of the existence of slavery and segregation in the heart of the land of freedom had nurtured a people who embodied the American experiment. In the blues, one found the paradigmatic example of the paradox, irony, and experimentation that defined democracy. Irreducible exclusively to race, the blues was "the very stuff of the human condition."[45]

Albert Murray's sense of the tragic—that the human condition was defined by contradiction and irresolution—shaped his analysis of the arts, its relationship to political struggles, and the role that religion might play in the realms of both art and politics. Like Ellison, he was highly critical of social science research as it informed arguments about literature and the arts. Whether such research took the form of an intellectual claim or an aesthetic vision, it was guided by assumptions that ignored complexity. The social sciences, and their preoccupation with resolving society's ailments, inadequately addressed the human condition. According to Murray, the consequence of this faulty reasoning was not simply that propaganda took the place of art; because such research inaccurately assessed the human condition, it failed to offer satisfactory solutions to social problems and misallocated resources.

In Albert Murray's estimation, racial discourse suffered from the prominence of the "pseudoscientific" analyses of the social sciences. Such an approach privileged "the fakelore of black pathology" and elevated a "folklore of white supremacy." In contrast, Murray argued that the logics of the racial binary did not pertain in social and cultural life. Americans were "all interrelated one way or another." Discussions that treated black and white life as mutually exclusive offered more insight into the art of interpretation than they revealed about the historical record. Because the politics of race in the United States overdetermined discussions of the vitality of American cultural life, Murray cast the national story as an amalgamated cultural epic.[46] Just as Ishmael Reed complicated the meaning of an American identity, Albert Murray posited that America was "irrevocably composite"; Americans—whether Euro, native, or black—were all "mulatto."

Despite the social order of segregation, and "for all their traditional antagonisms and obvious differences, the so-called black and so-called white people of the United States resemble nobody else in the world so much as they resemble each other," Murray surmised.[47] Giving primacy to antagonistic racial politics precluded the possibility of a more generative exploration of the "affirmative implications" of black culture in the United States. Instead, he suggested a creative synthesis. The heart of the matter was what he deemed to be common sense knowledge: "human nature is no less complex and fascinating for being encased in dark skin."[48] Paraphrasing a popular song of the day, Albert Murray mused, "The time for accentuating the positive and eliminating the negative is long overdue."[49]

The failure of the arts and of intellectual life to acknowledge the "affirmative elements of U.S. Negro life," Murray noted, also led to an impoverished account of the essential cultural ingredient of faith.[50] He recognized that there was more to black faith than what was acknowledged in popular functionalist accounts of the day. Afro-Protestantism was not simply a matrix of "otherworldly" concerns that put African Americans at odds with the demands of modern society.[51] As was the case with the blues, the religious rituals of ordinary black Americans revealed an awareness of the inconsistencies and limitations of the human condition. Recalling

Langston Hughes's writing of decades earlier, Murray celebrated spirituals for cultivating a religious sensibility that was able to distinguish between social power and human freedom. Black faith traditions, he argued, maintained a sense that while whites were the arbiters of political power in the United States, they were no more "free" than black people. The everyday practices of Afro-Protestantism provided an arsenal of aesthetic resources for sustaining black lives even if they did not scale the "racial mountain."

To illustrate his point, Murray turned to the American literary canon, attempting to overturn common caricatures, both black and white. T. S. Eliot's masterful diagnosis of the American spiritual crisis in the wake of World War I provided his evidence.[52] On the pages of *The Wasteland*, he found proof that some white folks sang the blues as well. It was a white blues note that allowed Murray to call attention to the resources of black faith. Having witnessed the white despair that Eliot put on display, Murray described the experience by writing of himself in the third person:

> But he is not cheered by the fix they're in; he is sobered by it—as his great great grandfather was sobered by the spirituals that sometimes whispered *nobody knows the trouble I seen when I seen what was really happening in the* BIG HOUSE. No wonder great great grandpa took religious salvation so seriously.[53]

With no small dose of sarcasm, Murray posited that an intimate engagement with white social worlds would shine light in the shadows of legal freedom and racial privilege. Calling attention to the blues in the "big house" was not a strategy intended to produce sympathy for the master. Rather, it effectively revealed the limits of the racial binary, the folly of reducing the work of religion and culture to the categories of politics.

Blurring the boundaries of race and religion—the presumably sacred spirituals and the secular blues—Murray playfully parodied the spirituals even as he accented the persuasive powers of "religious salvation." Acknowledging religion's capacity to address quotidian human needs, he refused to assess the merits of black faith solely on political terms. Whether or not religion adequately opposed or overturned white supremacy was beside the point. The faith embraced by his "great great grandpa" spoke deeply to the tragic nature of the human condition. There were certain predicaments, and possibilities, that were not reducible simply to the exclusions attached to black identity in American society.

In the introduction to *The Omni-Americans*, Albert Murray referred to his book as "a brief for the affirmative." As an account of "black assets," it would counter popular perspectives that began with an assumption of either white oppression or black pathology. To signal this trajectory, Murray invoked a song that was originally inspired by none other than Father Divine, the God of Harlem, and was more or less a standard by 1970. While he was no doubt familiar with the evolution of the song over the preceding two decades, Murray was perhaps unaware of its religious history.

Johnny Mercer, the popular American lyricist, first wrote the words to "Accentuate the Positive" in 1944. He was inspired to do so by his agent, who had attended an event hosted by the Peace Mission, which by then had moved to Philadelphia. During the service, Father Divine exhorted the expectant congregation about his own brand of New Thought preaching.[54] "You've got to accentuate the positive and eliminate the negative," announced the preacher. Eight years before the publication of Norman Vincent Peale's bestseller *The Power of Positive Thinking*, Father Divine's words were put to music and became the chorus of a chart-topping song.[55]

Mercer first performed the song himself, along with the Pied Pipers and Paul Weston's orchestra, in October 1944. Before the end of the year, both Bing Crosby and the popular bandleader Kay Kyser had recorded versions. The following year Dinah Washington teamed up with the jazz percussionist Lionel Hampton and his orchestra to cover the song. At the 1945 live recording, Washington performed "Accentuate the Positive," in the styles of a preacher, as if the song were the original Father Divine sermon.[56] Over the next decade the tune was taken up by a long line of popular performers, including Perry Como, Connie Francis, Johnny Green, and Artie Shaw. By the end of the 1960s, even as the "age of blackness" dawned, Sam Cooke, Ella Fitzgerald, and Aretha Franklin had all recorded the number as well.

It is unclear whether Albert Murray had Aretha Franklin, Johnny Mercer, or Father Divine in mind when he paraphrased the popular song on the first few pages of *The Omni-Americans*. He was just the kind of eclectic literary provocateur to cite a single source with the aim of revealing the surprising connections between a presumably unrelated trio of American performers. It would also have been a classic Albert Murray move to enlist an infamously unconventional black preacher, who eschewed almost every social category, as proof of the transcendent powers of black faith. By all accounts, Divine stood outside the religious orthodoxies of organized Afro-Protestantism and on the margins of Harlem's history of black cultural achievement. For Murray, this fact would only have made him a more perfect candidate for illustrating the contradictions at the heart of the American experience and its "black dimensions."[57]

Although the two men never lived in Harlem at the same time—Divine left for Philadelphia in 1942, and Murray arrived two decades later—both utilized the resources of language to resist the demands of traditional race politics. Where the former swore off the word "Negro," the latter was not especially fond of "black" or "African-American."[58] Murray also marked his difference more subtly, when he named his adopted neighborhood in New York in the front matter of his first book. Even though at the time he had called Harlem home for almost a decade, in the preface to *The Omni-Americans*, he signed off from "Uptown Manhattan."[59] In this simple writerly sleight of hand, Murray could unsettle years of cultural mythology and race politics. In effect, he refused to cordon off the storied streets of Harlem—whether as the stage of a literary renaissance or as the location of ghetto pathology—that were once known as the "mecca of the New Negro" and, more recently, had become the launching pad for the Black Arts. Harlem may have been his beloved home, but it was still on the island of Manhattan.

Perhaps Albert Murray was entirely unaware of the divine origins of "Accentuate the Positive." Even if this was the case, laying claim to such a simple message of positive thinking was in and of itself a herculean feat in the face of all that the 1960s had wrought. And Father Divine represented one clear example of many black efforts to turn the negative, by way of theological ingenuity, into a positive. In the absence of political liberation or wholesale revolution, black faith might just have to be good enough.

While Larry Neal suggested that a Blues God could become the mythological force to inspire an oppositional racial aesthetic, Murray maintained a different perspective. The same circumstances that catalyzed the creation of the blues inspired the push toward transcendence in religious life. Both of these cultural expressions—religion and the arts—bore witness to the fact that black people were quintessentially American and deeply human. Oppressive political orders, like slavery and segregation, did not preclude cultural exchange or aesthetic ingenuity. In fact, oppression and exclusion were often the very terms that occasioned and inspired innovation and improvisation. Indeed, it was the problem of Christianity that set the course for the creative possibilities that animated Afro-Protestantism.

Black faith was, in truth, a blues note.

EPILOGUE

You Can't Keep a Good Church Down!

Despite the declaration of Alain Locke and others in the 1920s, the dawn of the New Negro movement did not occasion a definitive breaking point when the rule of black churches was replaced by secular concerns, commitments, and institutional arrangements. Neither emancipation nor Reconstruction entirely achieved a black secularism. The push from slavery to freedom and then toward segregation did, however, set in motion a series of struggles that eventually culminated with the Supreme Court ruling in *Plessy v. Ferguson*. That decision, in turn, created circumstances that meant that a diverse set of black institutions (e.g., churches, businesses, banks, etc.) had to be established even as their flourishing was undermined by the law of Jim Crow. Indeed, legal segregation simultaneously required and reinforced the central role of an institutional Afro-Protestantism in organizing a segregated black life. This remained so from the days of the New Negro until the era of the Black Arts.

Afro-Protestant commitments did not exclusively follow the path of independent black churches, which grew exponentially during the final decades of the nineteenth century. Nor did secular concerns unfold exclusively on black political platforms, the budget sheets of black businesses, or the pages of African American literature. African American cultural, political, and religious traditions both flourished and floundered on their own terms even as they remained entangled across the presumed divisions of sacred and secular that marked the twentieth century as modern. There was never any definitive break between "the Black Church" and the range of other independent "secular" black institutions that emerged later. Church presses published secular (i.e., non-Christian) literature, while secular (i.e., African American) literature remained driven by religious ambitions. In the 1930s, Benjamin Elijah Mays was one of the first to observe this entanglement and interpret the relationship between these two spheres—religion and literature—of culture. Mays also worried that a significant crack was beginning to form in the armor of the liberal Afro-Protestantism that presided over black social life.

Roughly thirty years later, Mays's *The Negro's God as Reflected in His Literature* was revised and republished amid the radical ethos of the late 1960s. If Mays had been unduly anxious about a declining black church tradition in the 1930s, the aesthetics and politics of Black Power appeared poised to finally supplant the authority of a fading Christian hegemony in 1968. Ironically, the triumph of secularism in the West was announced at precisely the same moment when laws were being passed to secure equality for black people in the United States. With the death of Jim Crow, perhaps there would actually no longer be a need for the kind of prophetic religion that Mays had called for three decades earlier. And maybe now Negro literature as such would also actually finally disappear, as Richard Wright had prematurely speculated it would a decade earlier.[1] Indeed, a causal connection had frequently been asserted between religious decline and the rise of racial equality; the latter was often assumed to require the former. The same logic was also often applied to literature. Social equality, it was believed, would be the end of racial aesthetics. Some worried that the newfound freedoms occasioned by the demise of legal segregation might signal the end of both black churches and black literature. Quite the contrary would prove to be true, in fact, in both cases.

Nobody knew this better or more intuitively than Aretha Franklin. She was in the midst of making a way back to her own religious roots when she recorded "Spirit in the Dark" in May 1970. The song drew upon the ritual aesthetics and affective rhythms and cadences of black churches. It was a powerful testament to what Albert Murray, in *The Omni-Americans*, observed as the affirmative powers of black faith. Franklin appeared to personify one take on the visions of black feminism announced in Toni Cade Bambara's anthology *The Black Woman*. Both Bambara and Murray's books went to print the same year that Franklin took "Spirit in the Dark" on the road. Franklin had undergone great change, both musically and personally, during the turbulent decade of the 1960s. With eighteen top ten songs on the soul charts and eight Grammy awards in the same category, Aretha swiftly became the undisputed "Queen of Soul."[2] Yet by the end of the decade, she was moved by the revolutionary fervors of recent years. By 1970, Aretha Franklin was singing a different tune, and the "Queen of Soul" moniker carried added meaning.

Her own evolution was paradigmatic of the age—and of the persistence of the Black Church. By the 1970s, doors that had previously barred black people from direct access to markets and media outlets were being pried open. Afro-Protestantism would flourish anew under the novel circumstances of neoliberalism, in forms that were age-old even as they were entirely modern. It should have been no surprise that Aretha would soon go back to gospel music or that, in doing so, she would record the one album that would outsell all of the rest. The album Aretha Franklin recorded in 1972, *Amazing Grace*, grew out of the aesthetic innovations and intellectual developments of the 1960s, which the Black Arts articulated in spiritual terms. Aretha Franklin's journey from *Spirit in the Dark* to the Los Angeles sanctuary where she recorded *Amazing Grace* was a harbinger of something new on the horizon that was not yet fully understood.

"Spirit in the Dark," then, was a bridge over troubled waters, from the nightclub back to church, a passageway into a post-soul era that, once again, might never quite become the Promised Land some hailed it to be.[3] In the realm of black literature, an even newer generation of "new black" writers would rise to make claims that were in many ways reminiscent of Alain Locke's spiritual musings in his classic 1926 anthology *The New Negro*. Yet at the same time, they shared much in common with the sentiments of James Stewart, who had declared in 1968, in the lead essay to *Black Fire*, "That spirit is black!"[4] In laying claim to a "new blackness," the late Joe Wood could have been summing up the history of racial aesthetics when, in the introduction to his 1992 anthology on the meaning of Malcolm X for his generation, he wrote, "Black spirit has never meant one thing, or anything concrete, which is its great power *and* failure."[5]

Afro-modernity in the likeness of a black church, even still. Saturday nights, Sunday mornings. Sacred spaces, secular places. Black congregations, white audiences. Other-worldly preoccupations, this-worldly powers. Converted souls, financial gains. Religious salvation, racial transcendence. Old-time religion, modern literary visions. All of these modes, moods, and meanings were entangled, along with many more, in the history of racial aesthetics—a genealogy of spirit (in the dark). Whether positive or negative, church and spirit were all inseparably encoded, brilliantly deciphered, and masterfully enacted in Aretha Franklin's performance of Afro-Protestant modernity. Chasing the *spirit in the dark*. Or, as it's been said, "You can't keep a good church down!"[6]

NOTES

INTRODUCTION

1. Benjamin Elijah Mays, *The Negro's God as Reflected in His Literature* (New York: Atheneum, 1968), 218.
2. Ibid., 244.
3. Ibid.
4. Stuart Hall, "What Is This 'Black' in Black Popular Culture?," in *Black Popular Culture*, ed. Gina Dent (Seattle: Bay Press, 1992), 21–33.
5. Victoria Earle Matthews, 'The Value of Race Literature: An Address' Delivered at the First Congress of Colored Women of the United States at Boston, Mass., July 30, 1895," *The Massachusetts Review* (Summer 1986): 170–185.
6. Kenneth Warren, *What Was African American Literature?* (Cambridge, MA: Harvard University Press, 2011), 10.
7. Gene Jarrett, *Deans and Truants: A New Political History of African American Literature* (New York: New York University Press, 2011); John Ernest, *Liberation Historiography: African American Writers and the Challenge of History, 1794–1861* (Chapel Hill: University of North Carolina Press, 2004); Curtis Evans, *The Burden of Black Religion* (New York: Oxford University Press, 2008).
8. Robert Hayden, "We Have Not Forgotten" (April 7, 1940, in Hayden, *Heart-Shape in the Dust: Poems* (Detroit, MI: Falcon Press, 1940); Barbara Dianne Savage, *Your Spirits Walk Beside Us: The Politics of Black Religion* (Cambridge, MA: Harvard University Press, 2009), 5–6.
9. For an excellent account of the plurality of modernism, see Mark Wollaeger and Matt Eatough, eds., *The Oxford Handbook of Global Modernisms* (New York: Oxford University Press, 2013).
10. This is not exclusive to black literature and culture, as Peter Kerry Powers points out in his academic framing of "modern" American literature. See Peter Kerry Powers, *Recalling Religions: Resistance, Memory, and Cultural Revision in Ethnic Women's Literature* (Knoxville: University of Tennessee Press, 2001).
11. For a recent discussion of the relationships between religion and literature in American history (and the study thereof), see Jonathan Ebel and Justine Murison, eds., "American Religions, American Literature," *American Literary History* 26, no. 1 (2014): 1–5. Also see Giles Gunn, *The Interpretation of Otherness* (New York: Oxford University Press, 1987).
12. Nancy Ammerman, "Spiritual but Not Religious?: Beyond Binary Choices in the Study of Religion," *Journal for the Scientific Study of Religion* 52, no. 2 (2013): 258–278. Courtney Bender, "Religion and Spirituality: History, Discourse,

Measurement," report submitted to the Social Science Research Council, 2007. For a discussion of the history of American spirituality, see Leigh Schmidt, *Restless Souls: The Making of American Spirituality* (Berkeley and Los Angeles: University of California Press, 2013). For the ways in which history shapes the practice of contemporary spirituality, see Courtney Bender, *The New Metaphysicals: Spirituality and the American Religious Imagination* (Chicago: University of Chicago Press, 2010).

13. I have advanced this argument concerning the Harlem Renaissance, in particular, in Josef Sorett, "We Build Our Temples for Tomorrow: Racial Ecumenism and Religious Liberalism in the Harlem Renaissance," in *American Religious Liberalism*, ed. Leigh Schmidt and Salley Promey (Bloomington: Indiana University Press, 2011), 190–206.

14. Frances Smith Foster and Chanta Haywood, "Christian Recordings: Afro-Protestantism, Its Press, and the Production of African American Literature," *Religion & Literature*, special issue, "Giving Testimony: African-American Spirituality and Literature," 27, no. 1 (Spring 1995): 15–33.

15. W. E. B. Du Bois, *The Gift of Black Folk: The Negroes in the Making of America* (New York: Washington Square Press, 1970), 178–179.

16. Alain Locke, foreword to Alain Locke, ed., *The New Negro: Voices from the Harlem Renaissance* (New York: Simon and Schuster, 1992).

17. Langston Hughes, "The Negro Artist and the Racial Mountain," *The Nation* 122, no. 3181 (June 1926): 693.

18. To be clear, I use the term "racial spirit" as a rubric for placing in conversation the many ways that black artists and critics employed spirit-talk (spirit, spiritual, spirituality, etc.) and to refer to the range of race terms used (Negro, darker-skinned, Aframerican, African, etc.) to explain the particular racial quality of black art and culture.

19. Wallace Thurman, *Infants of the Spring* (Boston: Northeastern University Press, 1992), 235–237.

20. Daylanne K. English, "Selecting the Harlem Renaissance," *Critical Inquiry* 25, no. 4 (Summer 1999): 807–821.

21. Langston Hughes, "Art and the Heart," in *Langston Hughes and the Chicago Defender: Essays on Race, Politics and Culture, 1941–1962*, ed. Christopher C. De Santis (Champaign: University of Illinois Press, 1995), 203.

22. Langston Hughes, "Art and Integrity," in *Langston Hughes and the Chicago Defender*, 200–202.

23. Romare Bearden, "The Negro Artist's Dilemma," *Critique* (November 1946): 20–21.

24. James Baldwin, "Everybody's Protest Novel," in *Notes of a Native Son* (Boston: Beacon Books, 1955), 13–23.

25. James Baldwin, "Autobiographical Notes," in *Notes of a Native Son*, 7.

26. Larry Neal, "The Black Arts Movement," *The Drama Review: TDR*, special issue, "Black Theatre," 12, no. 4 (Summer 1968): 28.

27. Larry Neal, "Afterword: And Shine Swam On," in *Black Fire: An Anthology of Afro-American Writing*, ed. Amiri Baraka and Larry Neal (Baltimore: Black Classic Press, 2007), 636–656.

28. Amiri Baraka, foreword to *Black Fire*, xiv.

29. Henry Louis Gates Jr., "Harlem on Our Minds," *Critical Inquiry* 24, no. 1 (Autumn 1997): 1–12. English, "Selecting the Harlem Renaissance." For several great books on black writers during this period, see Farah Jasmine Griffin,

Harlem Nocturne: Women Artists and Progressive Politics during World War I (New York: Basic Civitas, 2013); Mary Helen Washington, *The Other Blacklist: The African American Literary and Cultural Left of the 1950s* (New York: Columbia University Press, 2014); and Lawrence P. Jackson, *The Indignant Generation: A Narrative History of African American Writers and Critics, 1934–1960* (Princeton, NJ: Princeton University Press, 2010).

CHAPTER 1

1. Rayford Logan, *The Betrayal of the Negro: From Rutherford B. Hayes to Woodrow Wilson* (New York: Da Capo Press, 1997).

2. Reverdy C. Ransom, "The New Negro," *New York Amsterdam News*, January 3, 1923, 12.

3. Calvin Morris, *Reverdy C. Ransom: Black Advocate of the Social Gospel* (Lanham, MD: University Press of America, 1990).

4. Anthony B. Pinn, ed., *Making the Gospel Plain: The Writings of Bishop Reverdy C. Ransom* (Harrisburg, PA: Trinity Press International, 1999), xiii–xv.

5. Ralph Luker, *The Social Gospel in Black and White: American Racial Reform, 1885–1912* (Chapel Hill: University of North Carolina Press, 1991).

6. Morris, *Reverdy C. Ransom*, 10–12.

7. Jon Michael Spencer, "The Black Church and the Harlem Renaissance," *African American Review* 30, no. 3 (1996): 453–460; Frances Smith Foster and Chanta Haywood, "Christian Recordings: Afro-Protestantism, Its Press, and the Production of African-American Literature," *Religion & Literature*, special issue, "Giving Testimony: African-American Spirituality and Literature," 27, no. 1 (Spring 1995): 15–33.

8. Morris, *Reverdy C. Ransom*, 40–72. Wallace Best refers to clergy who sought to blend the traditional with the modern as "mixed-type preachers." See Wallace D. Best, *Passionately Human, No Less Divine: Religion and Culture in Black Chicago, 1915–1952* (Princeton, NJ: Princeton University Press, 2005). For a discussion of uplift politics, see Kevin K. Gaines, *Uplifting the Race: Black Leadership, Politics, and Culture in the Twentieth Century* (Chapel Hill: University of North Carolina Press, 1996).

9. Cleveland pastor W. E. C. Wright published an essay that emphasized the centrality of "Christian Education" in making a "new Negro"; see W. E. C. Wright, "The New Negro," *American Missionary* 48, no. 1 (January 1894): 8–12. I have written elsewhere on the coalescence of religious liberalism and racial ecumenism. See Josef Sorett, "We Build Our Temples for Tomorrow: Racial Ecumenism and Religious Liberalism in the Harlem Renaissance," in *American Religious Liberalism*, ed. Leigh Schmidt and Salley Promey (Bloomington: Indiana University Press, 2012), 190–206.

10. Laurie Maffly-Kipp, *Setting Down the Sacred Past: African American Race Narratives* (Cambridge, MA: Harvard University Press, 2009).

11. Discussions of primitivism were often closely connected to interpretation of African American religion. For the significance of primitivism in the aesthetics of the Harlem Renaissance, see David Levering Lewis, *When Harlem Was in Vogue* (New York: Oxford University Press, 1981), 224, 239, 257; Ann Douglas, *Terrible Honesty: Mongrel Manhattan in the 1920s* (New York: Noonday Press/ Farrar, Straus and Giroux, 1995), 282–288, 506–507; and George Hutchinson, *The Harlem Renaissance in Black and White* (Cambridge, MA: Harvard University Press, 1995), 284–285.

12. "'Marcus Garvey Mightiest Prophet': Bishop Ransom Calls Him Greatest Leader in 50 Years," *New York Amsterdam News*, December 21, 1927.

13. Ransom, "The New Negro."

14. George Frederickson, *The Black Image in the White Mind: The Debate on Afro-American Character and Destiny, 1817–1914* (Middletown, CT: Wesleyan University Press, 1987), 97–129.

15. For a discussion of *A New Negro for a New Century*, see Henry Louis Gates Jr., "The Trope of a New Negro and the Reconstruction of the Image of the Black," *Representations*, special issue, "America Reconstructed, 1840–1940," 24 (Autumn 1988): 136–140.

16. For a discussion of the salience of the term "New Negro" from the 1930s to the 1960s, see Angela Dillard, *Faith in the City: Preaching Radical Social Change in Detroit* (Ann Arbor: University of Michigan Press, 2007).

17. Gates, "The Trope of the New Negro," 134–135. Significantly, Gates explains, "the name has implied a tension between strictly political concerns and strictly artistic concerns," as evidenced in the different figures—from Washington to Locke—who have used the term.

18. Robert Hayden, "Preface to the Atheneum Edition," in *The New Negro*, ed. Alain Locke (New York: Atheneum, 1968), ix.

19. Much has been done to historicize different constructions of "New Negro" rhetoric, highlighting the fact of its mythic quality rather than its veracity as an actual measure of black life. For an excellent discussion of the construction of Alain Locke's anthology *The New Negro*, see Hutchinson, *Harlem Renaissance in Black and White*, 387–434.

20. Morris, *Reverdy C. Ransom*. Although Morris narrates Ransom's theological evolution, for a more thorough treatment of the impact of modern culture on Protestant Christianity, see William R. Hutchison, *The Modernist Impulse in American Protestantism* (Durham, NC: Duke University Press, 1992).

21. Spencer, "The Black Church and the Harlem Renaissance," 453–460. See also Best, *Passionately Human, No Less Divine*. See also Adam Clayton Powell Sr., *Against the Tide: An Autobiography* (1938; repr., New York: Arno Press, 1980).

22. I have defined New Negro clergy in this way, but some black preachers found other ways of fusing the old and new to reimagine black Christianity. For example, see Lerone Martin's discussion of the emergence of recordings of black preachers in *Preaching on Wax: The Phonograph and the Shaping of Modern African American Religion* (New York: New York University Press, 2014). Martin's research is in keeping with arguments that foreground the market in making the New Negro. See also Davarian Baldwin, *Chicago's New Negroes: Modernity, the Great Migration, and Black Urban Life* (Chapel Hill: University of North Carolina Press, 2007).

23. Perhaps a prime example of the efforts of black clergy to represent African American religion (and all of the race, for that matter) to the American public was the Fraternal Council of Negro Churches, which was founded in 1934. For a good discussion of the formation of this council, see Mary R. Sawyer, "The Fraternal Council of Negro Churches, 1934–1964," *Church History* 59, no. 1 (March 1990): 51–64.

24. Gates, "The Trope of a New Negro," 129–155. For a discussion of the tensions between black churches in the North and the folk religion of black migrants from the South, see Best, *Passionately Human, No Less Divine*, 71–93.

25. Milton Sernett's work on religion during the Great Migration initiated what he referred to as an instrumentalist approach to the Negro Church. See Milton Sernett, *Bound for the Promised Land: African American Religion and the Great Migration* (Durham, NC: Duke University Press, 1997). For a more recent discussion of the rise of this instrumentalist approach to black religion, see Curtis Evans, *The Burden of Black Religion* (New York: Oxford University Press, 2008).

26. William R. Hutchison, *The Modernist Impulse in American Protestantism* (Durham, NC: Duke University Press, 1992).

27. Leigh Schmidt, *Restless Souls: The Making of American Spirituality*, 2d ed. (Berkeley and Los Angeles: University of California Press, 2011).

28. For a sustained discussion of religious liberalism in the context of the Harlem Renaissance, see Sorett, "We Build Our Temples for Tomorrow," 190–206.

29. Lewis, *When Harlem Was in Vogue*, xxi, 89–94; Hutchinson, *Harlem Renaissance in Black and White*, 39.

30. Rampersad, "Introduction," to *The New Negro: Voices of the Harlem Renaissance*, ed. Alain Locke (New York: Touchstone, 1999), ix–xi, xxii–xxiii. Rampersad explains that the origin of the anthology in the issue of *Survey Graphic* reveals that this publication's mission was more concerned with social work than with art.

31. *Survey Graphic*, special edition, "Harlem: Mecca of the New Negro," ed. Alain Locke, 4, no. 6 (March 1925).

32. Hutchinson, *Harlem Renaissance in Black and White*, 396–433. Other recent works that shed fascinating new light on the New Negro but give very little attention to religion include Erin Chapman, *Prove It On Me: New Negroes, Sex, and Popular Culture in the 1920s* (New York: Oxford University Press, 2012); Daphne Lamothe, *Inventing the New Negro: Narrative, Culture and Ethnography* (Philadelphia: University of Pennsylvania Press, 2008); Martha Nadell, *Enter the New Negro: Images of Race in American Culture* (Cambridge, MA: Harvard University Press, 2004); Davarian Baldwin and Minkah Makalani, ed., *Escape from New York: The New Negro Renaissance beyond Harlem* (Minneapolis: University of Minnesota Press, 2013); and Shannon King, *Whose Harlem Is It Anyway? Community Politics and Grassroots Activism during the New Negro Era* (New York: New York University Press, 2015).

33. Marlon Ross, *Manning the Race: Reforming Black Men in the Jim Crow Era* (New York: New York University Press, 2004), 162–166. Samuel K. Roberts Sr., "Crucible for a Vision: The Work of George Edmund Haynes and the Commission on Race Relations, 1922–1947" (PhD dissertation, Columbia University, 1975).

34. Rudolph Fisher, "The South Lingers On," *Survey Graphic* 6, no. 6 (1925): 644–647. In the transition to *The New Negro*, Fisher's group of five untitled short stories was shortened to four and retitled "Vestiges." See Rudolph Fisher, "Vestiges," in *The New Negro: Voices from the Harlem Renaissance*, ed. Alain Locke (New York: Simon and Schuster, 1925), 75–84. The restructured series included the four short stories "Shepherd! Lead Us," "Majutah," "Learnin'," and "Revival." The fifth (untitled) story in the *Survey Graphic* number, which was not reprinted in *The New Negro*, focused on workplace discrimination that recently arrived migrants faced in New York City. *The New Negro: Voices from the Harlem Renaissance*, ed. Alain Locke (New York: Simon and Schuster, 1925), 75–84.

35. Fisher, "Vestiges."

36. Ibid.

37. Farah Jasmine Griffin, *"Who Set You Flowin'?": The African-American Migration Narrative* (New York: Oxford University Press, 1995).
38. Alain Locke, "The Ancestral Arts," in *The New Negro*, 255.
39. For further discussion, see V. F. Calverton, introduction to *An Anthology of American Negro Literature*, ed. V. F. Calverton (New York: Modern Library, 1929), 4–5; and Henry Louis Gates Jr., "The Master's Pieces: On Canon Formation and the African American Tradition," *South Atlantic Quarterly* 89 (1990): 97. Hutchinson, *Harlem Renaissance in Black and White*, 278–288.
40. Alain Locke, "The Negro Spirituals," in *The New Negro*, 199.
41. Ibid., 199–200.
42. Ibid.
43. Locke, *The New Negro*, 2, 345.
44. Benjamin Mays and Joseph Nicholson, *The Negro's Church* (New York: Institute of Social and Religious Research, 1933).
45. Best, *Passionately Human, No Less Divine*, 71–94.
46. For more background on Haynes, see Daniel Perlman, "Stirring the White Conscience: The Life of George Edmund Haynes" (PhD dissertation, New York University, 1972).
47. George Edmund Haynes, "The Church and the Negro Spirit," *Survey Graphic*, special edition, "Harlem: Mecca of the New Negro," ed. Alain Locke, 4, no. 6 (March 1925): 695–697, 708–709.
48. Locke's Ethical Culture background is discussed in Hutchison, *Harlem Renaissance in Black and White*, 39. For more on Locke as a Baha'i, see Derek Smith, "Love's Lonely Offices" (PhD dissertation, Northwestern University, 2004), 177–197; and Christopher Buck, *Alain Locke: Faith and Philosophy* (Los Angeles: Kalimat Press, 2005). There is, in fact, a debate in the literature as to whether Alain Locke can be claimed as Baha'i. Where both Smith and Buck claim that Locke was Baha'i, Leonard Harris disagrees. See Leonard Harris and Charles Molesworth, *Alain L. Locke: The Biography of a Philosopher* (Chicago: University of Chicago Press, 2010).
49. Locke, foreword to *The New Negro*, xxvii.
50. Locke, "The New Negro," in *The New Negro*, 3–4. Here I mean to locate the New Negro movement within current trajectories in African American religious studies. For instance, Anthony Pinn's definition of religion as the "quest for complex subjectivity" shares much with Locke's claim that the New Negro was breaking out of existing racial stereotypes in order to acknowledge the complexity and humanity of black people. See Anthony Pinn, "Black Bodies in Pain and Ecstasy: Terror, Subjectivity, and the Nature of Black Religion," *Nova Religio* 7, no. 1 (July 2003): 76–89.
51. Locke, *The New Negro*, 6–7.
52. Ibid.
53. See Milton Sernett, *Bound for the Promised Land: African American Religion and the Great Migration* (Durham, NC: Duke University Press, 1997); and Best, *Passionately Human, No Less Divine*.
54. Although Alain Locke is the better known of the two men, after the *Survey Graphic* number, George Haynes continued his work in this vein largely through service to the church. His primary contribution to ending the problem of the color line was in his capacity as secretary of the Federal Council of Churches' Commission on Church and Race Relations for more than two decades. See Samuel K. Roberts, "Crucible for a Vision: The Work of George

Edmund Haynes and the Commission of Race Relations" (PhD dissertation, Columbia University, 1974).

55. Jeffrey B. Ferguson, *The Sage of Sugar Hill: George S. Schuyler and the Harlem Renaissance* (New Haven, CT: Yale University Press, 2005), 33.

56. George S. Schuyler, "The Negro-Art Hokum," in *The Norton Anthology of African American Literature*, ed. Nellie McKay and Henry Louis Gates Jr. (New York: Norton, 1997). Originally published as "The Negro-Art Hokum," *The Nation*, June 16, 1926, 1171.

57. Schuyler, "The Negro-Art Hokum," 1172.

58. Schuyler's comments presaged the later work of Joseph Washington, who argued that there was no such thing as "black religion" because blacks made no unique theological contribution to the Christian tradition. See Joseph R. Washington, *Black Religion: The Negro and Christianity in the United States* (Boston, MA: Beacon Press, 1964).

59. David W. Wills, "The Central Themes of American Religious History: Pluralism, Puritanism, and the Encounter of Black and White," in *African American Religion: Interpretive Essays in History and Culture*, ed. Timothy Fulop and Albert Raboteau (New York: Routledge, 1997), 7–20.

60. Ferguson, *The Sage of Sugar Hill*, 32.

61. George S. Schuyler, "Ten Commandments," *Views and Reviews*, October 16, 1926.

62. Ibid. See also Ferguson, *The Sage of Sugar Hill*, 34–35.

63. Ferguson, *The Sage of Sugar Hill*, 119–120; Jeffrey B. Ferguson, "The Newest Negro: George Schuyler's Intellectual Quest in the Nineteen Twenties and Beyond" (PhD dissertation, Harvard University, 1998), 340–368.

64. Schuyler, "The Negro-Art Hokum," 1172.

65. Langston Hughes, "The Negro Artist and the Racial Mountain," in *The Norton Anthology of African American Literature*, ed. Nellie McKay and Henry Louis Gates Jr. (New York: Norton, 1997), 1267–1271. Originally published as Langston Hughes, "The Negro Artist and the Racial Mountain," *The Nation*, June 23, 1926.

66. Arnold Rampersad, "Future Scholarly Projects on Langston Hughes," *Black American Literature Forum* 21, no. 3 (1987): 10. Rampersad cites religion as an underdeveloped area in existing scholarship on Langston Hughes. To date, relatively few works exist on this topic. Noteworthy articles are Leslie C. Sanders, "I've Wrestled with Them All My Life: Langston Hughes' *Tambourines to Glory*," *Black American Literature Forum* 25, no. 1 (Spring 1991); Carolyn P. Walker, "Liberating Christ: Sargeant's Metamorphosis in Langston Hughes's 'On the Road,'" *Black American Literature Forum* 25, no. 4 (Winter 1991); James A. Emanuel, "The Christ and the Killers," in *Langston Hughes: Critical Perspectives, Past and Present*, ed. Anthony Appiah and Henry Louis Gates Jr. (New York: Amistad Press, 1993).

67. The City of Boston, for one, maintains an annual tradition that spans more than thirty years.

68. Victor Anderson, *Beyond Ontological Blackness: An Essay on African American Religious and Cultural Criticism* (New York: Continuum, 1999); William Hart, *Edward Said and the Religious Effects of Culture* (New York: Cambridge University Press, 2000).

69. Langston Hughes, "Salvation," in *The Big Sea: An Autobiography* (1940; repr., New York: Thunder's Mouth Press, 1986), 18–21.

70. Arnold Rampersad, *The Life of Langston Hughes*, vol. 1, *1902–1941, I, Too, Sing America* (New York: Oxford University Press, 1986), 134.

71. Lewis, *When Harlem Was in Vogue*, 191.

72. Hughes, "The Negro Artist and the Racial Mountain," 1267–1268.

73. Deborah McDowell, ed., *Quicksand* and *Passing*, by Nella Larsen (1928 and 1929; repr., New Brunswick, NJ: Rutgers University Press, 1986).

74. Hughes, "The Negro Artist and the Racial Mountain," 1268.

75. Ibid.

76. Ibid., 1312.

77. Hughes's romance with folk culture—a common source of inspiration for both black and white artists and intellectuals in the United States during the 1920s—in part affirmed Schuyler's emphasis on a shared American terrain. See Ann Douglass, *Terrible Honesty: Mongrel Manhattan in the 1920s* (New York: Noonday Press/Farrar, Straus and Giroux, 1995).

78. Hughes, "The Negro Artist and the Racial Mountain," 1314.

79. Ibid., 1270–1271.

80. Leigh Eric Schmidt, "Introduction: The Parameters and Problematics of American Religious Liberalism," in *American Religious Liberalism*, ed. Sally Promey and Leigh Schmidt (Bloomington: Indiana University Press, 2012).

81. Charles S. Johnson specifically used the term "orthodoxy" to refer to artistic representation that called attention to "racial foibles." See Charles S. Johnson, introduction to *Ebony and Topaz: A Collectanea*, ed. Charles S. Johnson (Freeport, NY: Books for Libraries Press, 1971).

82. W. E. B. Du Bois, "Criteria of Negro Art," *The Crisis* 32, no. 6 (October 1926): 290–297.

83. Du Bois, "Criteria of Negro Art," 294–295, 297.

84. W. E. B. Du Bois, *Black Reconstruction in America* (1935; repr., New York: Free Press, 1998). *Black Reconstruction* took on the Dunning School's account of Reconstruction. See William Archibald Dunning, *Reconstruction: Political & Economic, 1865–1877* (New York: Harper and Brothers, 1907).

85. Darwin T. Turner, "W. E. B. Du Bois and the Theory of a Black Aesthetic," in *Harlem Renaissance Re-Examined: A Revised and Expanded Edition*, ed. Victor A. Kramer and Robert A. Russ (Troy, NY: Whitston Publishing Company, 1997), 52–58. For an excellent historical study of the race in the American popular imagination at the time, see George M. Fredrickson, *The Black Image in the White Mind: The Debate on Afro-American Character and Destiny, 1817–1914* (Middletown, CT: Wesleyan University Press, 1971).

86. Du Bois, "Criteria of Negro Art," 296–297.

87. Turner, "W. E. B. Du Bois and the Theory of a Black Aesthetic," 46–47.

88. W. E. B. Du Bois, *The Souls of Black Folk* (1903; repr., New Haven, CT: Yale University Press, 2015). *Souls* includes chapters titled "Of Our Spiritual Strivings" and "Of the Faith of the Fathers," and a discussion of the spirituals, "Of the Sorrow Songs." Du Bois's original prayers have been compiled in Herbert Aptheker, ed., *Prayers for Darker People*, by W. E. B. Du Bois (Amherst: University of Massachusetts Press, 1980).

89. W. E. B. Du Bois, "The Conservation of the Races," in *The Oxford W. E. B. Du Bois Reader*, ed. Eric J. Sundquist (1897; repr., New York: Oxford University Press, 1996).

90. Du Bois, *The Souls of Black Folk*, 189.

91. W. E. B. Du Bois, *The Gift of Black Folk: Negroes in the Making of America* (1924; repr., New York: Washington Square Press, 1970), 158–190.

92. Ibid., 158, 178.

93. Frederickson, *The Black Image in the White Mind*, 97–129.

94. Du Bois, "Criteria of Negro Art," 290–292.

95. Locke, "The New Negro," 7. Locke elsewhere claimed that Christianity was a source of alienation for black artists looking for aesthetic cues in African cultures. Locke, introduction to *The New Negro*, 176–178.

96. Du Bois, "Criteria of Negro Art," 758.

97. Ibid.

98. Evelyn Brooks Higginbotham, *Righteous Discontent: The Women's Movement in the Black Baptist Church, 1880–1920* (Cambridge, MA: Harvard University Press, 1994), 185–230. Black people who advocated a "politics of respectability," Higginbotham has argued, sought to advance the interests of the race by cleaning up aspects of black culture associated with the vestiges of slavery.

99. W. E. B. Du Bois, "The Problem of Amusement," in *Du Bois on Religion*, ed. Phil Zuckerman (New York: Rowman and Littlefield, 2000), 19–28; Tracy Fessenden, *The Puritan Origins of American Sex* (Princeton, NJ: Princeton University Press, 2000).

100. Du Bois, "Criteria of Negro Art," 758; Edward J. Blum, *W. E. B. Du Bois: American Prophet* (Philadelphia: University of Pennsylvania Press, 2007), 123. Blum provides a discussion of how global white supremacy led to a devaluing of black religious and cultural practices by Africans and blacks living in the United States. Also, for a discussion of the historical forces that created a white normative gaze, see Cornel West, *Prophesy Deliverance! An Afro-American Revolutionary Christianity* (Louisville, KY: Westminster John Knox Press, 2002).

101. Du Bois, *The Souls of Black Folk*, 142–155.

102. Phil Zuckerman, introduction to *Du Bois on Religion*; Turner, "W. E. B. Du Bois and the Theory of a Black Aesthetic," 44–62. Such apparent inconsistencies have led some scholars to describe Du Bois as schizophrenic in his opinions regarding religion. In less dramatic terms, Turner describes Du Bois's thinking on aesthetics as riddled with inconsistencies and contradictions. Du Bois's critique of the irrational qualities of black religious culture was consistent with the models of Christian leadership he lauded. His celebration of black Christian leaders such as Alexander Crummell and Daniel Payne in other writings underscored Du Bois's privileging of an educated clergy who relegated "the problem of amusement" to other black institutions (schools, social clubs, etc.). See W. E. B. Du Bois, "The Problem of Amusement," in *Du Bois on Religion*, ed. Phil Zuckerman (Walnut Creek, CA: Alta Mira Press, 2000), 19–28.

103. Du Bois, "Criteria of Negro Art," 297.

104. Ibid.

105. Richard Bruce Nugent and Thomas Wirth, *Gay Rebel of the Harlem Renaissance: Selections from the Work of Richard Bruce Nugent* (Durham, NC: Duke University Press, 2002).

106. Lewis, *When Harlem Was in Vogue*, 194–200. For an extended discussion of *Fire!!*, see Yvonne Elizabeth Price, "What Beauty Is Their Own: Fire's Significance in the Harlem Renaissance" (PhD dissertation, Stanford University, 2003).

107. Arthur Huff Fauset, "Intelligentsia," in *Fire!! A Quarterly Devoted to Younger Negro Artists*, ed. Wallace Thurman (1926; repr., Metuchen, NJ: The Fire!! Press, 1982). Well before *Black Gods of the Metropolis*, Fauset was critical of the Afro-Protestant establishment. In "Jumby" (Caribbean vernacular for ghost or spirit), a short story he wrote for *Ebony and Topaz*, Fauset highlighted Afro-Caribbean spiritual traditions.

108. Thurman, *Fire!!*. See also Johnson, "Introduction."

109. Wallace Thurman, "Negro Artists and the Negro," *The New Republic*, August 31, 1927, 37–39.

110. For a book-length treatment of Schuyler, see Ferguson, *The Sage of Sugar Hill*. Also, Ferguson provides a more in-depth account of Schuyler's writings on religion in a chapter from the dissertation that preceded the book. See Ferguson, "The Newest Negro," 340–368.

111. Hall Johnson, "Fi-yer!," in *The Hall Johnson Collection* (New York: Carl Fischer, 2003). See also Eugene Simpson, *Hall Johnson: His Life, His Spirit, and His Music* (Metuchen, NJ: Scarecrow Press, 2008); Nugent and Wirth, *Gay Rebel of the Harlem Renaissance*, 31; Eleonore van Notten, *Wallace Thurman's Harlem Renaissance* (Amsterdam: Rodopi/Brill, 1994), 137.

112. Theophilus Lewis, "The Negro Actor's Deficit," in *Ebony and Topaz: A Collecteana*, ed. Charles S. Johnson (Freeport, NY: Books for Libraries Press, 1971), 125–127.

113. Johnson, "Introduction," 11–13.

114. James Weldon Johnson, *God's Trombones: Seven Negro Sermons in Verse* (1927; repr., New York: Penguin Books, 2008), 1–2.

115. James Weldon Johnson, preface to *The Book of American Negro Poetry*, ed. James Weldon Johnson (1922; repr., New York: Harcourt Brace Jovanovich, 1931), 47.

116. Johnson, *The Book of American Negro Poetry*, 16.

117. Ibid., 9.

118. Ibid., 41–42.

119. Ibid., 4–6. For example, see Langston Hughes, *The Weary Blues* (1927) and Sterling Brown, *Southern Road* (1932).

120. James Weldon Johnson, preface to *God's Trombones*, 5–8, italics in original. Here Johnson was quoting himself from his preface to *The Book of American Negro Poetry*, 41–42, italics in original.

121. James Weldon Johnson, *Along This Way: The Autobiography of James Weldon Johnson* (New York: Viking, 1933), 30, 105.

122. Spencer, "The Black Church and the Harlem Renaissance," 455. Also see Johnson, *Along This Way*, 30; James Weldon Johnson, *Negro Americans, What Now?* (New York: Viking, 1934), 21–23; and James Weldon Johnson, *The Autobiography of an Ex-Coloured Man* (New York: Hill and Wang, 1912), 24–25.

123. James Weldon Johnson, *Black Manhattan* (1930; repr., New York: Da Capo, 1991), 3.

124. Ibid., 24–26. Before undertaking the topic of religion during the 1920s and 1930s, Johnson provides a discussion of the founding of black denominations in eighteenth-century New York. Additionally, he argues that in contrast to the pattern of increasing integration within schools, black and white churches have become increasingly segregated and separate.

125. Johnson, *Black Manhattan*, 160, 255, italics added. See also Randall K. Burkett, *Garveyism as a Religious Movement: The Institutionalization of a Black Civil Religion* (Metuchen, NJ: Scarecrow Press, 1978).

126. Johnson, *Black Manhattan*, 14.

127. Evans, *The Burden of Black Religion*, 105–140.

128. Johnson, *Black Manhattan*, 164–167.

129. For a book-length discussion of the politics of racial uplift, see Kevin Gaines, *Uplifting the Race: Black Leadership, Politics and Culture in the Twentieth Century* (Chapel Hill: University of North Carolina Press, 1996). James Weldon Johnson's analysis of churches squares well with the uplift ideologies Gaines details, which organized black political life in the Progressive Era.

130. Johnson, *Black Manhattan*, 164–167.

131. Ibid., 167.

132. Wallace Thurman, *Infants of the Spring* (New York: Dover Publications, 1932); Nathan Huggins, *The Harlem Renaissance* (New York: Oxford University Press, 1971); Lewis, *When Harlem Was in Vogue*; Gerald Early, *My Soul's High Song: The Collected Writings of Countee Cullen* (New York: Anchor Books, 1991).

133. Amritjit Singh, ed., *The Collected Writings of Wallace Thurman: A Harlem Renaissance Reader* (New Brunswick, NJ: Rutgers University Press, 2003), 5.

134. Lewis, *When Harlem Was in Vogue*, 13.

135. For a comprehensive discussion of the political and historical context in which the study of African American religion took shape, see Evans, *The Burden of Black Religion*.

136. Best, *Passionately Human, No Less Divine*; Sernett, *Bound for the Promised Land*.

137. Eddie S. Glaude, "Babel in the North: Black Migration, Moral Community, and the Ethics of Racial Authenticity," in *A Companion to African American Studies*, ed. Lewis Gordon and Jane Gordon (Malden, MA: Blackwell Publishing Group, 2006), 494–511. Interestingly, Glaude's argument strongly resembles claims Alain Locke made in 1925 in his introduction to *The New Negro*.

138. Leonard Harris, "Harlem Renaissance and Philosophy," in *A Companion to African-American Philosophy*, ed. Tommy L. Lott and John P. Pittman (Malden, MA: Blackwell Publishing Group, 2003), 381–385.

CHAPTER 2

1. William J. Maxwell, *New Negro, Old Left: African American Writing and Communism between the Wars* (New York: Columbia University Press, 1999); James Smethurst, *The New Red Negro: The Literary Left and African American Poetry, 1930–1946* (New York: Oxford University Press, 1999).

2. James Weldon Johnson, introduction to *Southern Road*, by Sterling Brown (Boston: Beacon Press, 1974), xxxvi–xxxvii.

3. Maxwell, *New Negro, Old Left*, 92, 153–179.

4. Jean Toomer, *Cane* (New York: Liveright, 1975), 17.

5. Farah Jasmine Griffin, *"Who Set You Flowin": The African American Migration Narrative* (New York: Oxford University Press, 1995). Griffin borrowed her book's title phrase from Jean Toomer's *Cane*, 39. Griffin's treatment of the impact of migration on African American literature and cultural expression highlights how the rural South served as a site of ancestral spirituality in opposition to the secularizing forces of the urban North. See also Houston A. Baker Jr., *Afro-American Poetics: Revisions of Harlem and the Black Aesthetic* (Madison: University of Wisconsin Press, 1988), 100–110.

6. Curtis J. Evans, *The Burden of Black Religion* (New York: Oxford University Press, 2008), 203–222. Evans argues that in the midst of the migration era, white anxieties and religious identities were mediated through representations of rural southern black religion, as seen in such plays as *The Green Pastures*.

7. Evelyn Higginbotham, "Rethinking Vernacular Culture: Black Religion and Race Records in the 1920s and 1930s," in *The House That Race Built*, ed. Wahneema Lubiano (New York: Vintage, 1998), 157–177.

8. George Hutchinson, *The Harlem Renaissance in Black and White* (Cambridge, MA: Harvard University Press, 1995), 1–28. Hutchinson locates the Harlem Renaissance movement within the context of an American cultural field that includes the development of cultural nationalism. This nascent nationalism no doubt included a religious dimension. For instance, Leigh Schmidt outlines a tradition of American spirituality that was "a search for a religious world larger than the British Protestant inheritance." See Leigh Eric Schmidt, *Restless Souls: The Making of American Spirituality* (New York: HarperSanFrancisco, 2005), 5.

9. Wallace Thurman, *Infants of the Spring* (Boston: Northeastern University Press, 1992), 235–237.

10. Claude McKay, "A Negro Writer to His Critics," in *The New Negro: Readings on Race, Representation, and African American Culture, 1892–1938*, ed. Henry Louis Gates Jr. and Gene Andrew Jarrett (Princeton, NJ: Princeton University Press, 2008), 391. Originally published in *New York Herald Tribune Books* 6 (March 6, 1932): 1, 6.

11. Romare Bearden, "The Negro Artist and Modern Art," in *The New Negro Readings on Race, Representation, and African American Culture, 1892–1938*, ed. Henry Louis Gates Jr. and Gene Andrew Jarrett (Princeton, NJ: Princeton University Press, 2008), 555. Originally published in *Opportunity* 12 (December 1934): 371–372.

12. Charles Long, *Significations: Sign, Symbols, and Images in the Interpretation of Religion* (Aurora, CO: Davies Group Publishers, 2004), 188; Laurie Maffly-Kipp, *Setting Down the Sacred Past: African American Race Narratives* (Cambridge, MA: Harvard University Press, 2009), 154–200.

13. Ann Douglas, *Terrible Honesty: Mongrel Manhattan in the 1920s* (New York: Farrar, Straus, and Giroux, 1995), 272–282; Nancy Cunard, ed., *Negro: An Anthology* (1934; repr., New York: New York University Press, 1969). See also Brent Hayes Edwards, *The Practice of Diaspora: Literature, Translation and the Rise of Black Internationalism* (Cambridge, MA: Harvard University Press, 2003), 309–320.

14. See H. de los Dias, "Obeah, Fetishism of the British West Indies"; Marcellino Bottaro, "Ritual and 'Candombes'"; H. Kwesi Oku, "The Kind of Christianity We Have in Akan and Akwapim Districts"; and n.a., "Experience of the Black Man with the Missionaries," in *Negro: An Anthology*, ed. Nancy Cunard (1934; repr., New York: New York University Press, 1969), 452–454, 519–522, 769–771, and 790–791, respectively.

15. See Zora Neale Hurston, "Characteristics of Negro Expression, Conversions and Visions, Shouting, The Sermon, Mother Catherine. Uncle Monday"; Anthony J. Buttitta, "Negro Folklore in North Carolina"; Rev. Arthur E. Massey, "My Experiences of Colour Prejudice in America," 163–166; all in *Negro: An Anthology*, ed. Nancy Cunard (1934; repr., New York: New York University Press, 1969), 62–66, 163–166, respectively.

16. See Nancy Cunard, "Foreword"; "Harlem Reviewed"; "A Reactionary Negro Organization"; "The American Moron and the American of Sense"; "Scottsboro—and Other Scottsboros"; "Southern Sheriff"; "Jamaica, the Negro Island"; "Colour Bar," in *Negro: An Anthology*, ed. Nancy Cunard (1934; repr., New York: New York University Press, 1969), 142–148, 197–200, 243–268, 429, 437–449, and 551–553, respectively.

17. Cunard, "Harlem Reviewed," 67–75. For the influence of Adam Clayton Powell Jr. and Abyssinian Baptist Church on Dietrich Bonhoeffer, see Reggie Williams, *Bonhoeffer's Black Jesus: Harlem Renaissance Theology and an Ethic of Resistance* (Waco, TX: Baylor University Press, 2014).

18. Douglas, *Terrible Honesty*, 94.

19. Evans, *The Burden of Black Religion*, 177–202.

20. Cunard, "Harlem Reviewed," 51.

21. Langston Hughes, "Good-bye Christ," in *Good Morning, Revolution: Uncollected Social Protest Writings by Langston Hughes*, ed. Faith Berry (New York: Lawrence Hill, 1973), 36. Originally published in *Negro Worker* (November–December 1932), 51.

22. Cunard, "Harlem Reviewed," 50–51.

23. Ibid., 51.

24. Ibid., 67–75. Cunard's observations were consistent with studies exploring the colonial encounter between Europeans and indigenous peoples in Africa and Latin America. While some colonizers expressed an appreciation for the vitality of the religious and cultural practices of the black "other," they simultaneously rendered such practices as not true religion. For a more in-depth discussion, see David Chidester, *Savage Systems: Colonialism and Comparative Religion in Southern Africa* (Charlottesville: University of Virginia Press, 1996).

25. Cunard, "Harlem Reviewed," 52.

26. Douglas, *Terrible Honesty*, 272. Father Divine and Elder Michaux had been featured in *Time* magazine in recent years. See "God in Sayville," *Time* (June 6, 1932), 40; "Disorderly Heaven," *Time* (August 7, 1933), 26; and "Happy Am I," *Time* (June 11, 1934), 37. Cunard could not have anticipated that Divine (whom she mentioned in passing) would be the subject of an extended story in *The New Yorker* just two years later and that a number of book-length treatments would follow. See St. Clair McKelway and A. J. Liebling, "Who Is This King of Glory?" (in three parts), *The New Yorker*, June 13, 20, and 27, 1936.

27. For one of the most thoroughly researched and persuasive accounts of relationships between black political organizing and the Popular Front, see Robin Kelley, *Hammer and Hoe: Alabama Communists during the Great Depression* (Chapel Hill: University of North Carolina Press, 1990).

28. Cunard, "Harlem Reviewed," 52.

29. Ibid., 53.

30. Ibid., 54–55. See also David Levering Lewis, *When Harlem Was in Vogue* (New York: Oxford University Press, 1981).

31. Sections IX, X, and XI of Cunard's anthology included five essays on Communism. See B. D. Amis, "The Negro Nation Oppression and Social Antagonisms"; Michael Gold, "A Word as to Uncle Tom"; Eugene Gordon, "Blacks Turn Red"; "'*Afro-American* Editor Is for Communists,' from *The Liberator*"; and William Herberg, "Marxism and the American Negro."

32. Herberg, "Marxism and the American Negro," 131–135.

33. Smethurst, *The New Red Negro*.

34. The only other contributor to write as many pages as Cunard or Hurston was Raymond Michelet, who authored several essays on Africa and whom Cunard described as "my chief collaborator" in developing the anthology. See Edwards, *The Practice of Diaspora*, 313.

35. Zora Neale Hurston, *Dust Tracks on the Road* (New York: HarperPerennial, 2006), 215. In recent years the religious dimensions of her novels have

attracted significant scholarly attention. One dissertation goes so far as to conclude that "the black church formed the foundation for Hurston's aesthetic vision, stimulated her fertile imagination, and provided the basis for imaginative re-creation of folk experience." Gloria Grace Holmes, "Zora Neale Hurston's Divided Vision: The Influence of Afro-Christianity and the Blues" (PhD dissertation, State University of New York at Stony Brook, 1994), 145. For other explorations of religion in Hurston's work, see Leslie Elizabeth Wingard, *The Sacred and Secular Reconciled: Crossing the Line in Twentieth Century African American Literature* (Berkeley and Los Angeles: University of California Press, 2006), 28–57; and Nicholas Birns, *Spirits Lingering: Christianity and Modernity in Twentieth-Century American Literature* (New York: New York University Press, 1992), 468–557.

36. Zora Neale Hurston, "Spirituals and Neo-Spirituals," in *Negro: An Anthology*, ed. Nancy Cunard (1934; repr., New York: New York University Press, 1969), 223–225.

37. Zora Neale Hurston, "Characteristics of Negro Expression," in *Negro: An Anthology*, ed. Nancy Cunard (1934; repr., New York: New York University Press, 1969), 24–46.

38. Toni Cade Bambara, ed., *The Sanctified Church: The Folklore Writings of Zora Neale Hurston* (Berkeley, CA: Turtle Island Foundation, 1981).

39. Evans, *The Burden of Black Religion*, 177–202.

40. Langston Hughes, "The Negro Artist and the Racial Mountain," *The Nation*, June 23, 1926, 693.

41. Hutchinson, *Harlem Renaissance in Black and White*, 65–70; Robert E. Hemenway, *Zora Neale Hurston: A Literary Biography* (Urbana: University of Illinois Press, 1977), 134.

42. For a discussion of the unfinished comedic play *Mule Bone*, see Henry Louis Gates Jr., introduction to *Mule Bone: A Comedy of Negro Life*, by Langston Hughes and Zora Neale Hurston, ed. George Houston Bass and Henry Louis Gates Jr. (New York: HarperPerennial, 1991).

43. Zora Neale Hurston, "Characteristics of Negro Expression," in *The Norton Anthology of African American Literature*, ed. Henry Louis Gates Jr. and Nellie McKay (New York: Norton, 1997), 1026.

44. Ibid.

45. Ibid., 1024.

46. Ibid. Marion A. Thomas, "Reflections on the Sanctified Church as Portrayed by Zora Neale Hurston," *Black American Literature Forum* 25, no. 1 (Spring 1991): 35. Jack refers to the highest cultural hero, High John the Conqueror. Charles Long has suggested that scholars of African American religious studies explore folklore as a site of inquiry. See Long, *Significations: Sign, Symbols, and Images in the Interpretation of Religion* (Aurora, CO: Davies Group, 1995).

47. Hurston, "Characteristics of Negro Expression," 1024. Seven years later, Herskovits offered the most thorough argument to date on the resilience of African cultural retentions in black communities in the United States. See Melville Herskovits, *The Myth of the Negro Past* (1941; repr., Boston: Beacon Press, 1990). Like Herskovits, Hurston's arguments for a distinct black culture drew upon new theories of cultural pluralism advanced by Franz Boas, who had taught them both at Columbia. See Hutchinson, *Harlem Renaissance in Black and White*, 70.

48. Cunard, "Harlem Reviewed," 51.

49. Daphne Lamothe, *Inventing the New Negro: Narrative, Culture, and Ethnography* (Philadelphia: University of Pennsylvania Press, 2008), 1–9.

50. Erik D. Curren, "Should Their Eyes Have Been Watching God? Hurston's Use of Religious Experience and Gothic Horror," *African American Review* 29, no. 1 (Spring 1995): 18.

51. Thomas, "Reflections on the Sanctified Church as Portrayed by Zora Neale Hurston," 35.

52. Hurston, "Characteristics of Negro Expression," 46.

53. Hurston, "Spirituals and Neo-Spirituals," 360–361.

54. Robert Hemenway, *Zora Neale Hurston: A Literary Biography*; Valerie Boyd, *Wrapped in Rainbows: The Life of Zora Neale Hurston* (New York: Scribner, 2004).

55. See Mark Huddle, ed., *Roi Ottley's World War II: The Lost Diary of an African American Journalist* (Lawrence: University Press of Kansas, 2012); Arnold Rampersad, *Ralph Ellison: A Biography* (New York: Knopf, 2007), 111.

56. *New York Panorama: A Comprehensive View of the Metropolis, Presented in a Series of Articles by the Federal Writers' Project of the Works Progress Administration in New York City* (1938; repr., St. Clair Shores, MI: Scholarly Press, 1976).

57. Richard Wright, "A Portrait of Harlem," in *New York Panorama*, 142–146.

58. Miles Mark Fisher, "Organized Religion and the Culture," *The Crisis* (January 1937): 8–10, 29–30.

59. Wright, "A Portrait of Harlem," 140.

60. Michel Fabre, *The Unfinished Quest of Richard Wright*, 2d ed. (Urbana: University of Illinois Press, 1993), 156–168.

61. Harriet Beecher Stowe, *Uncle Tom's Cabin* (New York: Dover, 2005).

62. By "Marxist" I refer to a broad umbrella of ideas that might be gathered under the umbrella of Communism, much in the same way that William J. Maxwell refers to an "ecumenical, unscientific Marxism" that shaped and was deeply shaped by black artists associated with the New Negro Movement. See Maxwell, *New Negro, Old Left*.

63. See discussion of *Challenge* and *New Challenge* in Robert Bone and Richard Courage, *The Muse in Bronzeville: African American Creative Expression in Chicago, 1932–1950* (New Brunswick, NJ: Rutgers University Press, 2011), 165–170.

64. Benjamin Mays and Joseph Nicholson, *The Negro's Church* (New York: Institute for Social and Religious Research, 1933).

65. Hutchinson, *Harlem Renaissance in Black and White*, 271ff.; Douglas, *Terrible Honesty*, 466.

66. Gerald Early, *My Soul's High Song: Countee Cullen, Voice of the Harlem Renaissance* (New York: Anchor Books, 1991).

67. Smethurst, *The New Red Negro*.

68. Bone and Courage, *The Muse in Bronzeville*, 168.

69. Marian Minus, review of *Their Eyes Were Watching God*, by Zora Neale Hurston, *New Challenge* 2, no. 2 (Fall 1937): 85–87.

70. Alain Locke, review of *A Long Way from Home*, by Claude McKay, *New Challenge* 2, no. 2 (Fall 1937): 81–84.

71. Bone and Courage, *The Muse in Bronzeville*, 168.

72. Richard Wright, "Blueprint for Negro Writing," in *The Norton Anthology of African American Literature*, ed. Henry Louis Gates Jr. and Nellie McKay (New York: Norton, 1997), 1267–1271 and 1380–1381. Originally published in *New Challenge* 2, no. 2 (Fall 1937).

73. Wright's critique of the Harlem Renaissance presaged the work of early scholarship on the period by Nathan Huggins and David Levering Lewis, both of whom deemed the movement a failure. See Huggins, *The Harlem Renaissance* (New York: Oxford University Press, 1972); and Lewis, *When Harlem Was in Vogue*.

74. Kelley, *Hammer and Hoe*, 13.

75. Wright, "Blueprint for Negro Writing," 1404; Kelley, *Hammer and Hoe*. Kelley's work on the shared spaces Communist activists and black communities in Alabama occupied leading up to the Popular Front movement captures the conflicts and creativity that emerged from black/Communist exchanges. Moreover, Kelley demonstrates that many black churches worked together with Communist Party members to organize black workers in the South.

76. Wright, "Blueprint for Negro Writing," 1404.

77. James W. Coleman, *Faithful Vision: Treatments of the Sacred, Spiritual, and Supernatural in Twentieth-Century African American Fiction* (Baton Rouge: Louisiana State University Press, 2006), 17–24. Coleman goes so far as to argue that Wright's work "misrepresents the black cultural tradition by denying the effect of Christianity." See also Sylvester Johnson, "Tribalism and Religious Identity in the Work of Richard Wright," *Literature and Theology* 20, no. 2 (June 2006): 172.

78. Richard Wright, *Black Boy: A Record of Childhood and Youth* (New York: Harper and Brothers, 1945). For a helpful account of the influence of Christianity on Wright's personal and professional life, see Johnson, "Tribalism and Religious Identity in the Work of Richard Wright," 171–188; and Robert L. Douglas, "Religious Orthodoxy and Skepticism in Richard Wright's *Uncle Tom's Children* and *Native Son*," in *Richard Wright: Myths and Realities*, ed. C. James Trotman (New York: Garland Publishing, 1988), 79–88.

79. Wright, "Blueprint for Negro Writing," 1407.

80. Ibid., 1381.

81. Wright's argument that African American religion had declined from a "struggle for human rights" to complacency with the status quo predicts later academic interpretations that read "black religion" through the lens of liberation struggle. See Gayraud S. Wilmore, *Black Religion and Black Radicalism* (New York: Doubleday, 1972); and James H. Cone, *Black Theology and Black Power* (New York: Seabury Press, 1969). More recently, Eddie Glaude's argument concerning "the problem of history in black theology" helps situate the work of Wilmore, Cone, and others in the political climate of the 1960s and illuminate how such "narratives of decline" occlude the diversity of African American religious life. See Eddie S. Glaude, *In a Shade of Blue: Pragmatism and the Politics of Black America* (Chicago: University of Chicago Press, 2007), 66–88.

82. Wright, "Blueprint for Negro Writing," 1405. For a thoughtful discussion of Wright's complicated relationship with religion, see Johnson, "Tribalism and Religious Identity in the Work of Richard Wright," 171–188.

83. Wright, "Blueprint for Negro Writing," 1381.

84. Ibid., 1383.

85. Du Bois, *The Souls of Black Folk*, 1.

86. Wright, "Blueprint for Negro Writing," 1383, italics in original.

87. Kelley, *Hammer and Hoe*, 181.

88. Wright, "Blueprint for Negro Writing," 1384.

89. Ibid.
90. Kelley, *Hammer and Hoe*, provides numerous examples of the workers Wright was encouraging writers to model themselves after. For example, Kelley cites several instances in which organizers rewrote the lyrics to popular hymns in order to recruit black Christians in the South for the Communist Party. See also Michael K. Honey, *Southern Labor and Black Civil Rights: Organizing Memphis Workers* (Urbana: University of Illinois Press, 1993).
91. Wright, "Blueprint for Negro Writing," 1383.
92. James N. Gregory, *The Southern Diaspora: How the Great Migrations of Black and White Southerners Changed America* (Chapel Hill: University of North Carolina Press, 2005).
93. Wright, "Blueprint for Negro Writing," 1407.

CHAPTER 3

1. Michel Fabre, *The Unfinished Quest of Richard Wright* (Urbana: University of Illinois Press, 1993), 184. *Native Son* was criticized on this count in a forum in the Communist publication *New Masses* in 1940.
2. Theodore Stanford, review of *The Negro Caravan*, ed. Sterling A. Brown, Arthur Davis, and Ulysses Lee, *Philadelphia Tribune*, January 24, 1942, 11, col. 6.
3. Sterling A. Brown, Arthur Davis, and Ulysses Lee, eds., *The Negro Caravan: Writings by American Negroes* (New York: Dryden Press, 1941), vi.
4. "Book-Authors," *New York Times*, January 17, 1942.
5. Read Bain, review of *Color and Human Nature: Negro Personality Development in a Northern City*, by W. Lloyd Warner et al., *Color, Class, and Personality*, by Robert Sutherland, and *The Negro Caravan*, ed. Sterling A. Brown et al., *American Sociological Review* 8, no. 1 (February 1943): 106–108.
6. David Daiches, review of *The Negro Caravan: Writings by American Negroes*, ed. Sterling A. Brown, Arthur P. Davis, and Ulysses Lee, *American Journal of Sociology* 48, no. 3 (November 1942): 435–436; Robert Park, "Negro Race Consciousness as Reflected in Race Literature," *American Review* 1, no. 5 (September–October 1923): 505–517; Benjamin Mays, "The Idea of God in Negro Literature" (PhD dissertation, University of Chicago, 1934). Ironically, though he was a sociologist, Bain accented the book's aesthetic value. Meanwhile David Daiches, a literature scholar at the University of Chicago, highlighted its evidentiary weight. According to Daiches, *The Negro Caravan* was "equally important to students of literature, sociology and politics," perhaps reflecting the way these fields were coming together at that time in Chicago. As mentioned in the introduction to this book, Benjamin Mays's dissertation, which became *The Negro's God,* was perhaps the best evidence of the convergence of these fields.
7. Brown, Davis, and Lee, *The Negro Caravan*, v.
8. William Shands Meacham, "Negro Writers Speak for Themselves," *New York Times*, March 29, 1942, 3, 20.
9. Howard Hintz, review of *The Negro Caravan: Writings by American Negroes*, ed. Sterling A. Brown, Arthur P. Davis, and Ulysses Lee, *College English* 4, no. 4 (January 1943): 267–268.
10. Brown, Davis, and Lee, *The Negro Caravan*, 7.
11. Lorenzo Turner, review of *The Negro Caravan: Writings by American Negroes*, ed. Sterling A. Brown, Arthur P. Davis, Ulysses Lee, *Journal of Negro History* 27, no. 2 (April 1942): 219–222. In this regard, Turner's analysis was aligned with the recent research of such anthropologists as Franz Boas and his students

Melville Herskovits and Zora Neale Hurston. As was noted in chapter 2, each of these ethnographers gathered evidence in support of a claim for the persistence of West African cultural practices in the Americas. As a founder of Gullah studies, Turner had come to such conclusions in his own research on the black communities of South Carolina's Sea Coast Islands. See Turner's landmark text, *Africanisms in the Gullah Dialect* (Columbia: University of South Carolina Press, 1949); and Margaret Wade-Lewis, *Lorenzo Dow Turner: Father of Gullah Studies* (Columbia: University of South Carolina Press, 2007).

12. Meacham, "Negro Writers Speak for Themselves," 20.

13. Julius Lester, Review of *The Negro Caravan, New York Times*, November 30, 1969.

14. Brown, Davis, and Lee, *The Negro Caravan*, 7.

15. By "artworld" I am referring to Arthur Danto's classic definition of the institutional structures that developed to sustain the practice, reception, and criticism during the twentieth century. Danto's definition squares well with the kind of sociological critique Bearden and other black artists offered at this time. See Danto, "The Artworld," *Journal of Philosophy* 61 (1964): 571–584.

16. Tracy Fessenden, *Culture and Redemption: Religion, the Secular, and American Literature* (Princeton, NJ: Princeton University Press, 2008), 111–136.

17. Matthew Frye Jacobsen, *Whiteness of a Different Color: European Immigrants and the Alchemy of Race* (Cambridge, MA: Harvard University Press, 1999); Karen Brodkin, *How Jews Became White Folks and What That Says about Race in America* (New Brunswick, NJ: Rutgers University Press, 1998).

18. Robert Orsi, *Between Heaven and Earth: The Religious Worlds People Make and the Scholars Who Study Them* (Princeton, NJ: Princeton University Press, 2005), 167–170.

19. Thomas Sugrue, *Origins of the Urban Crisis: Race and Inequality in Postwar Detroit* (Princeton, NJ: Princeton University Press, 2014), 33–56; John T. McGreevy, *Parish Boundaries: The Catholic Encounter with Race in the Twentieth-Century Urban North* (Chicago: University of Chicago, 1998), 77–110.

20. McGreevey, *Parish Boundaries*, 134.

21. Cyprian Davis, "In the Beginning, There Were Black Catholics," The National Black Catholic Congress, http://www.nbccongress.org/features/in-the-beginning.asp. See also Cyprian Davis, *The History of Black Catholics in the United States* (New York: Crossroads Publishing, 1996).

22. Albert J. Raboteau, *A Fire in the Bones: Reflections on African-American Religious History* (Boston: Beacon Press), 133.

23. A great example of the convergence of Catholicism and black international developments can be found in the first of issue of *Phylon: The Atlanta University Review of Race and Culture* 1 (1940), which included a profile of the first African bishop, Joseph Kiwanuka, who was cast as evidence of the Catholic Church's commitment to racial equality and democracy. See *Phylon* 1 (1940): 31–35. For a work that is attentive to the ways Catholicism informed the work of Negritude writers, see Gary Wilder, *Freedom Time: Negritude, Decolonization, and the Future of the World* (Durham, NC: Duke University Press, 2015).

24. Derek Smith, "Love's Lonely Office: Robert Hayden and the African-American Literary Tradition" (PhD dissertation, Northwestern University, 2004).

25. "Fellowship Church History," The Church for the Fellowship of All Peoples, http://www.fellowshipsf.org/about-us/, accessed September 2, 2015.

26. Theophilus Lewis, "The Negro Actor's Deficit," in *Ebony and Topaz: A Collectanea*, ed. Charles Spurgeon Johnson (New York, 1927), 125–127.

27. Darryl Dickson-Carr, "Theophilus Lewis," in *Encyclopedia of the Harlem Renaissance*, vols. 1 and 2, ed. Cary Wintz and Paul Finkelman (New York: Routledge, 2004); Theodore Kornweibel Jr., "Theophilus Lewis and the Theater of the Harlem Renaissance," in *The Harlem Renaissance Remembered*, ed. Arna Bontemps (New York: Dodd, Mead & Company, 1972), 171–189.

28. Farah Jasmine Griffin, *Harlem Nocturne: Women Artists and Progressive Politics during World War II* (New York: Basic, 2013).

29. Claude McKay, "If We Must Die," in *Complete Poems: Claude McKay*, ed. William J. Maxwell (Urbana: University of Illinois Press, 2004), 177.

30. Claude McKay to Max Eastman, October 16, 1944, in Wayne F. Cooper, ed., *The Passion of Claude McKay* (New York: Schocken, 1973), 304–305.

31. Cooper, *The Passion of Claude McKay*, 1.

32. McKay to Eastman, October 16, 1944, in Cooper, *The Passion of Claude McKay*, 304–305.

33. Ibid.

34. Ibid.

35. Giles Gunn, *The Interpretation of Otherness: Literature, Religion, and the American Imagination* (New York: Oxford University Press, 1979), 52–91.

36. McKay to Eastman, October 16, 1944, in Cooper, *The Passion of Claude McKay*, 305.

37. McKay himself wrote at the time that his conversion "cannot be defined." McKay to Eastman, October 16, 1944, and August 28, 1946, in Cooper, *The Passion of Claude McKay*, 304–305, 310–312.

38. George Hutchinson, *The Harlem Renaissance in Black and White* (Cambridge, MA: Harvard University Press, 1995).

39. McKay to Eastman, September 16, 1946, in Cooper, *The Passion of Claude McKay*, 312–313.

40. McKay's entrance into the Catholic Church was largely facilitated by his relationship with Bishop Bernard Sheil. Sheil would come to be known as the "Red Bishop" because of his pro-labor activism and opposition to Senator Joseph McCarthy's surveillance of Communist activism. Cooper, introduction to *The Passion of Claude McKay*, 40–41.

41. McKay to Eastman, September 16, 1946, in Cooper, *The Passion of Claude McKay*, 312–313.

42. Claude McKay to James Weldon Johnson, February 1, 1929, James Weldon Johnson Collection, Beinecke Rare Book and Manuscript Library, Yale University, New Haven; David Goldweber, "Home at Last: The Pilgrimage of Claude McKay—Black Poet Converted to Christianity," *Commonweal: A Review of Religion, Politics and Culture* 126, no. 15 (September 10, 1999). See also discussion of Islam in Claude McKay, *A Long Way from Home* (New Brunswick, NJ: Rutgers University Press, 2007), 254–255. One of the earliest readings of McKay and religion can be found in Jean Wagner, *Black Poets of the United States* (Urbana: University of Illinois Press, 1973), 197–258.

43. Ellen Tarry, *The Third Door: The Autobiography of an American Negro Woman* (London: Staples Press, 1956).

44. Ibid., 212, 248.

45. Bernard Sheil, "If I Were a Negro" (November 1942) and "Eyes on the Future," (February 1943), both in *Negro Digest: A Magazine of Negro Comment*.

46. McKay to Eastman, November 27, 1944; January 26 and March 21, 1945; and August 28, 1946, in Cooper, *The Passion of Claude McKay*, 306–308, 312.

47. Cooper, *The Passion of Claude McKay*, 325.

48. Claude McKay, untitled poem, in *Complete Poems: Claude McKay*, 247.

49. Claude McKay, untitled poem, in *Complete Poems: Claude McKay*, 253, originally published as "Look Within," *Catholic Worker* 11 (January 1945): 8.

50. Primus quoted in Helen Fitzgerald, "A Glimpse of a Rising Young Star," *Daily Worker*, June 3, 1943, 7. Quoted in Griffin, *Harlem Nocturne*, 30.

51. Barbara Savage, *Broadcasting Freedom: Radio, War and the Politics of Race, 1938–1948* (Chapel Hill: University of North Carolina Press, 1999), 231.

52. Raboteau, *Fire in the Bones*, 117–140.

53. Langston Hughes, *The Big Sea: An Autobiography* (New York: A. A. Knopf, 1940).

54. See Barbara Jackson Griffin, "Claude McKay's Unpublished 'Cycle Manuscript,'" *MELUS* 21, no. 1 (Spring 1996): 55n18.

55. Claude McKay, "A Negro Writer to His Critics," *New York Herald-Tribune Books*, March 6, 1932, reprinted in Cooper, *The Passion of Claude McKay*, 134.

56. Alain Locke, "Spiritual Truancy," in *The Works of Alain Locke*, ed. Henry Louis Gates Jr. and Charles Molesworth (New York: Oxford University Press, 2012), 224–227, originally published in *New Challenge* (Fall 1937).

57. Lawrence Jackson, *The Indignant Generation: A Narrative History of African American Writers and Critics, 1934–1960* (Princeton, NJ: Princeton University Press, 2010), 3.

58. Richard Powell, *Black Art: A Cultural History*, 2d ed. (New York: Thames & Hudson, 2003), 89.

59. Brent Hayes Edwards, *The Practice of Diaspora: Literature, Translation, and the Rise of Black Internationalism* (Cambridge, MA: Harvard University Press, 2003).

60. Ibid., 187–240.

61. Arthur Huff Fauset, *Black Gods of the Metropolis: Negro Religious Cults in the Urban North* (Philadelphia: University of Pennsylvania, 1945). The distinction between denominational churches and cults drove Fauset's analysis in *Black Gods*.

62. Claude McKay, *Harlem: Negro Metropolis* (New York: E. P. Dutton, 1940), 31, 73–85.

63. Ibid., 73–75.

64. Ibid., 82.

65. Langston Hughes, "Good-Bye Christ," in *Good Morning, Revolution: Uncollected Social Protest Writings*, ed. Faith Berry (New York: Lawrence Hill, 1973).

66. McKay, *Harlem*, 82–85.

67. St. Clair Drake and Horace R. Cayton, *Black Metropolis: A Study of Negro Life in a Northern City* (1945; repr., Chicago: University of Chicago Press, 1993).

68. McKay, *Harlem*, 32.

69. Ibid., 16.

70. Ibid., 101, 106.

71. Ted Poston, "A Book on Harlem," *New Republic* 103 (November 25, 1940): 732; Roi Ottley, "Claude McKay's Picture of Harlem," *New York Times*, November 24, 1940, 5.

72. Jonathan Walton's *Watch This!: The Ethics and Aesthetics of Black Televangelism* (New York: New York University Press, 2009) provides an especially astute analysis of the significance and mass appeal of three more recent religious figures. McKay's arguments suggest that he came to see Communism as a false religion and black adherents to its propaganda as the true dupes. As the final line of his book put it, they were "the black butt of Communism."

73. Catherine Albanese, *A Republic of Mind and Spirit: A Cultural History of American Metaphysical Religion* (New Haven, CT: Yale University Press, 2008).

74. For a more in-depth discussion of African American religion and American New Thought traditions, see Darnise C. Martin, *Beyond Christianity: African Americans in a New Thought Church* (New York: New York University Press, 2005).

75. Ron Alexander, "Chronicle," *New York Times*, May 31, 1994.

76. McKay, *Harlem*, 32–72.

77. For the most extensive study of religion and the UNIA, see Randall K. Burkett, *Garveyism as a Religious Movement: The Institutionalization of a Black Civil Religion* (New York: Scarecrow Press, 1978).

78. See Devon Dick, "Marcus Garvey Praised AME Church," *The Gleaner*, http://jamaica-gleaner.com/gleaner/20111110/cleisure/cleisure2.html; William E. Montgomery, *Under Their Own Vine and Fig Tree: The African-American Church in the South, 1865–1900* (Baton Rouge: Louisiana University Press, 1994); Burkett, *Garveyism as a Religious Movement*, 136–149.

79. McKay, *Harlem*, 143–180.

80. Burkett, *Garveyism as a Religious Movement*, 178.

81. For an excellent discussion of the rise of Methodism in the Atlantic World, see David Hempton, *Methodism: Empire of the Spirit* (New Haven, CT: Yale University Press, 2006).

82. Burkett, *Garveyism as a Religious Movement*.

83. Courtney Bender and Pamela E. Klaasen, eds., *After Pluralism: Reimagining Religious Engagement* (New York: Columbia University Press, 2010); McKay, *Harlem*, 20.

84. McKay, *Harlem*, 210.

85. Ibid., 181–262. For a discussion of the ways Communist ideologies were blended with black church culture, see Robin D. G. Kelley, *Hammer and Hoe: Alabama Communists during the Great Depression* (Chapel Hill: University of North Carolina Press, 1990).

86. McKay, *Harlem*, 214. For a biographical sketch of Hamid, see Mark Thomson, "Sufi Abdul Hamid," in *Encyclopedia of the Harlem Renaissance*, vols. 1 and 2, ed. Cary D. Wintz and Paul Finkelman (New York: Routledge, 2004), 459–460.

87. McKay, *Harlem*, 181.

88. Ibid., 211.

89. Ibid., 219.

90. Ibid., 220.

91. Ibid., 229–230, 257–258.

92. Richard Wright, "Blueprint for Negro Writing," *New Challenge*, October 1937. What McKay described in Harlem was consistent with Wright's claims, although he was less sanguine about the possibilities for transcendence on social terms, especially via Communism.

93. McKay, *Harlem*, 255.

94. Ibid., 181.

95. I define "alternative modernities" as the range of recent works in postcolonial theories that capture modernity itself as a site of contested social worlds. For an introduction to these debates, see Dilip Gaonkar, ed., *Alternative Modernities* (Durham, NC: Duke University Press, 2001).

96. McKay, *Harlem*, 73.

97. Roi Ottley, *New World A-Coming* (Boston: Houghton Mifflin, 1943), 347.

98. Ibid., 343.

99. Ibid., 40–41.

100. Ann Pellegrini and Janet R. Jakobsen, "Introduction: Times Like These," in *Secularisms*, ed. Ann Pelligrini and Janet R. Jakobsen (Durham, NC: Duke University Press, 2008), 10.

101. K. Healon Gaston, "Interpreting Judeo-Christianity in America," *Relegere: Studies in Religion and Reception* 2, no. 2 (2012): 291–304. See also Mark Silk's earlier essay, "Notes on the Judeo-Christian Tradition in America," *American Quarterly* 36, no. 1 (Spring 1984): 65–85.

102. Ottley, *New World A-Coming*, 75.

103. Ibid., 73, 80.

104. Ibid., 83.

105. Ibid., 86, 88.

106. Ibid., 82, 86.

107. Victor Francis Calverton, *Where Angels Dared to Tread* (New York: Bobbs Merrill Company, 1941), 332. This quote appears in *New World A-Coming* as the epigraph to chapter 7.

108. Deborah Dash Moore, *G.I. Jews: How World War II Changed a Generation* (Cambridge, MA: Belknap Press of Harvard University Press, 2006).

109. Two recent studies of black Jewish traditions that also track the genealogy of the study of black Jews are John Jackson, *Thin Description: Ethnography and the African Hebrew Israelite of Jerusalem* (Cambridge, MA: Harvard University Press, 2013); and Jacob S. Dorman, *Chosen People: The Rise of Black Hebrew Israelite Religion* (New York: Oxford University Press, 2013).

110. Ottley, *New World A-Coming*, 138.

111. Ibid., 139–141.

112. Ibid., 141–142. Abyssinian Baptist Church traces its own history to lower Manhattan in 1808. See Genn Rae McNeil, Houston Bryan Roberson, Quinton Hosford Dixie, and Kevin McGruder, *Witness: Two Hundred Years of African-American Faith and Practice at the Abyssinian Baptist Church of Harlem, New York* (Grand Rapids, MI: Eerdmans, 2013), 5–8.

113. Evelyn Brooks Higginbotham, *Righteous Discontent: The Women's Movement in the Black Baptist Church, 1880–1920* (Cambridge, MA: Harvard University Press, 1994).

114. Ottley, *New World A-Coming*, 146.

115. Ibid.

116. Dorman, *Chosen People*, 3–23.

117. For a discussion of the processes of Jewish inclusion in the United States, see Deborah Dash Moore, *At Home in America: Second Generation New York Jews* (New York: Columbia University Press, 1981), and Moore, *G.I. Jew.*

118. Mark Silk, "Notes on the Judeo-Christian Tradition in America," *American Quarterly* 36, no. 1 (1984): 65–85; Mark Silk, *Spiritual Politics: Religion and America since World War II* (New York: Simon and Schuster, 1988), 40–53.

119. Ottley, *New World A-Coming*, 236, 237.

120. W. E. B. Du Bois, *The Souls of Black Folk* (1903; repr., New Haven, CT: Yale University Press, 2015), 143.

121. Ottley, *New World A-Coming*, 221.

122. Ibid., 231.

123. Ibid., 233.

124. Ibid., 235.

125. Helen R. Houston, "Ottley, Roi," in *The Concise Oxford Companion to African American Literature*, ed. William L. Andrews, Frances Smith Foster, and Trudier Harris (New York: Oxford University Press, 2001), 317. Mark Huddle, "Roi Ottley's War: Black Internationalism and the Long Freedom Struggle," in *Roi Ottley's World War II: The Lost Diary of an African American Journalist*, ed. Mark Huddle (Lawrence: University Press of Kansas, 2011), 6.

126. Ottley, *New World A-Coming*, 222.

127. Barbara Dianne Savage, *Your Spirits Walk beside Us: The Politics of Black Religion* (Cambridge, MA: Belknap/Harvard University Press, 2012); Curtis J. Evans, *The Burden of Black Religion* (New York: Oxford University Press, 2008).

128. Ottley, *New World A-Coming*, 222.

129. Ibid., 223.

130. Arnold Rampersad, *Ralph Ellison: A Biography* (New York: Knopf, 2007), 111.

131. Ottley, *New World A-Coming*, 236. For discussion of Powell's campaign, see 233–235.

132. Roi Ottley, "Claude McKay's Picture of Harlem," *New York Time Book Review*, November 24, 1940, 5.

133. Ottley, *New World A-Coming*, 240.

134. Wright, "Blueprint for Negro Writing."

135. Ottley, *New World A-Coming*, 343–344.

136. Ibid., 345.

137. Ibid., 347.

138. Guy Johnson, untitled review, *Social Forces* 22, no. 2 (December 1943): 235–236; Rackham Holt, "A Tenth of a Nation," *New York Times*, August 15, 1943.

139. In a 1994 profile in *The New Yorker*, Ellington is quoted as saying, "I don't write jazz. I write Negro folk music"; "Profiles: The Hot Bach," *The New Yorker*, June 24, 1944. Also, on the occasion of what would have been Ellington's 111th birthday, his granddaughter is quoted as saying, "He never labeled his music. It was not jazz, he said it was 'American music.'" Quoted in Greg Goodsell, "Duke Ellington's Accomplishments Remembered," *Catholic Online*, April 21, 2010. http://www.catholic.org/news/ae/music/story.php?id=36244.

140. Duke Ellington, *Music Is My Mistress* (New York: Da Capo, 1973), 183.

141. Langston Hughes, "The Negro Artist and the Racial Mountain," *The Nation*, June 23, 1926.

CHAPTER 4

1. Alain Locke, foreword to *The New Negro: Voices of the Harlem Renaissance* (New York: Touchstone, 1997), xxvii.

2. Roi Ottley, *New World A-Coming: Inside Black America* (Boston: Houghton Mifflin, 1943), 347.

3. Gladys P. Graham, "Book Reviews," *Atlanta Daily World*, November 26, 1948, 6.

4. No author listed, untitled review of *Black Odyssey*, *The New Yorker*, November 6, 1948, 133.

5. Langston Hughes, "Here to Yonder: Art and the Heart," *The Chicago Defender*, April 6, 1946, 12.

6. Ibid.

7. Ibid.

8. Romare Bearden, "The Negro Artist and Modern Art," *Opportunity: Journal of Negro Life* 12 (December 1934): 371–372.

9. Romare Bearden, "The Negro Artist's Dilemma," *Critique*, November 1946, 16.

10. Ibid., 18.

11. Ibid., 19.

12. Ibid.

13. Ibid., 20.

14. Ibid., 22.

15. Robert Hayden, "Counterpoise," in *Collected Prose: Robert Hayden*, ed. Frederick Glaysher (Ann Arbor: University of Michigan Press, 1984), 41–42. Glaysher describes the statement as a "manifesto . . . written in about 1948 for an introductory leaflet to the Counterpoise Series (Nashville: Hemphill Press, ca. 1948)." According to Hayden's biographer, John Hatcher, the statement appeared in a subscription flier for the series in April 1948. See John Hatcher, *From the Auroral Darkness: The Life and Poetry of Robert Hayden* (Oxford: George Ronald, 1984), 314n6.

16. Selden Rodman, "Negro Poets," *New York Times Book Review*, October 10, 1948, 27.

17. Hatcher, *From the Auroral Darkness*, 16–17; "Robert Hayden," in *The Oxford Encyclopedia of American Literature*, ed. Jay Parini (New York: Oxford University Press, 2004), 2:177–181.

18. As Ed Pavlic has noted, some critics have gone so far as to argue that in Hayden's "best poems," race, religion, and art "converge and confirm each other." See Ed Pavlic, "'Something Patterned, Wild, and Free': Robert Hayden's Angles of Descent and the Democratic Unconscious," *African American Review* 36, no. 4 (Winter 2002): 535.

19. James Smethurst, *The Black Arts Movement: Literary Nationalism in the 1960s and 1970s* (Chapel Hill: University of North Carolina Press, 2005), 76.

20. Pavlic, "'Something Patterned, Wild, and Free,'" 537.

21. Hayden, "Counterpoise," 41, italics added.

22. Ibid.

23. Ibid.

24. Robert Hayden, "A Certain Vision," in *Collected Prose*, 111.

25. Hatcher, *From the Auroral Darkness*, 160.

26. Brian Conniff discusses the influence of Niebuhr's Christian realism on W. H. Auden before Hayden became his student, suggesting that for Auden poetry "could be a religious vocation." Conniff, "Answering 'The Wasteland': Robert Hayden and the Rise of African American Poetic Sequence," *African American Review* 33, no. 3 (Autumn 1999): 494–495.

27. As explained on the official website of the Baha'is of the United States, "The principle of the oneness of humankind is the pivot around which all the teachings of Bahá'u'lláh revolve." See "The Oneness of God, Religion and Humanity," Bahá'ís of the United States, https://www.bahai.us/beliefs. See also "Principles of the Baha'i Faith," http://www.bahai.us/welcome/spiritual-concepts/. See also http://www.bahai.com/Bahaullah/principles.htm#THE%20ONENESS%20OF%20MANKIND.

28. See *The Promulgation of Universal Peace*, http://reference.bahai.org/en/t/ab/PUP/.

29. Samuel Moyn, *The Last Utopia: Human Rights in History* (Cambridge, MA: Belknap Press of Harvard University, 2010).

30. For an excellent religious reading of Baldwin, see Clarence E. Hardy III, *James Baldwin's God: Sex, Hope, and Crisis in Black Holiness Culture* (Knoxville:

University of Tennessee Press, 2003). Also, Michael L. Cobb highlights the complicated way Baldwin drew on religious rhetoric to explore black churches as a site of sexual violence. See Michael L. Cobb, "Pulpitic Publicity: James Baldwin and the Queer Uses of Religious Words," *GLQ* 7, no. 2 (2001): 285–312.

31. Langston Hughes, "The Negro Artist and the Racial Mountain," *The Nation* (June 26, 1926), 692–694; Hurston, "Characteristics of Negro Expression," in *Negro: An Anthology*, ed. Nancy Cunard (London: Nancy Cunard at Wishart & Co., 1934), 39–46.

32. For a literary treatment of "the South in the City," see Farah Jasmine Griffin, *"Who Set You Flowin'?": The African American Migration Narrative* (New York: Oxford University Press, 1996), 48–99. For a historical and religious studies analysis, see Wallace D. Best, *Passionately Human, No Less Divine: Religion and Culture in Black Chicago, 1915–1952* (Princeton, NJ: Princeton University Press, 1996), 35–70.

33. Greg Miller, "James Baldwin," in *The Oxford Encyclopedia of American Literature*, ed. Jay Parini (New York: Oxford University Press, 2004), 120.

34. Ibid., 117–124.

35. James Baldwin, "Everybody's Protest Novel," in *Notes of a Native Son* (Boston: Beacon Press, 1984), 18.

36. Ibid., 15, 18.

37. Ibid., 13.

38. Ibid., 17.

39. Ibid., 23.

40. Ibid., 21.

41. Ibid., 19.

42. Ibid., 15–16.

43. Ibid., 7–8.

44. Baldwin, "Many Thousands Gone," 25, 44.

45. Ibid., 36–39.

46. Ibid., 34, 39.

47. Ibid., 24.

48. Ibid., 42.

49. Ibid., 37. For a comprehensive discussion of the social life that surrounded lynchings, see Koritha Mitchell, *Living with Lynching: African American Lynching Plays, Performance, and Citizenship, 1890–1930* (Champaign: University of Illinois Press, 2012).

50. Baldwin, "Autobiographical Notes," in *Notes of a Native Son*, 8.

51. Farah Jasmine Griffin refers to Petry's time in Harlem as her "most prolific period." See Farah Jasmine Griffin, *Harlem Nocturne: Women Artists and Progressive Politics during World War II* (New York: Basic Books, 2013), 89.

52. Ibid., 86; Alan Wald, *Trinity of Passion: The Literary Left and the Antifascist Crusade* (Chapel Hill: University of North Carolina Press, 2007), 111.

53. For a more detailed discussion and a listing of Petry's short story publications during this period, see Griffin, *Harlem Nocturne*, 103–106, 209–210.

54. Indeed, because of the commercial track record of this literary form (i.e., Wright's *Native Son*), Petry had benefited from the full backing of Houghton-Mifflin when her first book was released.

55. Griffin, *Harlem Nocturne*, 113.

56. Helen R. Hull, ed., *The Writer's Book* (New York: Harper and Brothers, 1950).

57. Wald, *Trinity of Passion*, 118–122; Griffin, *Harlem Nocturne*, 115–118.

58. Griffin, *Harlem Nocturne*, 88, 224.

59. Earl Conrad, "American Viewpoint: A Woman's Place in Harlem," *The Chicago Defender*, February 2, 1946, 13.

60. Writers such as Olaudah Equiano, Omar Ibn Said, Mariah Stewart, David Walker, and numerous others can be counted in this number. This lens led Frederick Douglass to note the difference between "the Christianity of this land, and the Christianity of Christ." "Appendix to the *Narrative of the Life of Frederick Douglass*," in *The Classic Slave Narratives*, ed. Henry Louis Gates Jr. (New York: Penguin, 2002), 397.

61. Ann Petry, "The Novel as Social Criticism," in *The Writer's Book*, ed. Helen R. Hull (New York: Harper and Brothers, 1950), 32.

62. Ibid., 33.

63. Ibid., 35.

64. Harold Cruse, *The Crisis of the Negro Intellectual: A Historical Analysis of the Failure of Black Leadership* (1967; repr., New York: New York Review of Books, 2005).

65. Ellison believed that Himes had underestimated the rising Red Scare politics. Ralph Ellison to Richard Wright, February 1, 1948, RW, box 97, folder 1314. For further discussion, see Lawrence P. Jackson, *The Indignant Generation: A Narrative History of African American Writers and Critics, 1934–1960* (Princeton, NJ: Princeton University Press, 2010), 267, 535n29.

66. Griffin, *Harlem Nocturne*, 116.

67. Petry, "The Novel as Social Criticism," 36.

68. Baldwin, "Autobiographical Notes," in *Notes of a Native Son*, 5; Hayden, "Counterpoise," 41; Petry, "The Novel as Social Criticism," 37.

69. Petry, "The Novel as Social Criticism," 38.

70. For a helpful discussion of Ann Petry's work in the context of postwar American literary politics, see Alex Lubin, ed., *Revising the Blueprint: Ann Petry and the Literary Left* (Jackson: University Press of Mississippi, 2007).

71. Griffin, *Harlem Nocturne*, 127. Despite Wright and Brooks's Chicago ties, Wright only supported Brooks's work from a distance. He had positively reviewed several of her poems for editors at Harper, but that was only after he had moved to New York. George E. Kent, *A Life of Gwendolyn Brooks* (Lexington: University Press of Kentucky, 1990), 62, 266.

72. Gwendolyn Brooks, "They Call It Bronzeville," *Holiday* 10, no. 4 (October 1951): 61–67.

73. Brooks followed Petry's work, and in some instances it informed the way she thought through publication opportunities. Additionally, her editor at Harper, Elizabeth Lawrence, shared with her a note that Ann Petry had written praising Brooks's novel *Maud Martha*. See Kent, *A Life of Gwendolyn Brooks*, 107, 112.

74. Langston Hughes, "Just in Case You Haven't Heard, I Would Like to Call Your Attention To," *The Chicago Defender*, October 13, 1951, 10.

75. Arnold Rampersad, *The Life of Langston Hughes*, vol. 2, *1941–1967, I Dream a World* (New York: Oxford University Press, 2002), 223–244; Langston Hughes, *Good Morning, Revolution: Uncollected Writings of Social Protest*, ed. Faith Berry (New York: L. Hill, 1973).

76. In truth, she had been cultivating a distinctive literary voice since her grade school days. Her first published poem, "Eventide," had appeared in *American Childhood* in 1930, when she was just thirteen. Over the course of Brooks's life, seventy-five of her poems were published in the *Chicago Defender*. William

Nash, "Gwendolyn Brooks," in *The Oxford Encyclopedia of American Literature*, ed. Jay Parini (New York: Oxford University Press, 2004), 211.

77. Kent, *A Life of Gwendolyn Brooks*, 59–64.

78. Langston Hughes, "Pulitzer Prize to Gwendolyn Brooks Accents Upsurge of Negro in Arts," *The Chicago Defender*, May 13, 1950, 6.

79. Ralph Ellison, "Editorial," *Negro Digest* 4, no. 1 (Winter–Spring 1943).

80. Gwendolyn Brooks, "Poets Who Are Negroes," *Phylon* 11, no. 4 (1950): 312.

81. Brooks was not alone in this regard, by any stretch. Nick Aaron Ford's essay in the same issue of *Phylon*, "A Blueprint for Negro Authors," captured this best. His title made clear that Ford was revising Richard Wright's 1937 "Blueprint for Negro Writing," which had foregrounded the political responsibility of black writers. In making his case, Ford wrote, "The first of my requirements is a mastery of craftsmanship. . . . The chief weakness of these writers has been in the area of craftsmanship." Nick Aaron Ford, "A Blueprint for Negro Authors," *Phylon* 11, no. 4 (1950): 374.

82. Margaret Walker, "New Poets," *Phylon* 11, no. 4 (1950): 354. In talking about these "young poets," Walker singled out M. Carl Holman as possessing these virtues. Holman was a poet, playwright, and professor who went on to serve as deputy director of the U.S. Civil Rights Commission. Albin Crebs, "Carl Holman, 69, a Major Figure in Civil Rights Movement, Is Dead," *New York Times*, August 11, 1988.

83. Walker, "New Poets," 350.

84. Two books that inform my thinking on the influence of this internationalism on American politics and cultural expression are Mary Dudziak, *Cold War Civil Rights: Race and the Image of American Democracy* (Princeton, NJ: Princeton University Press, 2000); and Penny Von Eschen, *Satchmo Blows Up the World: Jazz Ambassadors Play the Cold War* (Cambridge, MA: Harvard University Press, 2004).

85. Caroline Roth (the wife of *Holiday* illustrator Arnold Roth) is quoted in Michael Callahan, "A *Holiday* for the Jet Set," *Vanity Fair*, May 2013, http://www.vanityfair.com/culture/2013/05/holiday-magazine-history.

86. Ibid.

87. Adam Green, *Selling the Race: Culture, Community, and Black Chicago, 1940–1955* (Chicago: University of Chicago Press, 2007), 141–147.

88. According to Marsha Bryant, "A Street in Bronzeville" was recommended in *Ebony* in 1945. Brooks was interviewed for a celebrity story in 1950 and was mentioned in editorials later in the decade. Marsha Bryant, "Gwendolyn Brooks, *Ebony*, and Postwar Race Relations," *American Literature* 79, no. 1 (March 2007): 113.

89. Deborah Willis, *Reflections in Black: A History of Black Photographers, 1840 to the Present* (New York: Norton, 2002). See also Deborah Willis-Thomas, *Black Photographers, 1840–1940: A Bio-Bibliography* (New York: Garland Publishing, 1989). Saunders is also mentioned in *The Oxford Companion to the Photograph*, ed. Robin Lenman (New York: Oxford University Press, 2005), 17.

90. Brooks, "They Call It Bronzeville," 114.

91. Ibid., 61.

92. Ibid., 116.

93. Ibid., 67.

94. Roberts served the church from 1937 to 1952 before climbing the AME Church's hierarchy. Coincidentally, his son would follow him into Christian ministry and

eventually assume the pulpit of Atlanta's Ebenezer Baptist Church after the assassination of its more famous pastor, Martin Luther King Jr.

95. Brooks, "They Call It Bronzeville," 67.

96. Ibid., 63.

97. This was most likely also the name of a character in the novel that was never published, "American Family Brown," but which eventually evolved into *Maud Martha*. For an extensive discussion of "American Family Brown,", see D. H. Melhem, *Gwendolyn Brooks: Poetry and the Heroic Voice* (Lexington: University Press of Kentucky, 1987), 16–19, 79–83.

98. Brooks, "They Call It Bronzeville," 114.

99. Ibid., 116.

100. Ralph Ellison, "Brave Words for a Startling Occasion," in *The Collected Essays of Ralph Ellison*, ed. John Callahan (New York: Modern Library, 2003), 154.

101. Ibid., 151.

102. Lawrence Jackson, *Ralph Ellison: Emergence of Genius* (Athens: University of Georgia Press, 2007), 180.

103. Ibid., 186. See also Joyce Durham, "Dorothy West and the Importance of Black 'Little' Magazines of the 1930s: Challenge and New Challenge," *The Langston Hughes Review* 16, nos. 1–2 (Fall 1999–Spring 2001): 19–31.

104. Jackson, *Ralph Ellison*, 187.

105. Ralph Ellison, "Creative and Cultural Lag," *New Challenge* 2 (1937): 90.

106. Jackson, *Ralph Ellison*, 187.

107. See discussion of Angelo Herndon in Jackson, *The Indignant Generation*, 12, 112.

108. Jackson, *Ralph Ellison*, 368.

109. "Editorial," *Negro Quarterly* 4, no. 1 (Winter–Spring 1943): 295–296.

110. Ibid., 296–297.

111. Jill Watts, *God, Harlem, U.S.A.: The Father Divine Story* (Berkeley and Los Angeles: University of California Press, 1995). Three essays on Divine ran in *The New Yorker* in 1936–1937. See chapter 3 for my discussion of how Father Divine figured as a major character in several key interpretations of black life, including Claude McKay's *Harlem: Negro Metropolis* (1940) and Roi Ottley's *New World A-Coming* (1943).

112. "Editorial," *Negro Quarterly*, 297, 298.

113. Ibid., 298–300.

114. Ibid., 300.

115. Jackson, *Ralph Ellison*, 368.

116. Ralph Ellison, "The Blues," *New York Review of Books*, February 6, 1964.

117. Ellison, "Brave Words for a Startling Occasion," 151.

118. Ibid., 153.

119. Ibid., 152.

120. Ibid., 153.

121. Ralph Ellison, *Invisible Man* (New York: Vintage Books, 1972), 8–9, all italics added for emphasis.

122. Henry Louis Gates Jr., *Figures in Black: Words, Signs, and the "Racial" Self* (New York: Oxford University Press, 1987); Bruno Latour, *We Have Never Been Modern* (Cambridge, MA: Harvard University Press, 1993); Curtis Evans, *The Burden of Black Religion* (New York: Oxford University Press, 2008); Dolan Hubbard, *The Sermon and the African American Literary Imagination* (Columbia: University of Missouri Press, 1994). Interestingly, Congress had passed the

Boggs Act the previous year (on November 2, 1951) establishing a mandatory minimum sentence for the use of marijuana.

123. Ellison to Albert Murray, September 28, 1958, in *Trading Twelves: The Selected Letters of Ralph Ellison and Albert Murray*, ed. John Callahan (New York: Modern Library, 2000), 195.

124. Ralph Ellison, "The Minton Movement: Seventeen Years Later," *Esquire* (January 1959): 107–111.

125. Ellison to Albert Murray, September 28, 1958, in *Trading Twelves*, 195.

126. Ibid., 194.

127. See Emily J. Lordi, *Black Resonance: Iconic Women Singers and African American Literature* (New Brunswick, NJ: Rutgers University Press, 2013). Lordi insightfully points out that one significant difference between Ellison and Richard Wright was that the former anticipated "a readership that will corroborate his complex vision" (66). However, his letter to Murray and his essay on Mahalia Jackson suggest that he perhaps had some doubts on this count. See Ralph Ellison, "As the Spirit Moves Mahalia," in *The Collected Essays of Ralph Ellison*, ed. John F. Callahan (New York: Modern Library Classics, 2003), 250–255.

128. Ironically, the festival billed gospel music as "the roots of jazz"—when it began to include the genre gospel in 1957. See Lordi, *Black Resonance*, 67.

129. For a thoughtful discussion of the influence of religion in Ellison's life and how the theme is evident across his writings, see Laura Saunders, "Ellison and the Black Church: The Gospel According to Ralph," in *The Cambridge Companion to Ralph Ellison*, ed. Ross Posnock (Cambridge: Cambridge University Press, 2005), 35–55.

130. "Editorial," *Negro Quarterly*, 4, no. 1 (Winter–Spring 1943): 301.

131. Even the language he used to describe the women in *Invisible Man* and Mahalia is similar: "flamenco." It is also interesting that although Louis Armstrong (whose music is playing on the phonograph in *Invisible Man*) and Mahalia Jackson were originally southerners who participated in the Great Migration to the North, both claimed New Orleans as their original home.

132. Ralph Ellison, "As the Spirit Moves Mahalia," Ibid., 253; "Editorial," *Negro Quarterly*, 297.

133. Ellison, "As the Spirit Moves Mahalia," 252, 255.

134. Ellison to Albert Murray, September 28, 1958, in *Trading Twelves*, 194.

135. Ellison, "As the Spirit Moves Mahalia," 254–255. Ellison uses the term "Afro-American Episcopal Church." Ellison had grown up in an AME Church in Oklahoma, so perhaps this error was a reflection of his disinterest in the specific varieties of black Protestant churches. Saunders, "Ellison and the Black Church," 37.

136. Ellison, "Brave Words for a Startling Occasion," 153.

137. William R. Hutchison, *The Modernist Impulse in American Protestantism* (Durham, NC: Duke University Press, 1992).

138. I agree with Robert O'Meally's assessment of Ellison's views on this matter. O'Meally writes, "There can be no doubt that Ellison believed in the American melting pot and the universality of the arts. Still, jazz comes from the black side of the tracks, and white or other nonblacks who want to play the music must pay their dues to their artistic parents just as surely as Ellison the novelist must pay his to Melville, Hemingway, Joyce, and the rest." See Robert O'Meally, *Living with Music: Ralph Ellison's Jazz Writings* (New York: Modern Library, 2002), 235.

139. Ellison, "As the Spirit Moves Mahalia," 251. On the next page Ellison clarified that Jackson's voice was not "simply the expression of the Negro's 'natural' ability as is held by the stereotype" (252).
140. Ellison, "Brave Words for a Startling Occasion," 153.

CHAPTER 5

1. Richard Wright, "The Literature of the Negro in the United States," in *White Man, Listen!* (1957; repr., New York: HarperCollins, 1995), 108.
2. Adam Green, *Selling the Race: Culture, Community, and Black Chicago, 1940–1955* (Chicago: University of Chicago Press, 2009).
3. Gwendolyn Brooks wrote two poems inspired by the murder of Emmett Till. Both "A Bronzeville Mother Loiters in Mississippi. Meanwhile, a Mississippi Mother Burns Bacon" and "The Last Quatrain of the Ballad of Emmett Till" were published in her book *The Bean Eaters* (1960).
4. Vincent Harding, "Preface to the Atheneum Edition," in Benjamin E. Mays, *The Negro's God as Reflected in His Literature*, 2d ed. (New York: Atheneum, 1968).
5. James C. Hall, *Mercy, Mercy Me: African-American Culture and the American Sixties* (New York: Oxford University Press, 2001).
6. For a concise explanation of the black aesthetic, see Carolyn Fowler, *Black Arts and Black Aesthetics: A Bibliography* (Atlanta, GA: First World Foundation Press, 1981), v–xlii; Addison Gayle, introduction to *The Black Aesthetic*, ed. Addison Gayle (New York: Anchor Books, 1971); and James Edward Smethurst, *The Black Arts Movement: Literary Nationalism in the 1960s and 1970s* (Chapel Hill: University of North Carolina Press, 2005). Like Addison Gayle, I understand the black aesthetic as more of a question than a fixed category. Furthermore, as Smethurst argues, the Black Arts Movement (typically defined as the period from 1965 to 1973) was not constituted by one uniform position or a single organizational entity. Throughout this chapter I employ the term "Black Arts" as a broader rubric to link these concerns and writers across the decade. I also use it to highlight what were generally the oppositional aims of the black aesthetic and to play with the obvious normative connotations associated with "the Black Arts" as an occult practice in opposition to "religion."
7. Mary Helen Washington, *The Other Blacklist: The African American Literary and Cultural Left of the 1950s* (New York: Columbia University Press, 2014).
8. Brent Hayes Edwards, *The Practice of Diaspora: Literature, Translation, and the Rise of Black Internationalism* (Cambridge, MA: Harvard University Press, 2003).
9. Horace Cayton references sympathy for the "West African or the Mau Mau" specifically. Horace Cayton, "World at Large," *Pittsburgh Courier*, March 21, 1959, A6.
10. Ibid.
11. Ibid.
12. Ibid.
13. Ibid.
14. In 1959, the New York Drama Critics' Circle named it the play of the year, and in 1960 it received four Tony Award nominations. In 1973, a musical inspired by the original play won the Tony for best musical. Twenty-five years after the original debut, after seeing a revival of the play at Chicago's Goodman

Theater, *New York Times* critic Frank Rich declared that Hansberry's *A Raisin in the Sun* had "changed American theater forever."

15. Lorraine Hansberry, "Gold Coast's Rulers Go, Ghana Moves to Freedom," *Freedom* 1, no. 12 (December 1951): 2; Lorraine Hansberry, "Egyptian People Fight for Freedom," *Freedom* 2, no. 3 (March 1952): 3; Lorraine Hansberry, "Kenya's Kikuyu: A Peaceful People Wage Heroic Struggle against British," *Freedom* 2, no. 12 (December 1952): 3; Lorraine Hansberry and Stan Steiner, "Cry for Colonial Freedom Jolts Phony Youth Meet," *Freedom* 1, no. 9 (September 1951): 6. For an insightful discussion of Hansberry's writing during this period, see Fanon Che Wilkins, "Beyond Bandung: The Critical Nationalism of Lorraine Hansberry, 1950–1965," *Radical History Review* 95 (Spring 2006): 191–210. Hansberry's writing on colonialism is also discussed in Jackson, *The Indignant Generation*, 345.

16. Lorraine Hansberry, "The Beauty of Things Black—Towards Total Liberation: An Interview with Mike Wallace, May 8, 1959," in *Lorraine Hansberry Speaks Out: Art and the Black Revolution*, cassette recordings (New York: Caedmon, [1972]); Jackson, *The Indignant Generation*, 471, 478.

17. Lorraine Hansberry, "The Negro Writer and His Roots: Toward a New Romanticism," *The Black Scholar*, special issue, "Black Literature: Criticism," 12, no. 2 (March/April 1981): 2–3.

18. Ibid., 5.

19. Ibid., 6.

20. Wilkins, "Beyond Bandung," 191–210.

21. John A. Davis, preface to *The American Negro Writer and His Roots: Selected Papers from the First Conference of Negro Writers* (New York: American Society of African Culture, 1960), iv.

22. Peter Abrahams, "The Blacks"; and Nadine Gordimer, "Apartheid," *Holiday*, April 1959, 74ff. and 94ff., respectively.

23. Arnold Rampersad, *Ralph Ellison: A Biography* (New York: Vintage, 2008), 274, 398.

24. Ralph Ellison, "Editorial," *Negro Digest* 4, no. 1 (Winter–Spring 1943). I do not intend to claim that Baldwin's growing political engagement compromised his aesthetics. Rather, *The Fire Next Time* was clearly on a continuum with Baldwin's earlier essays that had begun to lay bare the theology of white supremacy that circulated in so much of American literature.

25. Of course, the Chicago protests did lay the groundwork for fair housing legislation in northern cities, and Stokely Carmichael first called for "Black Power" in the Deep South, while speaking at a rally in Greenwood, Mississippi, that King attended, just a few months after the Chicago campaign ended. Thomas Sugrue, *Sweet Land of Liberty: The Forgotten Struggle for Civil Rights in the North* (New York: Random House, 2008), 289.

26. Angela Dillard, *Faith in the City: Preaching Radical Social Change in Detroit* (Ann Arbor: University of Michigan Press, 2007).

27. James Campbell, *Talking at the Gates: A Life of James Baldwin* (London: Faber and Faber, 1991), 149–150.

28. James Baldwin, *The Fire Next Time* (New York: Vintage Books, 1962), 106.

29. Lawrie Balfour, *The Evidence of Things Not Said: James Baldwin and the Promise of American Democracy* (Ithaca, NY: Cornell University Press, 2001), 11–13. See also Darryl Pickney, "The Magic of James Baldwin," *New York Review of Books*, November 19, 1998.

30. Sacvan Bercovitch, *The American Jeremiad* (Madison: University of Wisconsin Press, 1980). For a discussion of the jeremiad in the African American context, see David Howard-Pitney, *The African American Jeremiad: Appeals for Justice in America* (Philadelphia, PA: Temple University Press, 2005). For a specific focus on African American religion, see Eddie S. Glaude Jr., *Exodus!: Religion, Race and Nation in Early Nineteenth-Century Black America* (Chicago: University of Chicago Press, 2000), 34–43.

31. Baldwin, *The Fire Next Time*, 105. Also see Clarence E. Hardy III, *James Baldwin's God: Sex, Hope, and Crisis in Black Holiness Culture* (Knoxville: University of Tennessee Press, 2003). In chapter 5, Hardy offers an analysis of how Baldwin drew on the apocalyptic rhetoric of Christian scripture to condemn white supremacy as it was practiced in the United States.

32. "U.S. Agency Studies Reports on News Coverage of Rioting," *New York Times*, September 6, 1967.

33. Baldwin, *The Fire Next Time*, 44.

34. Ibid., 44–45.

35. Ibid., 47.

36. Andrew Shin and Barbara Judson, "Beneath the Black Aesthetic: James Baldwin's Primer of Black American Masculinity—African American Gay Author," *African American Review* 32, no. 2 (1998): 147.

37. Edith Blumberg, *Civil Rights: The 1960s Freedom Struggle* (Boston, MA: Twayne Publishers, 1984); Aldon Morris, *The Origins of the Civil Rights Movement* (New York: Free Press, 1986); Clayborne Carson, In Struggle: SNCC and the Black Awakening of the 1960s (Cambridge, MA: Harvard University Press, 1981); Robin D. G. Kelley, ""We Are Not What We Seem': Rethinking Black Working-Class Opposition in the Jim Crow South," *Journal of American History* 80, no. 1 (June 1993): 75–112. Kelley argues that scholars must pay more nuanced attention to religion, particularly to the ways "the sacred and the spirit were also often understood and invoked by African Americans as weapons to protect themselves and attack others," 88–89.

38. Recent works on Black Power that have problematized earlier periodizations include Timothy Tyson, *Radio Free Dixie: Robert F. Williams and the Roots of Black Power* (Chapel Hill: University of North Carolina Press, 1999); Kelley, ""We Are Not What We Seem'"; Peniel Joseph, *Waiting 'Til the Midnight Hour* (New York: Henry Holt, 2006); and Dillard, *Faith in the City*.

39. For work on religion and politics in the 1960s, see David Chappelle, *Stone of Hope: Religion and the Death of Jim Crow* (Chapel Hill: University of North Carolina Press, 2007); Adolph Reed, *The Jesse Jackson Phenomenon: The Crisis of Purpose in African American Politics* (New Haven, CT: Yale University Press, 1986); William L. Van Deburg, *New Day in Babylon: The Black Power Movement and American Culture, 1965–1975* (Chicago: University of Chicago Press, 1992). While working within the historical framework established by early periodizations, Van Deburg devotes a brief section of his analysis to the impact of Black Power on African American religious culture (236–247).

40. Dillard, *Faith in the City*, 7–11.

41. Mark L. Chapman, *Christianity on Trial: African American Religious Thought before and after Black Power* (Maryknoll, NY: Orbis Books, 1996). Chapman provides a thorough discussion of the interactions between Christianity and Black Power. See also James H. Cone and Gayraud S. Wilmore, eds., *Black Theology: A Documentary History*, vol. 1, 1966–1979 (Maryknoll, NY: Orbis Books, 1979),

23–34. A number of African American clergy worked strategically to reconcile their Christian faith with the new racial discourse of Black Power, thus rejecting the premise that Black Power was inherently opposed to religious claims. In fact, one month after Stokely Carmichael raised the cry for Black Power in Mississippi, Dr. Benjamin Payton, executive director of the National Council of Churches' Commission on Religion and Race, convened a group of ministers at New York's Riverside Church with the hope of forming the northern equivalent of King's Southern Christian Leadership Conference. This initial gathering led to the founding of the National Council of Negro Churchmen, whose first act was to issue a full-page statement on Black Power in the July 31, 1966, edition of the *New York Times*. The Council, which changed its named to the National Council of Black Churchmen the following year, published a series of statements on race and religion in American life over the next five years. Similar developments took place in academia, where Black Theology emerged as an intellectual enterprise.

42. Baldwin, *The Fire Next Time*, 57.

43. Arguably the two most popular advocates of Black Theology during the late 1960s and 1970s were James Cone in the academy and Albert Cleage in the church. In 1969, James Cone—a systematic theologian, a minister in the AME Church, and a professor at Union Theological Seminary in New York City— published his first book, *Black Theology and Black Power*, which he quickly followed up with *A Black Theology of Liberation* in 1970. Drawing on the ideas of the same theologian, Karl Barth, who had captured Albert Cleage's imagination, Cone simultaneously critiqued white Christianity and declared that God had a decided loyalty to society's dispossessed. Cone's theology allowed for the possibility that anyone who identified with the oppressed could achieve blackness. See James H. Cone, *Black Theology and Black Power* (Maryknoll, NY: Orbis Books, 1969); James H. Cone, *A Black Theology of Liberation* (Philadelphia: Lippincott, 1970); and Albert Cleage, *The Black Messiah* (Trenton, NJ: Africa World Press, 1989).

44. Dillard, *Faith in the City*, 237–285. While building his congregation in Detroit, Cleage's social ministry led him into circles frequented by Detroit's young black radical activists and artists. He partnered with such organizations as The Group on Advanced Leadership (GOAL) and UHURU to sponsor political campaigns and protest police brutality. He also collaborated with local organizations to co-sponsor Detroit's Black Arts conventions, events attended by a number of young Black Arts Movement writers. For a collection of Cleage's sermons, see Cleage, *The Black Messiah*.

45. Craig Werner, *A Change Is Gonna Come: Music, Race, and the Soul of America*, 2d ed. (Ann Arbor: University of Michigan Press, 2006); Nick Salvatore, *Singing in a Strange Land: C. L. Franklin, the Black Church, and the Transformation of America* (Urbana: University of Illinois Press, 2006). Not insignificantly, even to this day, Franklin's gospel album *Amazing Grace* (1972) remains her best-selling record.

46. Salvatore, *Singing in a Strange Land*, 230, 287–291. Salvatore reveals that even though Franklin disagreed with the nationalist posture of Cleage and many BAM artists, he preached his own brand of Black Power, which he laid out most thoroughly in a series of sermons he delivered during the first Negro History Month after Martin Luther King Jr.'s assassination. While Franklin frequently integrated scripture and social criticism (most often on race matters) over the

course of his preaching career, in February 1969 he more explicitly articulated what might be called an organic theology of Black Power. As Salvatore has noted, Franklin's three-part series was a departure from his typical preaching, both in form and content. First, he traded in his customary outlines for three fully written manuscripts. Second, he gave priority to a trinity of black male heroes over any particular biblical text as the inspiration for each sermon. The title of Franklin's third and final Negro History Month sermon was entitled "On the Meaning of Black Power," acknowledging that the theme of Black Power had a much longer history in black America. Like his friend Martin Luther King Jr., Franklin rejected the nationalist reading of this term as the inverse of white supremacy. He informed his black congregation that true power rested not in social recognition or equality but in the fact that their humanity was imprinted with the divine seal.

47. For a full discussion of the Black Arts Movement in Detroit, see Julius Eric Thompson, *Dudley Randall, Broadside Press, and the Black Arts Movement in Detroit, 1960–1995* (Jefferson, NC: McFarland, 1999); Smethurst, *The Black Arts Movement*, 179–246; and Melba Joyce Boyd, *Wrestling with the Muse: Dudley Randall and the Broadside Press* (New York: Columbia University Press, 2003).

48. Cyprian Davis, *The History of Black Catholics in the United States* (New York: Crossroad, 1990), 238–260.

49. Larry Neal, "My Lord, He Speaks to Me in the Thunder," in *Visions of a Liberated Future: Black Arts Movement Writings by Larry Neal*, ed. Michael Schwartz (New York: Thunder's Mouth Press, 1989), 124.

50. Harding, "Preface to the Atheneum Edition," n.p.

51. Ibid.

52. This law is sometimes called the Immigration and Naturalization Act of 1965.

53. Glaude, *Exodus!*. According to Glaude, the Exodus trope provided a "common grammar of faith" through which African Americans constructed a national identity during the early nineteenth century.

54. Here I am thinking of George M. Fredrickson's work on "romantic racialism." See George M. Fredrickson, *The Black Image in the White Mind: The Debate on Afro-American Character and Destiny, 1817–1914* (Middletown, CT: Wesleyan University Press, 1987), 97–129.

55. Charles H. Long, *Significations: Signs, Symbols, and Images in the Interpretation of Religion* (Minneapolis, MN: Fortress Press, 1986); Victor Anderson, *Beyond Ontological Blackness: An Essay on African American Religious and Cultural Criticism* (New York: Continuum, 1999).

56. Ingrid Monson, *Freedom Sounds: Civil Rights Calls Out to Jazz and Africa* (New York: Oxford University Press, 2007), 311.

57. My thinking is influenced by the work of Eddie S. Glaude Jr. He writes, "This way of thinking about race bound African Americans to one another, grounded the work of cultural recovery, and steadied their lives by way of a reverent attachment to the putative sources of their being. ... Blackness came to be recognized as the source of black individual existence, and efforts to be cognizant of this source and to act appropriately toward it (whatever that might entail) became a critical feature of the politics of the Black Power era." See Glaude, "Introduction: Black Power Revisited," in *Is It Nation Time? Contemporary Essays on Black Power and Black Nationalism*, ed. Eddie S. Glaude Jr. (Chicago: University of Chicago Press, 2002), 7.

58. Maulana Karenga, "Blackness Is Our Ultimate Reality," quoted in ibid., 3.

59. Glaude, "Introduction," 7; Victor Anderson argues that during the 1960s many black artists and intellectuals reified race by imbuing it with ultimate significance. See Victor Anderson, *Beyond Ontological Blackness: An Essay on African American Religious and Cultural Criticism* (New York: Continuum, 1999).

60. Werner Sollors, *Amiri Baraka/Leroi Jones: The Quest for a "Populist Modernism"* (New York: Columbia University Press, 1978), 13. According to Sollors, "Baraka often ridiculed the hypocrisy of the Baptist Church, but retained a deep seated sense of religion and used Christic references and biblical language through-out his writings." In pointing to this tension in Baraka, Sollors helps frame a broader reading of the complexities of how religion was treated by artists in this historical moment. More broadly, many black artists took up Malcolm X's popular critique of Christianity as "the white man's religion" as part of their efforts to articulate what they perceived to be a more "authentic" black spirituality.

61. Tracey E. Hucks, *Yoruba Religion and African American Nationalism* (Albuquerque: University of New Mexico Press, 2012).

62. Amiri Baraka, "The Black Arts Movement," in *The Leroi Jones/Amiri Baraka Reader*, ed. William J. Harris (New York: Thunder's Mouth Press, 2000), 501.

63. Although only acknowledged in passing here, gender—often mediated through and by appeals to religion—figured as a crucial fault line for Black Arts men and women alike.

64. Smethurst, *The Black Arts Movement*, 132. Smethurst argues that "while the spir-itualistic impulse that Neal, Toure, Baraka, James Stewart, and others helped popularize in their *Liberator* essays was not always clearly defined, a commit-ment to a generally non-Christian, sometimes Islamic (or Islamic-influenced), sometimes neo-African or syncretic African spirituality became a hallmark of the Black Arts movement." In general I agree with Smethurst's assessment, but I think the relationship between the Black Arts and Christianity was more com-plicated and often included a re-reading (rather than a rejection) of Christianity. Furthermore, their reading of each of these religious traditions was informed by a particular vision of blackness, which ordered their interpretation of the specific religious practices they gravitated toward in each tradition.

65. Frederick Douglass, *Narrative of the Life of Frederick Douglass, an American Slave*, edited with an introduction by Deborah McDowell (Oxford: Oxford University Press, 1999), 66.

66. "Conjure," in *The American Heritage Dictionary of the English Language*, 4th ed. (Boston: Houghton Mifflin, 2004). For a compelling religious studies analysis of conjure, see Theophus H. Smith, *Conjuring Culture: Biblical Formations in Black America* (New York: Oxford University Press, 1995).

67. Robert Orsi, *Between Heaven and Earth: The Religious Worlds People Make and the Scholars Who Study Them* (Princeton, NJ: Princeton University Press, 2005); Jonathan Z. Smith, *Imagining Religion: From Babylon to Jamestown* (Chicago: University of Chicago Press, 1982), chs. 2 and 3.

68. Baldwin, *The Fire Next Time*, 50.

69. Ibid., 66–68.

70. Amiri Baraka, "The Black Arts (Harlem, Politics, Search for New Life)," in *The Leroi Jones/Amiri Baraka Reader*, ed. William J. Harris (New York: Basic Books, 2000), 367–399.

71. Baraka, "The Black Arts Movement," 495–505.
72. Dudley Randall, *For Malcolm: Poems on the Life and the Death of Malcolm X* (Detroit, MI: Broadside Press, 1965).
73. Maulana Karenga, best known for creating the African American cultural celebration Kwanzaa, also wrote extensively on religion. For a good introduction to his thinking on this subject, see Maulana Karenga, "Black Religion," in *African American Religious Studies* (Durham, NC: Duke University Press, 1989), 271–300.
74. Gwendolyn Brooks, *Report from Part One* (Detroit: Broadside Press, 1972), 83–86. For further discussion see Smethurst, *The Black Arts Movement*, 48.
75. Smethurst, *The Black Arts Movement*, 101.
76. Ibid., 379.
77. Ibid., 100–101.
78. "U.S. Agency Studies Reports on News Coverage of Rioting," *New York Times*, September 6, 1967.
79. Smethurst, *The Black Arts Movement*, 8.
80. Albert Cleage, "Dr. King and Black Power," in *The Black Messiah*, ed. Albert Cleage (Trenton, NJ: Africa World Press, 1989), 209.
81. Ibid., 211.
82. Larry Neal, "The Black Arts Movement," in *The Black Aesthetic*, ed. Addison Gayle (New York: Doubleday, 1972), 273.
83. Ibid.
84. Ben Caldwell, "Prayer Meeting, or, the First Militant Minister," in *Black Fire: An Anthology of Afro-American Writing*, ed. Amiri Baraka and Larry Neal (New York: William Morrow, 1968), 589–594.
85. For a discussion of Nat Turner, see Stephen B. Oates, *The Fires of Jubilee: Nat Turner's Fierce Rebellion* (New York: HarperPerennial, 1990). Larry Neal also cites Nat Turner as a model of religious resistance in "My Lord, He Speaks to Me in the Thunder," in *Visions of a Liberated Future: Black Arts Movement Writings by Larry Neal*, ed. Michael Schwartz (New York: Thunder's Mouth Press, 1989), 122.
86. Neal, "The Black Arts Movement," 273; and Neal, "My Lord, He Speaks to Me in the Thunder," 118.
87. Harold Cruse, *The Crisis of the Negro Intellectual: A Historical Analysis of the Failure of Black Leadership* (New York: New York Review of Books, 2005), 182.
88. Wright, "Blueprint for Negro Writing," in *The Norton Anthology of African American Literature*, ed. Henry Louis Gates Jr. and Nellie McKay (New York: Norton, 2003), 1382; Ann Petry, "The Novel as Social Criticism," in *The Writer's Book*, ed. Helen Hull (New York: Harper and Brothers, 1950).
89. Washington, *The Other Blacklist*.
90. Additionally, it was through Wright that the Popular Front aesthetics of the 1930s directly influenced the Black Arts movement. See Smethurst, *The Black Arts Movement*, 27–28.
91. Wright, "Blueprint for Negro Writing," 1384.
92. Larry Neal, "The Black Writer's Role, I: Richard Wright," in *Visions of a Liberated Future: Black Arts Movement Writings* (New York: Thunder's Mouth Press, 1989), 24.
93. William L. Van Deburg, *A New Day in Babylon: The Black Power Movement and American Culture, 1965–1975* (Chicago: University of Chicago Press, 1993), 236–247. See also Glaude, *Is It Nation Time?*

94. Ishmael Reed, "Can A Metronome Know the Thunder or Summon a God?" in *The Black Aesthetic*, ed. Addison Gayle (New York: Anchor Books, 1971), 381–382.

CHAPTER 6

1. Vincent Harding, preface to Benjamin E. Mays, *The Negro's God as Reflected in His Literature*, 2d ed. (New York: Atheneum, 1968), n.p.
2. Robert Earl Hayden, "Introduction to *The New Negro: Voices of the Harlem Renaissance*, Atheneum Edition," in *The Collected Prose of Robert Hayden*, ed. Robert Earl Hayden and Frederick Glaysher (Ann Arbor: University of Michigan Press, 1984). For a discussion of the impact of Hayden's Baha'i faith on his aesthetics, see Derek Jalal Smith, "Love's Lonely Offices: Robert Hayden and the African-American Literary Tradition" (PhD dissertation, Northwestern University, 2004).
3. Julius Lester, "Journey through Black Literature," *New York Times*, November 30, 1969.
4. Ibid.
5. Werner Sollors, *Amiri Baraka/Leroi Jones: The Quest for a "Populist Modernism"* (New York: Columbia University Press, 1978), 194. In his analysis of Baraka's embrace of a black aesthetic, Sollors offers an interesting discussion of the relationship between black aesthetic critics, like Baraka, and "the masses." According to Sollors, the rhetoric of "the people" often obscured "a struggle between the elitist writer and the people who are to learn the right Black consciousness from him. Writing for the people may mask a deep seated opposition to the people."
6. Clarence Major, ed., *The New Black Poetry* (New York: International Publishers, 1969), 15. Major cites Du Bois's interpretation of spirituals in *The Souls of Black Folk*, where Du Bois describes "Sorrow Songs" as the "singular spiritual heritage of the nation and the greatest gift of the Negro people."
7. Dudley Randall, introduction to *The Black Poets*, ed. Dudley Randall (New York: Bantam Books, 1970), xxiii.
8. Sylvia Winter, "The Black Aesthetic," in *The Encyclopedia of Aesthetics* (New York: Oxford University Press, 1998), 1:274.
9. Harding, preface to *The Negro's God*, n.p.
10. Andrew Hill, *Black Fire*, 33⅓ rpm, Blue Note, 1964.
11. Amiri Baraka, foreword to *Black Fire: An Anthology of Afro-American Literature*, ed. Amiri Baraka and Larry Neal (New York: Morrow, 1968), xvii.
12. Ibid., xvii–xviii.
13. Sollors, *Amiri Baraka/Leroi Jones*, 188, 210.
14. James A. Miller, "'I Investigate the Sun': Amiri Baraka in the 1980s," *Callaloo*, no. 26 (Winter 1986): 184; Kimberly W. Benston, *Baraka: The Renegade and the Mask* (New Haven, CT: Yale University Press, 1976), 144. It is important to note the performative quality of his self-naming, as the title page listed him as "Leroi Jones," but his foreword to *Black Fire* is credited to "Ameer Baraka." On the cover and title page of *In Our Terribleness* (1970), Leroi Jones is also identified as "IMAMU AMIRI BARAKA."
15. "Black Design" is a gloss of the translation of the Swahili ("Weusi Mchoro") to English: "Black sketch, design, diagram or figure." Translation from Google Translate. Weusi was also the name of a Black Arts group in New York City. See James Smethurst, *The Black Arts Movement: Literary Nationalism in the 1960s and 1970s* (Chapel Hill: University of North Carolina Press, 2005), 144.

16. See Baraka's recollection of this intention in his "New Introduction" to the reissued edition of *Black Fire* (Baltimore, MD: Black Classic Press, 2007).

17. Larry Neal, "Afterword: And Shine Swam On," in *Black Fire: An Anthology of Afro-American Literature*, ed. Amiri Baraka and Larry Neal (New York: Morrow, 1968), 638.

18. Ibid., 656.

19. Ibid.

20. Stephen E. Henderson, "Take Two—Larry Neal and the Blues God: Aspects of the Poetry," *Callaloo*, no. 23 (Winter 1985): 215; Richard Wright, "Blueprint for Negro Writing," in *The Norton Anthology of African American Literature*, ed. Henry Louis Gates Jr. and Nellie McKay (New York: Norton, 1997), 1267–1271 and 1380–1381.

21. Neal, "Afterword," 647.

22. W. E. B. Du Bois, *The Souls of Black Folk* (1903; repr., New Haven, CT: Yale University Press, 2015).

23. Neal, "Afterword," 647.

24. Ibid., 648–649.

25. Ibid., 650; Henderson, "Take Two—Larry Neal and the Blues God," 215, italics added.

26. Larry Neal, "The Black Arts Movement," in *Visions of a Liberated Future: Black Arts Movement Writings* (New York: Thunder's Mouth Press, 1989), 272–273.

27. Smethurst, *The Black Arts Movement*, 58.

28. Ibid., 357. Smethurst acknowledges that other black aesthetic theorists saw Gayle's hard-line nationalist analysis as "an overly rigid sense of ideological and aesthetic blackness." Although Gayle advances this nationalist perspective, in the essay he also acknowledges that black identity in the United States was an inherently hybrid form. He thus seems to support Neal's claim that a desire to demolish the double-consciousness was a defining feature of the movement.

29. Addison Gayle Jr., introduction to *The Black Aesthetic*, ed. Addison Gayle Jr. (New York: Anchor Books, 1971), xxi.

30. For an introduction to similar arguments about the Harlem Renaissance, see Nathan Huggins, *The Harlem Renaissance* (New York: Oxford University Press, 1971); and David Lewis, *When Harlem Was in Vogue* (New York: Penguin Books, 1987).

31. Gayle, introduction to *The Black Aesthetic*, xxii.

32. Eddie S. Glaude, "Introduction: Black Power Revisited," in *Is It Nation Time? Contemporary Essays on Black Power and Black Nationalism*, ed. Eddie S. Glaude Jr. (Chicago: University of Chicago Press, 2002), 6–10.

33. Amiri Baraka/Leroi Jones, *Blues People: Negro Music in White America* (New York: William Morrow, 1963).

34. Jason Robinson, "The Challenge of the Changing Same: The Jazz Avant-Garde of the 1960s, the Black Aesthetic, and the Black Arts Movement," *Critical Studies in Improvisation* 1, no. 2 (2005): 20–37.

35. Amiri Baraka, "The Changing Same," in *The Leroi Jones/Amiri Baraka Reader*, ed. William J. Harris (New York: Thunder's Mouth Press, 2000), 187.

36. Robinson, "The Challenge of the Changing Same," 20.

37. Of course, this "roots" versus "routes" distinction has been commonly used to interpret the process of cultural transmission. See, for example, Shalva Wail, *Roots and Routes: Ethnicity and Migration in Global Perspective* (Jerusalem: Magnes, 1999); and Elizabeth DeLoughrey, *Roots and*

Routes: Navigating Caribbean and Pacific Island Literatures (Honolulu: University of Hawai'i Press, 2007).

38. Baraka, "The Changing Same," 187.
39. Ibid., 188.
40. Wright, "Blueprint for Negro Writing," 1381–1382.
41. Baraka, "The Changing Same," 177.
42. Ibid., 188.
43. Robinson, "The Challenge of the Changing Same," 21–22.
44. Baraka, "The Changing Same," 190, 196.
45. Ibid., 192.
46. Ibid., 178.
47. Ibid.
48. Ibid., 204. *United States v. Seeger*, 380 U.S. 163 (1965); James McBride, "Paul Tillich and the Supreme Court: Tillich's 'Ultimate Concern' as Standard in Judicial Interpretation," *Journal of Church and State* 30, no. 2 (1988): 245–272.
49. For a discussion of the importance of Africa (real and imagined) in Black Power art and politics, see Gerald Horne, "Reflecting Black: Zimbabwe and U.S. Black Nationalism," in *Is It Nation Time? Contemporary Essays on Black Power and Black Nationalism*, ed. Eddie S. Glaude Jr. (Chicago: University of Chicago Press, 2002); and E. Francis White, "Africa on My Mind: Gender, Counter Discourse, and African American Nationalism," also in *Is It Nation Time?* An excellent example of Black Arts literature that appeals directly to both Africa and American ghettos as sites of an oppositional black culture is Ishmael Reed, "Neo-Hoodoo Manifesto," in *Los Angeles Free Press* (September 18, 1970), 42.
50. James T. Stewart, "The Development of the Black Revolutionary Artist," in *Black Fire: An Anthology of Afro-American Literature*, ed. Amiri Baraka and Larry Neal (New York: Morrow, 1968); Smethurst, *The Black Arts Movement*, 64–66.
51. Stewart, "The Development of the Black Revolutionary Artist," 3.
52. Ibid., 3–4.
53. Ibid., 6.
54. Ibid., 6–8. Stewart acknowledges the Nation of Islam elsewhere in the essay with a reference to "one of our 'negro' writers" who "failed to understand the historicity" of the NOI. Perhaps this was a subtle critique of Baldwin, who had rejected the NOI in *The Fire Next Time*.
55. Stewart, "The Development of the Black Revolutionary Artist," 9–10.
56. Ibid., 10.
57. Other authors who contributed more than one essay were Addison Gayle (the anthology's editor), Hoyt Fuller, and Alain Locke, the New Negro theorist par excellence.
58. Neal, "The Black Arts Movement," 257. Of note, Neal sounds strangely similar to Charles Long, who in the essay "Perspectives for the Study of Afro-American Religion in the United States" laid out an "initial ordering" of the religious experiences of black people in the United States. There he sought to delineate indigenous categories that expanded the familiar Christian language. See Charles Long, *Significations: Signs, Symbols, and Images in the Interpretation of Religion* (Aurora, CO: The Davies Group, 1999), 187–198.
59. Larry Neal, "Some Reflections on the Black Aesthetic," in *The Black Aesthetic*, ed. Addison Gayle Jr. (New York: Anchor Books, 1971), 12. Smethurst outlines similarities between aesthetic and political visions of Neal and Stewart in *The Black Arts Movement*, 64.

60. Sollors, *Amiri Baraka/Leroi Jones*, 200.

61. Henderson, "Take Two—Larry Neal and the Blues God," 226.

62. Neal, "Some Reflections on the Black Aesthetic," 12–15.

63. Larry Neal, "Any Day Now: Black Art and Black Liberation," in *Black Poets and Prophets*, ed. Woodie King and Earl Anthony (New York: Mentor, 1972), 152, italics added.

64. George Edmund Haynes, "The Church and the Negro Spirit," *Survey Graphic*, special edition, "Harlem: Mecca of the New Negro," ed. Alain Locke, 4, no. 6 (March 1925): 695–697, 708–709. In some ways, Neal's interpretation had more in common with Nancy Cunard's essay, "Harlem Reviewed," in *Negro: An Anthology*. See discussion of Haynes and Cunard in chapters 1 and 2, respectively.

65. Seven of the seventy-seven contributors to *Black Fire* were women.

66. Gail Bederman, *Manliness and Civilization: A Cultural History of Race and Gender in the United States, 1880–1917* (Chicago: University of Chicago Press, 1996); Hazel Carby, *Race Men* (Cambridge, MA: Harvard University Press, 1998).

67. Margaret Walker's epigraph quoted in *The Black Aesthetic* is from Walker, "For My People," in *This Is My Century: New and Collected Poems* (Athens: University of Georgia Press, 1989), 7.

68. Glaude, "Introduction: Black Power Revisited," 5–6.

69. For work focusing on the contributions of women to the Black Arts Movement, see Cheryl Clarke, *"After Mecca": Women Poets and the Black Arts Movement* (New Brunswick, NJ: Rutgers University Press, 2005); and Madhu Dubey, *Black Women Novelists and the Nationalist Aesthetic* (Bloomington: Indiana University Press, 1994). Also see Andrew Shin and Barbara Judson, "Beneath the Black Aesthetic: James Baldwin's Primer of Black American Masculinity—African American Gay Author," *African American Review* 32, no. 2 (Summer 1998): 247–261. In their analysis of James Baldwin's exclusion from black aesthetic criticism, Shin and Judson highlight the movement's privileging of heteronormativity and patriarchy.

70. Neal, "Afterword: And Shine Swam On," 636–656.

71. Smethurst, *The Black Arts Movement*, 120–121. Smethurst argues that from the earliest stages of the Black Arts Movement, black women pointed out the patriarchal sensibilities of many of their brothers in the struggle, thus making gender a central issue throughout the evolution of the movement. To make the case, he points to Sarah Wright's presentation on "The Negro Woman in American Literature" from 1965. Wright asserted that "far too many of our Afro-American men are walking around begging for a popular recognition of what is fictitiously called 'manhood,' a begging which takes the form of attacks on women launched from many different directions."

72. Earl Lewis, "To Turn as on a Pivot: Writing African Americans into a History of Overlapping Diasporas," *American Historical Review* 100, no. 3 (1995): 765–787. Lewis uses the term "pivot" to explain the places (class, gender, region, etc.) where the complexity of black identities is revealed.

73. Farah Jasmine Griffin, "Conflict and Chorus: Reconsidering Toni Cade's *The Black Woman: An Anthology*," in *Is It Nation Time? Contemporary Essays on Black Power and Black Nationalism*, ed. Eddie S. Glaude Jr. (Chicago: University of Chicago Press, 2002), 117. As Griffin explains, the book was a feminist text, but not in the sense that feminism is typically understood. Rather, it contained

a debate among black women about the appropriate norms for black women's efforts at self-determination.

74. Ingrid Monson, *Freedom Sounds: Jazz Calls Out to Civil Rights and Africa* (New York: Oxford University Press, 2005), 283–311.

75. Toni Cade Bambara, "On the Issue of Roles," in *The Black Woman: An Anthology*, ed. Toni Cade Bambara (New York: Penguin Books, 1970), 103.

76. Ibid.

77. Carby, *Race Men*; Evelyn Brooks Higginbotham, "African American Women's History and the Metalanguage of Race," *Signs* 17, no. 2 (Winter 1992): 251–274.

78. Carolyn F. Gerald, "The Black Writer and His Role," in *The Black Aesthetic*, ed. Addison Gayle Jr. (New York: Anchor Books, 1971), 349–350. For a discussion of Gerald's work, see Dubey, *Black Women Novelists and the Nationalist Aesthetic*, 1–32.

79. Gerald, "The Black Writer and His Role," 353.

80. Ibid.

81. Smethurst, *The Black Arts Movement*, 78, 92.

82. Gerald, "The Black Writer and His Role," 354–355.

83. Sarah Webster Fabio, "Tripping with Black Writing," in *The Black Aesthetic*, ed. Addison Gayle Jr. (New York: Anchor Books, 1971), 181.

84. Ishmael Reed, *Conjure* (Amherst: University of Massachusetts Press, 1972).

85. James Stewart, "The Development of the Revolutionary Black Artist," in *Black Fire: An Anthology of Afro-American Literature*, ed. Amiri Baraka and Larry Neal (New York: Morrow, 1968), 6.

86. Joyce Green, "Black Romanticism," in *The Black Woman: An Anthology*, ed. Toni Cade Bambara (New York: Penguin Books, 1970), 139.

87. W. E. B. Du Bois, *The Souls of Black Folk* (1903; repr., New Haven, CT: Yale University Press, 2015).

88. Green, "Black Romanticism," 172.

89. Ibid., 171–172. In the afterword to *Black Fire*, Larry Neal positions black men similarly. He begins the essay by quoting a brief story of the African American trickster figure Shine. In the story, Shine is forced to choose between freedom and the opportunity to have sex with a white woman. Neal, "Afterword: And Shine Swam On." See also Smethurst, *The Black Arts Movement*, 259. Smethurst argues that Cook advocated a form of black cultural nationalism similar to that of Maulana Karenga but "without the subordination of women."

90. Ann Cook, "Black Pride? Some Contradictions," in *The Black Woman: An Anthology*, ed. Toni Cade Bambara (New York: Penguin Books, 1970), 155. Cook extended her analysis from religion to geography, writing, "By the same token, I wonder why we spend so much of our discourse about Africa emphasizing the great kingdoms Songhai, Bornu, Ghana, and Mali. Could it be because these kingdoms were similar in structure and size to European ones and serve as reassurance to us that we had the same things they had, even if, like Islam, these kingdoms were not the norm?"

91. Tracy Fessenden, *Culture and Redemption: Religion, the Secular, and American Literature* (Princeton, NJ: Princeton University Press, 2006).

92. Cook, "Black Pride? Some Contradictions," 155–156.

93. Baraka, "The Black Arts Movement," in *The Leroi Jones/Amiri Baraka Reader*, 501.

94. Bambara, "On the Issue of Roles," 109.

95. Ibid., 105. For a discussion of Father Divine, see Jill Watts, *God, Harlem U.S.A.: The Father Divine Story* (Berkeley and Los Angeles: University of California Press, 1995).

96. Robert Weisbrot, *Father Divine and the Struggle for Racial Equality* (Urbana: University of Illinois Press, 1983), 100–102; "Platform Drafted by Father Divine," *New York Times*, January 13, 1936, 19.

97. Lewis, *When Harlem Was in Vogue*, 300; Mark Chapman, *Christianity on Trial: African-American Religious Thought before and after Black Power* (Maryknoll, NY: Orbis Books, 1996).

98. Linda Janet Holmes, "Poised for the Light," in *Savoring the Salt: The Legacy of Toni Cade Bambara*, ed. Linda Janet Holmes and Cheryl A. Wall (Philadelphia: Temple University Press, 2008), 10, 25n5. See also Linda Janet Holmes, *A Joyous Revolt: Toni Cade Bambara, Writer and Activist* (Santa Barbara, CA: Praeger, 2014), 182.

99. Holmes, "Poised for the Light," 9.

100. Bambara, "On the Issue of Roles," 103.

101. Wright, "Blueprint for Negro Writing," 1384.

102. Alain Locke, *The New Negro* (New York: Touchstone, 1999), 1.

CHAPTER 7

1. Larry Neal, "My Lord, He Calls Me by the Thunder," in *Visions of a Liberated Future: Black Arts Movement Writings by Larry Neal*, ed. Michael Schwartz (New York: Thunder's Mouth Press, 1989), 124.

2. In the "Neo-HooDoo Manifesto," Reed names several figures—including Ted Joans, Quincy Troupe, and Sarah Fabio—whom he referred to as "HooDoo's 'Manhattan Project' of writing." Reed also participated in the Umbra Writers Workshop, which produced a number of key figures in the Black Arts movement, and he maintained relationships with several others. Reed's work was also published in a major text of the movement, *The Black Aesthetic*, which included a short excerpt from Reed's 1970 compilation *Nineteen Necromancers from Now* (1970). Reed, "Neo-HooDoo Manifesto," in *The Norton Anthology of African American Literature*, ed. Henry Louis Gates Jr. and Nellie McKay (New York: Norton, 2004), 2062–2066. Originally published as Ishmael Reed, "Neo-HooDoo Manifesto," *Los Angeles Free Press*, September 18–24, 1969, 42. For a more detailed discussion of Reed's relationship to the Black Arts movement, see James Smethurst, *The Black Arts Movement: Literary Nationalism in the 1960s and 1970s* (Chapel Hill: University of North Carolina Press, 2005), especially chs. 3 and 5.

3. Shamoon Zamir, "The Artist as Prophet, Priest and Gunslinger: Ishmael Reed's Cowboy in the Boat of Ra," *Callaloo* 17, no. 4 (Autumn 1994): 1207–1209. "Neo-HooDoo Manifesto" is similar to Reed's other work, as Zamir illustrates, where myths of "divine conflict" are used to cast an opposition to black spiritual force.

4. Ishmael Reed, "Bring It Down Front: Ending the Western Established Church of Art," *Essence*, January 1971, 15.

5. Reed, "Neo-HooDoo Manifesto," 2297–2301; James Lindroth, "Images of Subversion: Ishmael Reed and the Hoodoo Trickster," *African American Review* 30, no. 2 (Summer 1996): 185–196.

6. Reed, "Neo-HooDoo Manifesto," 2301.

7. See Amiri Baraka, "The Changing Same," in *The LeRoi Jones/Amiri Baraka Reader*, ed. William J. Harris (New York: Thunder's Mouth Press, 2000),

186–209; Langston Hughes, "The Negro Artist and the Racial Mountain," in *The Norton Anthology of African American Literature*, ed. Henry Louis Gates Jr. and Nellie McKay (New York: Norton, 1997), 1267–1271; Zora Neale Hurston, "Characteristics of Negro Expression," in *The Sanctified Church: The Folklore Writings of Zora Neale Hurston*, ed. Toni Cade Bambara (New York: Turtle Island Foundation, 1981).

8. For excellent interpretations of black culture as fundamentally "polycultural," see Henry Louis Gates Jr., *The Signifying Monkey: A Theory of African-American Literary Criticism* (New York: Oxford University Press, 1989); and Robin Kelley, "People in Me," *Colorlines Magazine* 1, no. 3 (Winter 1999): 5–7.

9. Ishmael Reed, *catechism of d neoamerican hoodoo church* (London: P. Breman, 1970); Nicolas Barker, "Paul Breman: Bookseller, Writer and Publisher of Black Poetry," *The Independent*, November 24, 2008.

10. Reed, "Neo-HooDoo Manifesto," 2298.

11. Ibid., 2299.

12. Hughes, "The Negro Artist and the Racial Mountain," 693.

13. Lindroth, "Images of Subversion," 185. Lindroth argues that Reed's aesthetic is "driven by a mocking wit that subverts white authority and destroys white illusions of superiority while simultaneously promoting numerous value-laden symbols of black culture."

14. Jason Berry, *The Spirit of Black Hawk: A Mystery of Africans and Indians* (Jackson: University Press of Mississippi, 1995); Milo Rigaud, *Secrets of Voodoo* (New York: Arco Publishing, 1953).

15. For an academic discussion of Tituba, see Elaine G. Breslaw, *Tituba, Reluctant Witch of Salem: Devilish Indians and Puritan Fantasies* (New York: New York University Press, 1995). Given Ishmael Reed's long-standing public dispute with black women writers and feminism (generally over their portrayal of black men), it is a bit ironic that his own efforts to craft an oppositional aesthetic would include foregrounding a long list of powerful black women. Robert Towers, "Good Men Are Hard to Find," *New York Review of Books*, August 12, 1982; Ishmael Reed, "Complaint," *New York Review of Books*, October 21, 1982; Brent Staples, "Media-Lashed and Sex-Listed," *New York Review of Books*, March 23, 1986.

16. See Yvonne P. Chireau, *Black Magic: Religion and the African American Conjuring Tradition* (Berkeley: University of California Press, 2003); and Theophus H. Smith, *Conjuring Culture: Biblical Formations of Black America* (New York: Oxford University Press, 1995), 4–5. I discuss the salience of the conjuring tradition in African American culture and the arts in chapter 5.

17. Here I mean to suggest that what Reed celebrates in Neo-Hoodoo is ordered by a logic that runs counter to what has been understood as "good religion" in the West. For a discussion of the normative distinction between "good" and "bad" religion, see Robert A. Orsi, *Between Heaven and Earth: The Religious Worlds People Make and the Scholars Who Study Them* (Princeton, NJ: Princeton University Press, 2004), 177–204.

18. "Black Priest Leaves Order to Marry St. Louis Woman," *Jet*, July 20, 1970, 49. Cunningham married another professor, the German American Lois Fassbinder. See Ishmael Reed, *Dispatches from the Race War* (New York: Basic Books, 2003), 122.

19. Reed, *catechism*, n.p.; Ishmael Reed, *The Reed Reader* (New York: Basic Books, 2008), xiv. Other dedicatees after Cunningham were Peter Bradley, Walter Harris, and Winnie Stowers.

20. Reed, "Black power poem," in *catechism*, 3.
21. Reed, *catechism*, 27.
22. Reed, "Neo-Hoodoo Manifesto," 2062. On the back of *catechism of d neoameri-can hoodoo church*, Reed explained that his next novel was due out the next year and would be titled "Mumbo Jumbo Kathedral" (with a backward K). This book was published in 1972 as *Mumbo Jumbo*.
23. *19 Necromancers from Now* was originally listed in manuscript form as "The Black Revival and 19 Necromancers from Now." See Ishmael Reed, "The Black Revival and 19 Necromancers from Now," four typescript drafts, August 10, 1970, F550, University of Delaware Archives, Newark.
24. Joseph E. Holloway, *Africaisms in African American Culture*, 2d ed. (Bloomington: Indiana University Press, 2005).
25. Here my thinking is informed by Robert Orsi's work on Catholic alterity. See Orsi, *The Madonna of 115th Street: Faith and Community in Italian Harlem*, 3d ed. (New Haven, CT: Yale University Press, 2003), xxvii–lvi.
26. Ishmael Reed, "Bringing It Down Front: Ending the Western Established Church of Art," *Essence*, January 1971.
27. Alice Walker, "Zora Neale Hurston: A Cautionary Tale and Partisan Review," and "Looking for Zora," in *In Search of Our Mothers' Gardens: Womanist Prose*, ed. Alice Walker (New York: Harcourt, Brace, Jovanovich, 1983), 87, 93–116. These essays were originally published in 1973 and 1975, respectively.
28. Alice Walker, review of *Gifts of Power: The Writings of Rebecca Cox Jackson (1797–1871), Black Visionary, Shaker Eldress*, edited with an introduction by Jean McMahon Humez, *The Black Scholar*, September–October 1981, 64–67.
29. Alice Walker, "The Unglamorous but Worthwhile Duties of the Black Revolutionary Artist, or of the Black Writer Who Simply Works and Writes," in *In Search of Our Mothers' Gardens: Womanist Prose*, ed. Alice Walker (New York: Harcourt, Brace, Jovanovich, 1983), 132.
30. James Stewart, "The Development of the Black Revolutionary Artist," in *Black Fire: An Anthology of Afro-American Writing*, ed. Amiri Baraka and Larry Neal (New York: William Morrow, 1968), 3–10.
31. Walker, "The Unglamorous but Worthwhile Duties of the Black Revolutionary Artist," 134.
32. Richard Wright, *Native Son* (New York: Harper Perennial, 2005); James Baldwin, "Everybody's Protest Novel," in *Notes of a Native Son* (Boston: Beacon Press, 1983), 13–23. For a discussion of how religion figured into Baldwin's critique of Wright's *Native Son* and protest literature in general, see chapter 4.
33. Walker, "The Unglamorous but Worthwhile Duties of the Black Revolutionary Artist," 137.
34. Amiri Baraka, "The Changing Same: R&B and the New Black Music," in *The Leroi Jones/Amiri Baraka Reader*, ed. William J. Harris (New York: Thunder's Mouth Press, 2000), 186–209.
35. Reed, *catechism of d neoamerican hoodoo church*, 3.
36. Ralph Ellison, "Editorial," *Negro Quarterly* 4, no. 1 (Winter–Spring 1943): 297–298; and "Brave Words for a Startling Occasion," in *The Collected Essays of Ralph Ellison*, ed. John Callahan (New York: Modern Library, 2003), 153.
37. Ralph Ellison, "Blues People," in *The Collected Essays of Ralph Ellison*, ed. John Callahan (New York: Modern Library, 2003), 279. Originally published as "Blues People," *New York Review of Books*, February 6, 1964.

38. Ralph Ellison to Albert Murray, September 28, 1958, in *Trading Twelves: The Selected Letters of Ralph Ellison and Albert Murray*, ed. Albert Murray and John F. Callahan (New York: Modern Library, 2000), 195.

39. For writing on Ellison and Baraka's respective experiences with black churches, see Laura Saunders, "Ellison and the Black Church: The Gospel According to Ralph," in *The Cambridge Companion to Ralph Ellison*, ed. Ross Posnock (Cambridge: Cambridge University Press, 2005), 35–55; and Jerry Gafio Watts, *Amiri Baraka: The Politics and Art of a Black Intellectual* (New York: New York University Press, 2001), 1.

40. James Hall, *Mercy, Mercy Me: African American Culture and the American 1960s* (New York: Oxford University Press, 2001), 39–77; Andrew Shin and Barbara Judson, "Beneath the Black Aesthetic: James Baldwin's Primer of Black American Masculinity," *African American Review* 32, no. 2 (Summer 1998): 247–261.

41. Albert Murray, *The Omni-Americans: Black Experience and American Culture; Some Alternatives to the Folklore of White Supremacy* (New York: Da Capo Press, 1970), 17, 47, 50.

42. Ibid., 152.

43. Ibid., 153.

44. Ibid., 166.

45. Ibid., 165.

46. Jared Sexton, *Amalgamation Schemes: Anti-Blackness and the Critique of Multiracialism* (Minneapolis: University of Minnesota Press, 2008).

47. Murray, *The Omni-Americans*, 22.

48. Ibid., 4.

49. Ibid., 7.

50. Ibid., 158.

51. E. Franklin Frazier, *The Negro Church in America* (New York: Schocken Books, 1974).

52. Giles Gunn, *The Interpretation of Otherness* (New York: Oxford University Press, 1979).

53. Murray, *The Omni-Americans*, 157–158.

54. John Gilliand, *Pop Chronicles of the 40s: The Lively Story of Pop Music in the 40s*, audiobook, Soundelux Audio, 1994.

55. The song reached number two on the Billboard charts in 1945, where it lasted for thirteen weeks.

56. Dinah Washington, "Accentuate the Positive," *Live-the Early Years*, CD, Mr. Music, 2014.

57. Murray, *The Omni-Americans*, 153.

58. Charles Rowell, "'An All-Purpose, All-American Literary Intellectual': An Interview with Albert Murray," *Callaloo* 20, no. 2 (1997): 399–414. See also Mel Watkins, "Albert Murray, Scholar Who Saw a Multicolored American Culture, Dies at 97," *New York Times*, August 19, 2013.

59. Murray, *The Omni-Americans*, 9.

EPILOGUE

1. Richard Wright, "The Literature of the Negro in the United States," in *White Man, Listen!* (1957; repr., New York: HarperCollins, 1995), 108.

2. Craig Werner, *A Change Is Gonna Come: Music, Race, and the Soul of America* (New York: Penguin, 1999), 122.

3. Mark Anthony Neal, *Soul Babies: Black Popular Culture and the Post-Soul Aesthetic* (New York: Routledge, 2002).

4. Alain Locke, *The New Negro* (New York: Touchstone, 1992); James Stewart, "The Development of the Revolutionary Black Artist," in *Black Fire: An Anthology of Afro-American Writing*, ed. Amiri Baraka and Larry Neal (Baltimore, MD: Black Classics Press, 2007), 6.

5. Joe Wood, ed., *Malcolm X in Our Image* (New York: St. Martin's Press, 1992), 7; Trey Ellis, "The New Black Aesthetic," *Callaloo*, no. 38 (Winter 1989): 223–243; Kevin Powell, ed., *Step into a World: A Global Anthology of the New Black Literature* (New York: John Wiley, 2000).

6. Ishmael Reed, "Neo-HooDoo Manifesto," in *The Norton Anthology of African American Literature*, ed. Henry Louis Gates Jr. and Nellie McKay (New York: Norton, 2004), 2066.

INDEX